D1154665

WITHDRAWN

The Original Misunderstanding

*The English, the Americans and the Dialectic of
Federalist Jurisprudence*

Stephen B. Presser

Carolina Academic Press
Durham, North Carolina

Carolina Academic Press
700 Kent Street
Durham, North Carolina 27701
919-489-7486

Dedication

*To Vivian Leiber, the greatest of the Leibers
and my beloved muse.*

Contents

Preface

The work that you hold in your hands, gentle reader, is not exactly a work of history nor a work of law nor a work of biography, but something approaching all three and torn in three directions by its multiple aims. Please make allowances if it seems to suffer from a literary multiple personality disorder, or if there seems to be too many false starts along these diverse paths. I teach in a law school, and wanted to produce something that answered a particular need—to arrive at a lawyer's understanding of some of the historical and personality elements that have created a current constitutional dilemma. I set out to find the roots of some current controversies over constitutional interpretation, and think that I have found them in the experience of the first Federal judges, particularly that of the much maligned and hapless Samuel Chase.

Having found something I believe to be of great value and greatly neglected by other interpreters of our constitutional history, and having been trained as an advocate, I realize that what we lawyers call "warm zeal" may have occasionally got the better of me in some of my treatment of Chase's contemporary and present critics. It could be argued that Thomas Jefferson and John Marshall, to pick but two examples, receive relatively short shrift here, and undoubtedly their present partisans will be troubled by some of what I have to say. Let it be acknowledged then, that I do not mean to relegate these two titans to the dustbin of legal history and put Chase in their place, but only to redress a bit of the balance.

A fuller explanation of what this study seeks to accomplish is offered in the introduction, but some disclaimers seemed called for because of the reaction of many of the readers of the manuscript who sought to save me from my own ideology, and to push me along one or the other of the multiple paths I have sought simultaneously to tread. These readers, friends, colleagues, and critics have been at it for some time now.

The beginning of this project was my work on the history of the United States Courts of the Third Circuit, which eventually resulted in the article *A Tale of Two Judges: Richard Peters, Samuel Chase, and the Broken Promise of Federalist Jurisprudence*, published in 1978 in the Northwestern University Law Review, an article in the public domain, and which has been cannibalized for inclusion at various points in the present work, particularly Chapters One, Two, Five, Six, and Seven. Chapter Six, which amounts to an essay within an essay of sorts, on the federal common law of crimes, begun in that first article, is probably the last word that I want to have on that subject, and may turn out to be the most useful contribution made here. Early phases of that first article

were given as workshops before the Legal History Group at the University of
Virginia, the American Society of Legal History, and the Legal History Group
at the University of Chicago. Three people who offered special help at that
stage were Professors Maxwell Bloomfield, Charles W. McCurdy, and G. Edward White. The Third Circuit's Bicentennial History Committee, Judges
Dumbauld, Marris, Gibbons, and Seitz, read many drafts and were unfailing
in their enthusiasm and encouragement. Valuable suggestions were also received from Gerhard Casper, James W. Ely, Jr., Kermit Hall, Wythe Holt, Morton Horwitz, Stan Katz, William Nelson, Mary K. Tachau, and Jamil Zainaldin. Financial support at that stage of the project was provided by a Summer
Stipend from the National Endowment for the Humanities. The Historical Society of Pennsylvania graciously granted permission for quotations from the
papers of Richard Peters, and helped me make my way through their manuscript collections.

The second stage of the project was the article, *Saving God's Republic: The
Jurisprudence of Samuel Chase*, which appeared in the University of Illinois
Law Review in 1984, and which was co-authored by Becky Bair Hurley, who
has granted her permission (as one of the dual copyright holders) for excerpts
of that article to appear here. They are to be found in Chapters Seven, Eight,
and Nine. Ms. Hurley was my research assistant and prepared two papers
which were used in the drafting of the article. One other Northwestern Law
Student Research Assistant who was invaluable at that stage was Donna Shra-
low, who unearthed further sources at the Pennsylvania Historical Society and
at the Historical Society of Maryland. Permission to quote from those sources
is again acknowledged, as is the help of Karen Stuart, of the Maryland Historical Society's Manuscript Division, who generously gave of her time in
teaching me to decipher what scholars have called Chase's "execrable" hand.
"Saving God's Republic" was given as a paper at the University of Chicago's
Legal History workshop and at a similar workshop at the University of Illinois. Important and useful critics at those events were Professors Gerhard
Casper, David Currie, Frank Easterbrook, Richard Epstein, Richard Helm-
holz, Dennis Hutchinson, John Langbein, and Cass Sunstein, at the University
of Chicago, and Michael Hoeflich, John Nowak, and Ronald Rotunda at the
University of Illinois. Research support for that article came from a Fulbright
Senior Scholarship for 1983-84 and from research grants from Northwestern
University's Law School authorized by its Dean David Ruder, and its then di-
rector of research, Robert Bennett.

A third piece that finds its way into these materials, principally in Chapter
Six, is *The Supra-Constitution, the Courts, and the Federal Common Law of
Crimes: Some Comments on Palmer and Preyer*, a response to articles by those
two scholars printed in the Fall 1986 volume of the Law and History Review,
and done with the encouragement of the then editor Russell Osgood. Kitty

Preyer and Robert Palmer helped in that piece not only by their works which prompted it, but by corresponding with me and by patiently and painstakingly explaining why I was wrong and they were right—so they can be absolved of errors caused by my obstinacy in refusing to recant my views. My research assistant at that time, Darsee Staley, helped with research on the internal law of nations, which represented the core of that piece. Support at about that time and for the next year was provided by the Washington Legal Foundation (WLF), a public interest law firm committed to the preservation of the free market, which was actually granted in support of a collateral project, an undergraduate text now nearing completion, but which was also crucial for my continuing work on Samuel Chase. I am particularly grateful to Daniel Popeo, the WLF's President and General Counsel, who made that support possible, and who has continued to offer his encouragement throughout the years.

The final piece incorporated here, which has the same title as this book, was published in 1989, in the Northwestern University Law Review, which has granted permission to reproduce it in this form. Parts of that Article appear in Chapters Three, Four, Eight, Nine, and Ten. Kitty Preyer, who has always been an inspiration, read the book manuscript and offered further bracing advice, some of which I followed. Stephen Conrad, Jefferson Powell, Carole Rose and my wife, ArLynn Leiber Presser, similarly made valuable critical comments. The paper which eventually became that fourth article was given at a panel of the American Society for Legal History. As eventually published, the article was part of a symposium on late eighteenth century Judicial Thought, and in revising the article for inclusion in this book I was influenced by many of the comments made on it by the symposium's commentators, Suzette Hemberger, Daniel Walker Howe, and Jennifer Nedelsky. Similar debts are owed to those who organized and edited the symposium, particularly Jonathan Turley and Leslie Sowle. I also presented talks based on the article, in 1990, at George Washington University School of Law, and at an institute for judges sponsored by the Liberty Fund in Sugarbush, Vermont. I am indebted for the comments and the assistance received at both places, and particularly for the help provided by Raoul Berger, Ed Berkowitz, James McClellan and Gary McDowell.

I am also grateful to the Carolina Academic Press, and, in particular, to Keith Sipe, who undertook to publish the book and to Mayapriya Long, who brilliantly guided it through the editing and designing process. My secretary, Suzanne Williams, did her usual matchless job in preparing the manuscript, and I occasionally pirated the time of Patricia Goffer, secretary to several of my colleagues. My law school colleagues Marty Redish, Tom Merrill, and Larry Marshall have given me the benefit of their understanding of the federal courts, and my colleague in Northwestern's history department, Tim Breen, has tirelessly sought to prove to me what a villain Chase actually was, and what a saint was Jefferson.

This book has been about fifteen years in the making, and, undoubtedly, the failing memory of an absent-minded academic has rendered me unable properly to note others who contributed. I ask them please to accept my unacknowledged thanks and my apologies. Fifteen years though it may have taken, and stentorian assertions to the contrary in the body of the text notwithstanding, I am not so bold as to declare that it is, as yet, completely right, but I hope that it might offer a useful contribution to turn of the century jurisprudence.

Stephen Presser
Northwestern University
Chicago, Illinois

The Original Misunderstanding

Introduction

Samuel Chase, the Broken Promise of Federalist Jurisprudence, and the Original Misunderstanding

It was April of 1800 in Philadelphia, the commercial and social capital of the young United States. John Fries was on trial for his life, and Richard Peters was furious with Samuel Chase. Each time Peters, the United States district court judge for Pennsylvania, sat on circuit with Supreme Court Justice Chase, the irascible and abrasive Chase plunged himself, and usually Peters, into some kind of trouble. Now, in spite of Peters's warnings, Chase had managed to precipitate an imbroglio that had just finished with both of the defendant's counsel quitting the case in an elaborately staged fit of pique. Judge Peters knew that Fries's trial was politically very sensitive. The presidential and congressional elections were only a few months away, and John Adams and the Federalist cause, of which both Peters and Chase were supporters, were in grave danger. The Federalists had lost much ground in the skirmishes over their ill-conceived Alien and Sedition Acts, and more and more they were perceived by the American voting public as the party of brutish reaction and pampered aristocracy. The spectacle of prominent Federalist judges leaving a man accused of the capital crime of treason (for protesting taxes, no less) without the assistance of counsel was going to give their enemies, the Republican[1] editors and their presidential candidate, Jefferson, a field day. How, the congenial and affable Peters probably wondered, had he and his party gotten themselves into such a mess? What had gone wrong?

In what follows, an attempt is made to answer Peters's hypothetical questions. This book is an examination of jurisprudence, primarily in the federal courts, and primarily during the years 1789 to 1800, the period between the inauguration of George Washington and the election of Thomas Jefferson. This story is one of both jurisprudential analysis and human drama. It is a story of several judges, but principally of Samuel Chase. It is also the story of what appeared to the American public in 1800 as a broken promise, the promise of popular sovereignty under the administrations of Washington and Adams. The perception that this promise was not kept, of course, resulted in the event that Richard Peters and other astute Federalists had seen foreshadowed in the spring of 1800: the victory of the Jeffersonian Republicans in the presidential and congressional elections of 1800 and the American public's large-scale repudiation of Federalist politics. What even Peters could not have foreseen, however, was what happened a scant few years after that—the impeachment of Samuel Chase by the House of Representatives, following an aborted attempt to impeach Peters himself.

The removal of Chase, as all students of early United States politics know, failed narrowly, but not before congressional Republicans had repealed important Federalist judicial reforms and had succeeded in setting a pattern of neglect of the lower federal judiciary that would persist for seventy-five years. This book is an attempt to remedy the results of that seventy-five years of neglect, augmented by another hundred or so years of misunderstanding. It is an attempt to look into the minds of Samuel Chase and other early American judges and to try to understand how they could have acted in the manner they did, and what might have been notable and worthwhile in their jurisprudential efforts, efforts that have usually only been excoriated since then. This effort to understand Chase and his fellows requires an attempt to look beyond the often distracting surface manifested, in particular, by the peculiar personality of Chase.

Soon after the *Fries* trial, for example, Associate Justice Chase journeyed to Virginia where he sat, in another hotbed of rabid Republicanism, on the Richmond circuit. There he tried a case of seditious libel against a particularly rebarbative Jeffersonian scribbler, *United States v. Callender*.[2] Even before the trial began, Chase had determined that he would himself chastise the obstreperous Virginia anti-Federalists who were using the *Callender* trial in the manner the Pennsylvania Republicans had used the *Fries* trial, to turn what should have been a neutral judicial proceeding into a political forum to be used to embarrass the Adams administration.[3] Unfortunately for Chase, the Republican press managed to paint Chase's conduct in the *Callender* trial as unfavorably as it had in the trial of Fries. Chase's handling of the two trials was to furnish the core of the impeachment charges brought against him by the Jefferson administration in 1804.[4]

Following the trial of Callender, Chase returned to Maryland, there actually to go out on the hustings on behalf of President Adams's campaign for reelection. Because Chief Justice Ellsworth was also absent (though on a diplomatic mission) during this period, the Supreme Court was forced to postpone its sessions. This earned some acid comments from the Jeffersonian organ, the *Philadelphia Aurora*, which observed:

> [T]he business of the nation [was held up] until Chase shall have disgorged himself. *O Tempora, O Mores!* ... The suspension of the business of the highest

court of Judicature in the United States to allow a Chief Justice to add nine thousand dollars to his salary and to permit Chase to make electioneering harangues in favor of Mr. Adams is a mere bagatelle.[5]

By January 1801 the *Aurora* would say of Justice Chase that his "disposition was so arbitrary and his temper so ferocious and disregardful of decorum" that "few men, perhaps, hold a humbler estimation among his fellow citizens."[6] In time, the *Aurora* was to refer to the federal prison as "Chase's repository of Republicans." The Jeffersonian press's opinion, which has come to be that of virtually all American historians, was probably best summed up in the "vicious little couplet" published shortly after the *Fries* trial, in August 1800: "Cursed of thy father, scum of all that's base. Thy sight is odious and thy name is _____ ."[7]

For the *Philadelphia Aurora*, for the Republican press generally, and for American historians for the next one hundred and seventy-five years, Chase became a convenient symbol for all the failings of the Federalists: Chase's shortcomings were generally portrayed as common to those of the entire federal judiciary.[8] The popular success of the Jeffersonian electors in 1800 undoubtedly owed much to the press campaign to discredit the federal judiciary,[9] a campaign that could not have been waged without the superb target provided by the conduct of Samuel Chase.[10]

In early 1801, following the election of Jefferson, the lame-duck Federalist Congress passed the Judiciary Act of 1801.[11] The act traditionally has been excoriated by historians sympathetic to the Jeffersonian Republicans (as most American historians have been) as a blatant attempt to entrench the Federalists on the bench before Adams's term ended, thus to secure the one branch of the national government not yet lost to the Federalists. This motive on the part of the Federalists seems clear, but often lost sight of is the fact that the Federalists were equally motivated by the need to create several badly needed reforms in the judiciary which would have made the delivery of federal justice more comprehensive and more convenient.[12]

Owing in part to the opposition to the Federalist judiciary that had been stirred up by the criticism of Chase, however, the Judiciary Act of 1801 was perceived as purely partisan, and was quickly repealed by the new Jeffersonian Republican-dominated Congress with the cooperation of the new president.[13] What may be worse, probably because of the popular opposition to the federal judiciary evoked by the presidential campaign of 1800, Congress regarded the efficient operation and expansion of the lower federal courts as a very low priority matter. Over the next few decades the lower federal courts grew much less effective, as they came increasingly to be under a crushing workload, and meaningful reform of them was not accomplished until almost three-quarters of a century later.[14] This essay is offered to aid in the revelation of what there was about Samuel Chase in particular, and the Federalist judiciary in general, that could have helped lead to such congressional neglect of the federal courts, and could have helped lead to the almost total neglect by historians of the valuable work that was performed by the first federal judges. There is, however, a contemporary relevance to this study of the earliest federal judges.

The celebration of the United States Constitution's bicentennial and the furor surrounding the nomination to the United States Supreme Court of Robert Bork have recently led to a vigorous reexamination of the United States Constitution's "original intention." Judge Bork was well known as an "intentionalist," a scholar who believed that it was appropriate and desirable to try to understand the aims of those who framed the 1787 document, in an attempt to implement their understanding of their words in interpreting the Constitution today.[15] Such an attitude toward desirable constitutional jurisprudence was also prominently displayed by former Attorney General Edwin Meese,[16] and by Chief Justice William Rehnquist,[17] who argued that by rendering decisions in accordance with the framers' "original intent" or "original understanding," modern judges could avoid the pitfalls of substituting their arbitrary policy preferences for the intended values established by the Constitution.

Critics of the views of Meese, Rehnquist, and Bork, occasionally called "noninterpretivists," or more recently "nonintentionalists," have argued that it is futile to seek to discover the "original understanding,"[18] either because the Constitution's framers' intentions are shrouded in deliberate secrecy or obfuscated by the passage of two centuries, or because the "intentions" of the drafters may have differed either from those of the delegates to the state constitutional conventions who actually adopted the Constitution,[19] or from those of the "sovereign people" who voted for the state delegates. It has also been maintained that "original understanding" or "original intent" is unimportant because the Constitution's framers deliberately used open-ended phrases and concepts, aiming thereby to create a "living document," which would be interpreted and shaped according to the variant needs and spirits of future times.[20]

In one of the most brilliant recent articles on original intent,[21] however, H. Jefferson Powell demonstrated that the men who attended the proceedings in Philadelphia in 1787, at which the Constitution was drafted, did not believe that it was appropriate for future constitutional interpreters to seek to divine the framers' particular "legislative intention," that is, the framers' own personal interpretations of their language. Instead, Powell has argued, the framers wanted the Constitution to be interpreted in the manner of English statutes at English common law, according to the "plain meaning" of the words the legislature used and in accordance with judicial precedent. While Powell does not stress it, I think it is fair to say that his work also suggests that the framers also believed that it was possible to arrive at an "objective" interpretation of the Constitution by the method he explicates.[22]

Powell's views, then, offer no comfort for those seeking to revise constitutional law to be more in accordance with the demonstrable subjective beliefs of particular framers, as their critics accused Bork, Meese, and Rehnquist of desiring. Nevertheless, Powell's study of original intention does suggest the validity of an approach to constitutional interpretation which seeks to understand the foundation, the underlying assumptions inherent in the plain meaning of the words used in that document. To put it slightly differently, it is still necessary for us to try to determine the political, linguistic, or cultural "structure" which the Constitution implied, on which the drafters and first interpreters of the document would have been expected to rely, and on which their claims for an objective interpretation of the Constitution would have been staked.[23]

A principal aim of this book is to help delineate that original "structural understanding" of the Constitution, to elaborate what might be called a set of "supraconstitutional" or metaphysical principles of government which I believe the Constitution's drafters meant to embody in their 1787 document.[24] I share with Professor Powell the notion that the interpretation put on the federal Constitution by the first federal courts to pass upon it was of great moment to its framers. Nevertheless, I seek here to go a bit beyond Professor Powell, and to demonstrate that we have neglected to too great an extent the interpretation of the document done in the 1790s, the period immediately following the adoption of the document and before the events of the early nineteenth century. Accordingly, the subject matter considered here will be the epic judicial battles between the Federalist judges and the Jeffersonian lawyers and defendants. This is primarily a study of constitutional interpretation before the election of Thomas Jefferson as president and before the ascendance to the Supreme Court of John Marshall.

It is possible and laudable to try to understand the original understanding of those who gave us the federal Constitution, but before that can be done, we must come to grips with an "original misunderstanding" which occurred at approximately the beginning of the nineteenth century. The idea of such an "original misunderstanding" at that time is another way of conceptualizing what has recently been referred to as the replacement of "republican" by "liberal" jurisprudence.[25] A subsidiary aim of this book is to explore the character of republican legal thought, and, in particular, to suggest two jurisprudential strains of republicanism in America, a "conservative" strain manifested by Federalist judges such as Samuel Chase, and an "opposition" or radical strain manifested by Jeffersonian "Republicans" such as Alexander James Dallas, John Taylor of Caroline, and Thomas Jefferson himself. It is probably true that American legal thought moved generally from a republican paradigm to a "liberal" paradigm, but I seek to show here the complexity and diversity in that republican paradigm, a complexity hinted at by a few recent writings,[26] but so far relatively undeveloped in American legal historiography. This book is offered to complement recent efforts by American historians to participate in a "massive reinterpretation of the years surrounding 1800 as a period of sweeping cultural and social change,"[27] as suggested in such recent works as Steven Watts, *The Republic Reborn* (1987), and Michael Lienesch, *New Order of the Ages: Time, the Constitution, and the Making of Modern American Political Thought* (1988).

The attempt to delineate the original understanding, the original structural conception of the United States Constitution, made here differs from most previous accounts of the period by legal historians, in at least two respects. First, I seek to show that the original understanding, at least as it manifested itself in the mind of one leading federal judge, Samuel Chase, was as much about culture, morality, and religion as it was about politics or law, and, second, I seek to demonstrate that this original understanding, this implicit set of notions about the proper structural interpretation for the United States Constitution, owed much more than is commonly recognized to the experience of the British in the seventeenth and eighteenth centuries. None of this will be treated as revolutionary by general American historians, but even they may find something of interest in carrying this usually political discussion into the legal doctrines examined here.

It might be appropriate to greet this effort with some skepticism, since it relies to such a great extent on the thought and work of Samuel Chase—a man still commonly regarded by those who ought to know better as nothing but a "rabid partisan," a brutal courtroom bully who wrongfully used the bench as a "political stump."[28] Be that as it may, for anyone who has read the opinions and the jury charges of the pre-Marshall justices, it is difficult not to conclude that Samuel Chase was the most brilliant of the first justices. Though it is undeniable that Chase had what might well have been a pathological and marked tendency toward embroiling himself in controversy, it seems clear that he did the best job of coherently stating the judicial principles of late eighteenth-century federalism.

If Chase's views on constitutional interpretation and his implicit belief that he was implementing the original understanding were typical of the earliest federal judges—and I think they were[29]—it suggests that the original understanding of the United States Constitution involved a greater measure of aristocracy and deference than is usually presumed, and suggests that the "republican" order forged by the Constitution, as understood by its earliest judicial interpreters, was much closer in spirit to the monarchy of England than it was to some of the more strictly American concepts of democracy that were to eventually dominate in the nineteenth century.[30]

I will, then, seek to show here some of the details I believe comprise the original misunderstanding, the abandonment of the first federal judges' "supraconstitutional" principles, the jettisoning and transformation of the original structural interpretation of the Constitution. With this I hope to present a model of the dynamic character of constitutional interpretation as it occurred in the late eighteenth century, which I think also has some present relevance. Most of my effort here, however, will be to analyze episodes in the judicial career of Samuel Chase, and it is to a somewhat more detailed treatment of his career, his world, his political philosophy, and his jurisprudential thought that we must next turn.

The chapters that follow first examine the main elements of political and cultural conflict during the crucial decade of the 1790s, the debate between the "Federalists" and the Jeffersonian "Republicans" (chapters 1 and 2), and then move on to an examination of the peculiar jurisprudential variant of federalism practiced by Samuel Chase (chapter 3). Next the English influences on Chase's thought and that of his persecutors, the Jeffersonian Republicans, are explored in the course of outlining two strains of English and American jurisprudence in the late eighteenth century, here called "conservative" and "opposition" (chapter 4). The conflict between conservative and opposition thought in the federal courts of Pennsylvania (chapters 5, 6, and 7) and Virginia (chapters 8 and 9) is discussed next, and particularly the contrasts between the views articulated by Samuel Chase on the one hand and Thomas Jefferson and his surrogates on the other. Some comparison is also made between the conservative jurisprudence of Samuel Chase and that of John Marshall, an amalgamation of "conservative" and "opposition" thought, which supplanted it.

In all the analysis and description which follows, I will explore the manner in which religious and ideological assumptions and beliefs were developed in the jurisprudential and personal writings of Samuel Chase and his contemporaries. All of this is offered in the belief that when legal historians recognize and fully understand the religious and "republican" conceptions the pre-Marshall justices brought to their task, there may be a somewhat more realistic appraisal of Marshall's accomplishments. Just as the English lawyers discovered a real English feudal past, and then realized the mythical nature of the English "Ancient Constitution,"[31] when American scholars understand the fundamental differences between Marshall and his predecessors, they may find their historical consciousness altered in a manner that makes belief in an unvarying Marshallian "American judicial tradition" more difficult. In the concluding chapter it is suggested that this new awareness may ultimately aid in refashioning our legal institutions, as it did centuries ago in England.

1

An Introduction to Samuel Chase and His Era

Samuel Chase's Instinct for Tumult

The source of many of the difficulties encountered by the Federalist judges, alluded to in the preface, was, simply stated, the peculiar personality of Associate Justice Samuel Chase. Richard Peters described it aptly in a letter written about the time of the Chase impeachment. "Of all others," Peters told his friend and fellow high Federalist Timothy Pickering, "I like the least to be coupled with him [Chase]. I never sat with him without pain, as he was forever getting into some intemperate and unnecessary squabble."[1] While Richard Peters was a person adept in the nuances of Pennsylvania politics, and a man who strove to avoid controversy whenever possible,[2] Samuel Chase actively sought it. Peters made efforts to restrain Chase,[3] but he was dealing with one who "had the singular instinct for tumult which scents [it] at a distance from whence it is imperceptible to other eyes, and irresistibly impels a participation in it."[4]

Chase conceived of one part of the judicial task to be the correction of errant politics, and he attempted to impose his conceptions of appropriate political virtue on the unruly Jeffersonian Republicans in Pennsylvania and Virginia. It may be, of course, that Samuel Chase was simply blissfully unconcerned or unaware of the potential hazards he faced from the Jeffersonians, but it seems clear that he made very little effort to accommodate to the particular jurisprudential climates in which he found himself.

Some of Chase's behavior might be explainable on the simple basis that jurisprudence in Maryland, his home state, was different from that in other states. Horace Binney, the nineteenth-century historian of the Pennsylvania bench and bar who was apparently present during some of Chase's controversial conduct on the Pennsylvania federal bench, wrote that Chase's tactical error in *Fries*, in making the rulings that resulted in defendant's counsel quitting the case, owed something to Chase's "greater familiarity with the Maryland practice, where the judge used to respond . . . more exclusively for the law, and the jury for the facts, or rather more dividedly or separately, than was, in point of form, the usage in Pennsylvania."[5]

Similarly, Chase seems to have believed, that he, as a justice of the United States Supreme Court, should have been allowed to proceed as did the contemporary judges in England. Deference, he believed, was owed to him by those before whom he presided.[6] To the more clear-eyed of Chase's contemporaries, even in Philadelphia, Chase's rulings and conduct may have been regarded not as "intended oppression," but rather as "great mistakes" resulting from his character and background.[7] Nevertheless, that same character and background made it easy for the Republican press to manipulate and use Chase to achieve their own ends. The public opinion that Chase apparently did not care to understand, or, as we will see is more likely, which he simply was not equipped to comprehend, was forcefully turned against him and his party.

Even Chase's calmer sometime colleague Richard Peters was caught in the political cross fire, when, in early 1803, the Jeffersonian-controlled House of Representatives authorized a committee to inquire into the conduct of *both* Chase and Peters. It is likely, however, that there was never a serious intention to attack Peters. The real goal of the Jeffersonians who introduced this resolution may have been simply to remove Chase from the Supreme Court and substitute a Jeffersonian Marylander.[8] Whether or not there was ever a serious attempt to impeach Peters, the House committee reported that "no cause of accusation existed" and that Peters's judicial conduct "had uniformly been marked by prudence, decorum and moderation."[9]

This conclusion of the congressional committee investigating the impeachment charges suggested for Peters and Chase raises rather serious questions about the motivation of those who pursued Chase and dropped Peters. Since Peters had acquiesced in several of the controversial rulings Chase made in the *Fries* case, which case stood at the core of the impeachment proceedings against Chase, if the congressional opponents of Chase intended to be completely principled in their arguments of judicial misconduct, they should have put Peters on trial before the Senate with Chase.[10] That Peters was not pursued suggests that the selection of a target was not done with an eye toward maximum correction of judicial misconduct, but rather to strike at an unpopular figure and to secure a seat for a fellow traveler of Jefferson's.

Nevertheless, the implied congressional approval for Peters's judicial conduct, which was surely as partisan as Chase's in content if not in style, needs further explanation. It may simply be that this again illustrates the personal contrast between Peters and Chase, and suggests some caution about interpreting events in the early history of the republic as a reflection of divergent ideologies. Nevertheless, such an ideological interpretation will be offered here, and before it is undertaken, it might be wise to stress the limitations of such an approach, and the powerful effect, instead, of haphazard personality considerations.

Even before the congressional committee decided to drop Peters from the impeachment proceedings, he did not appear to have been terribly concerned that they would result in harm to him. He wrote to his friend Pickering:

> I know I am brought into the Field, without premeditation. One not invited to the Hunt turned me out like a *Bag-Fox*, to amuse & wary the Hounds and divert them from the real *Chase*. One of them opened on a wrong scent, not being well broke in. I suspect the Huntsmen know better & will not be thrown out.[11]

Peters's nonchalance and the display of his famous sense of humor[12] are in grave contrast to the grim and combative resolve with which Chase fought the impeachment proceedings.[13]

It would appear that Peters's insouciance resulted from the knowledge that he could depend on his wide circle of friends and contacts, a circle that reached right into the new White House itself, to save him from any congressional enemies. Richard Peters was a wise and witty old American patrician; he habitually rubbed elbows not only with high Federalists like Timothy Pickering, but was also known to entertain Thomas Jefferson himself at his mansion on the outskirts of Philadelphia.[14] Chase was an abrasive Ciceronian "new man," was bereft of soft manners,[15] did not possess the wide circle of friends that Peters did, and was infinitely better than Peters at building a circle of enemies.[16] Peters was able to be rescued at an early stage, but Chase had to suffer the humiliation and agony of a protracted Senate trial.

Still, while much of what happened to Samuel Chase and his fellow Federalists in the early nineteenth century has a lot to do with particular and peculiar personality traits, it is important that Chase's particular combative personality not be allowed to obscure more significant matters, nor to cloud our ultimate judgment of the man. Though there may have been these surface dissimilarities between Chase and some cooler-headed judges, such as Peters, and though Chase's personal characteristics may have had much to do with the political storm he created or was used to creating, it is now time to discard the Jeffersonian fabrication that Chase was some sort of an "American Jeffreys." He was not the unrestrained ogre or "hanging judge" that he is still commonly made out to be in the work of virtually all late twentieth-century legal and constitutional historians. We may have lost sight of what was understood by some of the more astute of the historians of the nineteenth and early twentieth century who described Chase as one of the "greatest" of Maryland lawyers,[17] "one of the most conspicuous and able members of the Continental Congress," "an ardent lover of liberty and justice," "persuasive and where possible conciliatory,"[18] "[d]isinterested and consistent in all things," and "the torch that lighted up the revolutionary flame in Maryland."[19]

There is much that was appealing in Chase's judicial career. His whole judicial philosophy, when it is considered in context, can be seen to have a popular base to it. His rhetoric indicated that his extreme views on the rights of criminal defendants in libel trials sprang from a conviction that in a government based on popular sovereignty, to libel the government was to libel the people themselves, and therefore intolerable. In the matter of the common law of crimes, as we will see, Chase's states-rights judicial opinion in the *Worrall* case was used to great effect by popular Jeffersonian politicians. It represented a real contribution to their Republican political theory about the extent of federal sovereignty.

Even Chase's conduct in the *Fries* trial, which figured so prominently in the invective hurled against him and in his impeachment trial, may not have been nearly as outrageous as the Jeffersonians have been successful in making most historians believe. Fries was subsequently pardoned by the popularity-seeking John Adams, and following his pardon, Fries himself was reported to have visited Chase at his home in Maryland "for the avowed purpose of thanking him for his impartial, fair and equitable conduct" during the trial.[20]

Most puzzling of all, perhaps, after his acquittal on impeachment charges, Chase appears to have attracted relatively little notice. One theory is that of Francis Wharton, the reporter of the American *State Trials*, who wrote in 1849 that "By the impeachment, his proud spirit seemed finally broken, and though when on the circuit he completed the business of the term with scrupulous exactness, he remained on the bench a silent judge."[21] I think a simpler explanation than Wharton's is possible. I think it was not so much a matter of Chase's spirit having been broken, but simply that his temper had cooled, and the exigencies of the period from 1800 to 1803 appeared to have passed. This is suggested by the fact that even before the impeachment trial, Chase had apparently chosen to return to what I believe to be, for him, a more profound jurisprudential principle than outspoken defense of the Federalist cause, and this was a rather restricted sense of what judges ought to be doing, what might be called Chase's "jurisprudence of restraint." Chase was prepared to propound this modest judicial role, even if this involved rejecting some aspects of the English example which Chase usually sought to emulate. While sitting on the Delaware circuit in June 1804, Chase wrote:

> I know that in England construction of the words of Statutes has gone a great way. This doctrine I explode. If the words of Statutes are clear, I am bound, tho' the provision be unjust. This I hold to be the duty of an American Judge. [A] Judge has in this country only to say *Sic lex est scripta*.[22]

It would seem, then, that Chase's wildest overreaction, his stepping out of appropriate judicial bounds in a manner that made him a bad judicial joke for so many Jeffersonians, and for so many modern American historians, was of relatively short duration. Chase's notorious behavior was only manifest for a brief period, from about 1798 to 1803, and the worst excesses were probably reached only during the 1800 term, when Chase sat on the fateful circuits in Pennsylvania and Virginia.

Popular Politics and Federalist Paranoia

Even a cursory examination of contemporary accounts and the best recent writing on the late 1790s and early 1800s makes clear, however, that this was a period marked by paranoia and overreaction, particularly among Federalists like Chase, but also among zealots on the Jeffersonian side, particularly the Republican editors whom Chase tried for seditious libel. If Chase seemed at times to exceed the other political actors in impact, it was a quantitative and not a qualitative difference.

Even Richard Peters, who was a relatively cautious and fair man, seems to have swung decidedly to favor the government in several of the criminal trials that will be reviewed here—by eschewing the technical niceties of federal law mandating the following of state procedure in the *Whiskey Rebels* trials,[23] by virtually ignoring the purpose of a provision in the Judiciary Act in the first trial of John Fries,[24] and by callously deprecating the necessity of a retrial in that latter case.[25] Like Chase, Peters perceived, in the late 1790s, dark designs forming in the United States, and he felt he was required to act accordingly. In a letter written in 1793 Peters mentioned that he was "convinced that the greater part of Europe is Scourged by War and Agitated with discordant political opinions." Nevertheless, in these early years, he thought there was relatively little cause for concern. "Although we have, like other nations," he conceded, "some uneasy spirit and tempers among us, yet the great body of the Nation is determined on Peace with all the World."[26] But by 1798, at the height of the Federalist hysteria over the threat posed to conservative governments everywhere by the success of Napoleon, and at the height of concern over rebellion in Ireland, Peters had become more worried. His friend Timothy Pickering told Peters on August 28, 1798:

> Mr. Rawle [the Federalist District Attorney for Pennsylvania] has written me about the secret projects of the United Irishmen: I now send him an answer. [P]ut this under cover to him. . . . It will perhaps be useful for you to see him, as both of you have at the same time had your attention excited by the same discontented characters which infest our country.[27]

When Peters was on official business concerning the Northampton insurgency of 1799 (an armed uprising in a Pennsylvania county not far from Philadelphia which resulted in the treason trial of John Fries), he assessed the situation and concluded: "I did believe that unless the army had gone through the whole county, there would have been the most atrocious instances of violence."[28] American historians have tended to belittle the significance of the Whiskey Rebellion and the Northampton insurrection, but there is very good reason to believe that there was a firm basis in fact for treating them seriously and for supporting Peters's gloomy assessment.[29] Finally, convinced that the country was in the direst peril, Peters assured Pickering that he [Peters] would make all necessary efforts "to get rid of a Set of villains who are ready to Strike when they think the Crisis arrives,"[30] and thus he and Chase appear to have been acting on many of the same impulses, even if Chase acted overtly while Peters (and Pickering and Rawle) performed more covertly.

Similarly, Supreme Court Justice William Paterson, who in an early judicial review case, *Van Horne's Lessee*,[31] had lauded the independence of the jury as the finder of *both* law and fact,[32] went out of his way to tell the jurors in the trial of the whiskey rebels exactly what they should conclude on legal and factual questions.[33] Another Supreme Court justice, a southerner, North Carolinian James Iredell, who seemed to be quite sympathetic to the defendant in the first trial of John Fries,[34] and who took great pains to tell the petit jury in that trial that he had no right to comment on the question of treasonable intention or overt acts,[35] had expressed grave concern to the grand jury that indicted Fries. "Some seem to have taken it for granted that credit could be obtained without justice, money without taxes, and the honor and safety of the United States only preserved by a disgraceful foreign dependence [on France],"[36] he said. "If you suffer this government to be destroyed," Iredell cautioned his grand jurors, "anarchy will ride triumphant, and all lovers of order, decency, truth and justice will be trampled under foot."[37] The same views that were reflected on the bench, of course, prompted Washington and Adams to send in thousands of federal troops to quell the two Pennsylvania insurrections during this period.

At this time also, a majority of Congressmen could be persuaded to vote for the passage of the Alien and Sedition Acts, giving rise to some of the trials soon to be reviewed involving Paterson, Peters, and Chase. By 1800 there were those in Congress who seemed to be actively seeking drastic methods to avoid the increasing possibility that Jefferson's popularity (or his demagoguery, as they saw it) would carry him into the presidency.[38] In this year of crisis even the wily Alexander Hamilton seems to have lost most of his self-control, hatching his ill-conceived plan to thwart the will of the legislature in New York by imposing a scheme that would take away their power to select presidential electors. One of Hamilton's best biographers concludes that this plan, which Hamilton eventually must have abandoned, was originated because Hamilton believed that "to save the country from the fangs of Jefferson, 'guile sophistry and fraud were lawful.' "[39] In those years Hamilton noted, "In times like these in which we live, it will not do to be over-scrupulous. It is easy to sacrifice *the substantial interests of Society by a strict adherence to ordinary rules.*"[40]

Even more surprising for the usually subtle Hamilton, in the course of the 1800 election campaign Hamilton was careless in expressing his feelings that President Adams had lost his judgment by such actions as making peaceful overtures to France and by pardoning John Fries. The publication of these sentiments, to which Hamilton apparently did not even object, probably did as much as anything else to weaken the Federalist cause from within and thus lose the presidential election of 1800.[41]

It was not, however, merely the exit of its own rats which eventually sank the Federalist ship of state. The chief problem, aspects of which will be explored here, had to do with a basic difference in political philosophy between the Federalists and the Jeffersonian Republicans. While the Federalists argued that their government was set up by the actions of the people in approving the federal Constitution and was thus bottomed on the concept of popular sovereignty, their political philosophy, in practice, left very little room for ongoing popular participation in government. The people could vote in elections and on constitutions, but once the people had cast their votes, at least according to the Federalist judges, the people were henceforth to refrain from harmful criticism of their properly constituted officials and were to obey them unquestioningly. Any other course, the Federalists believed, would lead to exciting "the passions and jealousies of the mob," and eventually to the collapse of all government.[42]

Such a philosophy, of course, once it was exposed to derision in a popular press such as that operated by Jeffersonian editors, was not likely to continue to enlist great popular support. It revealed a basic distrust of the wisdom of the people, and a judiciary that saw its role as "preaching wisdom to the untutored masses."[43] The Jeffersonian Republicans, who managed to convince the public that they had a greater faith in the wisdom of the people and who claimed a greater willingness to tolerate ongoing public participation in government (at least in their election rhetoric) were thus easily able to discredit the Federalists when it came time in 1800 to vote for presidential electors and for members of Congress.

This philosophical struggle is well known to all students of American history, but much less noticed is that the struggle over the proper role of the people in American government was played out to perhaps the greatest degree in the courts of the early republic. The struggle over the popular nature of the American polity explains the surprising results of the trials for seditious libel, in one of which, the *Cooper* case,[44] Samuel Chase made rulings that, in effect, made it impossible for the defendant to engage in fair political comment without being able to demonstrate "beyond a marrow" the truth of his opinions.[45] Just as important, but perhaps somewhat subtler, was a struggle in the nation's courts during this period over the proper roles of judge and jury. There was a feeling in most quarters in the late eighteenth century in America that the expansive participation by the jury in legal decisions was an essential safeguard to the liberty of the people.[46] This required that the jury be given the latitude to pass on questions both of "law" and of "fact," and received at least lip service from both the Federalist judges and the Sedition Act of 1798 itself.[47]

Nevertheless, the conduct of the Federalist judges in closely instructing the jury in many of these cases as to the appropriate legal and factual conclusions and the tendency of Justice Chase, in particular, to remove "legal" issues from jury discretion opened the Federalist judges to charges of oppressing the people, and led to the popular victory of the Jeffersonians. To an extent that seems to have escaped virtually all the historians of the Federalist period, much of the discordant behavior of the Federalist Judges and the Jeffersonian lawyers on this point can be explained by the fact that they simply meant different things by the terms "law" and "fact."[48]

Unplanned Obsolescence

This difference over the meaning of basic jurisprudential terms on the part of the Federalists and Jeffersonians is a symptom of a deeper difficulty on the part of these political antagonists, an inability to cast off the preconceptions of the eighteenth century, particularly the preconceptions derived from English political thinkers, and English political struggles. Chase and his fellow Federalists, men like Hamilton, Adams, Peters, and Pickering, whatever their differences, believed in a structured society, the inevitability of different social classes, and the subordination of the lower orders to the upper. Their view was that the yeomen and the mechanics of America ought to be content with a system where their "betters," the large landowners, the members of the learned professions, and the titans of commerce ruled for the common good.[49] Accompanying this view, paradoxically, however, was probably an almost medieval pessimism about the chance for success of their conception of government. It is probable that among these "old Whigs" a real faith in progress was not firmly planted. The likelihood of things deteriorating loomed much larger. We have recently seen, in the work of Gerald Stourzh and other historians of republicanism in early America, how a Federalist like Hamilton was terrified by the force of the love of power and of the possibility of demagoguery leading inevitably to dictatorship.[50]

Jefferson's first administration in 1800 confirmed Hamilton's fears, and shortly after Jefferson's electoral victory, Cassandra-like, Hamilton predicted to his friends the inevitability of "bloody anarchy," and could offer no alternative but "grief and terror." At best, there was a slim chance, he believed, that like Napoleon rising out of the French terror, or like Caesar emerging from the chaos of Roman civil war, out of the coming American debacle "a strong, stable, and 'energetic' government would emerge."[51] Samuel Chase mirrored these views exactly. In March 1803, even before the impeachment efforts against him had resulted in charges being brought, he wrote John F. Mercer: "I believe nothing can save the *present* [Jeffersonian government] from dissolution. . . . The Seeds are sown, they ripen daily. Men without *sense* and without *property* are to be our *Rulers*. . . . Confidence is destroyed. . . . Things must take their natural course from *bad* to *worse*."[52]

There were influences at work here much broader than medieval Republican theory, however. Indeed, Chase's deepest feelings about the freedom of the press, which he invoked in favor of the Federalist cause, in two trials for seditious libel, actually bear the eighteenth-century stamp of French revolutionary philosophy. Like Robespierre in the French terror, Chase seems for some tortured months to have believed that "freedom consists not in doing what one wants to do, but in doing what is right." When Chase, like Robespierre, or his mentor Rousseau, perceived that he was confronted with an apostle of wickedness, he felt compelled to act to protect the rest of society, even if this contributed to his own downfall.[53] Alas, by 1800 the times had passed Chase and Hamilton by, and their conception of popular sovereignty, sincere though it may have been, was no longer acceptable to most Americans, or at least to those who influenced presidential and congressional elections.

With this outline of the peculiar personality of Samuel Chase, his political predilections and those of his Federalist colleagues, and the nature of the legal issues which resulted in political struggles in the late eighteenth century in America, it ought to become somewhat easier to understand why the record of the federal courts in the late eighteenth century must be read in light of the broader personal, political, and ideological struggles of the period. With this introduction to Samuel Chase and his time broadly sketched, we can move on to our principal object, the examination of jurisprudence in the early Republic. Our first task will be to describe in detail some of the differences between the popular Jeffersonian or Republican political and judicial theories and those of the Federalists, like Samuel Chase. Second, we will see how the efforts of the Federalist judges initially met with some success, but how eventually their thought was distorted by their opponents and used to discredit them. Third, we will see how there *were* some common threads in both Federalist and Jeffersonian jurisprudence and politics, but we will note how those common themes were lost sight of in the fierce struggle between the Federalists and Jeffersonians. Finally, we will see how our jurisprudence was, arguably, impoverished, when John Marshall concocted what might be described as a bastard synthesis of the two earliest American Republican jurisprudences.

The impeachment of Samuel Chase, which appears as a coda to the period here discussed, had a profound impact on the course of the federal judiciary. While this is widely recognized, the tendency on the part of American historians has been simply to focus on the outcome of the episode—Chase's eventual acquittal by the Senate. Since that time, of course, no justice of the Supreme Court has been impeached; neither has the impeachment remedy been used as "a means of keeping the courts in reasonable harmony with the will of the nation."[54] Nevertheless, the very institution of impeachment proceedings caused some major changes in judicial practice, Marshall's new jurisprudential "synthesis." John Marshall seems to have realized that had the Chase impeachment been successful, he would have been the next target.[55] This must have redoubled Marshall's tendency to appear above political controversy, and to avoid, where possible, the resolution of issues bound to plunge the court into the political thicket.[56]

Marshall's circumscription, learned from Chase's mistakes, and the substance of his jurisprudence, learned to a great extent from Chase's successes, enabled him to establish what has been called "the American judicial tradition"; and led to the notion current among American legal historians that the prestige of the national judiciary runs only from Marshall's tenure as chief justice.[57] According to this consensus view the Supreme Court was thus able to remain highly visible and to make its contribution to American development. Still, probably as a result of what happened during the 1790s, the lower federal courts atrophied and declined in importance over the next seventy-five years, as Congress refused to implement the remedies required for truly effective federal justice. More tragic still was the loss to our judicial and historical tradition, until recently, of a way of integrating jurisprudence with law, morality, and politics, a view in part shared by the Federalists and their Jeffersonian adversaries, and a view closer to the "original intention" of the Constitution's framers than may have been the jurisprudence of John Marshall.

2

The Federalists and the Challenge of Pennsylvania Radicalism

Revising the Conventional View
of Samuel Chase

According to the conventional view of Justice Samuel Chase, he was "a 'hanging judge' if such ever sat on the bench of the Supreme Court of the United States."[1] He is the only United States Supreme Court justice ever to have had impeachment charges brought against him by the House and to be tried in the Senate. He is almost universally described as "grossly partisan,"[2] an "American Jeffreys,"[3] or, at best, "a strange, inconsistent man"[4] and "stormy patriot."[5] His reputation as a partisan stems principally from his activities from 1800 to 1803 opposing the Jeffersonian Republicans and supporting the Federalist John Adams administration, and by implication supporting the "elitist" philosophy that the Federalists were perceived to represent. He has become virtually eponymous for the callousness and insensitivity to popular opinion that eventually lost political control for the Federalists.

Those who brought the impeachment charges against him argued that his conduct on the bench was too blatantly pro-prosecution to be tolerated and that he used his judicial position as nothing more than a convenient public forum for the propagation of partisan Federalist party positions. And yet, from time to time, legal historians examining Chase's jurisprudential record have noticed that he does not completely fit the Federalist mold. Morton J. Horwitz,[6] for example, while presenting Chase as a firm Federalist, noted that Chase's opinion that the United States had no common law of crimes was unlike that of any other Federalist.[7] The brilliant but erratic constitutional historian W. W. Crosskey even went so far as to assert flatly that "Chase was not a Federalist, as so often has been erroneously stated."[8] Crosskey based his conclusion primarily on Chase's opposition to the federal Constitution of 1787,[9] and asserted that Chase's partisanship in the early nineteenth century stemmed simply from the "personal animosity" between Chase and Thomas Jefferson.[10]

It was true that Chase was among the anti-Federalist opponents to the federal Constitution of 1787, but Chase altered his views on the propriety of a strong central government when the French Revolution created what he perceived to be a real threat to American liberty, and he became allied with the Washington and Adams administrations. Crosskey seems to have made the mistake of confusing the meaning of "Federalist" in 1787, which contemporaries and most historians used to refer to those who favored the proposed federal Constitution, with "Federalist" in 1800, which came to mean those who believed in the wisdom of the policies articulated, consistently or inconsistently, by Washington, Hamilton, John Adams, and others.[11]

Still, Crosskey was correct that some of Chase's practices, particularly regarding matters of procedure, did not always accord with those of his fellow Federalist judges. Not only did he differ on the issue of common law crimes, he also was inclined to issue subpoenas to members of Congress when at least one of his colleagues refused.[12] He was willing to take into account what he believed to be political partisanship when determining punishment, though his colleague on the bench, Richard Peters, refused to do so. Apparently alone among federal judges, he opposed reading presidential instructions into the record of judicial cases. He also seems to have been unique in his preparation of opinions on the law to be delivered to juries before defense counsel had an opportunity to argue the contrary.[13]

The conventional characterization of Chase, as a brutal unthinking Federalist partisan, accepted by virtually all American historians as the correct characterization of the man, is in error because it is a far too simplistic description of his judicial thought and conduct, and because it ignores too many complexities in the character of the man, in his political conceptions, and in the times in which he lived.

While some mystery still surrounds Chase's political career, it is apparent that during the revolutionary and early national years Chase was perceived as a magnificent champion of the people.[14] He was a signer of the Declaration of Independence, and served the patriot cause relatively honorably during the Revolutionary War.[15] During and after the war, Chase assumed an active role in Maryland state politics. His laudable initial service was as a principal architect of the Maryland Constitution of 1776. This document was "fraught with checks and balances, and with . . . powers so distributed between aristocracy and people, that destructive radicalism seemed impossible. Nevertheless, during Chase's service in the Continental Congress and in the Maryland legislature in the 1780s, he proved that a politician demagogically playing for the multitudes could launch the most outrageous schemes for private profit at public expense. While Chase's most daring schemes for personal financial aggrandizement were apparently regularly exposed, his success with Maryland popular politics, and in particular his attacks on the Maryland "aristocracy," usually insulated him from serious personal or political harm.[16] Chase's sensitivity to Maryland popular opinion, or possibly his sincere feelings about concentrated and centralized aristocratic authority, a sensitivity and feeling which he held in the late 1780s, led him to become a vehement opponent of the proposed federal Constitution.

Recent scholarship on the anti-Federalists of the late 1780s, the opponents of the federal Constitution, and a group that, by all accounts, included Samuel Chase, suggests that they were engaged in a profound ideological and philosophical struggle to understand the place of man in society. Influenced by the English experience of the seventeenth and early eighteenth centuries and the eighteenth-century colonial American experience, they were men "of little faith,"[17] men who looked backward in time and who believed that the principal lesson of history was that republics could only survive if local authorities with firm ties to the local community directly controlled governments and if unchecked power in a central government was never permitted. This was clearly the early view of Samuel Chase. He opposed the federal Constitution on the grounds that it tightly constricted the sovereignty of the individual states and left the way open for tyrants at the federal level.[18] Chase's early vision of the ideal American society was one in which there was communication among a ruling class at a national level, but also one in which local politics was the major force in government.[19]

Like his later foe Jefferson, Chase initially believed that landowners in a particular state ought to be primarily responsible for any political activity. Chase apparently concluded fairly early, however, that there was much more use and honor for those practicing commerce than Jefferson ever seemed willing to allow.[20] The sort of commerce Chase had in mind was agriculturally based; he never concluded that the produce of the land was anything but the primary source of wealth for a country. Unlike Alexander Hamilton, whose *Report on Manufactures*[21] accurately forecast the future, Chase probably concluded that the old ways of the eighteenth century were the best. Accordingly, one might best characterize Chase as a traditional English conservative, though his revolutionary era opposition to Great Britain and to "Tory" sympathizers seemed quite radical.[22]

As did so many of his American Whig colleagues of the late eighteenth century, Chase apparently believed that it was possible to construct a pristine social order in America.[23] This social order was to be a replica of what was thought to have once existed in England, where sturdy English yeomen imitated the civic virtue of the citizens of the Roman republic and selflessly participated responsibly in government by paying taxes, serving in militias, and serving on juries.[24] Further, according to this theory, once their temporary service to the community was over, citizens were expected, as did the Roman Cincinnatus, to go back happily to their farms.[25] Chase's earlier views were probably more democratic, but by the late 1790s they had changed. When he could see the havoc being wreaked in Europe in the name of democratic ideas, Chase came to share the Federalist notion that popular participation in the ongoing affairs of government ought to be limited to special occasions such as taxpaying, militia and jury service, and voting. Most affairs of the government, he came to believe, were best placed in the hands of those natural leaders whose ability was reflected in their greater accumulation of virtue, wealth, and education. In Chase's ideal deferential political system, even when individuals of lesser social standing participated in government through militia and jury service, or the payment of taxes, they were expected to be guided by the wisdom of their popularly selected leaders. Moreover, they were expected to choose leaders from the natural ruling class.[26]

After the Revolution secured America's independence from Great Britain, and following a visit to England in 1784, Chase apparently concluded that late eighteenth-century English society had much merit. As his biographers report, "The simple republican from Maryland clearly enjoyed seeing the pomp and magnificence of royalty, In fact, he was quite taken with England in general, reportedly speaking [of it] 'in raptures' upon his return to America."[27] Whether or not Chase ever was a "simple republican," and my reading of him indicates he was anything but simple, once he returned from England, for the rest of his professional life, Chase sought to implement some British deferential notions, particularly in his judicial activities. The trip to England, it seems fair to say, may have ended up spoiling him for increasingly democratic Maryland.

In the early 1790s, Chase served both as the chief judge on the Maryland General Court, the state court of highest jurisdiction, and as a judge on a lower level state criminal court. Concerned that lapses of public order in Maryland might presage conditions which would lead to excesses like those of the French Revolution, Chase vigorously punished breaches of the peace and mob action and became very unpopular as a result. Because there was some doubt about whether Chase's dual judicial service was constitutionally permissible in Maryland, his political enemies launched an impeachment drive against him. They asserted that his dual appointment violated the law and was a ground for removal from office. Although the effort failed, the increasingly popularly sensitive legislature did not renew his annually granted commission for the lower-level criminal court.[28]

The Maryland impeachment attempt and other democratic developments in late eighteenth-century Maryland politics convinced Chase to continue his earlier efforts to seek a more secure judicial position at the federal level. He and his sponsors renewed their requests, which they had begun in 1789, for a federal appointment for Chase, and assured Washington that Chase had become a firm friend of the Federalist administration.[29] In 1796, Washington rewarded their efforts by appointing Chase as an associate justice of the United States Supreme Court.

Chase already had a reputation as something of a difficult man. One of the chief causes of his rather unsavory reputation was his participation in what Alexander Hamilton and others perceived as a disgraceful commercial scandal. While he was serving as a member of the Continental Congress in 1778, Chase and some trading partners cornered the Baltimore market in flour futures. At about the same time Congress was confidentially ordering flour purchases in the mid-Atlantic states for troops in New England. This little misadventure in flour futures is the most difficult thing for one potentially sympathetic to Chase to comprehend or sanction. Still, it may be that Chase's activities were simply the result of shrewd business judgment rather than the use of confidential information received as a congressman. Indeed, "[n]o direct proof of Chase's breach of congressional trust or of his intention to engross was ever produced."[30] The coincidence of Congressman Chase's trades in flour and the congressional purchases was too much for Alexander Hamilton, however, who anonymously attacked Chase for such an egregious breach of duty. Writing as "Publius," Hamilton declared that Chase's actions made him "one public character as abandoned as any the history of past or present times can produce."[31]

The row over the flour purchases temporarily set back Chase's career as a state and federal politician. He lost his seat in Congress when the Maryland legislature failed to reelect him because of his reported speculation.[32] Nevertheless, it must be remembered that by the most prevalent standards of the day, it was not necessarily bad form to profit commercially while serving in a governmental capacity. Even as late as the 1830s, Justice Joseph Story, for example, served as a Supreme Court justice while he was simultaneously a chaired professor at Harvard and also the president of the Merchant's Bank of Salem.[33] Even the luminous John Marshall, while he was the chief justice of the Supreme Court, appears to have been able to profit handsomely from land speculation.[34]

Chase (and Story and Marshall, for that matter) might have logically rationalized commercial conduct, and perhaps holding dual offices, on the ground that political preeminence required that one project the assurance and independence of affluence. In this manner one could better gain the respect and cooperation of one's colleagues and constituents.[35] Chase, the son of a rather penurious preacher, must have quickly realized that he could not initially achieve such respect without commercial success, because he had not been born into the Maryland landed gentry. Chase must have assumed that it was not only convenient, but morally required, to amass a sufficient fortune to give him the financial independence that would enable him to make the highest civic contributions of which he was capable.

Perhaps not understanding this deeply avaricious altruism on Chase's part, some prominent Federalists strongly opposed his appointment, owing to what they perceived as his unsavory reputation.[36] One wonders, then, why the shrewd Washington would make such a nomination to the nation's highest court. Those who have studied this period have not been short on explanations for the Chase appointment. Their apologia for Washington's actions in appointing "The American Jeffreys" usually has three elements. Scholars have suggested that, first, the court was not very important at that early date. Second, they point out, almost no one was willing to serve on the court. Third, they suggest, with Chase's appointment the president was more or less scraping the bottom of the barrel.

This usual explanation is badly in need of revision, as it demonstrates a severe lack of familiarity with the actual facts and characteristics of federal jurisprudence in the early Republic. With regard to the importance and quality of the court: Despite John Jay's resignation as chief justice, and Washington's unsuccessful attempt to persuade the eminent John Cushing to accept appointment to the court, contemporaries apparently believed that the court *was* an important institution and important and impressive work was being done by the justices, although principally when they rode circuit. Taking into account all that we now know about the early court and its justices, Jay "seems to have stood almost alone in his opinion that the judiciary needed a complete reorganization to give it dignity and strength."[37]

Good and capable people were quite willing to serve on the early Supreme Court; Oliver Ellsworth, the chief justice Washington eventually selected after Cushing refused, was one of the most influential members of the United States Senate. Private correspondence about Ellsworth's appointment strongly suggests that Ellsworth and his fellow Federalists believed that his move to the court was a step up to a more prestigious position. More importantly, perhaps, it was a move that his Connecticut constituents could have regarded as in the best interests of the entire country.[38]

Chase was a man of very real talents, despite his being tarred with some scandal. He was a most knowledgeable judge, a sophisticated legal analyst, and a gifted conservative theoretician. Indeed, it appears that Chase was so talented that Washington was willing to ignore the strong advice against his appointment, based on Chase's thorny personality, which he received from Chase's critics. There is some clear evidence that those urging the appointment did so because of Chase's great skill as a legal and political scholar.[39] Still, while Washington probably regarded Chase's appointment to the court as an important event, the real purpose for the appointment is unclear because the wily Washington kept his motives to himself.[40] There is enough evidence in the correspondence about the appointment to suggest, however, that Washington made the appointment principally because he felt that he owed the South another high appointment, and Chase's background as a Marylander qualified him as a southerner.[41] Chase's status as a representative of the South may have inclined him in a particular direction in the course of rendering some of his early judicial decisions, although as he spent more time on the court his views lost their regional character and grew closer to those of his brethren on the bench.

Chase's joining the Federalists in the 1790s has been seen as a puzzle by his biographers, who have been struck by his earlier Republican activities in Maryland. As we have seen, though, this was a natural development spurred on in part by his contact with England, and by aging. Some of Chase's more uncharitable observers have suggested that his switch from democratic politician to Federalist may have merely reflected the kind of personal ambition that drove so much of his career. This factor cannot be discounted, although, as suggested, Chase may have seen his ambition as more altruistic than selfish. It seems more likely, however, that by this time, when he was well into middle age, his earlier democratic fire had cooled.[42]

As the events of the 1790s in Pennsylvania and elsewhere demonstrated significant popular dissatisfaction with the perceived policy of the ruling Federalists, Chase's political allegiance to the Federalists hardened still further until he was to engage in the activities that were to make him the hated symbol of partisanship. As explained in chapter 1, however, what happened to Chase was not unique. Chase's expressions of political sentiments may have had a particular style and force, but the environment to which he responded was not one which he inhabited alone. Viewed from what must have been the perspective of many other Federalists, Chase's actions have a certain inevitability about them and suggest that his motives were not uncharitable.[43]

Before examining what Chase did on the bench, then, before describing what came to be taken as his manifestations of extremism, it seems worthwhile further to consider their source, to expand the inquiry beyond him, to pause to explore the political atmosphere of the late 1790s in general, and the Federalist theories of politics in particular. Furthermore, we will soon see that many of the key events which influenced the nation, Chase, and his career took place in Pennsylvania, and we might, at this point, also consider what was happening in that state in the 1790s.

Consensus and Conflict 1776–1789

In order to understand the tensions that developed in the 1790s in Pennsylvania and elsewhere between the Federalist judges and the emerging opponents of the Federalist party, it is now necessary briefly to sketch the background of late eighteenth-century American politics. In the years leading up to the Declaration of Independence, men of fundamentally different mature political philosophies—John Adams, James Madison, Thomas Jefferson, and Alexander Hamilton—all considered themselves "Whigs." They were essentially in agreement in their political and legal conclusions that the British were failing to allow Americans the full liberties provided in the British "Constitution" as that political arrangement was understood in the colonies.[44]

Following the Revolution, however, this surface political hegemony broke down as a result of new political and economic forces. Men who had fought in the revolutionary army for "liberty" saw in this elusive value differing visions of what they had intended to achieve.[45] For some, like John Adams, American liberty ultimately may have meant little more than the implementation of his view of the British mixed constitution.[46] For others, however, like Benjamin Austin of Massachusetts and Benjamin Franklin Bache and William Duane of Pennsylvania, the separation from Great Britain presented the opportunity to place ultimate authority not in the person of a monarch in Parliament, as England had done, but in the American people themselves.[47]

As a result, during the years following the Revolution and preceding the federal Constitution, in Pennsylvania and in most other states, governments were set up to implement the principle of popular sovereignty through strengthening the legislatures at the expense of the executive. Of all the states, Pennsylvania went furthest in this direction, though it is still fairly typical of the tendency. The Pennsylvania Constitution of 1776 provided for no governor at all; instead, there was to be a popularly elected committee which would exercise executive functions. The legislature was also given control over the tenure and salary of judges, thus ensuring the legislature's ascendance as the premier political force. Nevertheless, to make the legislature more responsive to its theoretical master, the people, Pennsylvania required annual elections of representatives, required representatives to subject their acts to the instructions of their constituents, and required the legislature to submit proposed legislation to popular review.[48]

Immediately following the implementation of these new state constitutions, the new state legislatures proceeded to exercise not only legislative but also executive and judicial functions. This broad legislative activity had ramifications affecting many important economic and political interests. With varying degrees of frequency, state legislatures issued paper money and required its acceptance as legal tender, ordered confiscations of the property of suspected loyalists, and suspended or obliterated contractual debts and duties.[49] The threat to property and contract rights inherent in these activities (and the concomitant risk of legislative tyranny) was perceived fairly quickly by conservative Whigs, and they began to put together an alternative political system to replace legislative supremacy.

Federalist Political and Judicial Theory

The main principle of this new American political theory, as every schoolchild in America knows, the principle which reached its furthest expression in the federal Constitution of 1787, was that government should be composed of a number of powerful elements which could "check" and "balance" each other.[50] Because popular sovereignty had by this time become the essential prerequisite for success of any political theory in America, proponents of the federal Constitution, and of corresponding governmental changes in the states, saw that the success of their proposals depended upon popular approval of the new constitutions. Thus the proponents of the new constitutions argued that once the new governments were created pursuant to the new constitutions, each branch of government was still to regard itself as an agent of the people, and to behave accordingly.[51]

The judiciary's relationship to the people was more subtle than that of the executive or legislative branches, which were subject to popular vote. According to the new Federalist theory as embodied in the federal Constitution, judges were to be appointed, not elected, and they were to have tenure during good behavior. As the final arbiters of whether or not the other two branches were conforming their activities to the dictates of the Constitution, the written manifestation of the people's wishes,[52] the independence of the judiciary from the other two branches was thought to be crucial.

For many years in America there had been a fear of judicial discretion, and the fact that under the federal Constitution judges were to enjoy good behavior tenure while passing on the legitimacy of the acts of the other two branches rekindled some of these old fears about judicial arbitrariness.[53] The proponents of an enhanced judiciary had to counter these arguments by asserting that the judicial function, as it was to be exercised in the new American Republic, would simply be one of lawfinding, and not lawmaking. Judges were to guide their decisions only by the clear dictates of reason and common law precedent and, ultimately, by the plain words of the constitutions.[54] Judges' deviations from these guidelines, so the argument ran, could be readily perceived and the constitutional remedy of impeachment applied.[55]

The Federalists believed that once these new conceptions of political power could be implemented, the strong federal government which they envisioned would be able to restrain the dangerous majoritarian trends in some of the states. The federal Constitution would thus assure the necessary protection to the recently endangered individual property rights. Ultimately, it was hoped, the foundation thus erected could support the expanded trade, commerce, and development that Federalists like Alexander Hamilton or Samuel Chase thought were necessary to ensure the success and permanence of an independent American Republic.[56] The role of the judiciary was to be crucial in this enterprise, and federal judges were to be relied upon to see that justice, order, and dignity would take the place of anarchical confusion.[57]

The federal judicial experience, particularly in Pennsylvania and Virginia during the late 1790s, suggests that the Federalist theory about responsible, enhanced judicial power gave the impression of not working out in practice. Because of this gap between the Federalists' "popular" rhetoric and the public perception of actual federal judicial practice, the newest practitioners of popular politics, the Jeffersonian Republicans, could more easily discredit the national judiciary and Federalist politics generally. In order to understand this phenomenon, it is necessary to review in further detail events in the 1790s in Pennsylvania and Europe, and understand how these affected the temperament and outlook of Samuel Chase and his fellow Federalists.

The Pennsylvania Rebellions and the French Revolution

In the last section we observed how Pennsylvania, in 1776, had adopted a set of popularly based constitutional provisions which made it apparently the most unstable state in the country. As a means of redressing this instability, Pennsylvania conservatives managed, in 1790, to pass a new state constitution modeled on that of the federal government. This document reflected its framers' desire to lessen popular influence, to trim the power of the lower house, and to strengthen the senate and the executive.[58] While Pennsylvania's state government may thus have been made more conservative and stable in theory, in the years to follow the citizens of Pennsylvania proved that they were still the most rebellious in actual practice.

In 1794, when the United States government sought to collect long overdue revenues under an excise tax on whiskey originally passed by Congress in 1791,[59] the residents of western Pennsylvania resisted collection with violence. The tax struck hard at the economy of the region west of the Allegheny Mountains.[60] Many of the residents of that region engaged in armed attacks on federal excise officials in the summer of 1794, often resorting to the injudicious use of tar and feathers. For several months during 1794, federal authority was completely ended in western Pennsylvania. Federal commissioners sent to observe the situation concluded that "nothing less than the physical strength of the nation could enforce the law in western Pennsylvania."[61] Several thousand men of western Pennsylvania took up arms in opposition to the federal statute in one form or other,[62] and President Washington finally dispatched a contingent of fifteen thousand federal troops to restore the authority of the federal government to the affected area.[63]

Strikingly similar, although not as violent or extensive, citizen resistance to federal taxes broke out in eastern Pennsylvania in 1799, in the so-called "Fries Rebellion." This time the disturbances centered on a proposed federal assessment on houses, but the methods of opposition were close to those utilized in the Whiskey Rebellion of 1794. The Federalists also quelled the 1799 uprising by the dispatch of federal troops, this time authorized by President Adams.[64]

Compounding the problems caused to the Federalist administrations by the two outright rebellions in Pennsylvania during these years was the rise of a virulent opposition press. During the early 1790s two organs, Philip Freneau's *National Gazette* and Benjamin Franklin Bache's *Philadelphia General Advertiser* (the name was changed to *Philadelphia Aurora* in 1800), grew more and more openly hostile to the Federalists. By 1798, in fact, the Federalists sought to silence Bache by prosecution at common law for seditious libel.[65] Almost immediately following Bache's death, which short-circuited his prosecution, the editorship of the *Aurora* was taken up by William Duane, a confirmed antiaristocrat, who raged so bitterly against the Federalists that he may have had the major responsibility for the passage of the Sedition Law of 1798. In particular, Duane took the Federalists to task for their handling of the *Fries* trial and rebellion, and presented their conduct as a gross overreaction to the situation; according to Duane's *Aurora*, unnecessary brutality was used in subduing an already quiescent population.[66]

It seems to be the currently accepted wisdom of American historians that Federalist conduct in suppressing these two Pennsylvania insurrections did go too far. According to this view, the "overreaction" in the *Fries* affair was particularly instrumental in creating the perception that the Federalists were hopelessly out of touch with popular opinion and thus in helping the victory of the Jeffersonians in the elections of 1800.[67] To an extent that has escaped those adhering to the conventional view, it must be stressed that labeling the conduct of the Federalists in quelling these two rebellions as an "overreaction," if accurate, is only the wisdom of hindsight. It bears emphasis that to contemporaries, the Whiskey Rebellion and even the Fries Rebellion represented very real threats to the continued existence of an independent and complete United States.

Many responsible Americans, not all of them firm adherents to the Federalist faith, felt that the Whiskey Rebellion had the potential of developing into a full-scale civil war.[68] As even the critics of the Federalists among modern historians appear occasionally to acknowlege, the "Whiskey Rebellion had the potential to spread to several other states, and to affect a great many American citizens."[69]

The Fries Rebellion is habitually dismissed by modern American historians as a minor incident, almost of comic relief, involving principally unlettered German immigrants, mounting a feeble demonstration against what they believed to be unfair taxes. It is time we abandoned this view of the matter. In 1799, when the Fries Rebellion took place, judgments about the seriousness of the situation in that rebellion, judgments which viewed the events as of equal seriousness with the Whiskey Rebellion, were actually made, although the evidence of them is missing from virtually all modern histories of the period, and appears to have all but disappeared. This is probably because the current un-

derstanding of the Fries Rebellion appears to be based directly or indirectly on
F. M. Eastman, "The Fries Rebellion" (1922).[70]

Eastman's "history," which is really only a few pages from his longer work
on Pennsylvania lawyers, *The Courts and Lawyers of Pennsylvania* (1922), is
more or less lifted from an account that appeared in a Pennsylvania journal,
The Democrat, during 1860. This account is in W. W. H. Davis, "History of
the Rebellion in Milford Township, Bucks County in 1799" (1860) (which
now exists in the form of newspaper clippings in a bound volume in the Historical Society of Pennsylvania). A reading of this account suggests that it is
strongly influenced by what appeared in the *Philadelphia Aurora*, hardly an
unbiased source. Moreover, Davis's clippings collected in the Historical Society of Pennsylvania were annotated in longhand by one Jacob Rice, writing in
1860. Rice appears to have some firsthand knowledge of the Fries Rebellion
and writes

> This unfortunate affair happened at a period of great political excitement, and
> I do not believe that a strictly impartial history can at this time be furnished. The
> sources from which W. Davis has drawn his information appear to me to have
> been too favorable to the party opposing the measures of the United States Gov-
> ernment, as much of the blame, according to his statement, is laid to the charge
> of the assessors etc., which may be correct as it regards Bucks County. In North-
> ampton County [where Fries himself lived] such a charge cannot be
> sustained...
>
> My impression has always been that if the Federal authorities had not early
> surrendered captured prisoners when local insurgents demanded their release
> Bethlehem would have been burnt and razed to the ground.

So that to contemporary observers, then, the threat to peace in the 1799 rebellion was quite probably a real one.

It would have been easy, if not inevitable, for Chase and other Federalists to
see the events of the 1790s—particularly the Whiskey Rebellion, the Fries Rebellion, and the activities of the opposition press—as part of a pattern of
events they had seen many times before, and leading to a conclusion that they
knew only too well. This pattern could be observed in both the recent American and European experience. During the colonial period it was a fairly common occurrence for Americans seeking redress from perceived abuses to bring
their causes into the streets. Most of these demonstrations had been brought
about through well-organized committees of insurgents, and often those fomenting the disturbances implemented their schemes through written articles
or "constitutions" to which many citizens were persuaded to subscribe. In
some instances, the power of the insurgents was so great that they were able
to intimidate voters, to levy their own taxes, to dictate to colonial courts, and
to deploy their own militia. In several colonies, extralegal groups which had
started as popular resistance movements to royal government eventually me-

tamorphosed into provincial congresses. Representatives of these groups became the Continental Congress, the body that eventually declared American independence.[71]

For many years, and in particular during the period of the Confederation (the decade following the Declaration of Independence), men of wealth and influence in America had watched uneasily the increasing frequency of organized demonstrations by the "people out of doors."[72] While it was one thing, as Professor John Reid has shown, for Americans such as the "Sons of Liberty" to stage demonstrations against the British before the Revolutionary War,[73] it was quite another for these popular demonstrations to continue after the British enemy had been routed.[74] The Federalists of the late 1790s, men like John Adams and Samuel Chase, had once condoned and even participated in demonstrations of popular sentiment during the revolutionary years. Chase, for example, was a member of the Maryland Sons of Liberty, and was denounced by the colonial aldermen and mayor of Annapolis as a "busy, restless incendiary, a ringleader of mobs, a foul-mouthed and inflaming son of discord."[75] But once American independence had been won and governments presumably responsive to popular sentiment had been erected, the old "Whigs" began to worry about the continued popular discord.

During the later 1770s, mobs often roamed the streets intimidating merchants, dictating prices, and generally disturbing the peace. In the 1790s there were riots in Boston, New Haven, Philadelphia, and Charleston. Worst of all, in western Massachusetts in 1786, the popular uprising known as Shay's Rebellion ended the authority of the Massachusetts legislature and judiciary for several months until the state militia restored it. Even in conservative Virginia, courthouses were burned and tax collectors were stopped. In Pennsylvania during the Whiskey and Fries rebellions, the press and popular demagogues had inflamed the people with notions that no government had the right to tax them and that the Federalists were bent on crushing the people through the establishment of an American aristocracy and a monarchy.[76]

By the early 1790s these popular ideas and popular disturbances seemed to bear too close a resemblance to what was happening in France to be taken lightly. The 1794 Whiskey Rebellion, in western Pennsylvania, occurred two years after the September Massacres in France, where more than one thousand people had been executed, and approximately one year after the French regicide and the atrocities of the Terror, in which more than twenty thousand people lost their lives.[77] As was true in England, many contemporary Americans regarded the French Revolution as "a proletarian movement aiming at the destruction of private property" and feared a similar upheaval here.[78] The fact that the American "Democratic Societies," groups vocally supportive of the French Jacobins, appeared to have been implicated in fomenting the Whiskey Rebellion went far toward discrediting those societies. Moreover, the linkage in the minds of many concerned Americans between the Jacobins and the American "Democrats" encouraged the parallels between the disorder in contemporary France and the Whiskey Rebellion.[79] Apparently, American public opinion, including that of the more conservative Federalists, rapidly turned against the Democratic Societies and the whiskey rebels, particularly following President Washington's November 1794 denunciation of the societies for their role in the Whiskey Rebellion.[80] Most Americans appeared not to want a drama similar to the French betrayal and destruction of the French constitution of 1789 to occur here.

While the atrocities of the Terror abated in France after 1794, other French activities continued to alarm the Federalists. Even the somewhat more conservative French Directory, which held office in those years, did not appear to have abandoned the announced French goal of promising "French aid to all peoples wishing to regain their natural liberty."[81] Americans watched with increasing concern the French absorption of Belgium, the Rhineland, Savoy, and Nice, and the creation with French aid of "buffer republics" in Holland, Switzerland, and Italy.[82] All of this led to the "undeclared" naval war with France of 1797–1800. That war initially enjoyed great popular support following the disclosure of the French perfidy revealed by the "X,Y,Z" correspondence in 1796, when three French ministers demanded of American envoys that the French Directorate be given a colossal bribe in order to secure peace with France.[83]

Once news of the defeat of the French fleet at Trafalgar in August 1798[84] reached America, however, the political climate in the young Republic began once again to change. Fears of French invincibility dissipated. There began to be less alarm at the possibility of yielding to French force and thus risking a war with Britain. The collapse of commerce, public credit, and fiscal planning that would accompany such a war now seemed unlikely, at least to the general public and the opponents of the Federalist administration.

Nevertheless, it seems very likely that many Federalists continued to worry about events in France being repeated in the United States. In France, in June 1799, a parliamentary revolution overthrew the dictatorial French Directory, and legislation was passed imposing "a forced loan on the rich. . . . and a law which permitted the authorities to take hostages in the families of notorious *emigres* or suspects. . . . "[85] This news came just a year after the bloody Irish rebellion, against the established property owners in that unhappy place, and further played on the fears of the American propertied classes.

All of this must have added to perennial Federalist fears of an American popular uprising. It is not difficult to see, then, why John Adams could have been easily persuaded to send in troops to quell the Fries Rebellion in 1799, or to see how Chase and other Federalists could have been alarmed at this 1799 disturbance.

Francis Wharton, in the introduction to his *State Trials*, published in 1849, writes of the years of the late 1790s as "by far the gloomiest period in our history," and a period when there was actually a threat that part of the American west would fall under direct foreign domination.[86] As late as 1799 both the Federalist attorney general of the United States, Charles Lee, and Alexander James Dallas, a leading Republican (of whom more will be said later), carried sword canes, in fear of the general political fury.[87] Small wonder, then, that Adams might "overact" or that other Federalists might assume that the French experience might be repeated here. The postindependence popular mob actions, then (and in particular the Whiskey and Fries rebellions), profoundly enraged and perplexed Adams and his Federalist brethren. They could see the revolutionary justification for popular rebellion against British tyranny,[88] but they were determined to put a stop to rebellion against a government created by "the people" themselves. As it turns out, they were able to use the federal courts and the jurisprudential thought of men like Samuel Chase in their efforts.

Chase's English-influenced vision of the good society for America may not have accurately taken into account the emerging political realities of his native Maryland, to say nothing of Pennsylvania or Virginia, in the late eighteenth century. In the early 1800s, the Maryland "sons," whose "fathers" had erected a deferential republican constitution in 1776 under Chase's guidance, began to dismantle that structure in the name of participatory representative democracy. Deferential land-based politics, at least in the larger commercial cities, gradually gave way to popular participation. Correspondingly, the center of gravity for American economic and social life eventually became manufacturing and commerce rather than agriculture. In a series of developments which would reach fruition only at the end of the nineteenth century, new American species of city-dwellers, artisans, manufacturers, entrepreneurs, and "urban proletarians" began to accumulate in the cities. These new urban dwellers fostered direct political action and participation of a type that threatened Chase's vision of good government and republican virtue in America.[89] In England, similar phenomena eventually led to the passage of the Reform Bill of 1832.[90] Americans, however, who did not have a landed Whig aristocracy and who had less of a tradition of deferential politics than did England, insisted on electoral and economic reforms much earlier.[91]

Eventually, a new American republican theory arose to articulate the individualistic philosophy of the rising manufacturing-based commercial and entrepreneurial interests.[92] This new acquisitively individualistic republican, or, as it is more properly called, "liberal," theory had the potential to substantively transform the law.[93] Before this happened, however, judges such as Samuel Chase tried to control and reverse what they believed to be dangerous trends. Chase did not see some of these changes in American society for what they were—ineradicable alterations in the nation's economic and demographic structure. He regarded them, rather, as the reversible results of failures of will by insufficiently virtuous Americans, Americans beguiled by democratic French and alien rhetoric. The manner in which Chase sought to reinculcate virtue and reverse perceived lapses is the principal subject of the next chapter.

3

Samuel Chase and the Dialectic of Federalist Jurisprudence

Introduction: The Relevance of the Jurisprudence of a Conservative "Republican"

In the late 1790s, Samuel Chase strove to articulate a jurisprudence which could stave off the threat to American republican virtue posed by French atheism and French conceptions of democracy. Chase, who began his political career as a demagogic anti-Federalist and a virulent opponent of the federal Constitution, in the later years of his life, given what he could see happening in America and Europe, came to believe that some of his earlier political assumptions were dangerously inappropriate. The task of this chapter, then, is to outline the nature of Chase's early and late jurisprudence, in order to understand the reasons why he engaged in the judicial conduct to be reviewed in the next few chapters.

Chase's ideological odyssey may be put in the terms of analysis recently favored by American historians. He began as an adherent of what has recently been called American "country" republican ideology, with its attendant belief in the importance of guarding against strong central authority, drawing inspiration from the Harringtonian, Bolingbrokian, and Lockean English political philosophies. Chase eventually became, however, a champion of Burkean and Hobbesian ideas, believing in the necessity for a strong central authority to check inevitable tendencies in America (or in any popular republic) toward anarchy and chaos. Chase thus moved closer to what has been called the "court" strain of Anglo-American political ideology, as he became associated with the Federalists in their battles against the Jeffersonian Republicans.[1]

While the aspects of Chase's personal ideology which resulted in his opposing the federal Constitution in 1787 made him appear quite politically removed from the Federalist champions of the Constitution such as Madison, Hamilton, and Jay, Chase eventually became the very symbol of the Federalist judiciary. In much of the remainder of this book, we will seek to see how Chase cannot only be viewed as an exemplar of Federalist jurisprudence, but also consistently with the attempt made here to discover an "objective" manner of interpreting the Constitution in accordance with its framers' original structural intention, we should be able to see how Chase's opinions, and those of his fellow Federalist judges, articulated "objective" judicial principles that can lay some claim to being inherent in the 1787 document.

In the course of trying to demonstrate that a study of the evolution of Chase's jurisprudential thought can reveal a richness in Federalist jurisprudence in the 1790s which should belie the still-dominant notion that nothing worthwhile in the history of American judging occurred before John Marshall,[2] we will soon need to place Chase's jurisprudence somewhat more clearly in the context of other contemporary theories about the manner in which judges and juries ought to function, and the manner in which constitutional jurisprudence ought to be articulated.

In the remainder of this chapter, however, we will first examine the essential jurisprudential conclusions at which Samuel Chase arrived in the late eighteenth century and early nineteenth century, the notions which resulted in his impeachment by the Jeffersonians in 1805. Then the chapters which follow will compare and contrast Chase's ideas with those of some of his contemporaries, in particular the English, Pennsylvanians, and Virginians. The goal of all of this will be to articulate a particular ideological model, which offers an interpretation of American legal thought as proceeding along a dialectic with recurrent stages of thesis, antithesis, and synthesis.[3]

Essentially, what is suggested is that this American jurisprudential dialectic unfolded in the following manner: Chase and several of his Federalist colleagues drew many of their jurisprudential strategies from contemporary English sources, and their moves were then opposed by Jeffersonian Republicans whose jurisprudential rhetoric invoked some other, primarily English, jurisprudential or philosophical ideas. The ideas of the Jeffersonians were ostensibly antithetical to those of Chase and his colleagues, but a close examination reveals that they actually shared certain of Chase's philosophical premises. In reaction to this ostensible conflict between Chase and the Jeffersonians, however, those who followed them on the American benches, and in particular John Marshall, articulated a jurisprudential synthesis that purported to reflect earlier notions of constitutional law, but actually moved beyond them.

I do not seek to demonstrate that the jurisprudential dialectical straitjacket to be woven here fully reveals the richness of the jurisprudential struggles of the time, which are probably as complex and as eloquent as any in our history, and which, like all historical events, are incapable of complete reproduction. I do hope, nevertheless, that the dynamic model here offered has some heuristic value, and can add something to our appreciation of the dynamic character of American law.

It is frequently suggested that our political tradition is a moderate one[4] and perhaps if one took account, toting up an average, so to speak, of all the utterances of our principal political figures throughout their long lives, we could classify virtually all of them as moderates. Often in their careers, however, these same leaders—Jefferson, Hamilton, Calhoun, Lincoln, and both Roosevelts come to mind—took positions that would have to be classified as extreme, either in response to extreme assertions from others or on their own initiative. Whether or not the overall American experience, or even that since 1800, has been one of political pragmatism and moderation (although the Civil War and Reconstruction could hardly be so classified), there have certainly been periods in our history of real combat between extremist ideologies, when even our most famous moderate minds moved to the far reaches of the ideological spectrum.[5]

The 1790s and early 1800s, as described in the last chapter, was such a period of American and European immoderation, when the American revolutionary experiment seemed terribly threatened, when two rebellions wracked Pennsylvania, when Europe was ripped asunder by the French revolutionary wars, when twenty thousand lost their lives in the French Terror, when Philadelphia gentlemen carried sword canes for self-defense from the mob, and when some judges, like Samuel Chase, frantically issued jeremiads in a desperate attempt to save the Republic.

Chase's Jurisprudence of Restraint

Against Visionary Theories

Chase's principal jeremiad, and a full statement of his mature jurisprudence, was his charge before the Baltimore grand jury in 1803.[6] He was appalled by the fact that the Jeffersonians in the United States Congress had repealed the Judiciary Act of 1801 ("The Midnight Judges' Act");[7] he was dismayed that the Jeffersonians in Maryland had established universal male suffrage; and he was distressed that the Maryland democrats were threatening to abolish one of the important Maryland courts. Chase explained to his grand jurors that it appeared to him the country and the state were headed down the road to "mobocracy." He urged the grand jurors to realize and communicate to their fellow citizens that Americans could only enjoy true freedom if their persons and their property were protected by the laws, and that this protection could only be achieved if the judiciary was immune from the kind of tinkering the Jeffersonians were engaged in at the federal and local levels.

Chase further suggested that universal suffrage was a product of fanciful and "visionary theories" which erroneously maintained that all men should continue to enjoy the rights (presumably equality, fraternity, and liberty) which they possessed in a state of nature, and that it was equally erroneous to suggest that ownership of property should confer no superior political rights. Chase rejected these Jacobin, Lockean, Paineian,[8] or Jeffersonian notions, in stark Hobbesian terms. He explained to his grand jurors that there were no rights at all in a state of nature, that governments were formed not to protect all in the equal enjoyment of rights, but rather of necessity, when the weak in supplication sought the protection of the strong, because that was the only way open to the weak to assure even their existence, to say nothing of particular "inalienable" rights.

The cold, hard fact, according to Chase, who had taken to heart the lessons to be learned from the excesses of France during the Terror, from the Whiskey Rebellion, and from the Fries Rebellion, was that the only way to avoid mobocracy was to erect restraints around democracy. Suffrage, and thus the power to make laws, Chase explained, had to be limited to those with sufficient property and discretion (in his terms, "a sufficient interest in the community") to be able to exercise independent judgment. Voters, in short, had to have the resources and the judgment to prevent them from being the prey of designing demagogues.

In this grand jury charge in 1803, as he had been doing for several years, Chase also sought to reply to the assertions of some of these "visionaries," again probably Paine and Jefferson, that government was a matter completely secular, and that one's religious beliefs had no bearing on one's virtue as a citizen. Chase explained that the finest minds who had pondered the problem had all concluded that there could be nothing that really could be said to be "law" without a firm moral base, and that such a firm moral base could not exist without a religious foundation under it. In short, there could be no law without morality and no morality without religion.

By religion, Chase had made clear in several pronouncements, he meant a Christianity with an eschatology including a Day of Judgment when the Lord would mete out everlasting punishment or reward in a world to come according to one's conduct on earth.[9] While the First Amendment to the Constitution prohibited a church establishment supported by the public purse, Chase not only did not take that prohibition to mean that the Constitution forbade judges to infuse their jurisprudence with religion, he assumed such infusion was required.[10]

Chase's Early Decisions

Even before the Jeffersonians came to power, however, Chase had given evidence of the jurisprudential premises which he believed were necessary in order for the rule of law and its concomitantly required judicial independence to function. Curiously, these earliest decisions have much about them of antifederalism, or country republican theory. It is worth remembering at this point that when George Washington appointed Chase, he may have been as interested in appeasing the philosophical convictions of many southerners as he was in giving them a representative from their geographical territory. It appears likely, as well, that Chase's first few years on the federal bench may have pleased those southerners, the majority of whom once espoused "anti-Federalist" theories, particularly those in Congress who urged his appointment and who might have been expected to fear a diminution of the role of the people's representatives in the legislature at the hands of an overbearing executive.

In his first years on the national bench, for example, Chase avoided pronouncements which would suggest that Congress, the most popular branch of government, did not possess the power to effectively collect taxes. Indeed, Chase early appeared reluctant to exercise judicial review and quite willing to presume the constitutionality of congressional acts.[11] Further reflecting some of the traditional "country" fears of his fellow anti-Federalists of the previous decade, Chase seemed wary of deferring too much to the federal executive.[12] This attitude may explain his refusal to agree to the reading of *Executive Instructions* in the Supreme Court.[13]

For Chase, in these early years, the most important sources of law for the judiciary, and the most important sources of binding authority, were the Constitution itself and the acts of the federal and state legislatures. He would have looked askance at attempts by other organs of the federal government to formulate authoritative rules. Accordingly, in his first opinion on the federal common law of crimes, *United States v. Worrall*,[14] Chase concluded that the tenth amendment guaranteed that the federal courts could not punish criminal acts until the federal legislature had first defined such acts and apportioned punishments. In this case, then, and in his other early opinions, Chase reflected a conservative "country" strain clearly evident in the emerging Jeffersonian Republican party,[15] a party including in large part former anti-Federalists. The core ideas of the Jeffersonians continued the beliefs of the anti-Federalists; in particular, they emphasized the necessity of a strict separation of powers and cautioned against the accumulation of too much power in the executive.

Even in his early years on the bench, however, elements of Chase's jurisprudence suggested that it might be difficult to restrain his power as a judge, and even though these elements were common in the thought of some of the anti-Federalists, as we will see, they could eventually be turned to the hierarchical and centralizing ends of the Federalists. Most prominent in this vein is Chase's first published opinion on the Supreme Court, *Calder v. Bull* (1798).[16] Chase acknowledged that judges could rely on certain fundamental inherent, though not express, constitutional principles in order to overrule the acts of state or federal legislatures:

> There are acts which the federal or state legislature cannot do, without exceeding their authority. There are certain vital principles in our free Republican gov-

ernments, which will determine and overrule an apparent and flagrant abuse of legislative power; as to authorize manifest injustice by positive law; or to take away that security for personal liberty, or private property for the protection whereof the government was established. An act of the Legislature (for I cannot call it a law) contrary to the great first principles of the social compact, cannot be considered a rightful exercise of legislative authority.[17]

Chase's *Calder* opinion sets forth supraconstitutional principles of "free Republican governments" consisting of preventing "manifest injustice," and maintaining "security for personal liberty or personal property." He left the precise reach of these great principles vague. Nevertheless, Chase did give some examples of legislative "acts" which could not be dignified with the name "laws," and which these supraconstitutional principles would necessarily invalidate—*ex post facto* laws, laws which destroyed or impaired private contracts, laws which made men judges in their own cases, or laws which took the property of A and gave it to B. Chase's *Calder* opinion became a foundation for later theories of "substantive due process"[18] and for later convictions that there could be found "penumbras" and "emanations" from constitutional provisions or principles, as was done in our time by the Warren and Burger courts.

The notion that certain fundamental principles circumscribe every government's actions is also an element of Jeffersonian republicanism. This element, however, is usually associated with its more radical exponents, such as the young Thomas Jefferson who drafted the Declaration of Independence, or his Virginia colleagues, such as Virginia Chief Justice Spencer Roane.[19] A great tension existed in the jurisprudence of those such as Chase, who believed in fundamental principles of justice and yet who could not accept the argument of Federalists such as Richard Peters, who believed in the existence of other fundamental supraconstitutional principles. An example of one such principle that Peters offered, a principle without which Peters believed that none of Chase's cherished supraconstitutional maxims would be possible, was a national right to self-defense. Peters believed that this national right to self-defense dictated the existence of a federal common law of crimes,[20] but Chase, as we have seen, rejected this view. This acceptance of some supraconstitutional principles and rejection of others on the part of Chase created a tension too great to go unresolved for long in his work, and when he did resolve it, however briefly, it appears he accepted the notion of a federal common law of crime. Thus, Chase did not abandon his belief in fundamental principles of justice.

Moreover, at least rhetorically, Chase and Jefferson shared the same perception of the ultimate source of supraconstitutional principles as "nature's god."[21] More than Jefferson, however, Chase proceeded, in the late 1790s, to accept the arguments of his Federalist colleagues that atheistic France would seduce and corrupt America if American judges did not religiously stand firm and do all they could to protect Americans from the excesses of French and Francophilic democratic and rationalistic thought. The task of an American judge, Chase eventually understood, was to encourage the American people to exercise steadfastly and religiously their republican virtue in resisting atheistic democratic temptation.[22]

Chase's rationalistic, Lockean vision of inherent principles of justice as expressed in the *Calder* opinion soon shaded into the darker, more traditional Hobbesian, Haleian, or Burkean vision eventually fully expressed in his 1803 Baltimore grand jury charge. Chase arrived at this conservative metamorphosis or metempsychosis through a series of judicial steps that are briefly outlined in the section which follows, and which will be developed in subsequent chapters.

The Rule of Law and Required Restraints on Legislatures, Judges, and Juries

Chase's notions of the rule of law, his basic jurisprudential precepts outlined in *Calder v. Bull*, seemed to have a strong component of required restraint on the legislature, and, considering his opinion in the *Worrall* case, there was, at least initially, a similar component restraining the judiciary. In 1798, 1804, 1805, and 1806, Chase declared his belief that the lawmaking function was exclusively in the hands of legislatures and that the task of judges was simply to follow what the legislature laid down. Most controversially for a purported Federalist, as indicated, Chase applied this principle to mean that there was no federal common law of self-defense which permitted federal judges to punish crimes in the absence of a federal statute defining the crime and setting forth a penalty.[23]

Chase was the only Federalist appointee to issue an opinion to that effect before the victory of the Jeffersonians in 1800. In doing so, Chase may have seriously undermined the efforts of Federalist prosecutors and some other Federalist judges who believed that bringing indictments pursuant to a federal common law of crimes was the only effective means to protect the fledgling republic from the threat these Federalists perceived from Jacobin sappers and miners. Chase's arguments against the federal common law of crimes were rapidly picked up and used against the Federalists by Jefferson and Madison in the Virginia and Kentucky resolutions, and in the halls of Congress by Jeffersonians excoriating what they claimed to be the paranoid excesses of Federalists.

Somewhat later, in the course of the campaign for the presidency in 1800, when Chase's friend John Adams was locked in ideological struggle with the Jeffersonians (and the Hamiltonian Federalists), Chase elaborated on his jurisprudence in a manner that did not sit well with the Jeffersonians, and which formed the bulk of the case against him during his trial on impeachment charges before the Senate in 1805. This elaboration had to do with a third set of restraints, this time on the jury, a favorite political institution of English and American Whigs since at least the time of the *Seven Bishops*.[24]

It had become something of a major premise of legal lore that the jury in America was actually the judge of fact and law, but Chase interpreted this maxim to mean only that the jury had the job of making what we would now call "the law of the case," the application of the legal standard given by the judge to the unique facts, as found by the jury, in that particular case. This meant that in the trial of John Fries[25] Chase declared it was improper for defense lawyers to argue that the existing federal treason precedents were bad law, and it meant, at the trial of a particularly loathsome Jeffersonian party writer in Virginia,[26] that the jury could not pass on the constitutionality of the Alien and Sedition Acts of 1798.

Finally, and in the same Virginia trial wherein he rejected the attempt to make a jury a judge of constitutionality, Chase declared limits on the type of factual evidence which a jury could consider. Essentially declaring the principles of the rules of evidence as they now govern,[27] Chase held that evidence which went to prove only a part of a complex factual assertion made by the defense was inadmissible, unless evidence was offered of all the elements of the complex assertion. To admit such a partial proof, Chase suggested, would be to risk prejudicing the jury, who might erroneously believe that full proof had been offered. Chase's jurisprudence thus required that the judge sit as a careful monitor over the conduct of the counsel addressed to the jury. This was because Chase conceived of the jury, a popular institution, as an essentially passionate and easily misled fact-finding organ.

Competing Jurisprudential Models in America and England

Having thus glimpsed the basic elements of Chase's comprehensive jurisprudence of restraint, we must next examine from what sources it was derived and how it fared in application. These supraconstitutional matters, these principles of high politics, these circumscriptions of juries, legislatures, and judges were nowhere specified in fundamental written charters or statutes, and opinions could and did differ as to their validity.[28] These different jurisprudential opinions, while they, like Chase's, might well have been an attempt objectively to interpret the Constitution, had to flow from something more than an interpretation of the plain meaning of the words of Constitution and law, and, as we will see, the sources of these opinions of Chase's, and of his antagonists, were taken from the differing political, religious, and moral ideologies which flourished in the Anglo-American Atlantic community in the late eighteenth century. Most of the sources of Chase's jurisprudence of restraint and his supraconstitutional principles predate the 1787 United States Constitution, and thus might be argued to have been part of its structural interpretation.

In order, then, to illuminate the differences between the views of Chase, those of his antagonists, and those of his successors, and further to illustrate how Chase's and their jurisprudential and political paradigms worked, the next tasks are to discover the competing bases for the jurisprudence of Chase and his antagonists, which will be undertaken in the following chapter. Before moving on to examine this jurisprudential dialectic, some last words need to be said, however, about the differences between this dialectical approach to jurisprudential thought and the form of judicial analysis more commonly found among American legal historians.

The publication of such works as diverse as Roscoe Pound's *The Formative Era of American Law* (1936) and Morton Horwitz's *The Transformation of American Law: 1780–1860* (1977) have encouraged American legal historians to conceive of American legal evolution as a linear progression, with certain key legal personalities, such as James Kent, Joseph Story, Lemuel Shaw, or John Marshall transforming the law in accordance with new visions of what American culture required. This "transformation" model should be revised, however, to take account of the facts that "transformations" are rarely clearcut, that vestiges of old rules and old ideologies have a disturbing way of rising, phoenix-like, from their own ashes, and that major figures themselves may represent complex and conflicting legal or ideological strands. What follows is conceived in that spirit. The analysis presented here seeks to illustrate how Samuel Chase, his contemporaries, and his antagonists adhered to jurisprudential notions drawn from complex and competing ideologies, and how their adherence to these ideologies often led them to take inconsistent political or legal positions. Further, this study is designed to demonstrate how, in seeking to implement their competing views, Chase, his antagonists, and their successors produced jurisprudential transformations, reactions, and retransformations.

In the following chapters, the method that will be used will be to examine the beliefs of those whom Chase encountered in several different environments—in England (chapter 4), in Pennsylvania (chapters 5, 6, and 7), and in Virginia (chapters 8 and 9). As we are now beginning to realize, there seem to have been several identifiable different legal cultures in several of the states of the early republic, and several of these cultures had elements which clashed dramatically with Chase's beliefs, and caused him difficulty.[29] As the thought in the different jurisdictions in which Chase found himself is considered, it should become evident that Chase's notions of "Republicanism" came to differ from those of many of his contemporaries, particularly the Jeffersonians, many of whom had been his ideological colleagues during the late 1770s and 1780s, when they and he opposed the proposed federal Constitution.

When Chase's actions came to be judged within a framework of thought which differed substantially from his own, he may himself have despaired at the impossibility of realizing his values in nineteenth-century America. Worse, as will be explored in some detail in chapter 9, Chase may not have understood how much in common he shared with the jurisprudential antagonists he faced, particularly in Virginia. Nevertheless, elements of Chase's jurisprudence combined with the thought of his antagonists, in a dialectical manner, and eventually resulted in a jurisprudence which did finally win wide acceptance in nineteenth-century America.

This new legal ideology, represented by such figures as Story and Marshall, did not take the place of a simple or clear-cut "community" or "Republican" vision of the law,[30] but rather replaced several fragmented and highly ideological individual jurisprudences of several of the individual states. To an extent that has so far escaped most American legal historians,[31] these fragmented state jurisprudences owed their character to divisions over political and legal issues in late eighteenth-century England, divisions which Chase himself observed in a formative year in London, following the Treaty of Paris, in 1783. In order to begin to appreciate the influence of English ideas on Chase and his antagonists, then, we first examine the England Chase came to know.

4

An English Shield of Achilles

Chase was in England from September 1783 to August 1784 as an agent of the state of Maryland, in order to settle some claims resulting from the wartime confiscation of Maryland's assets in England. Very little of this trip was actually spent on Chase's legal mission, since it proved highly intractable, and in between bouts of attending to his business Chase took the opportunity to study what was happening in London. He seems to have been on terms with the great and the near great, spending a fortnight with Edmund Burke, and meeting William Pitt, Charles James Fox, Thomas Erskine, and other important English political and legal figures.[1]

The tableau that spread itself before Chase as he viewed eighteenth-century London and England must have been one as rich and lively as that on Achilles's Shield.[2] As G. M. Treveleyan's famous description ran, Chase saw "An age of aristocracy and liberty; of the rule of law and the absence of reform; of Latitudinarianism above and Wesleyanism below; of the growth of humanitarian and philanthropic feeling and endeavor; of creative vigor in all the trades and arts that serve and adorn the life of man."[3]

Chase could hardly have picked a richer time to be in England. Lord North's ministry had collapsed as a result of his losing the American war. The radical dissenters were hammering away at the need for parliamentary and other legal reform, and William Pitt was just beginning to launch his spectacular career as prime minister. Seventeen eighty-four was the year when Samuel Johnson died, when the English nation was poised uneasily between the loss of the American colonies and the acquisition of its new empire in India and Australia, and in a moment of peace before the long revolutionary wars with France. It was a time of national stocktaking, and Chase studied it all with relish.

He seems to have been dazzled by what he saw, and might be considered to be something of a late eighteenth-century Lincoln Steffens[4] from the other end of the political spectrum. Chase in England, as did Steffens in twentieth-century Russia, saw what he took to be the future. Chase saw the fusion of Pittite free marketism, rigorous Wesleyan piety, a confident and overbearing judiciary—and saw that it worked. He came back to America determined to profit from the insights he had gained in London, and, when the chances presented themselves on the bench in Maryland and on the federal bench, he did.

Chase followed events in London after his return and he could see, being played out on the stage of English public life, a drama that he assumed was being reenacted in America several years later, and with some of the very same actors. As we now know, much of the ideological conflict in England can be attributed to the rise of the middle-class manufacturing and mercantile interests, particularly in the great English cities, but when this ideology was transplanted to America it took root in rather incongruous places, such as the minds of the Virginia planter aristocracy. As a result of this use and manipulation of ideologies divorced from their social and cultural context, it becomes difficult to continue to describe what happened in either England or America in terms of such ancient divisions as court and country. It seems safest then, for a while at least, to abandon these terms and to call what happened simply an adoption and, in part, a dialectical transformation of a form of what might best be described as British political "radicalism," or the "English democratic movement."[5]

It is unlikely that in his brief visit Chase fully grasped the complex contours of British political and social change in the late eighteenth century, but eleven months was undoubtedly enough to give him some sense of the traditions, the divisions, and the direction of change in ongoing English politics. It seems likely that, once Chase returned to America, his sense that England was a more fully developed society than America led him to believe that what he saw in England could be used to clarify what was happening and what ought to be happening in America. Many Americans who visited or emigrated from England in the eighteenth century must have had similar experiences, and it thus seems legitimate to suggest that much of the social, legal, and political debate in England was imported to America. In order to understand how Chase and others could use elements of English experience and English thought, then, it is necessary to give a brief description of the late eighteenth-century constitutional and legal discourse which Chase would have been likely to encounter in England in 1784.

For our purposes we can posit two main strands of English political and jurisprudential thought in the late eighteenth century, which can be described as "Tory," "conservative," or even "court" beliefs on the one hand, and "Whig," "radical," or "opposition" thought on the other. These two schools of thought were both flourishing in 1784, although the "opposition" advocates had just begun to undergo persecution in seditious libel trials, were soon to encounter more serious trials for treason, and would, in the course of the next decade, be almost totally silenced as their thought was increasingly linked in the minds of the British "conservatives" with French Jacobinism.[6]

In the period in which Chase viewed these competing ideologies, several of the men he met, most notably Thomas Erskine[7] and Edmund Burke, could be seen to be sympathetic to the "opposition" ideology, particularly insofar as they believed "court" recalcitrance had resulted in unsympathetic treatment of the Americans and a loss of the colonies.[8] Burke, however, within six years would be perceived as having moved from the "opposition" camp to that of the "conservatives" or Tories, and it is likely that Chase took this move of Burke's as an inspiration for his own shift from left to right in the late 1790s.

In comparing these English ideologies, then, it is important to bear in mind that they reflected less the thought of particular individuals and more the diversity of possible assumptions about the most basic problems of human nature, society, and religion. It was entirely possible that the appeal of either of these sets of beliefs to particular individuals could increase or diminish with time, as particular events raised pressing questions about the assumptions of either model.

The "Conservative" Model

What, then, were the characteristics of these competing models which Chase would have been expected to see? Taking that of the "court" party, or "conservatives," first, they viewed themselves as the legitimate heirs of the Glorious Revolution of 1688, which they believed to have corrected an imbalance in the English Ancient Constitution.[9] They maintained that the sovereignty of England was vested, somewhat mysteriously, and certainly as a matter of divine inspiration, in the virtually holy trinity of commons, lords, and crown. None of the elements of this governmental trinity was supposed to dominate the others, and each was to contribute its particular genius to the solution of problems of the commonwealth—the crown its energy, the lords its wisdom, and the commons its honesty and equity. Each element of the constitution would check the weaknesses of the other, thus avoiding the tyranny of unchecked monarchy, the oligarchy of unchecked aristocracy, or the anarchy of unchecked democracy.[10]

The particular manner in which this balance was secured before and after the glorious revolution furnished essential components of conservative beliefs. Judicial independence, as manifested in such developments as good behavior tenure (achieved shortly after the revolution of 1688 and probably regarded in the conservative mind as a part of the Ancient Constitution), was one such component. Such independence of judges was everywhere conceded to be necessary in order to avoid the perceived excesses of a judiciary under crown domination. The classic example of such excesses were the "bloody assizes" performed at the direction of James II.[11] Presumably, such independence would guarantee an unbiased and objective interpretation of the law and "constitution." Finally, such independence of judges could encourage or permit phenomena like that of Powell's independent statement of constitutional principles in the *Seven Bishops* case, immediately before the revolution of 1688.[12]

Judicial independence was also perceived as putting the judge in the best position to understand the various complexities of the law. By the late eighteenth century, this notion that the judges understood the law best had resulted, in England, in the institutionalization of attitudes among the judiciary that an essential part of the judge's mission was to monitor and advise the deliberations of the jury. The judge was to pass on the benefit of his shrewder and more informed knowledge of the ways of the law and the ways of the criminal class,[13] and he was to prevent the jury from acting in a passionate or prejudiced manner.

Nevertheless, the actual result in the *Seven Bishops* case and in similar jury determinations in accordance with "liberty" and against "tyranny,"[14] where juries had reached results at odds with those an overbearing judiciary seemed to desire, required that the jury maintain its ultimate power to render determinations on the entire case, to render general rather than special verdicts. The ideology of the jury as a barrier against oppression was so strong that the theme of the criminal jury's "right" to find a general verdict is sounded loudly even in the bible of English legal conservatism, *Blackstone's Commentaries.*[15]

This power on the part of the jury was hedged, however, by the conservatives' firm belief that the jury was required by oath (and as late as 1765, still thought to be subject to punishment if it ignored the restriction) to follow the law as given to them by the judges.[16] Without this requirement, the conservatives maintained, the source of statute law in the trinity of crown, commons, and people would be undermined, as law would be made only by popular elements and the Constitution would degenerate into a mere "rope of sand."[17]

The conservatives' worry over jurors flowed from a deeper worry over the nature of the English people in particular and mankind in general. They probably believed, along with Thomas Hutchinson, who fought a losing battle to represent their interests in America, that no people were as easily excitable as the English, although they were also the people most likely, after calm reflection and admonishment, to return to their senses.[18]

More seriously, and of particular relevance with regard to restraints on jury discretion, the conservatives imbibed Hobbesian notions about the instability of the human character in a state of nature, understood the need for the strong restraints of the rule of law, and fretted about the inabilities of men to do the right thing because of the "corruption" of their souls on earth.[19]

The concern with the "corrupt" souls of the English people also manifested itself in a recognition that the glorious revolution was as much about the hegemony of a particular religion as it was about the establishment of a particular set of constitutional balances. Indeed, for the conservatives, the two, the constitutional balances and the Protestant religion, were fundamentally linked. The conservatives were thus not inclined to lift constitutional bars to the full enjoyment of citizenship by Catholics, Protestant dissenters, or Jews, because they believed that a limited franchise and religious tests for public office were necessary to maintain the constitutional balance struck when the Anglican Protestant adherents to the House of Orange expelled the Stuart Catholics. The Protestant religious foundation of the English constitution was continually stressed by English judges and other authorities in their instructions to English juries.[20] Those convicted of capital crimes were carefully advised as to how they might seek to secure their immortal souls, in accordance with orthodox Protestant doctrine.[21]

The jurisprudential world of the conservatives, in short, was a world of deference.[22] The triumph of the Revolution of 1688, the foundation and the most important political event for English conservative constitutional analysis,[23] was a triumph achieved by Protestant aristocrats, and a triumph achieved by an independent Parliament elected through a limited franchise. In the course of the American Revolution, English conservative politicians had sought to make this point through their theory of "virtual" representation in Parliament, whereby each and every member thought of himself as the representative of the entire British empire and reached decisions in a dispassionate manner, to the benefit of all. This made electoral reform and, in particular, parliamentary representation for the Americans, or for various unrepresented, or underrepresented, English constituencies, unnecessary. The conservatives, as would Burke in 1791, conceived of the state as an organic entity, with hierarchical control, and a single set of correct answers to political problems to be elaborated and pronounced from the top down. Sovereignty in England, in other words, rested not in the people but in the "holy trinity," of crown, lords, and commons.[24]

The "Opposition" Model

This hierarchical character of English conservative thought was its most characteristic contrast to English "opposition thought," which by the late eighteenth century had come increasingly to conceive of political power, and possibly the law as well, as properly flowing not from the top down, but from the bottom up. For example, in 1788, to mark the hundredth anniversary of the Glorious Revolution, the London Revolutionary Society, perhaps the key voice of English opposition ideology, passed a declaration of its political principles:

(1) That all civil and political authority is derived from the people; (2) That the abuse of power justifies resistance; (3) That the right of private judgement, lib-

erty of conscience, trial by jury, the freedom of the press, and the freedom of election ought ever to be held sacred and inviolable.[25]

Figures such as John Wilkes[26] dramatized the unrepresentative character of Parliament and argued for a broadening of the franchise and for notions of "actual" rather than "virtual" representation. These notions, borrowed from the English radicals, were, of course, the core theories which enabled the Americans, in the 1770s, to argue the injustice of parliamentary taxation without American representation.

Increasingly in the late eighteenth century in England, opposition or radical tracts, including reprints from the English seventeenth-century political upheavals as well as fresh treatments, set forth an English theory of popular sovereignty.[27] This meant that for the English opposition theorists the true English Ancient Constitution was not a matter of an irreducible trinity, and was less revealed in the theory of parliamentary sovereignty and the form of government put together at the time of the Glorious Revolution of 1688 than it was in the experience of the Saxons in England under Alfred and before the fixation of the "Norman Yoke."[28] One of the essential postulates of the radicals' reconstruction of an ancient constitution was an "elective" monarch who had to be perceived as a "servant," not a "sovereign," of his people,[29] and their model included also a Parliament made up of members who directly responded to the directions and wishes of their constituents.[30]

The importance of English opposition theory to the emergence of a theory of popular sovereignty in America is becoming increasingly well understood by American historians, but less frequently noticed is that the statements of English opposition theory also included a strong position on the jury and one which differed fundamentally from "conservative" theory. For the authors of English opposition tracts, such as those circulated initially by The Society for Constitutional Information, or later by the London Revolutionary Society,[31] the jury had the right as well as the power to make law, and this democratic check was essential to prevent tyranny or oppression.[32]

The focus for most of this writing on the jury at this time was the law of seditious libel, which the radicals realized was a profound impediment to the statement of their political views. In the trial of the dean of St. Asaph's, in 1783, when our protagonist Samuel Chase was most likely in the audience watching his new acquaintance Thomas Erskine argue for the defense, the radicals made the claim that the entire determination on the allegedly seditious character of a particular writing ought to be for the jury. Only in this manner, Erskine argued, could the jury serve as popular guardians of the right of popular critics of the ministry to be heard.[33] The three conservatives on the bench, Justice Barrington, Lord Kenyon, and the great Lord Mansfield, ruled against Erskine on this point[34] and declared, in keeping with conservative ideology, that such discretion on the part of the jury would detract from the certainty of the rule of law and endanger the stability of the English constitution.[35]

Nevertheless, so strong had the popularity of radical sentiments on the jury become, that Fox's libel act, which could be made to seem a bow to the radicals, soon passed Parliament. That act clarified the jury's legal right to make determinations, presumably including the question of the seditious character of particular utterances, and thus assured that the jury would do more than pass on the mere questions of "publication" and "innuendo" of the writing in question. It is important to stress, however, lest the influence of the "radicals" be blown out of proportion, that Fox's libel act still maintained that the jury was to make its determinations under the direction of the court, thus preserving the essential premise that the jury was obligated to follow the law as laid down by the judge.[36]

Much of the ardor of the English radicals, at least those who became the subject of treason prosecutions in England in the middle 1790s, men such as Thomas Paine, Horne Tooke, and Thomas Cooper (who was later to be prosecuted for seditious libel, and tried by Chase, following Cooper's emigration to America), flowed from a conception of human nature and of religion which differed fundamentally from that of the English conservatives. In the first place, a solid element of the opposition program, even as early as the 1780s, when Chase would have been in England, was the removal of civil disabilities at least from the Protestant dissenters, and in the program of some of the reformers, even from Catholics and Jews.[37] For the radicals, or "The Friends of Liberty" as they occasionally styled themselves, securing the benefits of the Glorious Revolution of 1688 could be done without Anglican hegemony, and should be done with the participation of all the English people. As "The Friends of Liberty" began to see their struggle as one in common with the people of revolutionary France, however, it was easier for conservative thinkers, like the newly converted Burke, to disparage and undercut their ecumenical efforts.

The radicals manifested a sunnier view of human nature than did the conservatives. Instead of brooding over the corruptibility of the temporal soul of man, the radicals touted man's perfectibility and borrowed their view of man in a state of nature from Locke or from Rousseau. The radicals' task, in line with that of their compatriots in France, became the overthrow, in most cases by peaceable means, of an English system which they found unrepresentative and tainted by ministerial, not psychical, corruption. Some of the radicals, notably Thomas Hardy, Thomas Walker, Thomas Cooper, or William Broomhead acted in order to safeguard what they believed to be essential economic interests, such as those of the largely unrepresented London merchant and entrepreneurial community, or those communities in other emerging English industrial centers, such as Norwich, Manchester, or Sheffield. Others, like Joseph Priestly, Richard Price, or Thomas Paine, probably acted from more religious, or more abstract philosophical, notions about the fraternal destiny of all humanity.[38]

Unfortunately for the opposition causes, however, when the excesses of ostensibly atheistic democracy in France, the regicides and the Terror, became clear, English public opinion turned against the radicals, and substantial English parliamentary reform did not come until the Reform Bill of 1832. The radicals were silenced for a while and not just by the utterances and writings of Burke, now clearly in the conservative camp. Their defeat was accomplished also by the exhortations of such popular spokesmen as the Methodist Wesley, who probably saw French atheism as such a great evil that it outweighed any good in French democracy. Even the mercurial Wilkes, who was probably always something of a trimmer, if not himself hopelessly corrupt by anybody's definition, eventually threw his hand in with the conservative forces, first helping George III to quell the popular discontent of the London mob manifested in the Gordon riots of 1780, and eventually declaring to his sovereign that whatever the excesses of his followers, he himself was not a "Wilkite."[39]

With the move of so many exponents of English opposition thought into a "Tory" embrace by the middle 1890s, it is no wonder that Samuel Chase, whose religion gave him a deep suspicion of what the French were doing, broke with Jefferson and other Americans who continued to believe in the tenets of English radical thought. By the 1790s Chase had moved, never really to leave, into the Federalist fold, where English conservative ideas continued to dominate.

In subsequent chapters we will study the clash of Chase's newly acquired conservatism with Jeffersonian or "Republican" radicalism as we move on to see what happened to Chase in the late eighteenth century when, as a federal judge, he visited the bastions of a transplanted English opposition thought in Pennsylvania and Virginia. We will also see something of the convoluted character of the American versions of English conservative and opposition legal thought, the strange manner in which political and judicial actors could move back and forth from one school of thought to another, and the tragic difficulties Chase (and others) had in perceiving common themes in the different schools of thought. The first of these bastions of American opposition thought to the Federalists was in Pennsylvania, and it is to that state we now turn.

Before we consider Chase's activities in that state, however, we need to review federal jurisprudence in Pennsylvania before Chase tried his hand at it. In the course of this review, in chapter 5, we will see that there were some significant accomplishments of that Federalist jurisprudence, accomplishments that have been obscured to us since they have been tarred or tarnished as a result of what Samuel Chase was perceived to have done to the federal courts.

5

Federal Jurisprudence in Pennsylvania: Part One

The Admiralty Decisions and the Civil Cases in the Circuit Court

The "California" of the Late-Eighteenth Century

Samuel Chase seems first to have attracted the attention of the anti-Federalist press in the jurisdiction of Pennsylvania. Certainly it was the place where the train of events began that eventually led to Chase's impeachment by the Jeffersonians. It was there that Chase's first profound judicial clash with an ideology that seemed different from his occurred, in the Pennsylvanian federal circuit court, held in Philadelphia in 1800.

Pennsylvania, in the late eighteenth century, seems to have been a sort of analogue to late twentieth-century California. It was the state where much of the advanced thinking of transplanted English and indigenous American radicals was taking place, it was the state that spawned two mini-revolutions against the federal government (the Whiskey Rebellion and the Fries Rebellion), and it was the state that seemed to offer the most sanctuary for radical or unusual styles of life.

It is some indication of the ideological orientation of Pennsylvania, and its coincidence with his own views, that Thomas Jefferson remarked in 1796, "With Pennsylvania we can defy the Universe!"[1] It was not just for its radicals that Pennsylvania was known, however. Philadelphia, where Chase sat on circuit, was the late eighteenth-century commercial capital of the nation, although it was soon to be surpassed by Boston and New York. It was also in the forefront in America of developing real class distinctions. As commercial growth accelerated, Philadelphia seems to have been among the first places in

America with a recognizable urban proletariat, and it was certainly among the first to have experienced differentiation in the labor market and primitive unionization, although that activity seems to have been quickly outlawed and suppressed.[2]

It is thus not surprising that in Pennsylvania, and in Philadelphia in particular, new legal styles of reasoning emerged, drawn from English examples, and these new legal styles seem to have been useful both in facilitating commerce and in implementing democracy. This chapter supplements our principal argument, the trials and tribulations of Samuel Chase in the course of the unfolding of the dialectic of Federalist jurisprudence, by demonstrating the positive accomplishments of Federalist jurisprudence, which were obscured by skillful Jeffersonian use of Chase's allegedly partisan Federalist conduct. In this chapter we will observe how the Pennsylvania federal courts and their Federalist judges, particularly Richard Peters, sought to implement the popular goal of commercial prosperity for the new nation. In the two chapters which follow, however, we will see how the Federalists in general, and Samuel Chase in particular, were perceived as failing to implement the professed Pennsylvania goal of democracy.

The Beginnings of an American Law of Admiralty

"The Federalists," wrote Robert Goodloe Harper in 1801, "laid it down as the cornerstone of their system, to support, cherish and invigorate commerce, as the best and indeed the only effectual means of promoting agriculture and every other branch of industry."[3] This program of building a commercial America was principally implemented in Pennsylvania by Federal District Court Judge Richard Peters, who was named to the bench in 1792.[4] He was not the first federal district court judge for Pennsylvania, but he was certainly the most notable and the most successful. We have already seen something of Peters's personal characteristics, and a little more information on his biography helps make it clear why he was more successful than was Chase at judging in Pennsylvania.

Peters had served as registrar of the Pennsylvania colonial admiralty court and was secretary and a member of the revolutionary board of war. After independence he served briefly as a United States congressman. In 1787 he was elected to the Pennsylvania assembly, and in 1790, to the Pennsylvania senate. Having served as speaker in both houses, he was thoroughly familiar with the workings of elective politics and popular opinion in Pennsylvania. Peters was also well versed in the classics and had a reading knowledge of Dutch, Spanish, French, and Italian, thus enabling him to make full use of civil law authorities.

A firm adherent of the Federalist doctrines, his education, family background, and previous experience uniquely suited him for the role of expositor of admiralty law.[5] For Judge Peters, the commercial success of America was an important value. In words much like Harper's, although in a more graphic maternal metaphor, he wrote: "If agriculture be . . . one of the breasts from which the state must draw its nourishment, then commerce is certainly the other. . . . The interests and comforts of the community will droop and finally perish if either be permitted to remain entirely at rest."[6]

The Constitution and the Judiciary Act had given admiralty jurisdiction to Peters's district court, but had not spelled out what substantive maritime law the federal courts were to apply. Solving this problem was a major task of the Pennsylvania Federal District Court. During the revolutionary period, Americans had strenuously argued that they were fighting to preserve the rights guaranteed to them by the English common law[7] and in time each state was to pass a statute indicating that the English common law, insofar as it was consistent with American institutions, was to be in force.[8] It might have thus been logical to expect that when the federal Constitution conferred admiralty jurisdiction on the federal courts, it was to be understood as granting the maritime jurisdiction of the English common law.

There were, however, historical difficulties in the English common law of admiralty that seemed to raise some problems for Americans. In particular, the jurisdiction of the admiralty courts in England was substantially less than in most maritime nations. This had resulted primarily from a struggle between the specialized admiralty courts and the more general law courts concerning which had jurisdiction over admiralty-related occurrences. The law courts gradually expanded their power at the expense of the admiralty courts. Hence, by the 1790s, many matters historically within admiralty jurisdiction had been taken over in England by the law courts.[9]

In any event, from the beginning, the Pennsylvania Federal District Court indicated that the sources of admiralty jurisprudence were to be as broad as necessary to accommodate American commerce. The first Pennsylvania Federal District Court judge, Francis Hopkinson, indicated in 1789 that he was prepared to decide admiralty cases, not simply on the basis of parties' contracts or any country's positive enactments but with reference to "law and reason" and the "rights of humanity" which, he said, were "superior" to the specific laws and customs of any one nation.[10]

Once Richard Peters came to the bench, the technique of admiralty jurisprudence of picking the best rule for America from a variety of sources was given full expression. This picking-and-culling technique, among the jurisprudential and legal records of a variety of nations, not simply English precedent, used by Peters in the admiralty cases was probably part of a "widespread feeling" among American legal scholars after the Revolution. It was reflected contemporaneously in the law lectures given by Supreme Court Justice James Wilson at the College of Philadelphia (later the University of Pennsylvania) in 1790–1792 and in James Kent's lectures at Columbia College at approximately the same time. Both Kent and Wilson stressed the need to incorporate into American jurisprudence not only rules of the English common law but also rules of the civil law.[11]

Pursuant to this line of jurisprudential reasoning, in one of his first cases Peters indicated that since America had become an independent nation, it could exercise the sovereign's prerogative of making its own law, and thus, as an American admiralty judge, he was not subject to the authority of the English common law. In *Jennings v. Carson*[12] Peters held that in a prize case his court had jurisdiction even if on the identical matter an English admiralty court would not.[13] For Peters, American admiralty law was to come rather from the maritime laws of the "law of nations." This required consulting many English and civil treatises, which Peters did with great gusto.

In *Warder v. LaBelle Creole*,[14] for example, a case during Peters's first term, he translated both "an authority out of Burlemaqui [a renowned Dutch scholar of international law]" and the marine ordinances of France to establish an American rule for admiralty salvage cases. According to "justice and policy," wrote Peters, owners of cargoes or ships had to reimburse seamen who had rescued their goods from "imminent danger, by great labor, or perhaps at the hazard of . . . life."[15] Peters subsequently developed this principle to hold that the amount of compensation for salvage should be varied according to the amount of risk assumed in the salvage operation.[16] This is an early illustration of what has been called an "actuarial consciousness" on the part of early American judges, and demonstrates that Peters was one of the earliest to mold American law according to a risk-reward calculus that took into consideration the needs of the marketplace.[17]

Although Peters drew his admiralty law from a wide variety of obscure and foreign sources, he also took pains to see that the law he pronounced in his court kept in step with the actual modern workings of commerce. After three years on the bench, the sweep of authorities Peters consulted had widened, and his purpose for their consultation had become clearer. In *Thompson v. The Catharina*,[18] for example, an action for wages brought by an American mariner against a Spanish shipowner, Peters laid out what had become his fundamental principles of admiralty jurisprudence. Where there was a choice of rules available to American admiralty judges, Peters wrote, "we must resort to the regulations of other maritime countries, which have stood the test of time and experience. . . . "[19] Peters appears to have believed that it would have been commercially unwise to ignore these other maritime countries' efforts: "We ought not to betray so much vanity as to take it for granted, that we could establish more salutary and useful regulations than those which have, for ages, governed the most commercial and powerful nations, and led them to wealth and greatness."[20] Peters then proceeded to rummage through the laws of the Rhodians, the Consolato Del Mare, the Amalphian code, the laws of Oleron, and the laws of the Hanse towns to find rules that would help Americans reach the "wealth and greatness" of those ancient maritime powers.

In a 1795 case, *Hollingsworth v. The Betsey*,[21] though he had plenary authority as an admiralty judge sitting without a jury, he ruled that damages were to be determined by a panel of "intelligent and disinterested merchants of this district."[22] In *Swift v. The Happy Return*,[23] on a point involving the time when seamen's wages were due, Peters looked first to the laws of Wisby, an ancient commercial power, but decided ultimately that "Philadelphia custom" as to the time of payment should govern. Finally, in *Pollock v. Donaldson*,[24] a dispute over the extent of coverage of a marine insurance policy, Peters took the testimony of Mr. Isaac Wharton, "an experienced insurance broker," and decided that the rule to be followed was "the general sense and usage of merchants."[25]

Still, and in keeping with the altruistic character modern American historians have said was inherent in early American theories of "civic republicanism" to which the Federalists were probably devoted, Peters was willing to protect the rights of merchants only insofar as they benefited the whole community. This was demonstrated in the 1800 case of *Willings v. Blight*.[26] The petitioners owned three-quarters of a vessel and were requesting a court order to compel the respondent, the owner of the remaining quarter interest in the ship, to permit the vessel's employment in a voyage. Peters held that the recusant owner could not prevent the voyage, although the other owners had to indemnify him from loss. Again Peters based his rulings on a survey of maritime authorities, drawn from both the English common and the European civil law. Peters announced: "[I]t is a principle discernible in all maritime codes, that every encouragement and assistance shall be afforded to those who are ready to give their ships constant employment; and this, not only for the particular profit of the owners, but for the general interests and prosperity of commerce." In these and other cases, Peters laid down principles which he believed would best promote commercial prosperity and economic development. Peters's creativity in articulating new principles for admiralty law seems to foreshadow the work of later nineteenth-century judges like Story, Kent, and Shaw, who would alter contract, tort, and corporation law to favor commerce by promoting a market economy.[27]

It has been suggested that in the late eighteenth and early nineteenth centuries most Americans would have favored agricultural over commercial interests, and would have rejected many procommercial doctrines that were implemented in the course of the nineteenth century.[28] Also, there is some evidence in the writings of Thomas Jefferson and others that many Americans feared and distrusted attempts to make the United States a great commercial power, and wished the country to continue as a preserve of simple yeomen.[29]

If there was such an anticommercial spirit in America and if public opinion was a significant force in American political and judicial affairs,[30] how was it that Peters was able so frankly to tailor his decisions in a manner to build commerce? One answer is that in Philadelphia at least, even the popular sentiment seemed to be procommercial,[31] and thus Peters's admiralty decisions were more likely applauded than condemned. Nevertheless, since the Philadelphia federal court normally operated its admiralty jurisdiction without juries and since the expanded jurisdiction of the colonial vice admiralty courts had been opposed for the very reason that they operated without juries, one might have expected to find at least some hostility to the expansive admiralty jurisdiction in the Philadelphia federal courts.[32]

Perhaps one strong contributing factor to Judge Peters's ability to promulgate procommercial doctrine was what appears to be his unwillingness to embroil his district court in issues that would inflame popular opinion. For example, in 1793, during a period when pro-French popular enthusiasm was at a high pitch in Philadelphia,[33] Peters refused to find that he had the jurisdiction to determine that French capture of British ships in American waters violated American neutrality even though there was a precedent allowing him so to rule.[34] Instead, and anticipating doctrines for which John Marshall would receive all the credit a decade letter, Peters circumspectly ruled that this was a question that should be left to the executive branch of American government and that the judiciary should abstain from acting.

Still another factor in Peters's success as a procommercial judge was his linkage of commerce with agriculture. Peters believed that the success of either commerce or agriculture in America would depend upon the constant encouragement of both endeavors. Peters's facility as a procommercial judge was probably considerably enhanced in the popular mind, even if public opinion leaned toward agricultural interests, because Peters practiced what he preached. While he was encouraging commerce from the bench, he was promoting agriculture from his vast country estate, Belmont, on the outskirts of Philadelphia.

Peters was probably well known to the farmers of Pennsylvania as the president of the first agricultural society in America. Based on his own experimentation at his farm at Belmont, Peters published in 1797 "A Statement of Facts and Opinions in Relation to the Use of Plaister of Paris (Gypsum)," a treatise which taught farmers how to increase their yields of clover, and thus enabled them more easily to produce good meadowlands to feed their livestock.[35] The pamphlet, which was dedicated to George Washington, proved so popular that the father of his country wrote Peters for additional copies so that he could pass one on to Sir John Sinclair, an English agriculturist.[36] Even before this publication, Peters was recognized as an agricultural expert. A few months prior to his acceptance of the district judgeship, no less a personage than Alexander Hamilton wrote Peters to solicit his advice on the productivity of agricultural lands. Hamilton stated: "I am persuaded no person can better assist in this object than yourself. . . . "[37] Thus, as a man who had literally written the book on American agriculture, Peters was entitled to a respectful ear when he spoke on the importance to agriculture of American commerce.

Finally, Peters's accomplishments as a judge and his sensitivity to popular feeling may stem in part from admirable personal qualities. If the testimony of his grandson can be believed, Peters's "witticisms were celebrated."[38] His good humor and generous hospitality were often exhibited at Belmont, where he and Mrs. Peters entertained a galaxy of the important political figures of the day. Peters was apparently on quite friendly terms with George Washington. The first president, who appointed Peters, even sat for a portrait at Peters's request, an honor which Washington reserved for a few of his intimate friends.[39] As indicated in chapter 1, Peters was also a close friend of perhaps the most acerbic and irascible of the arch-Federalists, Timothy Pickering.[40] In at least the early years of this period, however, Peters was also on easy social terms with Thomas Jefferson, and probably with James Madison as well.[41]

Since Jefferson and Madison were to become the leaders of the Republican party, the opposition to the Federalists, it might be inferred that Peters's personal associations, and, in stark contrast to other Federalists such as Chase, his affability, exposed him to a wide variety of political opinion, and that he was in a good position to sense the various currents of political and popular opinion and to accommodate to them where possible. Peters's progressive admiralty rulings and his sophistication in drawing on diverse sources compare favorably with the admiralty decisions of Joseph Story, commonly acknowledged to be the "father" of American admiralty law.[42] In any event, Peters's efforts on the district court, made possible in large part by his political and personal qualities, must be ranked as one of the great successes of Federalist jurisprudence. Since much of what Story was to do was anticipated by Peters and since Story himself freely acknowledged his debt to Peters's "rich contributions to the maritime jurisprudence of our country,"[43] perhaps it is time to accord Richard Peters the recognition he deserves as the real "father," or at least the "grandfather" of American admiralty law.

Civil Cases in the Pennsylvania Federal Circuit Court

At the same time Peters was at work in the federal district court building an admiralty law favorable to commercial progress, several important civil cases were litigated in the circuit court, where Peters sat with one or two members of the United States Supreme Court.[44] Like the jurisprudence in the district court, the civil decisions of the circuit court helped to promote the Federalist program. The main theme that can be found in these decisions is the preservation of the independence of the federal judiciary. These opinions, in frankly declaring the unique and important role the national judiciary was to play in American government, articulate basic Federalist theory. Further, these federal circuit court opinions clearly anticipate the best of the work of Chief Justice Marshall and show the real beginnings, much earlier than is usually reported, of what has been characterized as an "American judicial tradition."[45]

The first dramatic demonstration of judicial independence came in *Hayburn's Case*.[46] In March 1792 the United States Congress passed a statute[47] setting up a system for determining pensions for soldiers injured in the revolutionary war. The statute directed that the federal circuit court of the district where a particular applicant for a pension might reside was to determine the amount of the pension to be granted, according to the severity of the particular injury.[48] The act further imposed a duty on the circuit court judges to remain in session for five days at each sitting for the next two years, so that applicants for pensions "may have full opportunity to make their application for the relief proposed in this act."[49] Finally, the act gave the secretary of war the power to strike names forwarded to him by the circuit courts, where he should "have cause to suspect imposition or mistake."[50]

On April 18, 1792, Justices Wilson and Blair of the United States Supreme Court and District Judge Peters, sitting as the Circuit Court for the District of Pennsylvania, addressed a letter to President Washington, in which they set forth their determination to refuse to proceed under the act. The three noted, "It is a principle important to freedom, that in government the judicial should be distinct from, and independent of the legislative department." They observed that Congress, in requiring the circuit court to determine qualifications for pensions based on the degree of injury, was ordering these courts to perform a task outside the judicial power given by the United States Constitution. In addition, they indicated that since any determinations they made were subject to revision by the secretary of war, the scheme set up by the act was "radically inconsistent with the independence of that judicial power given which is vested in the courts; and, consequently, with that important principle which is so strictly observed by the Constitution of the United States."[51]

The Pennsylvania federal circuit court's refusal to play their part under the act resulted in an attempt to secure a mandamus from the Supreme Court to compel the judges to pass on the claim of one pension applicant, William Hayburn. The Supreme Court, however, merely took the request under advisement until the next term. The case was never decided, because Congress, perhaps sensing the delicate political issues involved, set up a new pension mechanism which did not involve the judges in such determinations.[52]

This declaration of judicial independence by the Pennsylvania federal circuit court is particularly striking because it was made in the face of what appears to have been strong public sentiment in favor of the pension program.[53] A decade earlier, angry Pennsylvanian revolutionary war veterans had actually caused members of the Continental Congress to withdraw from Philadelphia because of their failure to provide payment and pensions.[54] It must have taken some courage for the members of the Pennsylvania federal circuit court to risk a similar fate. So important was the principle of judicial independence to the federal judges of the Pennsylvania circuit that they appeared unwilling to proceed in the face-saving manner chosen by their brethren sitting on the New York and North Carolina circuits, who declared that they were merely acting as "commissioners"—and not judges—in performing their duties under the act.[55]

By their actions in refusing to proceed under the 1792 Pension Act, the judges of the federal circuit court of Pennsylvania not only indicated their belief in judicial independence, but also set a precedent for judicial exercise of the power to declare laws of Congress unconstitutional.[56] Two years later, in the unreported case of *United States v. Todd*,[57] the judges of the Pennsylvania circuit were vindicated in their refusal to proceed under the 1792 act. The United States Supreme Court apparently held that the actions of those judges from other circuits, who circumvented the independence problem by calling themselves "commissioners" when they ruled on pensioners' rights, had no legal validity.

In *Van Horne's Lessee v. Dorrance*,[58] the Pennsylvania federal circuit court again exercised the power of judicial review by declaring that a Pennsylvania state law violated the Pennsylvania constitution. In 1787 the Pennsylvania legislature had passed an act settling a long dispute over land in Luzerne County, Pennsylvania, between citizens of Pennsylvania and Connecticut; the former had been granted the land by the prerevolutionary Pennsylvania proprietors, and the latter took their title from Indians and from acts of the Connecticut legislature. The Pennsylvania legislature decided that the Connecticut claimants, who were then in possession, could remain in possession. Since the Pennsylvania group had good titles, however, the Pennsylvania legislature decided that they should be compensated for giving up their land. The compensation was to take the form of title to other parcels of Pennsylvania land, vacant property subject to the disposition of the state. Pursuant to the statutory scheme, the determination of the value of the land taken and the allocation of a parcel of corresponding value was to be accomplished by a group of specially appointed commissioners.[59] One of the Pennsylvania claimants whose title was to be given up brought suit to have the statute declared void. Since the dispute involved citizens of different states, the diversity jurisdiction of the federal circuit court was invoked.

In the course of the opinion for the court, Justice Paterson, sitting on circuit, made a strong statement of judicial powers and duties which anticipated the opinion of Justice Marshall in the great case of *Marbury v. Madison.*[60] In ringing words echoing Federalist political theory, he declared in his charge to the *Van Horne* jury that under American constitutions, unlike the variable practices in England, "[t]he frame of the government, delineated by the mighty hand of the people [establishes] certain first principles or fundamental laws [which are to be] the permanent will of the people, and the supreme law of the land." In England, Paterson explained, Parliament was theoretically omnipotent, but in America, the legislature had a duty to conform to the constitutional mandate. Moreover, it was the duty of American courts "as a co-ordinate, and not subordinate branch, to adhere to the constitution, and to declare the act null and void" where a statute transgressed the bounds specified for legislative action.[61] Thus, Paterson managed to restate the linkage of the judiciary with popular sovereignty—the strong selling point of Federalist political theory—and yet at the same time suggested that any "people" who set up a "Republican" government *ipso facto* intended to protect property rights.

In addition to reflecting the Federalist policies of judicial independence and judicial review, then, Paterson's charge emphasized the Federalist predilection for the sanctity of private property rights and the Federalist disgust over recent legislative excesses. "If this be the legislation of a republican government, in which the preservation of property is made sacred by the constitution," he declared, "I ask wherein it differs from the mandate of an Asiatic prince? Omnipotence in legislation is despotism."[62] "An Act of this sort deserves no favor;" he continued, "to construe it liberally would be sinning against the rights of private property."[63] In this opinion, of course, it is difficult to determine which is really guiding Paterson's reasoning—the asserted Federalist application of the principle of popular sovereignty that the Constitution circumscribes the activities of the legislature or merely the crypto-English conservative's (or the American Federalist "Republican" theorist's) high regard for private property rights. In any event, while we usually assume that the full delineation of the sphere of protected private property rights under the federal Constitution was not to take place until Marshall's tenure as chief justice,[64] Paterson was clearly drawing some of the first sketches in the Pennsylvania federal court years before.

Other cases involving private law questions which arose in the circuit court are not as dramatic as *Van Horne's Lessee* or *Hayburn's Case*, but several did seem to demonstrate the court's facility with commercial matters and its willingness to forge a body of modern commercial law. The modern American and English general principle of granting contract damages based on the expectation of the contracting parties seems to have been accepted in one case[65] and the doctrine of protecting holders in due course of bills and notes from makers' defenses was accepted in another.[66] The circuit court also clearly indicated its unwillingness to let important business transactions be defeated because of a failure to follow mere legal "technicalities," a development in commercial jurisprudence which occurred in many jurisdictions at this time.[67] Like Peters's work in the district court, then, some decisions of the circuit court facilitated American commerce, thereby furthering this Federalist goal.

Nevertheless, the convenience of commerce was clearly not the only important value to the Pennsylvania federal circuit court. For example, in *Searight v. Calbraith*,[68] the case which enunciated the rule allowing expectation damages, the jury instruction demonstrated the court's broad allowance of jury discretion, even in matters which might have been perceived as requiring commercial certainty. Justice Iredell instructed the jury.:

> As to the damages . . . though it is true that in actions for a breach of contract a jury should in general give the whole money contracted for and interest; yet in a case like the present they may modify the demand, and find such damages as they may think adequate to the injury actually sustained.[69]

The *Searight* case was settled before the verdict was announced, probably because the merchants involved were alarmed, after hearing Iredell's instruction, at the possibility that the jury might deliver a verdict not in accordance with their contract as made. The jury's actions would have borne out their fears, because it was later revealed that the jury would have exercised the discretion Iredell allowed it and awarded only six pence damages,[70] in a case where the "expectation" damages would have been much higher.

Justice Iredell's failure to insist on a judicially dictated certain standard for the measurement of damages is consistent with earlier eighteenth-century American jurisprudence, which emphasized discretion in the jury to decide contractual cases on the basis of the community's sense of "fairness," even if this differed from what might have been intended by the parties making the contract.[71]

Iredell's charge to the *Searight* jury reflected a strong sense of the jury's importance in this early period of the nation's history. This element of early Republican jurisprudence was a ticklish matter for the Federalists. Indeed, even in *Van Horne's Lessee*, the case representing the firmest defense of the Federalist conception of private property rights, Justice Paterson told the jury, "[I]n general verdicts, it frequently becomes necessary for the jurors to decide upon the law as well as the facts." Paterson was apparently prepared to give the jury this power even where great constitutionally protected rights were at stake and where it was the duty of the court to "adhere to the Constitution and declare [a statute] null and void."[72]

The older eighteenth-century view, favoring great jury discretion in determining both law and fact, eventually began to recede in commercial cases as more judges perceived that it should be the province of the jury merely to determine facts, leaving the pronouncement of the law for the court.[73] In these early years, however, the predilection for jury discretion was still strong. It seems likely that these Federalist judicial decisions in support of jury discretion are a manifestation of the same tendency to espouse the basic principle of popular sovereignty that was present in their "selling" of the federal Constitution. After all, the lack of a guarantee of jury trials in federal cases in the body of the Constitution of 1787 nearly led to its defeat and ultimately resulted in the guarantees of such trials in the Bill of Rights, adopted in 1791.

Again, as we saw was true with regard to the admiralty opinions of Judge Peters, these Federalist judicial pronouncements at least demonstrate Federalist awareness of and receptiveness to popular opinion. And yet, as we will see in the next chapter, the Federalist judges were by no means sanguine with regard to the popular conceptions about the role of the jury in passing on legal questions, or about the role of the people generally in participating in the making of all law. Indeed, as we will observe in subsequent chapters, the perception that the Federalist judges, particularly Samuel Chase, did not afford sufficient deference to the people all but obliterated the healthy work of the federal judges chronicled in this chapter. As we have seen, Peters, Paterson, Iredell, and their fellows all went far in establishing what was to be recognized as important characteristics for a national judiciary—the independence of the judges, the sanctity of the rights of private property, and the importance of national commerce. It is time that we recognized that these strides forward were made by the justices sitting on circuit and by the federal district courts and that this was done even before John Marshall came to preside.

6

Federal Jurisprudence in Pennsylvania: Part Two

The Federal Common Law of Crimes

As indicated in chapter 5, questions over the role of the jury surfaced sporadically in civil cases in the Pennsylvania federal circuit court, but it was in matters of criminal jurisprudence where the issue became most important, and indeed turned into a major political problem for the Federalists. In connection with the theory that the jury ought to function as a basic component of popular sovereignty, particularly in criminal cases, the jury's task was believed to include passing on law as well as fact. In perhaps the most important case of the early years under review here, *United States v. Henfield*,[1] jury acquittal was perceived, at least by the antiadministration press, as rejecting the law and policy of the federal government and as demonstrating popular disenchantment with Federalist rule.[2]

The acquittal in *Henfield* required an alteration in Federalist prosecutorial techniques and may have contributed something toward the Federalist predilection, most pronounced in the jurisprudence of Samuel Chase, to attempt to curtail the discretion of the criminal jury. Those attempts, to be explored in subsequent chapters, were a major cause of the fall from political grace of the Federalists. In particular, *Henfield* merits study for what it suggests about popular and judicial attitudes toward the existence of a federal common law of crimes, or, more generally, the propriety of the federal courts' punishing offenses which had not been proscribed by any federal statute.

By the late years of the period here under review, this issue had become of crucial significance. The emerging Jeffersonian Republicans took the position that there was no federal common law of crimes and saw dark designs in the Federalists' assertion that such crimes existed and could be punished. In the most extreme statement of this view, in a 1799 letter to Edmund Randolph, Thomas Jefferson suggested that all that the Federalist "monocrats," "aristocrats," and "monarchists" had done to harass the people—the creation of the bank of the United States, Jay's Treaty, the imposition of a standing army and navy, and the passage of the Sedition Act—were "solitary, inconsequential timid things in comparison with the audacious, barefaced and sweeping pretension to a system of law for the U.S. without the adoption of their legislature, and so infinitely beyond their power to adopt."[3] The Republican calumny against the Federalists for the latter's efforts to prosecute common law crimes probably had critical importance to Jefferson's electoral victory in 1800. Furthermore, the Federalist common law prosecutions served as justification for Jeffersonian attempts to cut back the influence of the national judiciary, and thus enabled the Jeffersonians more easily to overturn the judicial reforms of the 1801 Judiciary Act.[4]

To this day there is profound disagreement among legal scholars as to whether the Federalist common law prosecutions were legal or instead represented an unwarranted usurpation of power.[5] A review of the issue of the federal common law of crimes, particularly as it was debated in the Pennsylvania federal courts, suggests that the Federalist judges were legally correct in their assertion of jurisdiction over common law crimes. Still, it is argued here that the strict legal correctness of their position was much less important in the ultimate resolution of this issue than was the public perception of injustice in the Federalist position, a perception that arose out of the usual contemporary ideological and political struggles between the American "conservatives," the Federalists, and the American "opposition," the Jeffersonian Republicans.

The *Henfield* Case and Its Antecedents

The Judiciary Act of 1789 gave the federal circuit courts jurisdiction over "crimes and offenses cognizable under the authority of the United States,"[6] but the statute did not specify what acts were "crimes and offenses" nor did it specify the extent of the "authority" of the United States. Much of the prevailing jurisprudence can be derived from contemporary jury charges. The first official public interpretation of the federal grant of jurisdiction, in 1790, signaled that it was to be broadly construed. Chief Justice John Jay charged the grand juries of the eastern circuit in the spring of that year as follows: "In a word, Gentlemen! Your province and your duty extend . . . to the enquiry and presentment of all offenses of every kind, committed against the United States in this district, or on the high seas by persons in it."[7] Jay did not define the term "offenses," telling the jurors only: "[I]f in the performance of your duty, you should meet with difficulties, the court will be ready to afford you proper assistance." Nevertheless, Jay did provide some clues as to the scope of "crimes and offenses" against the United States.

First, he suggested that the jurors would

recollect that the laws of nations make part of the laws of this, and of every other civilized nation. They consist of those rules for regulating the conduct of nations towards each other, which, resulting from right reason, receive their obligation from that principle and from general assent and practice.[8]

"Right reason" is a term of art to lawyers, meaning little more, however, than enlightened common sense. In this charge Jay seems broadly to be asking that his jurors use their own common sense and their knowledge of world and national history to figure out what might be crimes according to the "law of nations," and then to sift the facts as presented to them to discover any violations of the way citizens of nations were to behave toward citizens of other nations.

Second, Jay acknowledged that some federal statutes defined crimes, but he maintained that these statutes would not serve alone as indicators of what offenses the jurors should present:

The penal statutes of the United States are few and principally respect the revenue. The right ordering and management of this important business is very essential to the credit, character, and prosperity of our country. On the citizens at large is placed the burthen of providing for the public exigencies. Whoever therefore fraudulently withdraws his shoulder from the common burthen necessarily leaves his portion of the weight to be born by the others, and thereby does injustice not only to the government, but to them.

It may be that Jay was simply talking picturesquely about failures to pay taxes and thus bear one's fair share of the operating costs of the government, but it seems possible also to find Jay's focus not to be on particular violations of the terms of revenue statutes but more broadly on "whoever fraudulently withdraws his shoulder from the common burthen."

Finally, Jay told the grand jurors, this time without a reference to a statute, to "direct your conduct also to the conduct of the national officers, and let not any corruptions, frauds, extortions or criminal negligence with which you may find any of them justly chargeable pass unnoticed."[9] In this last instance at least, and possibly in all three here quoted, Jay thus seemed to be defining "offenses against the United States" to include virtually any examples of wrongdoing against the nation, the government, or the public. Since the grand jury is and was in the business of inquiring only into the commission of criminal acts, the conclusion seems to be that Jay believed that more than the mere violations of the explicit texts of federal statutes constituted crimes against the United States.

Three years later, in a charge to the grand jury for the Middle Circuit in the District of Virginia, Jay had apparently refined his description of offenses. He told the jurors, "The laws of the United States admit of being classed under three heads (or) descriptions. 1st. All treaties made under the authority of the

United States. 2d. The laws of nations. 3dly. The constitution, and statutes of the United States."[10] Jay continued in a manner which suggests that conduct proscribed by any of these three "heads" of law was a matter into which the grand jury should inquire, but in this charge, at least, he seemed most concerned with violations of the "law of nations." This was a result of the outbreak of war between England and France in January 1793, which had violently split American public opinion and had just resulted in the "Neutrality Proclamation" issued by President Washington.[11] Jay quoted extensively from the proclamation and indicated that Washington's instructions to prosecute persons who committed, aided, or abetted hostilities against any of the belligerents, or who furnished them contraband, were "exactly consistent with and declaratory of the conduct enjoined by the law of nations."[12] Jay closed his charge with comments indicating that the United States' treaties of "firm and perpetual peace" also enjoined American citizens from aiding the belligerent powers, and that such conduct, as a violation of a treaty, was also punishable as a crime."[13]

Later, in July 1793, Justice James Wilson of the Supreme Court charged a grand jury for the middle circuit in Philadelphia. One of the matters which this grand jury was to investigate involved one Gideon Henfield, who was accused of engaging in acts hostile to nations at peace with the United States. Henfield had allegedly assisted in the capture of an English prize ship by a French privateer. As had Jay in 1790, and as was fairly common for federal judges at this time,"[14] Wilson used his grand jury charge as an opportunity to deliver a public lecture on the finer points of American jurisprudence. For Wilson, the basis of the American judicial system, and indeed the basis of any civilized system of jurisprudence, was what he called the "common law."

American common law, explained Wilson, was like English common law in that its "accommodating principle . . . will adjust its improvement to every grade and species of improvement . . . in consequence of practice, commerce, observation, study or refinement."[15] Unlike the contemporary English common law, however, Wilson suggested, American common law was closer to the common law of the ancient Saxons than it was to that of the Normans. The Saxons, like the Americans, had a more expansive notion of individual liberty and popular sovereignty.[16] Nevertheless, Wilson went on, the American common law, like every other, was "a social system of jurisprudence. She receives other laws and systems into a friendly correspondence; and associates to herself those who can give her information, or advice, or assistance."[17] Thus, when a court was faced with a problem involving the law of other countries, the law of merchants, or the law of nations, those bodies of doctrine would become assimilated into the common law and would be used in the disposition of particular cases.[18]

In this manner Wilson arrived at the same point Jay started with in his jury charge two months earlier: the United States law incorporated the law of nations. Unlike Jay, however, Wilson carefully explained that he had arrived at this destination through the vehicle of what he called the "common law." For Wilson, the law of nations (and by implication, the common law) was not simply a set of arbitrary rules. The law of nations was "the law of nature"; it was "of obligation indispensable" and "of origin divine."[19] This meant, then, that the law of nations was of binding force for the citizens of every country. Moreover, it was not simply limited to regulating the affairs of one nation with another. By becoming a nation, citizens created certain duties which they owed to each other and to the nation itself, duties specified by the law of nations.[20]

Among these duties which devolved on individuals (and on nations) was that of keeping "peace on earth," of living in amity with one's neighbors. Of course, it was true that "war and rumours of war" existed in "this imperfect state of things," but given the primary "law of nations"-mandated duty of citizens to be peaceful, the jurors were directed by Wilson to consider two questions:

> Into this unnatural state (of war) ought a nation to suffer herself to be drawn without her own act, or the act of him or them, to whom for this purpose she has delegated her power? Into this unnatural state should a nation suffer herself to be drawn by the unauthorized, nay by the unlicensed conduct of any of her citizens?[21]

Wilson immediately supplied the answer to both questions: "[A] citizen, who in our state of neutrality, and without the authority of the nation, takes an hostile part with either of the belligerent powers, violates thereby his duty, and the laws of his country...."[22]

Five days later, on July 27, 1793, Wilson's grand jury returned an indictment against Henfield. The indictment said that his conduct was "to the evil example of all others in like cases offending, in violation of the laws of nations, against the laws of the United States in such case made and provided, and against the Constitution of the United States, and against the peace and dignity of the said United States."[23] There is a boilerplate quality to the lengthy indictment. Nevertheless, the language just quoted certainly suggests that the prosecutors felt they were proceeding under an American law of nations. Moreover, since no statute was involved here,[24] the phrases "laws of the United States" and "peace and dignity of the United States" have a distinctly common law ring.

At Henfield's trial, held shortly after the indictment, the prosecutor, William Rawle, argued to the petit jury along the same lines that Wilson had charged the grand jury. He, too, explained that when individuals join to form a nation they give up the right to make war which *"in a state of nature"* adheres to the individual, but "is lost by *joining* society." Were this not so, Rawle argued, individuals might plunge the nation into unwarranted war. These propositions were not "only the speculations of the closet," explained Rawle to the jurors, "We see them carried into effect in England in affirmation of national common law, i.e., *the law of nations.*"[25]

Rawle acknowledged that in England such conduct [of making war against a nation with which one's nation was at peace] was expressly prohibited by statute, but he suggested that although "the English statute is not in force here, because the specific remedy [protecting England] for which alone it was made cannot be had, the *law* which it aided, not introduced, is in force." This was so because "the law of nations is part of the law of the land." The conduct of Henfield was "an offense against the laws of nations" and was punishable by "indictment or information as such."

Rawle acknowledged that it had been said that there was a "want of *precedent* for this prosecution." Nevertheless, stated Rawle, this should not deter the jury because "it is demonstrated that the law of nations is part of the law of the land," and second, "in numerous other instances, enumerated by Blackstone, the law of nations is enforced by the judiciary. In cases of this nature, we find provisions have been made by statute in *affirmance* of the law, providing more speedy and specific relief than the common course of the law will admit."[26]

In short, Rawle was advancing Wilson's theory—first, that the common law was the basis of jurisprudence for America as well as England; second, that American common law, like the English, incorporated the law of nations; and, finally, that American citizens were therefore answerable for violations of the law of nations. Unfortunately, there is no record of the argument made by counsel for Henfield, other than some notes taken by Rawle. These show that the defense stressed, inter alia, that Henfield's conduct "did not include an offense at common law," and that "independently" of other grounds "as there was no statute giving jurisdiction, the Court could take no cognizance of the offense."[27]

In his charge to the petit jury, Justice Wilson restated themes from his grand jury charge, and, in particular, he sought to answer the question raised by Henfield's counsel: "Against what law has he offended?" Wilson responded:

> As a citizen of the United States, he was bound to act no part which could injure the nation; he was bound to keep the peace in regard to all nations with whom we are at peace. This is the law of nations; not an *ex post facto* law, but a law that was in existence long before Gideon Henfield existed.[28]

All of this indicates, in short, that the Federalist prosecutor and judges believed in the existence of a federal common law of crimes which embraced violations of the law of nations. In addition, Wilson stressed that Henfield violated the terms of specific treaties, which were "expressly declared to be part of the supreme law of the land." After almost two days of deliberation and several consultations with the court, the jury delivered a verdict of not guilty.

The Meaning of the *Henfield* Case

Since there was absolutely no doubt that Henfield committed the acts with which he was charged,[29] it is tempting to read the acquittal as a rejection by the jury of the law as laid down in Justice Wilson's grand jury charge, his petit jury charge, and Rawle's argument to the petit jury. This temptation was too much for the antiadministration, or anti-Federalist press, to resist. A piece in the *National Gazette* of Philadelphia, the short-lived organ of the emerging opposition to the Federalist party,[30] proclaimed:

> By this verdict which according to the charge of the court indicates a decision on the *law* as well as the *facts*, it is now established that a citizen of the United States may by law enter on board a French Privateer and it is presumable that no other prosecution for this same cause can be sustained. . . . [31]

Thus the *National Gazette*, and its sister opposition newspaper, the *General Advertiser*,[32] proclaimed the doctrine that jury verdicts were to have precedential value. "[I]t would be contrary to the principles of impartial justice," the piece went on, "that any man should in future be convicted and punished for doing what in Gideon Henfield was no crime, and incurred no penalty." In the view of at least these commentators, then, the popular views of the jury were to be accorded more legal weight than the opinions of the Federalist prosecutors and judges.

The papers also criticized the Federalist doctrine that suggested that crimes could be punished without statutes:

> With respect to the charge of the court which declared explicitly, that the acts committed by Gideon Henfield were a violation of the land, and punishable, we can only lament that any occasion should arise for introducing motives of policy to influence the decisions of our courts of justice.[33]

This article closed with a stirring linkage of the *Henfield* jury's actions with those of a famous English liberty-loving jury:

> When the seven bishops (good and celebrated men) were tried for petitioning James the Second, a similar difference of opinion arose between the bench and the jury, the people then as the people now exulted in the verdict of acquittal; and our posterity will, probably, venerate this as we venerate that jury, for adding to the security of the rights and liberties of mankind.[34]

John Marshall wrote in his *Life of Washington* that the *Henfield* verdict was greeted with "extravagant marks of joy and exultation." According to Marshall the prosecution of Henfield had been perceived by the antiadministration popular press as pursuant to executive proclamation, not legislative act, nor established common law. "It was universally asked," he wrote, "what law had been offended, and under what statute was the indictment supported?"[35] Marshall's account would suggest that the opposition press, at least, was maintaining that a law of nations or common law could furnish no ground for the prosecution of Henfield, that the only colorable source of support was Washington's Neutrality Proclamation, and that since this was an executive, not a legislative, act, it could not be relied upon.

It is possible to read the verdict in the *Henfield* case as a popular rejection of the Federalist doctrine of the existence of common law crimes. It is doubtful, however, that the popular feeling against prosecutions at the law of nations or at common law was as great as these opposition newspapers made it out to be. First, the possibility that some sort of coercion was applied to at least one of the *Henfield* jurors cannot be dismissed. One of their number was reported to have declared to the court that "he was induced to the verdict because he heard threats made out of doors against any one who should oppose the acquittal."[36] Second, the jurors' acquittal of Henfield may have flowed more from Henfield's personal circumstances than from any hostility to the nature of the prosecution. Thomas Jefferson wrote shortly after the trial:

> It appeared on the trial, that the crime was not knowingly and willfully committed; that Henfield was ignorant of the unlawfulness of his undertaking; that, in the moment he was apprised of it he showed real contrition; that he had rendered meritorious services during the late war, and declared that he would live and die an American.[37]

Jefferson concluded: "The jury, therefore, in absolving him, did no more than the constitutional authority might have done, had they found him guilty."

This 1793 letter of Jefferson, written when he was still Washington's secretary of state, is very interesting insofar as it implicitly suggests that the prosecution of Henfield was a lawful undertaking. It states that Henfield's commission of hostilities against a nation with which the United States was at peace was an "unlawful act" and as such could not serve as a renunciation of American citizenship. Jefferson went on to note, without stating any disapproval, the opinions of the "Attorney General" (Jay) and of Wilson that Henfield's Conduct was punishable by law."[38] It is likely that Jefferson's 1793 letter to the financier Robert Morris, then in England, and the enclosed copies of the jury charges of Jay (at Richmond) and Wilson (at Philadelphia) were intended to mollify the British, and thus Jefferson was acting in a diplomatic capacity. Nevertheless, his attitude in this letter stands in marked contrast to the position he adopted in 1799. At that time, immediately before his presidential campaign, he violently excoriated the Federalists for the prosecution of "common law crimes." This was the way in which they, at least, seemed to view the Henfield prosecution, whether or not others (principally Jeffersonians) might later characterize it as a prosecution under a "treaty" or under the law of nations.

A final, and perhaps most convincing, explanation of Henfield's acquittal is
that the epidemic of Francophilia which had swept America shortly after the
revolutionary events of 1789 was apparently still fairly strong, and Henfield's
activities in aiding France may have been perceived by the majority of the jurors as "combating for liberty against the combined despots of Europe."[39]
Thus, admiration for the French Republicans rather than hostility to the form
of American conservative Federalist prosecution may have influenced the *Henfield* jury.

That there was at this time no overwhelming popular opposition to the doctrine that crimes could be prosecuted without statutes is also evident from the
proceedings in the case of *United States v. Ravara*,[40] tried one year after *Henfield*. Ravara was a consul from Genoa who was accused of sending threatening letters to the British minister and to several other persons "with a view to
extort money."[41]

At the trial, Ravara's defense was made on three grounds: first, that at common law what Ravara had done was no crime; second, that by virtue of his
being a consul, "the law of nations" (which was said to be a part of the law of
the United States) made him "independent of the ordinary criminal justice of
the place where he reside[d]"; and third, that the evidence was simply too circumstantial to support a verdict.[42] Thus, even the defense in this case appears
to have implicitly acknowledged the authority of the common law and the law
of nations, in the same manner as did Wilson's charge a year earlier.[43] The
prosecutor, again Mr. Rawle, maintained that "the offense was indictable at
common law; that the consular character of the defendant gave jurisdiction to
the circuit court, . . . [and] that the proof was as strong as the nature of the case
allowed."[44] The same position was taken by the court (Jay and Peters) in its
charge to the jury.

"[A]fter a short consultation," the jury "pronounced the defendant
guilty."[45] Like *Henfield*, *Ravara* was a case in which no statute proscribed the
criminal conduct. Devoid of the peculiar circumstances which may have
skewed the *Henfield* verdict, the guilty verdict in *Ravara* belies any overwhelming popular sentiment against such prosecutions. As we have seen in most of
the cases we have considered thus far, as late as the mid-1790s the tenets of
Federalist jurisprudence, including the advocacy of the existence of common
law crimes, do not appear to have met with decisive popular rejection.

Nevertheless, the *Henfield* verdict was apparently read by the wiser Federalists as a sign that prosecutions without statutes were risky. Henfield's acquittal "alarmed President Washington," who sought and obtained legislation
from Congress proscribing conduct like Henfield's.[46] A case under the new
law, *United States v. Guinet*,[47] was tried in the Pennsylvania federal circuit
court in 1795. Guinet was charged with helping to outfit a French privateer in
December 1794, a clear violation of the new statute. The jury apparently had

no trouble in rendering a guilty verdict. Since Henfield was acquitted of a similar charge when the prosecution was brought at common law, it would be possible to read the guilty verdict in *Guinet* as evidence of popular approval of Federalist prosecutions for the same act where it was outlawed by statute. This would have to be a tentative reading, however, since there were other differences in the two cases which might have influenced a jury. First, Guinet was apparently involved principally for money, whereas Henfield was at least arguably a disinterested lover of liberty. Also, the predominant pro-French mood of the country had largely dissipated by 1795, owing to the atrocities of the September Massacres of 1792, the Reign of Terror of 1793–1794, and George Washington's denunciation of the pro-French "democratic societies" in late 1794.[48]

As of 1795, then, it does not seem possible to conclude that American public opinion had reached a consensus on the legitimacy of prosecution in federal courts in cases without a statutory basis. Still, it does appear that there were several successful prosecutions of crimes at common law or the law of nations immediately after the *Henfield* case. Charles Warren wrote: "In spite of the result in the Henfield Case, the Federal Courts continued to indict persons for violations of neutrality, the indictments being based on common law and the law of nations."[49] Warren cited an account of three American citizens taken from the French privateer *Roland* in Boston and held for trial in the circuit court on a charge of "aiding and assisting in manning and fitting out vessels and piratically and feloniously capturing the vessels of nations with whom the United States are at peace"—in the *Connecticut Journal* for Sept. 4, 1793. Julius Goebel's examination of the manuscript records of the Circuit Court for the District of New York revealed the conviction for common law libel of a New York publisher named Greenleaf in 1797 (he was apparently indicted for the first time in 1795, but not prosecuted; then indicted, prosecuted, and convicted in 1797). According to the manuscript records of the Circuit Court for the District of Massachusetts of 1797, there were four indictments prosecuted for "counterfeiting or passing counterfeit bills of the Bank of the United States, not then a statutory offense."[50]

This means that the confident assertions by the opposition press that the *Henfield* jury's verdict would have legal precedential value were incorrect. None of these immediately post-*Henfield* federal common law prosecutions occurred in Pennsylvania, however, and the issue did not surface there again until 1798, in the strange case of *United States v. Worrall.*[51]

The *Worrall* Case

Robert Worrall was a businessman of sorts who in 1797 had unsuccessfully attempted to bribe the United States Commissioner of Revenue into awarding a contract for the construction of a government lighthouse. By this time, Congress had passed statutes providing punishments for bribing judges, officers of the "customs," or officers of the "excise," but there was no statute explicitly proscribing attempts to bribe the commissioner of revenue. Nevertheless, it was reasonably clear that at English common law such an attempt at bribery was an indictable crime.[52] Worrall was indicted by a grand jury and brought to trial in the Federal Circuit Court for the District of Pennsylvania before Judge Peters and Justice Samuel Chase, the man with whom we are primarily concerned.

The case is badly reported, but it appears that defense counsel threw out only the barest hint that there might be a problem in prosecution without a supporting statute.[53] The trial jury found Mr. Worrall guilty. Trial defense counsel's apparent failure to argue the illegality of indictments without supporting statutes, and the grand jury's previous indictment of Worrall, again suggest a lack of popular appeal of that legal argument, or at least Robert Worrall's lack of popular appeal. It might be of some significance that in early 1798 popular support for the Federalists was running fairly high in the wake of the XYZ affair and the atrocities of the French Reign of Terror.[54]

No sooner was Worrall found guilty than Alexander James Dallas, counsel for Mr. Worrall, rose to move in arrest of judgment on the grounds that the circuit court was without authority to take cognizance of the crime charged in the indictment. Mr. Dallas then made what appears to be the most complete legal argument against the prosecution of federal common law crimes yet advanced in public. Dallas suggested that all the judicial authority of the federal courts had to be derived either from the Constitution or from acts of Congress and that "the crime of attempting to bribe, the character of a Federal officer, and the place where the present offense was committed" were not specified in any constitutional provision, nor had there been an act of Congress which expressed these elements. Moreover, Dallas argued that the provision of the eleventh section of the Judiciary Act of 1789, giving the federal courts jurisdiction over "crimes and offenses cognizable under the authority of the United States," referred only to express constitutional provisions and statutes passed by Congress.[55]

Dallas took the position that a construction of the Judiciary Act more liberal than this would "destroy all the barriers between the judicial authorities of the state and the general government." If the present case were allowed, "anything which can prevent a Federal officer from the punctual, as well as from an impartial performance of his duty, an assault and battery or the recovery of a debt, as well as the offer of a bribe," said Dallas, "may be made a foundation of the jurisdiction of this court." He warned that "considering the constant disposition of power to extend the sphere of its influence, fictions will be resorted to, when real cases cease to occur."[56]

If the common law had been the "law of the United States," Dallas said that he would have been willing to acknowledge that Worrall's offense, though not specified in the Constitution nor defined in any act of Congress, could be punished in a federal court. However, Dallas maintained: "[T]he nature of our Federal compact will not . . . tolerate this doctrine."[57] The federal government, he argued, by virtue of the Tenth Amendment to the Constitution[58] was one of limited, enumerated, and delegated powers. Thus, since the Constitution spelled out in article 1, section 8, that Congress could pass statutes providing for the "punishment of counterfeiting . . . piracies and felonies . . . and offenses against the law of nations,"[59] and since the Constitution also provided that laws might be "necessary and proper for carrying into execution the powers of the general government,"[60] the federal courts were without power to act unless a specific statute were passed making bribing the commissioner a crime.

"Every power is a matter of definite and positive grant," Dallas went on, "but the very powers that are granted cannot take effect until they are exercised through the medium of a law." In short, in the Constitution as understood by Dallas, except for the reservation to the states in the Tenth Amendment, there "is no reference to a common law authority." Dallas then distinguished the indictment against Henfield as involving a violation of treaties (over which the Constitution expressly gave the federal government power) and that against Ravara as a proceeding against a consul (a proceeding also explicitly permitted in the Constitution).[61]

The prosecutor, Rawle, in support of the indictment and against the motion in arrest of judgment, argued that Worrall's offense was within the terms of the Constitution as an offense "arising under the laws of the United States." Because Coxe's office had been created by a federal law, said Rawle, an attempt to bribe him could be inferred to be an offense "arising under a law of the United States." This would have been grounds to support the indictment apart from the argument that there was a federal common law crimes jurisdiction. Fairly quickly, however, Rawle addressed the real controversy in the case—the existence of common law jurisdiction. He began by an attempt to demonstrate that *Henfield* and *Ravara* were indistinguishable from *Worrall* in that all had been proceedings at common law.[62] Following the jury charges of Wilson and Jay,[63] Rawle indicated that even though the prosecutions in *Henfield* and *Ravara* may have involved references to explicit constitutional grants of authority to the federal government, the methods of proceeding in the courts were not spelled out in the Constitution or in any federal statutes. Thus, the mere fact that indictments, trials, and (in the case of *Ravara*) sentencing took place demonstrated the existence of accepted common law guides which dictated procedure.[64]

As soon as Rawle had suggested that other federal cases had been brought by virtue of indictments sought at common law, Justice Chase, as he had a habit of doing, broke in. At this point he made the move that astonished his Federalist colleagues. "Do you mean, Mr. Attorney," Chase asked, "to support this indictment solely at common law? If you do, I have no difficulty upon the subject. The indictment cannot be maintained in this Court." Rawle answered "in the affirmative." Chase then delivered an opinion from the bench which seems to have been written anticipating Rawle's argument.

Chase's opinion was something of a treatise on the Tenth Amendment and ran along the lines of Dallas's presentation. Chase emphasized that the departments of the United States government could not assume any powers that were "not expressly granted by" the Constitution. Although the Congress clearly possessed the power to make bribery of the commissioner of revenue a crime by virtue of the "necessary and proper" clause of the Constitution, since it had not been done the courts could not yet act on the offense. For Chase it was "essential that Congress should define the offenses to be tried, and apportion the punishments to be inflicted. . . . "[65] Chase declared that it was impermissible to resort to the common law "for a definition and punishment of the offense which had been committed," because "in my opinion, the United States, as a Federal government, have no common law." Unlike the states, wrote Chase, the "United States" did not bring the common law with them from England, and neither the Constitution nor a federal statute had adopted it. Moreover, since the common law of each particular state varied according to its "local situation," there was no uniform body of common law that could be said to be applicable to the federal government.[66]

When Chase had finished, Judge Peters, who was sitting with Chase, expressed his opinion that Chase was wrong, and that the prosecutor had correctly stated the law. For Peters, the power "to preserve itself" was a "necessary and inseparable" feature of any government. The United States, he said, were "constitutionally possessed" of the "common law power" to punish misdemeanors in the exercise of such self-defense. While it was true that Congress could exercise this power in the form of a legislative act, the power could also "be enforced in a course of judicial proceeding." Peters used a sort of bootstrap reasoning which he summed up as follows:

> Whenever an offense aims at the subversion of any Federal institution, or at the corruption of its public officers, it is an offense against the well-being of the United States; from its very nature, it is cognizable under their authority; and, consequently, it is within the jurisdiction of this court, by virtue of the 11th section of the Judicial Act.[67]

Chase was the first federal judge to utter what might be regarded as Federalist heresy that there was no federal common law jurisdiction. Soon the Jeffersonian Republicans were to take up the claim and bandy it about the halls of Congress,[68] in private correspondence,[69] and in public manifestos.[70] As Republican suspicions grew that the Federalists were going to use a "federal common law" to harass and imprison critics of the administration, the issue of the existence of a federal common law became a red-hot political controversy. As the late Professor Julius Goebel pointed out, the debates in late 1798 and 1799 were filled more with political rhetoric than with legal analysis and did not resolve the question of the legal correctness of Peters's or Chase's views.[71] While the popular and judicial political reaction to the issue of federal common law crimes is of primary importance to us here, some consideration of the strictly legal aspects of the controversy may help to indicate the depth of the influence of political factors on the ultimate judicial resolution of this issue.

Was There a "Federal Common Law?" The Debate of the Scholars

The Intention of the Constitution's Framers

Professor Julius Goebel, of Columbia, one of the leading scholars of the legal history of the early Republic in the last generation, and a pretty thorough student of this problem, believed that it was not the intention of the framers of the Constitution to make the common law "the basic jurisprudence that would prevail in the new system." They intended, he believed, merely to take selected parts of the common law to fill out the definition of words like "Equity," "Jury," or "Treason."[72]

Goebel appears implicitly to be criticizing the view of Richard Peters, expressed in *Worrall*, although he does it by taking shots at an easier target. In particular, Goebel derided as "mere political bombast" the suggestion made in Congress in July 1798 by arch-Federalist Harrison Gray Otis that by incorporation of common law terms the United States Constitution implicitly incorporated the substance of the English common law.[73] In that 1798 political debate, which reflected the increasing ardor generated following the *Worrall* case, Jeffersonian Albert Gallatin of Pennsylvania disputed Otis by arguments similar to those of Dallas and Chase.[74]

Goebel seems to have believed that Gallatin had the better argument, since he (Goebel) maintained that the Constitution's framers intentionally did not incorporate the entire English common law, because they believed that if they had done so they would have been altering and homogenizing the jurisprudence of the states, and could have poured into American law all sorts of obscure and hateful English doctrines, including the establishment of the Anglican church.[75] Goebel's principal support for this notion is a letter from James Madison to George Washington (Oct. 18, 1797):

What could the [constitutional] Convention have done? If they had in general terms declared the Common law to be in force, they would have broken in upon the legal Code of every State in the most material points: they would have done more, they would have brought over from G[rea]t B[ritain] a thousand heterogeneous & antirepublican doctrines, and even the ecclesiastical Hierarchy itself, for that is a part of the common law.[76]

Madison was, of course, present at the creation, as he was at the Constitutional Convention itself, but his letter is written a decade later. Madison's after-the-fact rationalization, consistent with what became a Jeffersonian slippery-slope argument on the common law of crimes,[77] may prove too much, since the judicial proponents of a federal common law of crimes, like Richard Peters, never suggested that they believed that the federal Constitution incorporated the entire English common law, only that which was fit for the general government of a republican nation. This is implicitly suggested by a letter John Marshall wrote to the Virginia Jeffersonian St. George Tucker in November 1800. In that letter, as Kathryn Preyer has recently shown, Marshall

denied that anyone before 1798–99 seriously maintained the proposition that the common law of England had been adopted as the common law of the United States by the Constitution. This "strange and absurd doctrine," he charged, was first attributed to the federal judiciary by "some frothy newspaper publication in Richmond something more than twelve months past."[78]

Professor Preyer takes Marshall's letter as something casting doubt about a general common law crimes jurisdiction, but I read it differently. Since Marshall's letter is written two years after the *Worrall* case, and also after several Federalist prosecutions for common law crimes,[79] Marshall must have known that there was a Federalist belief in some "federal common law," though not the entire sanguinary English common law. His letter, then, simply explodes the Jeffersonian argument that the Federalists meant to impose the "entire" English common law on America.

Just what were the limits of the Federalist common law, however? The difficulty of drawing those limits has led some scholars in this generation, most notably Robert Palmer and Kathryn Preyer, to conclude that Peters and his Federalist colleagues who maintained the existence of a common law of crimes were either in a minority (Preyer) or in blatant constitutional error (Palmer).[80]

If there was an error, it appears that it was a pretty widespread one. Justices Jay, Wilson, and Ellsworth supported prosecution by way of indictments brought pursuant to a federal common law of crimes jurisdiction.[81] Professor Preyer cites comments from Justice James Iredell's writing that show that he, too, supported such jurisdiction.[82] Preyer explains that Iredell had, by 1794, "put aside his 'considerable doubts,' and charged a grand jury that a right of prosecution existed for breaches of neutrality even where the legislature had made no provision."[83] Moreover, and perhaps more to the point, as Professor Preyer elaborates, by 1796 Iredell had reached the conclusion that "the law of nations was a part of the laws of the United States 'in the same manner and upon the same principle as any other offense committed against the common law.' "[84]

Preyer believes that only these four Supreme Court justices can be said with certainty to have embraced the federal common law of crimes jurisdiction, but I think we can go further. First, we can add Justice Bushrod Washington, who declared in *U.S. v. James McGill* (1798)[85] that he had "often decided that the federal courts have common law jurisdiction in criminal cases."[86] Second, we can add William Paterson, whose biographer concluded in 1979 that "there is every reason to believe that Paterson went along with his Federalist colleagues and would have admitted common law indictments had they been presented to him,"[87] and whose manuscripts prior to 1794 have recently been demonstrated by Stewart Jay to contain a defense of the federal common law of crimes jurisdiction.[88] Finally, Charles Warren claimed that Justice Cushing, in his grand jury charges, had also embraced the federal common law of crimes jurisdiction.[89]

This would give us a majority of seven of the twelve justices who sat in the first decade of the Republic who believed in a jurisdiction for nonstatutorily defined crimes. This figure could conceivably be higher; no one has yet been able to refute Justice Story's statement that

> excepting Judge Chase, every Judge that ever sat on the Supreme Court from the adoption of the constitution until 1804 (as I have been very authoritatively informed) held a like opinion [on the legitimacy of the federal common law of crimes.][90]

More significant perhaps than the numbers is that three of the justices who invoked federal common law of crimes jurisdiction, Wilson, Ellsworth, and Paterson, were "prominent members of the [constitutional] convention; in fact the latter two served on the Senate Committee that drafted the Judiciary Act of 1789,"[91] and this brings us to consider another argument that Peters was right in the *Worrall* case and Chase was wrong.

The Intention of the Framers of the Judiciary Act

Even if Palmer, Preyer, Goebel, Chase, and Dallas were right about the Constitution not incorporating a federal common law, it is still at least theoretically possible that the incorporation of this jurisprudence could have been accomplished by a federal statute. Chase himself acknowledged this possibility in *Worrall*.[92] Peters, delivering his *Worrall* opinion immediately after Chase, made clear his belief in the jurisdiction of the federal circuit court to punish the kind of offense Worrall had committed. At this point it is worth quoting from that opinion at some length:

> Whenever a government has been established, I have always supposed, that a power to preserve itself, was a necessary and an inseparable concomitant. But the existence of the Federal Government would be precarious, and it could no longer be called an independent government, if, for the punishment of offenses of this nature, tending to obstruct and pervert the administration of its affairs, an appeal must be made to the State tribunals, or the offenders must escape with absolute impunity.
>
> The power to punish misdemeanors is originally and strictly a common law power; of which I think the United States are constitutionally possessed. It might have been exercised by Congress in the form of a legislative act; but it may also, in my opinion, be enforced in a course of judicial proceeding. Whenever an offense aims at the subversion of any Federal institution, or at the corruption of its public officers, it is an offense against the well-being of the United States; from its very nature, it is cognizable under their authority; and, consequently, it is within the jurisdiction of this court, by virtue of the 11th section of the judicial act.[93]

Peters's language is not unambiguous, but it does suggest his belief that the federal Constitution, by establishing an "independent" federal government, ipso facto mandated some common law of crimes jurisdiction. Having made this one step, Peters went on to state his belief that the language of the Judiciary Act giving the federal circuit court jurisdiction over "all crimes and offenses cognizable under the authority of the United States" was intended to create the federal common law of crimes jurisdiction in the circuit court.

This shifts the focus to the intention not of the framers of the Constitution, but to the framers of the 1789 Judiciary Act, Ellsworth and Paterson among them. Did the fact that they held for a federal common law of crimes jurisdiction reflect their understanding of the Judiciary Act? In his landmark 1923 article on the history of the 1789 Judiciary Act, Charles Warren argued that such incorporation of the federal common law of crimes jurisdiction was the intention of Congress.

Warren had discovered the draft of the bill that eventually became the 1789 act as it was introduced into the Senate. It defined the federal criminal jurisdiction as over "all crimes and offenses that shall be cognizable under the authority of the United States *and defined by the laws of the same.*"[94] When the bill was passed by Congress, the italicized language was deleted, and Warren infers from the deletion of these words that Congress meant not to restrict jurisdiction over offenses defined by statutes ("laws"), but instead intended to vest jurisdiction over crimes at common law and the law of nations.[95] That such jurisdiction was vested would be supportable by much of the evidence we have been reviewing in this chapter, beginning as early as Wilson's and Jay's jury charges, charges roughly contemporaneous with the 1789 act.[96]

Julius Goebel, however, would have none of this. As indicated already, he believed that there was no design to impose a federal common law of crimes jurisdiction by the Constitution, and he apparently believed that the Judiciary Act could not be interpreted to do so either. Goebel believed that the action in the Senate in deleting the phrase "and defined by the laws of the same" was taken simply because the phrase was considered redundant, "and defined by the laws of the same" apparently meaning the same thing, to Goebel at least, as "cognizable under the authority of the United States."[97] Goebel also pointed out that at the time of Senate consideration of the judiciary bill there was an expectation that the Senate would soon have before it a bill defining all possible crimes against the United States. Goebel takes this fact, coupled with the redundancy argument, to mean that the Senate probably did not intend to confer common law crimes jurisdiction.[98]

Given some rather startling ambiguities in Warren's treatment of congressional language, Goebel's redundancy justification for the deletion has some appeal. These ambiguities are revealed when one considers another part of Warren's "New Light" article, one more noted by American Constitution scholars, where he makes his celebrated announcement that Congress in section 34 of the act intended for the federal courts to follow state common law jurisprudence in civil matters (and that therefore *Swift v. Tyson*, 41 U.S. (16 Pet.) 1 (1942) was wrong).[99] In the article Warren infers that by the word "laws" Congress meant "to include the common law of a State as well as the statute law."[100] Yet, in the "New Light" article, when Warren discusses the Senate's deletion of the word "laws" from the draft of what became section 11, he argues that they meant to delete a reference to statutes only.[101]

It seems doubtful that when the drafters of the Judiciary Act used the word "laws," and when Congress considered "laws," Congress and the drafters meant one thing in leaving "laws" in section 34 and another in deleting it from the draft of section 11. If the word "laws" meant "statute and common law" in both places, then Warren is wrong about the significance of the deletion from section 11. If, in other words, "laws" meant "statute and common law," then it probably did mean the same thing as "cognizable under the authority of the United States," as Julius Goebel thought, and could have been deleted, as Goebel suggests, for redundancy. But the implication of this redundancy may not be what Goebel proposes, that is, it may not go to the existence or nonexistence of the federal common law of crimes. If, on the other hand, "laws" meant "statutes" in both places, then Warren is right about the importance of the deletion from section 11, that is, that the Senate meant to suggest a common law of crimes jurisdiction, but he is wrong about the meaning of section 34, which would then have meant only that federal courts were required to follow state statutes, and Story's opinion in *Swift* would have been correct. If, then, Warren was right about the existence of a federal common law of crimes, he might well have been wrong about Justice Story's effort in *Swift*, which would mean that the Supreme Court may have been wrong to follow Warren in *Erie R.R. Co. v. Tompkins.*[102]

One of these days, then, scholars are going to have to decide which Warren was right about, the existence of the federal common law of crimes or Story's "mistake" in finding a federal civil common law. In the meantime, however, if the reader is still following through this difficult thicket, it should be observed that Goebel's "redundancy" argument does not help solve the problems of the intention of the framers of the Judiciary Act any more than did Warren's article. This is because it is at least logically possible that the phrase "and defined by the laws of the same" was redundant not, as Goebel thought, because the words "cognizable under the authority of the United States" and "defined by the laws of the same" meant the same thing, but because both the phrase "crimes and offenses" and the word "laws" referred to both "statute and common law." If this last were the meaning of "laws," and this was a redundant meaning, then the phrase "cognizable under the authority of the United States" included statute and common law, and there was a federal common law of crimes by virtue of section 11 of the Judiciary Act. Thus it may be that Goebel's redundancy argument proves the very thing he disputed, and that he and his latter-day disciples Preyer, Palmer, and Samuel Chase were wrong and Judge Peters was right.

Even if the framers of the Judiciary Act intended to confer a "common law of crimes" jurisdiction, one might still argue that Section 11 of the Judiciary Act was unconstitutional insofar as it was intended to grant jurisdiction over common law crimes to the federal courts. This is the argument suggested both by Chase's opinion in *Worrall* and by Dallas's reference, in his argument, to what became the Tenth Amendment,[103] although this would mean that the statute became unconstitutional only after the ratification of the amendment in 1791.

In the final analysis, the Goebel-Warren controversy, which ultimately turns on the most arcane semantic hairsplitting, may be irrelevant because there is no way of knowing just what was intended by the framers of the Constitution and the Judiciary Act. The intentions of individual framers may have been completely different, depending upon their particular philosophical or political beliefs. In the Constitutional Convention of 1787, for example, the delegates apparently maintained different interpretations over just what had been proposed with regard to the questions of the extent of federal sovereignty and the role of the federal courts in judicial review, and a particular delegate's view was influenced by his predilection for what we used to call "nationalism" or "states' rights."[104] The Judiciary Act of 1789 was also a compromise and an ambiguous measure which did not give either those favoring "broad" jurisdiction in the lower federal courts or those favoring jurisdiction over federal questions in the state courts all they desired.[105] In this atmosphere, it seems at least possible that many key measures, like the provisions for federal criminal jurisdiction, may have been ambiguously worded compromises deliberately leaving room for different interpretations.[106]

Nevertheless, even where the legislative history is fairly certain, we should not be surprised to find partisans disagreeing about the meaning of particular phrases. For example, even though it was apparently clear that "states' rights" advocates "failed in their attempts to alter the proposal that was to become the tenth amendment so as to limit the federal government to those powers 'expressly' delegated by the Constitution," these advocates or their descendants were not above "frequently but incorrectly" insisting that the Tenth Amendment had made implied federal powers illegal.[107]

Something like this insistence seems to have happened right in the *Worrall* trial where both defense counsel Dallas and Justice Chase spoke as though the provisions of the Tenth Amendment forbade the application of a federal common law of crimes because the Constitution does not expressly grant such power.[108] In seeking an explanation for the divergence of judicial views in the *Worrall* case, then, the widespread division in opinion over the extent of the sovereignty of the federal government looks attractive. According to this view, Richard Peters, a believer in strong federal sovereignty,[109] would be expected to take the position he did, endorsing a strong federal government capable of exercising inherent powers of self-defense. But how, then, does one explain the views of Justice Chase, who seems to be taking a states' rights position in *Worrall*, but who later was to become the most blatant symbol of aggrandizing federalism? This is a puzzle that may never be solved, and has aready led to involved jurisprudential exegesis.

Jurisprudential Explanations

Horwitz's Rise of "Instrumentalism" Explanation. In one of the most provocative and brilliant presentations in recent years, one scholar, Morton Horwitz, has argued that the *Worrall* case turned on very abstract and relatively politically neutral jurisprudential concerns. Professor Horwitz saw in this split between Chase and Peters a divergence of philosophical views about the nature of the common law, a divergence which cut deeper than mere views on the extent of federal sovereignty.[110] Chase, he believed, reflected the recent eighteenth-century emergence of the notion that the common law, like all positive law, derived its authority only from its promulgation by the sovereign. According to this hypothesis, Chase's opinion in *Worrall* stands for the proposition that where the American sovereign (the legislature acting on behalf of the people or the people themselves in their Constitution) has accepted the authority of the English common law it is binding, but, where no such acceptance has taken place, the common law has no force.[111]

Horwitz would then, presumably, regard Peters as a representative of an older jurisprudential view that the English common law incorporated principles of the law of nature, which were everywhere in force whether or not they had been the subject of positive enactment or other promulgation by the sovereign. To a certain extent, then, the divergence of views on the nature of the common law would be a disagreement over the meaning of the two words. In Chase's view, as posited under this theory, the common law is no different from any other positive enactment of the sovereign will. The English or American common law, in short, is nothing more than a collection of arbitrary rules. To someone of Peters's persuasion as ascribed here, however, the words "common law" meant a collection of principles which were not arbitrary, but natural and perhaps eternal.[112]

According to this theory, then, Peters's notion about inherent rights to self-defense, including the power to prosecute for bribery, flows from his conception of the nature of the common law, the repository of such inherent rights. Horwitz's work suggests that for adherents to this view of the law, the common law was fixed and certain and may have even partaken of divine inspiration. Horwitz maintains that for Chase and other adherents to the newer jurisprudential view, the common law was seen to be a product of judicial discretion.[113] If the common law was a product of discretion, said these new jurisprudential theorists, then the choices made by English judges in accordance with the needs of the English system did not necessarily reflect what was acceptable in America.

Horwitz has used his theory of the emergence of what he believes to be Chase's "instrumental conception" of law at approximately the time of the *Worrall* case to explain, in part, why American law was able to develop so dramatically in the nineteenth century.[114] Based on both the nature of the cases and the behavior of the judges in the Pennsylvania federal courts, however, Horwitz's theory about the importance of jurisprudential premises to changes in the law is somewhat problematic, and this explanation for the divergence between Chase and Peters does not seem to be adequate.

First, Judge Peters in *Worrall* seems to exhibit the "preinstrumentalist" view of the common law, but his opinions in the admiralty cases[115] indicate that he was extremely policy oriented and had no hesitation in picking and choosing among judicial precedents. Second, as already noted, Justice Chase, in his Supreme Court opinion in *Calder v. Bull*,[116] issued at approximately this time, made a strong statement that there were certain unwritten "vital" or "fundamental" principles which circumscribed the activities of both state and federal legislatures and guaranteed the security of personal liberty and private property. The Chase of *Calder*, insofar as he insists on the presence of fundamental principles not derived from positive manifestations of the sovereign will, sounds as much like an advocate of eighteenth-century "natural-law" jurisprudence as does Judge Peters in the *Worrall* case. This suggests either that assumptions about the "instrumental" or "natural law" character of the law could switch on and off, or that a particular jurist's adherence to a jurisprudential view of the common law, at least in the terms used by Horwitz, may have had relatively little effect on the substance of his decisions.

An Internal Law of Nations and Other Supraconstitutional Matters.   It appears, then, that we must look beyond the instrumentalist/natural law dichotomy to explain what was going on in *Worrall*, and in the debate over a federal common law of crimes jurisdiction in particular. Nevertheless, I think Horwitz was basically on the right track, insofar as he believed that more than mere partisan politics was involved in the debate in the 1790s and that attitudes about the nature of the American legal system were at the heart of the judges' understanding. Moreover, I do not believe that a strictly technical legal form of analysis, of the type attempted by such scholars as DuPonceau in the nineteenth century[117] and Robert Palmer in the late twentieth century,[118] can solve this legitimacy problem either.

Palmer, for example, ingeniously draws distinctions among late eighteenth-century federal applications of state criminal law, federal jurisdiction based on the law of nations, and federal common law jurisdiction based on the law of treaties, all of which he finds to be legitimate exercises of federal common law jurisdiction, on the one hand, and application of a federal common law of crimes unsupported by any of these three bases, such as that attempted in prosecutions for seditious libel against the federal government[119] or prosecutions for other allegedly federal crimes unsupported by statute, as in the *Worrall* case, on the other hand, which he finds to be illegitimate.[120]

It is difficult not to admire the intellectual sophistication in an argument like Palmer's, but it is also difficult to believe that such a refined analysis would have appealed to many late eighteenth-century minds. Many of the early federal judges who held views like Peters's simply would not have found Palmer's distinctions meaningful. This is because they reached their jurisprudential judgment on the validity of a federal common law of crimes not as the result of the kind of legal analysis undertaken by Palmer and DuPonceau, but on the basis of what we might refer to as "supraconstitutional" factors, including, most prominently, writers on politics in general and the law of nations in particular. Horwitz is essentially correct that the political controversy over the common law of crimes, the charges from the Jeffersonians about the corrupt character of the Federalists' stand on the common law of crimes, has tended to overshadow the quite traditional basis in constitutional, or, perhaps more correctly, supraconstitutional, theory on which the notion of a federal common law of crimes was based.

This traditional supraconstitutional basis is most in evidence in the work of Richard Peters. As noted in chapter 5, Peters was learned in a plethora of languages and thoroughly conversant with the law of nations.[121] Moreover, Peters believed that the common law, the reports of decisions by the judicial and scholarly interpreters of the English customs and unwritten law, had an innate superiority over statutes:

> The feudal parts of [the English common] law, and such as are inconsistent with the principles of our [American] government are not, nor can they be, in force. Those who are best acquainted with its wise and just principles, as they relate to contracts, and the property, as well as the personal rights of individuals, admire the common law as the venerable and solid bulwark of both liberty and property. Statute laws innovating upon it have seldom been found, on experience, to be real improvements.[122]

Continuing in the same note to the admiralty opinion where he made these comments, Peters proceeded to take a swipe at the enemies of the common law, probably firing a broadside at those who would soon launch the Jeffersonian popular attack on the federal common law of crimes jurisdiction:

> Those who do not know the common law suppose it to be everything that it is not. Its rules and principles are not arbitrary, but fixed and settled by the wisdom and decisions of the most respectable and intelligent sages, of both ancient and modern times. Many of the objections raised against it shew a want of acquaintance with its system and principles. Some of these objections are founded in innovation made by statutes altering or obscuring the common law. Others have nothing in either common or statute law to support them.[123]

Peters, as did his fellow Pennsylvanian James Wilson, for example, believed that the American common law, insofar as it incorporated the law of nations, gave a very broad basis for criminal jurisdiction, even without the aid of statutes.[124]

In Peters's *Worrall* opinion, it will be remembered, he referred to a national right to self-defense, which the federal courts could invoke to punish an individual who sought to bribe a commissioner of revenue, though no federal statute had yet prohibited such conduct nor specified a punishment. It seems certain that this right to national "self-defense" which Peters invoked was viewed by him, given his familiarity with the law of nations jurisprudence of the great civilians, as a manifestation of what might best be described as the "internal" dimension of the "law of nations" remarked on by Grotius and Vattel.[125] This internal law of nations for the civilians flowed from the people of each nation's obligation "to preserve themselves,"[126] and was consonant also, as observed by Vattel and later by Wilson in his *Henfield* grand jury charge, with the law of nature.[127]

This duty of self-preservation found in an internal law of nations, also described as the "necessary law of nations,"[128] appears to have included the duty to punish treason,[129] as well as the duty to restrain individuals who usurped the nation's exclusive right to wage war.[130] It was this last duty that Wilson invoked in his grand jury charge, and that federal prosecutors and judges invoked to support a common law of crimes jurisdiction in the *Henfield* case. Similarly, a 1799 South Carolina grand jury charge given by United States Supreme Court Chief Justice Oliver Ellsworth, as recently noted by Kathryn Preyer, seems to embrace the same theory. Ellsworth suggested that offenses against the United States and therefore within the jurisdiction of federal grand juries and circuit courts:

> ... are chiefly defined in the statutes ... or they are acts manifestly subversive of the national government, or of some of its powers specified in the constitution. ... An offense consists in transgressing the sovereign will, whether that will be expressly or obviously implied. Conduct, therefore, clearly destructive of a government or its powers, which the people have ordained to *exist* [emphasis in the original] must be criminal. It is not necessary to particularize the acts falling within this description, because they are readily perceived, and are ascertained by known and established rules; I mean the maxims and principles of the common law of our land.[131]

Ellsworth, like Peters and Wilson, seems to have been tracking the theory expressed by the civilians of an internal law of nations, which could support the wide variety of criminal prosecutions for acts "manifestly subversive of the national government." Such a jurisdiction would permit prosecutions of attempts to bribe officials, prosecutions for treason, prosecutions for seditious libel, and for any other "offenses" which might be construed as "transgressing the sovereign will" or "clearly destructive of a government or its powers." Like Peters, Ellsworth appears to have believed that this did not confer unlimited jurisdiction on the federal courts, however, and that the jurisdiction was "ascertained by known and established rules," the "maxims and principles of the common law of our land."

It appears, then, that Peters, Ellsworth, Wilson, and virtually all of the other Federalist judges who believed in a federal common law, like their Pennsylvania prosecutor William Rawle, would not distinguish between common-law prosecutions under the law of nations, under treaties, or implied from other statutes (as in *Worrall*, where Rawle sought to imply a right to punish bribery from the federal statute creating the office of the commissioner of revenue). Nevertheless, for modern scholars such as Robert Palmer and for his forbears, the Jeffersonians such as Alexander James Dallas (and later, Peter S. Du-Ponceau), the *Henfield* case, which involved treaties and the law of nations, had a firmer constitutional basis than did the *Worrall* case. The Federalists would have disagreed. They might have agreed with the Jeffersonians that the

Constitution had created a government based on popular sovereignty, but they would have suggested that even under a government created by the people there was a great deal of deference required toward those in positions of authority, like federal judges, and a great deal of discretion to authorize common-law prosecutions which went along with that authority and deference. In accordance with those views, then, they must have seen both *Worrall* and *Henfield* as similar and necessary exercises of jurisdiction which manifested this deference and discretion.

Such deference and discretion would have been seen by the Federalists as flowing from the nature of nationhood itself then, even popular nationhood, and these prosecutions would therefore have been legitimized by the internal law of nations, the natural right of the nation to self-defense, without which the United States simply could not enjoy true nationhood. Their basis for these views, again, was civilian jurisprudence, which, as we saw in chapter 5, had a profound effect on early American jurisprudence in general and the work of Richard Peters in particular.[132]

Indeed, more than respect for the civilians was at work in the Federalist jurisprudence of national self-defense. It is likely that the notions of an internal law of nations, a supraconstitutional law of self-defense which could be invoked to give nonstatutory jurisdiction to the federal courts, could also be found in the literature of the Anglo-American tradition itself, in the work of the greatest of the modern political writers, Thomas Hobbes. In his *Elements of Law* (1640), Hobbes wrote that it was impossible for legislators to promulgate laws for all contingencies and that "in such cases where no special law is made, the law of nature keepeth its place, and the magistrates ought to give sentence according thereunto, that is to say, according to natural reason."[133] Hobbes, elaborating, went on to say that "as for the law of nations, it is the same with the law of nature."[134]

For the Jeffersonians all of this would be regarded as constitutional heresy, since they had a grudging conception of the federal government as one of inherently limited and enumerated powers and since they took their cue on federal common law of crimes jurisdiction, as Kathryn Preyer has demonstrated,[135] from that fabulous and complex Federalist Samuel Chase, who claimed in *Worrall* that there was no federal common law and that for a crime to be punished in the federal courts the federal legislature had first to speak.

Indeed, as suggested earlier,[136] the Jeffersonians believed that the invocation of a jurisdiction based on a federal common law of crimes was inherently unlimited and would lead inexorably to all the sanguinary and feudal barbarities of the English common law. This Jeffersonian slippery-slope argument, however, should be recognized by dispassionate scholars as extraordinarily self-serving, since no Federalist ever maintained that the federal common law included each and every English common law crime. No Federalist ever argued that there were no limits on federal common law of crimes jurisdiction, and it would seem that some limits could be expected even from the Federalists. I think that some such thought must have motivated John Marshall's 1800 letter, quoted above.[137]

No Federalist ever clearly demarcated the American federal common law of crimes jurisdiction, probably because they believed, pursuant to the common law method, that such things could never be presented with utter precision, but the Federalists must have believed that whatever these limits were, they could be consistently followed, and the common law of crimes could be consistently interpreted in accordance with the spirit of American republicanism, and in a manner somewhat different from that of any English monarchical excesses.

The Two English Political Philosophies Revisited   It remains to be explained how the Jeffersonians and the Federalists could so differ over a question of constitutional interpretation such as the existence of a Federal common law of crimes, how the Federalists could trust in their own discretion while the Jeffersonians did not, and why the issue cannot readily be resolved in favor of one or the other view. The answer, I think, lies in the fact suggested in chapter 4, that in the 1790s at least two basic political philosophies or ideologies borrowed from England were operating in America and influencing attitudes toward constitutional and legal interpretation and the necessary existence of supraconstitutional principles.

For purposes here we can refer to two strands of English jurisprudential theory, one strand which we might label "Tory," "court," or, perhaps most validly, "conservative" beliefs, and the other of which we could call "radical," "democratic," or simply "opposition" thought.[138] These two jurisprudential strands had been developing in England since the sixteenth century, but their differences came into sharper focus in the 1780s and then became most pronounced in the 1790s as the conservative English judiciary reacted to the radicalism of the French revolution and its adherents in England. Indeed, as we will see in subsequent chapters, when many English radicals, men such as Thomas Cooper, James Thomson Callender, and Joseph Priestly, were forced out of England, they came to America and continued to fight their ideological battles, enlisting with the Jeffersonians in their war of words against the Federalists and ensuring that the American ideological and legal debate would bear a strong resemblance to that in England.

Much of the focus of the English radicals' writing on the jury was the law of seditious libel. While, as we will see in chapter 7, after independence from Great Britain virtually all national prosecutions for seditious libel were done in this country pursuant to a statute; in England until 1792, and in the colonies, prosecutions for seditious libel were conducted pursuant to jurisdiction conferred by the English common law of crimes. It was this fact that lay behind much of the Jeffersonian opposition to the federal common law of crimes jurisdiction. The Jeffersonians were here following in the footsteps of the English radicals. The English opposition thinkers had correctly realized that the English law of seditious libel was a profound impediment to the statement of their political views, because the English conservatives employed it and the treason doctrines to silence many of them in the time of the French Revolution.

The English radicals argued in court and in Parliament that the jury's role in seditious libel cases ought to be expanded in order for the juries, who they believed would be more sympathetic to opposition complaints, to serve as popular guardians of the right of popular critics of the ministry to be heard. Over the objections of conservative judges like Lords Kenyon and Mansfield, the Parliamentary statute, Fox's Libel Act of 1792, codified part of the radicals' views and was later incorporated, even by the Federalists, into American seditious libel doctrine. Nevertheless, Fox's Libel Act (and the Federalists' Alien and Sedition Acts of 1798) were compromises between radical and conservative views, and both made clear that a deferential jury should make its determinations under the direction of the court.

Once the English radicals could be identified, by Burke and by John Wesley among others, with the Regicide and the Terror in an atheistic France, their influence rapidly deteriorated in England, and true English radical change had to wait until the Reform Bill of 1832. The struggle the English radicals began was continued in America, however, as their ideas were picked up by those who led the two rebellions in Pennsylvania in the 1790s and by those like Alexander James Dallas, who struggled against the federal common law of crimes and who sought to implement the English radicals' understanding of the prerogatives of the jury. As we will see, Dallas even tried to remove from the Pennsylvania bench in 1803 one Alexander Addison, a Federalist state supreme court judge who had been outspoken in his criticism of the radical principles of the Virginia and Kentucky resolutions of 1798 (the two most famous public attacks on the notion of the federal common law of crimes). Other Pennsylvania radicals attacked even the state common law, demanding codification and provoking the sort of irate response from American conservatives like Richard Peters that we have already observed in defense of the common law against statutes.[139]

As we will see in chapter 8, similar battles took place in Virginia, where the Virginians, for quite different purposes from those of the Pennsylvanians, mouthed the platitudes of the English radicals and argued for broad jury prerogatives, including the right to judge the constitutionality of the federal Alien and Sedition Acts themselves. It was also from Virginia that Madison and Jefferson made their most articulate arguments against the common law of crimes, in their Virginia and Kentucky resolutions. These resolutions, in a bold departure from the "original intention" of the federal Constitution's framers, set forth the notorious Jeffersonian (and later Calhounian) states' rights "compact" theory of the Constitution, which undercut the very sovereignty of the federal government the Constitution's framers thought they had established and furnished the South a constitutional justification for its secession in 1861.[140]

By 1800 the Jeffersonians were able to capture the presidency by their skillful publicizing of Federalist errors such as the zealous prosecution of seditious libel and the other blatant examples of transplanted English conservative and deferential jurisprudence employed by the newly converted Samuel Chase in the *Fries* and *Callender* cases and in his celebrated grand jury charges. The essence of the Jeffersonians' presentation, often made by transported British radicals like Cooper and Callender, was that if there was any corruption in American society it was not in the people, but in the Federalist government. The thrust of the Virginia and Kentucky resolutions was that the federal government had succumbed to tyranny and selfishness and was bent on enslaving the states. Profoundly important evidence of such corruption for the Jeffersonians were what they perceived as judicial excesses such as the common law of crimes and the legislative excesses of the Alien and Sedition laws.

Believing that the Virginia and Kentucky resolutions were invitations to anarchy, having seen such anarchy in the two Pennsylvania rebellions, in revolutionary France, and in mob agitation in late eighteenth-century England, it is no wonder the Federalists sought to invoke the deferential, essentially English, conservative jurisprudence which many of them believed that they had of necessity incorporated into the federal Constitution, or at least the Judiciary Act of 1789. Their articulation of a federal common law of crimes, based on a traditional reading of the law of nations, on a particular view of human nature, and as a matter of political necessity seems quite natural, and quite in keeping with English conservatism. Whether or not simple partisan politics lay behind the debate on the common law of crimes, then, it is clear that divergent ideologies, prompted by the late eighteenth-century experience in England, is at the foundation of the differences between the Federalists and the Jeffersonians.

The Resolution and Aftermath of the *Worrall* Case

What then was going on in *Worrall* and how do we explain the divergence of views between Chase and Peters? We have seen how Peters, as an American "conservative" and as a Federalist, would favor a common law of crimes, but what about Chase? We have seen that the division between the Federalists and the Jeffersonians, a division prompted by the acceptance of different English political and judicial ideologies (or looked at in the traditional manner of

American historians, a division over the extent of powers that the Constitution granted to the central government), might explain differences over the common law of crimes. On the other hand, since Chase is the traditional American historian's symbol of the Federalists' zeal, something more than the traditional explanation is called for.

The incongruity of a Federalist such as Chase being against the common law of crimes led Professor Horwitz to suggest that more was involved here than merely a debate over the extent of the powers of the federal government. However, a consideration of Chase's background and political views and his subsequent behavior in the *Worrall* case itself suggests that the Chase/Peters split was not over the kind of jurisprudential concepts which interested Horwitz, but was instead a vestige of the usual political or ideological opinions that distinguished the Federalists and Jeffersonian Republicans. The split in *Worrall*, though, probably reflected the vestiges of divisions within the Federalist party itself, divisions which persisted until about 1798. As it became clearer to Samuel Chase, following this initial opinion, that the current political situation called for political hegemony, he may have "purified" his views to be more in accord with his newfound Federalist brethren, and he may have been transformed, as was Edmund Burke, to an adherent of transplanted English conservative jurisprudential thought.

Immediately after the opinions were delivered in *Worrall*, when it became clear that Chase and Peters were divided over the existence of a federal common law, the two judges suggested that Worrall's counsel bring the matter to the Supreme Court for a definitive ruling.[141] The defendant, probably realizing that he stood little chance with his arguments in the Supreme Court, refused to appeal. Apparently surprised by this refusal, Chase and Peters withdrew for "a short consultation."[142]

There is no hard evidence on what happened during this time, but Wharton, as a note to his report of the case, suggests that Chase and Peters consulted other members of the Supreme Court who were conveniently present in Philadelphia.[143] According to this hypothesis, Chase was then informed of the belief of the other justices, particularly the chief justice and coauthor of the Judiciary Act, Oliver Ellsworth, that prosecutions under a federal law of crimes were permissible and desirable.[144] Chase and Peters returned to the circuit court, reconvened, and sentenced Worrall to a term of imprisonment of three months and a fine of $200, using the venerable common law punishment of discretionary fine and imprisonment. This sentence could not have been meted out to Worrall unless both judges agreed upon it.

The fact that Chase was ultimately willing to join in the imposition of punishment certainly suggests that his views on the law were at least malleable, if not a complete turnaround. A complete reversal in his position on a federal common law is very possibly what happened, however. A year after *Worrall*, in 1799, Chase "presided in the case of *United States v. Sylvester,* a common-law prosecution for counterfeiting, which ended in a conviction and a sentence of one year in jail and a $100 fine."[145] If Justice Chase turned around on the existence of the federal common law of crimes, or even if he was willing to go along just once in the *Worrall* case, how is this reversal to be explained? If Justice Chase did confer with his brethren, it is very likely that he then would have been informed by one or more of his new Federalist friends that the political necessities of the time required a federal common law jurisdiction, and not just the punishment of those who bribed federal officials.

Federalist hysteria was beginning to run high in 1798, and the Alien and Sedition Acts were shortly to be passed. Even before these acts, however, the need was felt to prosecute for seditious libel at common law. One such prosecution was begun in Philadelphia a scant few weeks after the *Worrall* case. On June 26, 1798, Benjamin Franklin Bache, who had long been the most strongly anti-Federalist newspaper publisher,[146] was arrested. Since the federal Alien and Sedition Acts had not yet been passed by the United States Congress, the offense was one at common law for seditious libel. Bache's counsel appeared before Judge Peters to argue that there was no legal support for prosecution of a federal common law offense and cited the opinion of Justice Chase from the *Worrall* case. It is not difficult to imagine Judge Peters's ire as he replied to Bache's counsel that he had not changed his opinion from the *Worrall* case, and that as far as he was concerned, the law was as he (Peters) had stated it. Unfortunately for the early resolution of the federal common law of crime issue, Bache died in a yellow fever epidemic before he could even be formally indicted. Since the federal Sedition Act was soon passed and had the appearance of a more "liberal" measure, there were no further attempted Federalist prosecutions in the federal courts for common law seditious libel.[147]

Given the close proximity in time of the Bache arrest and the *Worrall* case, it is probable that Chase was made aware by his brother judges of the desirability of prosecuting Bache at common law and that this had some influence over him. Chase tended to be quick on the trigger, and he may not have realized all the political implications when he issued his *Worrall* opinion. He may have subsequently altered his view, and agreed to participate in the sentencing of Worrall when he was reminded that he had promised Washington when he (Chase) was appointed to the Supreme Court that the president "shall never have reason to regret the nomination."[148]

In any event, Chase's "mistake" about the existence of a federal common law was not repeated by any other federal judge in the period with which we are concerned. The intensity with which the Federalist judges maintained that there was a federal common law of crimes became more and more useful to the Republicans, who argued that the Federalist judiciary was abusing federal power at the expense of the rights of the states and the people. For example, in what may have been the most important case in these years on the federal common law of crimes, one that further developed the common law principles inherent in *Henfield* and *Worral*, Chief Justice Ellsworth ruled in *Isaac Williams's Case*[149] that the United States, by virtue of what he found to be its adoption of the criminal common law, had accepted the English principle that no subject could renounce his allegiance. This doctrine was particularly ridiculed by Jeffersonian Republicans when it was pointed out that it was this very principle that the British were maintaining in their impressment of American seamen before and after the American Revolution.[150] A few months before the trial of Isaac Williams, Ellsworth had charged a grand jury in much the same terms as those used earlier by Wilson in his *Henfield* grand jury charge, and then later by Peters in his *Worrall* opinion, suggesting that conduct "clearly destructive of a government or its powers ordained to exist by the people must be criminal."[151]

Ellsworth argued that the common law's adoption was evidenced through "those frequent references in the Constitution to the common law as a living code."[152] Since Ellsworth was either the "leading projector" or one of the principal draftsmen of the Judiciary Act ten years earlier[153] and since (at least in his grand jury charge of 1799) Ellsworth based his acceptance of a federal common law on the Constitution and not the Judiciary Act,[154] Charles Warren's conclusion about the Judiciary Act's being intended to adopt a federal common law is open to further question.[155] It seems more likely, then, that the Federalists, the jurisprudential heirs of the English conservatives, believed that a federal common law of crimes jurisdiction was inherent in any American national government worthy of the name, and thus inherent in the Constitution.

The constitutional aspects of this issue were finally decided by the Supreme Court in 1812 in the case of *United States v. Hudson & Goodwin*.[156] In *Hudson*, Mr. Justice Johnson, speaking for the Court, stated that the question "whether the Circuit Courts of the United States can exercise a common-law jurisdiction in criminal cases" was then before the Supreme Court "for the first time." Nevertheless, said Johnson, "we consider it as having been long since settled in public opinion," and he proceeded to rule, in accordance with what he said was this "public opinion," that there was no federal common law criminal jurisdiction.

Johnson sought to justify his ruling by reference to general concepts of limited American government, including the proposition that "whatever is not expressly given to the [federal government] the states expressly reserve." Johnson also summarily rejected Judge Peters's old argument that "upon the formation of any political body, an implied power to preserve its own existence and promote the end and object of its creation" necessitated a federal common law. In essence, Johnson's opinion seemed to be founded on little more than the bald assertion, much like that of Chase in *Worrall*, that before an act can be constitutionally prosecuted as a crime in the federal courts "[t]he legislative authority of the Union must first make an act a crime, affix a punishment to it, and declare the court that shall have jurisdiction of the offense."[157]

Conclusion: Public Opinion and the Jeffersonian Victory

Since there was a perfectly valid jurisprudential defense for the constitutionality of the federal common law of crimes, or at least a constitutional defense powerful enough to convince virtually all of the Supreme Court justices and federal judges who passed on its jurisdiction in the eighteenth century but Chase, the real source of the rejection of the constitutionality of the federal common law of crimes must not be the Tenth Amendment, but, as Johnson suggested, "public opinion." By 1812, in short, public opinion had decidedly turned against the position of the Federalist judges in 1798 and 1799. All of this suggests that the problem of the federal common law of crimes, in the sense that the issue was intimately tied in with popular opinion, was much more a political than a legal problem.

It remains to be explored here, however, why the position of the Federalist judges of 1799 was so decisively rejected by the "public opinion" Justice Johnson referred to in 1812. The conduct of one man, Samuel Chase, probably had as much to do with directing public opinion against the Federalist judges as all the other factors combined.[158] It was Chase who, in a view that has been accepted by virtually all twentieth-century American historians, was to bring "such odium upon the court, as to work a repeal of what ever about it was repealable, and to involve the rest in a degree of unpopularity from which it was only slowly relieved by the stern public and private virtues of [John Marshall]."[159] In the next few chapters we discover what it was that Chase did to cause such excoriation, and try to determine whether the opprobrium he has been under for generations really was merited.

This study of the federal common law of crimes problem has revealed two strange aspects of the work of the early federal judges, aspects all but ignored by most scholars. The first is that Chase, a man tarred as the most violent of the Federalists, supplied the Jeffersonians with their most cogent argument against a vital jurisprudential principle that the Federalists defended. The second is that even though the Supreme Court embraced this Jeffersonian view first pronounced by Chase, it will not do simply to accept the Supreme Court's reasoning in *United States v. Hudson & Goodwin*, even though it did represent a final Jeffersonian triumph on this issue. By the time this case was decided in 1812, the most knowledgeable early federal judges had left the scene and even Chase had retired from the court. The triumph of the Jeffersonians in *Hudson* should be viewed not as a triumph of law, but as a triumph of their politics, philosophy, and jurisprudence, which finally rejected the conservative English strain in order to declare that the constitutional structure of separated, limited, and enumerated powers created a general government in which a federal common law of crimes was impossible. The Jeffersonians may have represented the future, but their victory must not be taken as a demonstration that they possessed the only valid jurisprudential argument.

The persuasive nature of the Federalist jurisprudence in general and the Federalist view of the common law of crimes in particular needs to be accorded more attention than current scholars seem willing to grant. The late eighteenth-century understanding of the Constitution should be seen against the background of supraconstitutional principles drawn principally from the law of nations, as well as from English political ideologies, and ultimately from an understanding of the inevitable shortcomings of humankind. Such an understanding was expressed by Hobbes in his *Leviathan*, but was also a staple of common conservative English and American political theory and jurisprudence. This staple theory was also to be found in such well-known works as Allan Ramsay's *Thoughts on the Nature of Government* (1769), Burke's widely circulated *Reflections on the Revolution in France* (1791), or in the jury charges of the Federalist judges, including, as we shall see, those of Samuel Chase.

These Hobbesian human shortcomings, the knowledge of which was so important to many in the framing of the federal Constitution, suggested both that no governmental structure sprung from the mind of man could anticipate every power that would be needed to deal with his foibles and that every national government, even a federal one, needed a power to deal with unanticipated threats. For many of our Federalist framers, the federal common law of crimes, based on supraconstitutional principles, or, if we like, an unwritten Constitution, was as necessary to the preservation of our early Republic as was the supraconstitutional jurisprudence of our own time, the learning based on penumbras and emanations from the Bill of Rights, of the Warren and Burger courts, employed in its efforts to safeguard and perfect the Republic in the mid-twentieth century.

7

Federal Jurisprudence in Pennsylvania: Part Three
Trials for Treason and Violations of the Alien and Sedition Acts

The Treason Trials

The Trials of the Whiskey Rebels

In 1795, several men were apprehended by federal troops in the effort to stop the Whiskey Rebellion,[1] an armed and incendiary protest in western Pennsylvania against the United States's excise task on spirits, which involved thousands of persons. The apprehended rebels were brought to trial before Judge Peters of the Pennsylvania district court and Justice Paterson of the United States Supreme Court—together sitting as the Federal Circuit Court for the District of Pennsylvania. The reports of these trials are not particularly detailed. This plus the fact that the two defendants convicted of treason were pardoned and that popular sympathy generally ran with the Federalists on their treatment of the whiskey rebels[2] make these trials of relatively limited importance to an understanding of the eventual popular disenchantment with the federal judiciary, the principal concern of this book. Moreover, the entire affair of the Whiskey Rebellion has received fairly adequate historical treatment,[3] so there is no need to go into great detail about the events of the rebellion.

Nevertheless, an understanding of the events of those trials does help clarify some of the workings of Federalist jurisprudence, and some retelling of the story may still be useful, since the historians of the Whiskey Rebellion have not placed the trials of the whiskey rebels into the broader scheme of Federalist jurisprudence, as they will be here. In particular, those trials are valuable to our analysis insofar as they suggest the great debt owed by the presiding federal judges to English conservative jurisprudence.[4]

The first significant point about these trials is that they were the first trials for treason in the federal courts. The court adopted what has been called the English rule of "constructive levying of war,"[5] in establishing the precedent that armed opposition to execution of a United States statute (in this case the excise tax on whiskey) amounted to "levying war" against the United States, and thus came within the constitutional definition of treason.[6]

The Federalist judges made it clear that there was nothing uniquely American or "Republican" in their attitude toward the offenses committed. Justice Paterson's opinion on the law in one of these cases as delivered to the jury clearly accepted the notion of the Federalist prosecutor, William Rawle: "What constitutes a levying of war . . . must be the same, in technical interpretation, whether committed under a republican, or a regal form of government; since either institution may be assailed and subverted by the same means."[7] Rawle's English common law authority providing that "raising a body of men to obtain, by intimidation or violence, the repeal of a law, or to oppose and prevent by force and terror, the execution of a law, is an act of levying war" was clearly reflected in Justice Paterson's summation to the jury, and thus passed into American law.[8] In these trials, it appears that any attempts by counsel for the defense to refute this doctrine were rather flabby, as no frontal attack on the broad construction of the Constitution's treason clause was mounted. This had to await the trial of John Fries, to be considered next.

Second, these trials reflected a willingness on the part of the judges to act in a manner that clearly aided the national government, a manner that seems to owe much to English conservative deferential jurisprudence, and which has much in common with the Federalist judges' attitude toward the federal common law of crimes, considered in chapter 6. In some early pretrial skirmishing in the *Whiskey Rebels* trials, for instance, Judge Peters advanced his opinion that the federal judiciary should not be hamstrung by delicate niceties of state procedure. Counsel for some of the prisoners had argued that the prosecutions were not conforming to the requirements of section 29 of the Judiciary Act, which expressly ordered that certain matters of jury selection should be in accordance with state practice. For example, defense counsel objected that the federal marshal had returned a greater number of jurors than the Pennsylvania law authorized, that copies of captions of the indictments had not been delivered to the prisoners as required by Pennsylvania law, and that there was insufficient specification of "the addition [occupation] and places of abode of the jurors and witnesses," as required by Pennsylvania court procedure.[9]

Peters diplomatically accepted some of these objections and accordingly postponed the trials until compliance with state law could be accomplished, but he rejected arguments based on other technical infractions of state law:

> Although, in ordinary cases, it would be well to accommodate our practice with that of the state, yet the judiciary of the United States should not be fettered and

controlled in its operations, by a strict adherence to state regulations and practice. . . . The legislature of a state have in their consideration a variety of local arrangements, which cannot be adapted to the more expanded policy of the nation. It never could have been in the contemplation of congress, by any reference to state regulations, to defeat the operation of the national laws.[10]

Peters cited no authority in support of these propositions and seems to have been manifesting almost a contempt for the express provisions of the 1789 Judiciary Act, in refusing to follow its plain directives where he personally felt the national interest dictated otherwise. This is probably not surprising in a man who held the rather low opinion of statutes that he did.[11]

In any event, the desire to aid the national security efforts of the federal prosecution looms even larger in Justice Paterson's jury charges in the two cases that did result in treason convictions. In the first, *United States v. Vigol*,[12] Paterson appears to the modern eye to have usurped the jury's fact-finding function by declaring at the outset of this charge:

> With respect to the evidence, the current runs one way. It harmonizes in all its parts. It proves that the prisoner was a member of the party who, at each place, committed acts of violence and devastation. . . . With respect to the intention to suppress the office of excise, likewise, there is not, unhappily, the slightest possibility of doubt.[13]

Paterson's charge in the second case, *United States v. Mitchell*,[14] is no more restrained in its conclusions. Paterson told the jury that the first question for them to consider was whether the object of the insurrection was the treasonous intention to prevent the execution of an act of Congress. He then concluded: "Taking the testimony in a rational and connected point of view, this was the object." Commenting on the purposes for which the insurgents had assembled, Paterson said:

> They were arrayed in a military manner; they affected the military forms of negotiation by a flag; they pretended no personal hostility to General Neville; but they insisted on the surrender of his commission. Can there be a doubt, than [sic] that the object of the insurrection was of a general and public nature? . . .
> Upon the whole, . . . the prisoner [Mitchell] must be pronounced guilty. The consequences are not to weigh with the jury:—it is their province to do justice; the attribute of mercy is placed by our Constitution in other hands.[15]

Paterson's conduct in these jury charges has been branded by the latest writing on the *Whiskey Rebels* trials as "heavy-handed by the standards of the day,"[16] but I think this characterization goes too far. Paterson was not really departing from what might be viewed as mainstream English conservative practice, which the Federalist judges were clearly swimming in. Paterson's commenting on the evidence and dictating conclusions to the juries had been sanctioned by English conservative tradition for hundreds of years and could

still be regarded as consistent with allowing the jury the final decision on determining the facts of the case.[17] Nevertheless, as the misconstruction of Paterson's conduct by modern historians shows, Paterson's actions could very easily be portrayed as objectionable when we take into consideration the
emerging American, particularly Jeffersonian, standards of great discretion
for juries in criminal cases.[18] In a scant few years, summary conduct like Paterson's, although it seems to have passed relatively without notice in the trials
of the whiskey rebels, would meet with great popular resistance when it was
indulged in by Justice Chase at the trials of Fries and Cooper.

The First Trial for Treason of John Fries

Five years after the Whiskey Rebellion in western Pennsylvania, the Fries Rebellion took place in eastern Pennsylvania. The federal levy which was the object of the Fries Rebellion, a tax on houses, had become necessary because of
the high cost of troops used to quell the Whiskey Rebellion[19] and also because
of the expenditures for anticipated hostilities against France. The yeomen of
Northampton, Montgomery, and Bucks counties in eastern Pennsylvania organized protests against the new federal taxes and succeeded in preventing
their collection. Although there was no real bloodshed, there was, during the
months of 1799, much marching around by armed troops in uniform and at
least one overt act of rebellion—the liberation of prisoners from the custody
of a federal marshal by means of armed militia.

The 1799 rebellion is often referred to as the "Fries Rebellion," because
John Fries, a coroner from Northampton County, was reported to be the most
notorious of the defendants. The disturbance is also known as the "hot water
war," to commemorate the actions of at least one sturdy matron of Northampton County. She poured scalding water over the federal tax inspector who had
come to count her windows, such window-counting being the traditional
method of fixing an amount for a house tax.[20] Fries had engaged in a more
dangerous activity; he had led an armed assault to free federal prisoners arrested for resisting the collection of the tax and was then charged with the
capital crime of treason. This charge could be construed to come within the
precedent set a few years earlier at the trials of the whiskey rebels, when Justice
Paterson and District Judge Peters held, following English precedent, that
armed opposition to a United States tax statute was treason.[21]

The chief perpetrators of agitation, including John Fries, were brought to
trial for treason before Judge Peters and Justice Iredell in 1799. The case
aroused interest in the Pennsylvania press, and the trial immediately took on
dramatic political overtones. Acting as lawyers for the defense were William
Lewis, a former federal judge, and Alexander James Dallas, fast becoming the

kingpin of the emerging Pennsylvania Republican organization. Their arguments were designed to stir popular sympathies.

Once again the beginnings of the trial reveal the judges' tendency to favor the prosecution. On April 30, 1799, Lewis moved for the *Fries* trial to be removed from Philadelphia to Northampton County, the place where Fries's offense was alleged to have been committed. His motion was made pursuant to section 29 of the Judiciary Act, which mandated trial in the county where the offense had occurred.[22] The motion was denied by Iredell and Peters. In his opinion, Peters announced, considering fairness to the prosecution, that "a fair and impartial trial ought to be had, which he was certain could not be held in the county of Northampton."[23] Similarly, Iredell questioned: "If nearly one whole county has been in state of insurrection, can it be said that a fair trial can be had there?"[24] If there was anything in the spirit of the Judiciary Act that sought to give the defendant the benefit of a sympathetic trial among his neighbors, it was not of paramount importance to Peters or Iredell.

Most of the arguments of Fries's counsel at trial went to the law of the case. The thrust of their defense was to persuade the jury that armed resistance to a federal officer's execution of a federal statute was not a crime of treason. Lewis and Dallas, in short, were exhorting the jurors in Fries's case to arrive at the opposite legal conclusion from that laid down by Justice Paterson, Judge Peters, and the jurors in the trials of the whiskey rebels.

The technique of arguing the law to the jury was tacitly approved by Peters and Iredell. Peters was later to write that the latitude permitted counsel in this trial was "unbounded" or even "unjustifiable" as to "both Law & Fact."[25] Peters described this first *Fries* trial as one in which "I had more than my share of trouble." It had been his policy, he wrote, to "rather err on the side of indulgence, as I had generally perceived that more time was lost & irritation produced in attempts to contain, than in suffering counsel to take their own course." Still, Peters noted, these were "9 or 10 toilsome & irksome days."[26] Indeed, Peters later remembered that in this first *Fries* trial defense counsel was even permitted to charge that the law laid down in the *Whiskey Rebels* trials (a trial, it will be remembered, over which Peters had also presided) was as "unsound as the worst opinion, delivered in the worst of times in England."[27]

Taking advantage of the broad latitude Peters and Iredell permitted them in 1799, Fries's counsel did not argue that their client was innocent of all crimes, but simply that he was not guilty of the heinous crime of treason. The bold and popular strategy which Lewis and Dallas employed was to parade before the jury a series of "horribles" drawn from the English common law. They sought to show that employment of the "constructive treason" doctrine, used in the *Whiskey Rebels* trials to find armed opposition to a statute to be the crime of "levying war," inevitably led to gross tyranny. Judge Peters's reflection on this tactic was: "All the abominable and reprobated cases on constructive treason in England were suffered to be read."[28] That Peters's negative evaluation of counsel's conduct was sound—indeed, that Lewis and Dallas's tactics were little more than a demagogic diversion—is strongly suggested by the fact that they did not limit themselves to examples of the English "constructions" of the "levying war" or "giving aid and comfort to enemies" phrases, the only examples of treason permitted in the American Constitution. Instead, they concentrated on English abuses construing other common law treason doctrines, such as "compassing" (scheming for or plotting) the death of the king. They ignored the fact that the Constitution's framers had been careful to omit those parts of the treason doctrine from the 1787 document.

Two such examples from the odious English "compassing" doctrine were cited by Lewis and Dallas with great gusto. For one, defense counsel described how once, in the "dark ages of English jurisprudence" when a sporting king had killed a yeoman's stag, the yeoman, in a fit of anger "wished the horns of the stag in the king's belly." The yeoman was swiftly, and apparently successfully, prosecuted for the treasonous crime of compassing the death of the king. As an even more egregious travesty, the case was given of an innkeeper who kept an inn called "the sign of the crown." In a loose moment of levity, the publican had bragged that he would make his son "heir to the crown," and so he was similarly convicted of treason.[29]

In contrast to the abuses of the treason doctrine Lewis and Dallas cited from England, they argued that in a "free republic" like America, the application of the doctrine of treason should be so limited that the phrase "levying war" would only apply to cases where armed men sought "to put an end to the government," where a part of "the Union" sought to "throw off the authority of the United States," or where rebels actually marched on the national legislature or the executive. It should not be treason, they argued, where insurgents simply opposed the implementation of the Republic's laws. The latter activity, they urged, might constitute "sedition," or, when a release of prisoners was involved, the crime of common law "rescue," but not the capital crime of treason. Lewis and Dallas used their catalog of abuses from the English common law to disparage the only direct English factual precedent for Fries's prosecution, a holding that the "rescue" of prisoners from official hands was a levying of war which would amount to treason. They argued that since that case came from the time of the absolute monarchy of Henry VIII, it should be ignored by the jury as one more reflection of English monarchical despotic excess.[30] Lewis and Dallas were, of course, aware that they were arguing contrary to the five-year-old precedent of the Whiskey Rebellion trials; but, in a frankly political argument, they urged that in the new American Republic there was a need for a maximum freedom of expression of political sentiments and that a broad application of the treason doctrine was inconsistent with this need.[31]

After more than a week of impassioned arguments by Lewis and Dallas, Iredell and Peters charged the jury. Peters stated his opinion first. He maintained that the *Vigol* and *Mitchell* cases (the Whiskey Rebellion trials) governed: "It is treason to oppose or prevent by force, numbers or intimidation, a public and general law of the United States, with intent to prevent its operation or compel its repeal." By opposing a law, said Peters, "the rights of all are invaded by the force and violence of a few" and "a deadly blow is aimed at the government, when its fiscal arrangements are forcibly destroyed, distracted and impeded; for on its revenues its very existence depends."[32] In short, nothing could be more dangerous than armed opposition to taxes.

Justice Iredell opened his charge by declaring: "Gentlemen, it is with great satisfaction to me, on the present occasion, that my ideas on the points of law directing our conclusions, upon which it is the duty of the court to give opinion, absolutely coincide with that of the respectable judge with whom I have the honor to sit."[33] In sharp contrast to the attitude of Justice Paterson in the *Whiskey Rebels* trials,[34] however, and suggesting that he saw some merit in the American "opposition" theories on the jury, Iredell indicated that he would not usurp the role of the jury and thus implied his acceptance of emerging popular Jeffersonian attitudes about the scope and importance of jury verdicts, at least with regard to matters of fact. "[I]t is not for the court," Iredell stated, "to say whether there was treasonable intention or act as charged in the indictment; that is for the jury to determine; we have only to state the law, we therefore should have no right to give our opinion on it."[35] For Iredell, then, as for the judges in the years to follow, a trade-off had begun to emerge. The jury would lose its popular right, sanctioned by English opposition theory, to determine law, but in return, as a concession to those favoring jury prerogatives, the jury's discretion in matters of fact would not be hamstrung by the judge's own conclusions.

A verdict of "guilty" was rendered. Given the latitude that Lewis and Dallas were allowed by the judges in arguing the law to the jury, and given the force of their arguments that their client at most had committed sedition or "rescue," but not treason, the verdict is somewhat surprising. It may be that public opinion in the city of Philadelphia, where the trial took place, was strongly against the rural insurgents and influenced the jury. It may be, however, that the federal marshal, who had some discretion in picking the jury, was careful to choose members sensitive to the need for peace and good order. Or, after all, it may simply be that the jurors were most impressed with the precedent of the whiskey insurgents' case, and were willing to extend its holding that armed opposition to federal law was treason to the case of an armed rescue of a prisoner from federal custody.

The possibility of a biased jury is strongly suggested, however, by subsequent events. Five days after the verdict was announced, Mr. Lewis moved for a new trial for Fries on the ground that a Mr. John Rhoad, one of the jurors, had "declared a prejudice against the prisoner after he was summoned as a juror on the trial." Though Rhoad denied it under oath, five sworn witnesses stated that Rhoad, after he was summoned for jury duty but before the trial, had said that Fries "ought to be hung" and that "it would not be safe at home unless they hung them all."[36]

This seemed to be the excuse to terminate this trial that the troubled Justice Iredell may have been looking for. Justice Iredell had earlier written his wife that when the jury's verdict was announced, "I could not bear to look upon the poor man [the defendant, Fries], but, I am told he fainted away.... I dread the task I have before me in pronouncing sentence on him."[37] Iredell, probably much relieved by the evidence of possible juror bias, pronounced his view that Fries was entitled to a new trial. Judge Peters gave his opinion that there was no reason to grant a new trial, perhaps again demonstrating his tendency to favor the prosecution of those who disrupted the orderly functioning of the young Republic. Peters implied that even if Rhoad had made the statement attributed to him, he only reflected "the facts" as they "appeared then to the public." In any event, Peters finally concluded that "as a division in the court might lessen the weight of the judgment if finally pronounced and the great end of the law in punishments being example," he reluctantly went along with Iredell's opinion, and the new trial was granted.[38] Some years later Peters put something of a better face on this: "Their client then was saved, by my coming round to Mr. Iredell's opinion, as to a Juror to whose conduct (fatal to the Verdict) objections were made. In a capital case I Yielded, in Favor of Life. Tho' my judgement & his did not coincide in the Point."[39]

The Second Trial of Fries

John Fries came up for retrial during the next term, in April 1800, when Justice Samuel Chase had arrived to sit on circuit with Judge Peters. This second *Fries* trial is perhaps the most interesting of Chase's judicial experiences for us, because it shows how he differed from the more politically-in-tune-with-Pennsylvania-popular-politics Peters, because it contains clear and dramatic expressions of what Chase believed to be the central tenets of a conservative American republican jurisprudence, and because Chase's conduct during the *Fries* trial was later the subject of the first part of the articles of impeachment brought against him. Indeed, at the time of the first rumblings in Congress for Chase's impeachment, it looked as if his presiding over the *Fries* trial was the most important factor leading to his impeachment.[40]

Before the second *Fries* trial, Chase had indicated to Peters that the judges needed to devise some way to "get through all the business which had accumulated on the civil side" as a result of the great amount of time spent in the last year's circuit with the criminal trials resulting from the Fries Rebellion.[41]

In particular, Chase wanted to keep the *Fries* retrial short. He had been informed about the latitude Peters and Iredell had permitted Lewis and Dallas. He apparently believed that they had been too generous to counsel, and he had informed Peters of his belief that what took ten days in the first trial should have been accomplished in no more than "one-third" of the time.[42]

Chase was determined that this second time around there should not be so much leeway in citing "irrelevant authorities & unnecessary discussions." Chase therefore drafted an opinion, which he hoped to use as the opinion of the court on the law, and thus prevent counsel from straying. He showed the draft opinion to Peters, who approved of it, later indicating that "he had expressed what I had before delivered as my opinion better than I had done it myself." Chase had apparently not yet settled on the manner of delivering this opinion, and Peters had told him that it should be done with "prudence." Peters was left with the impression that Chase would consult him about the "time & manner of delivery" of the opinion. Peters, who believed in circumspection, had begun to be uneasy, "lest a premature Declaration of the Opinion of the Court might be made."

As the proceedings opened, a juror came up to Judge Peters on the bench "to make some excuses for nonattendance." Peters then noticed some commotion and discovered to his surprise that while his "attention had been thus engaged" Chase had distributed copies of his opinion, one to defense counsel, one to the district attorney, and one to the jury. "I felt uneasy," Peters later wrote, "& silently waited to see the effect, which did not surprize me." Chase had apparently engaged in the very "premature" conduct that Peters had feared.

In the same manner he had in the *Worrall* case, Chase had arrived at an opinion beforehand which he was anxious to release as soon as possible. He apparently made it clear to defense counsel that his opinion contained the court's view of the law of treason, which he said was that articulated by Judge Peters and Justice Paterson in the *Whiskey Rebels* trials and Judge Peters and Justice Iredell in the first *Fries* trial: armed opposition to United States statutes was treason. Since this was the law, Chase went on, the court would not permit arguments that such conduct was not treason to be made to the jury. In particular, Chase was determined that the jury not be distracted with odious English treason cases like that of the yeoman who wished the stag's horns in the king's belly or that of the boastful innkeeper.[43] There seems to be no other recorded example in early republican American judicial history of counsel being thus circumscribed in advance of the trial, and Chase's tactics appeared to be inconsistent with the widely prevalent opposition attitude that the jury's role extended to finding both fact and law.

As will be explained in some detail soon, however, Chase probably did not regard his conduct as infringing any rights properly belonging to juries, and, indeed, he was quite willing to concede the traditional truism that juries ought to decide on both matters of law and fact. In Chase's eventual answer to the impeachment charges brought against him five years later, for example, he conceded that juries did have the power to decide matters of both law and fact, although judges had a duty "to guard the jury against erroneous impressions regarding the law of the land."[44] Perhaps even more significant, in the opinion that caused him so much trouble, the one he precipitously delivered to Fries's defense counsel, the prosecutor, and the jury, Chase stated: "It is the duty of the court in this, and in all criminal cases, to state to the jury their opinions of the law arising on the facts, but the jury are to decide on the present, and in all cases, both the law and the facts on their consideration of the whole case."[45]

In any event, when Mr. Lewis, one of Fries's two lawyers, realized that the tactics he and Alexander James Dallas had used in the first *Fries* trial would be foreclosed, he threw down Chase's opinion in anger. Peters whispered to Chase that he believed that Fries's counsel would "take the studs & abandon the Cause, or take advantage of [the delivery of this statement of Chase's view] to operate on public opinion, or on that of the jury at least." Peters reprimanded Chase and reminded him of "my having 'told him so' or 'predicted it!' " Chase, demonstrating that he was not as familiar with the operation of Philadelphia public opinion or the Philadelphia bar as Peters, replied: "[H]e did not think the counsel would quit the Cause," and "it was only a *Threat* or some such expression." Peters, however, was right, and Chase was wrong. Lewis and Dallas announced their intention of withdrawing from the case, since the court had prejudged what they wished to argue.

Chase and Peters then repaired to the office of Mr. Rawle, the prosecutor. (Some measure of their detachment from the prosecution might be taken from their choice of meeting place.) The politically astute Rawle, sitting in on the meeting, and Peters persuaded Chase that his opinion "should be recalled." Chase, not actually wishing to create trouble, "readily consented, declaring his intention to be merely to save time & accelerate business." At this point Peters was satisfied, and "thought all matters rectified & in *statu quo*." The next morning Lewis and Dallas were again in court, and Peters told them that "they might proceed in the Cause." He assured them expressly that "you may, & I hope will, proceed in your own way, as if nothing had happened." Peters was perfectly prepared to sit through the same "toilsome & irksome" discussion of cases he had listened to in the first trial.

Chase was not quite as conciliatory as Peters, and though he did not contradict Peters, Chase "administered no Emollients." Chase, wrote Peters later, appeared "animated—if not irritated." He declared: "The council [sic] could not embarrass him. He knew what it was about!" According to Peters's account of the event, Chase went on to state that

> As to every Turn they might give to the Declaration of the opinion of the court (which being recalled was as if not made) he valued it not. It was an opinion he adopted on great Consideration it having been settled by the Judges [Paterson, Iredell, and Peters] who still continued in that opinion. If he could not make up an Opinion without Argument on the general Principles of Law, he was not fit to Sit there. All Judges of law did this."[46]

Nevertheless, Chase proceeded to point out that he was "*willing* and *desirous to hear*" counsel's opinion on the law, and that "it might be controverted either with the Jury or any other Way." Chase cautioned Lewis and Dallas, however, that "he would not permit improper or irrelevant authorities," and he probably told them that if they stepped out of bounds in their citation of authority they would be proceeding "at the hazard of [their] reputation." Dallas later said: "This had the contrary effect rather than to induce me to proceed," and he and Lewis remained firm in their determination to leave the case.[47]

The events surrounding Chase's pretrial release of his opinion reveal the dilemma he faced in trying to apply his version of American conservative jurisprudence in Pennsylvania, a state dominated by closer adherence to the opposition theories favored by the Jeffersonians. The principal difficulty centered around the truism that the American jury was to be the judge of both fact and law, and the political underpinnings of that notion. For Lewis and Dallas, their wish to refer to the odious English cases meant that they believed that the jury's power and right to decide the law meant that the jury could determine that it was proper to overrule present or past judges on the legal issues. This does not seem to have been what Chase meant when he referred to the jury's ability to pass on the "law and the facts" pursuant to their consideration "of the whole case."[48]

Lewis and Dallas, as would twentieth-century lawyers, used the term "law" to denote the general substantive legal rule which governs the case at hand, and which might be applied in similar cases. For Chase, however, the jury's task in finding the law of a case was probably no more than simply applying the judge-supplied rule to the facts of the case. The jury could, then, find the law (the application of legal standards) for the particular case, but it could not determine the legal rule to be applied, as that task was to be reserved for the judge. In Chase's world, then, it made no sense to allow defense attorneys to confuse the jury by suggesting that they were free to fashion their own legal rules, ignoring previous precedents. In short, defense attorneys like Lewis and Dallas had no business confusing the jury by suggesting that the jury members were free to ignore the legal rules that the judges supplied.

This makes more understandable Chase's seemingly belligerent comments, when in exasperation he agreed to let Lewis and Dallas argue whatever they wanted to the second *Fries* jury. He withdrew his pretrial opinion from the jury and from counsel, and was prepared to proceed as if his pretrial opinion on the law had never been circulated, but he warned Lewis and Dallas that they would be "proceeding at the hazard of their reputation."[49] This simply meant that, as he usually did, Chase assumed that all right-thinking men shared his views on the nature of law and on the need to defer to constitutionally erected governments with their official jurisprudential voices, the sitting judges. Perhaps Chase never quite grasped that Lewis, Dallas, and perhaps even Peters, meant different things by "law" than he did. He also never understood that the difference in meaning flowed from an almost intuitive understanding of indigenous Pennsylvania democratic practices that was at odds with Chase's English and Maryland-influenced conservatism.

The results of Chase's misunderstanding of this were dire, because although Peters and Rawle had persuaded Chase to withdraw his opinion and to let Lewis and Dallas proceed at will, Lewis and Dallas used Chase's supposed prejudgment of the law as a pretext to abandon the case. Their real motive in this enterprise does not appear to have been, as Julius Goebel suggested, to maintain "the honor of the bar," but instead to create popular (and perhaps jury) sympathy for Fries, by presenting Chase as a harsh and cruel judge who had driven off counsel for a man accused of a capital crime.

When Lewis and Dallas withdrew, Chase and Peters offered to appoint other counsel for Fries. Fries declined, because the departing Lewis and Dallas had persuaded him that if he faced the mercurial Chase alone, unassisted by lawyers, public sympathy for him would lead to a presidential pardon.[50] Fries's counsel correctly predicted that the beleaguered and popularity-craving John Adams would seize the chance, following Fries's conviction, to make such a demagogic gesture.

In the meantime, however, Chase and Peters had the difficult assignment of trying a criminal for treason without counsel for his defense. At this point, Chase made what looks to us to be the extraordinary gesture of declaring that the court would proceed to act both as counsel for the defense and as judges. "[B]y the blessing of God," said Chase to Fries, invoking the religious basis of his jurisprudence, "the court will be your counsel, and will do you as much justice as those who were your counsel."[51] Peters, who was, as we have seen, a rather stern critic of Chase, conceded that Chase was true to his word, and "[a] more impartial, fair and humane proceeding I never witnessed. Mr. Chase conducted himself with Ability, Kindness, and impartiality."[52]

Both the notion of Chase announcing that the court would act as counsel for the defense and Peters's praise of Chase's conduct in this role appear incongruous to our eyes, and this incongruity again can point us toward the sources of Chase's jurisprudence and the distance between our views of appropriate criminal procedure and those of an eighteenth-century conservative such as Chase (or Peters).

First, it was Chase's familiarity with English practice and theory which allowed him instantly to assume that he could act as counsel for the defense as well as judge. The idea of judges as "counsel" to prisoners was a staple English criminal law maxim. Moreover, the practice of trying defendants for capital crimes without counsel to defend them was fairly common in England in the eighteenth century. Indeed, Blackstone, the writer of the bible of the English conservatives, had stated that "it is a settled rule at common law, that no counsel shall be allowed a prisoner upon his trial, upon the general issue in any capital crime, unless some point of law shall arise proper to be debated."[53] It will be remembered that Chase thought the law in Fries's case was perfectly settled, suggesting no counsel was really needed. Blackstone himself manifested some ambivalence about this English rule, explaining that what happened at most felony trials was "that noble declaration of the law, when rightly understood, that the judge shall be counsel for the prisoner; that is, shall see that the proceedings against him are legal and strictly regular. . . . "[54] It is fair to say, then, as one close reader of the *Fries* trials has, that Chase was doing no more than "following common law tradition."[55]

In any event, the real significance of Chase's conduct here for us, and the significance of the English rule itself, one suspects, is that Chase was able to accept what seem to us to be the contradictory roles of judge and defense counsel, because for him they were not contradictory. Chase, and judges like him, simply did not see the pursuit of justice in criminal cases as an example of an adversarial enterprise—in sharp contrast to modern courtroom notions. As his opinion in *Calder v. Bull*[56] indicates, Chase believed in the existence of clear principles of justice, which led to clear rules of law. This clarity, he must have assumed, particularly where, as in *Fries*, the law had been laid down in two previous treason trials, would allow him to proceed and protect the interest of Fries as well as those of the government. These were interests, again, which Chase simply did not believe diverged.

During the trial Chase made several efforts to allow testimony favorable to Fries, and in at least one instance prompted Fries to speak out in his own defense. But Chase did not abandon his protection of the prosecution's interests.[57] When William Rawle, the Federalist district attorney, declined to sum up the evidence against Fries on the ground that this would be unfair because Fries had no counsel to give a countersummary, Chase announced that fairness to the government required a summing up, and if Rawle did not do it, then he, Chase, would. Chase was not only willing to be judge and counsel to Fries, then, but also counsel to the government.

Finally, in one incredible part of the proceeding, Chase reminded the current jury that the previous jury had found Fries guilty—conduct that surely would be grounds for a mistrial if it occurred today. Remarkably, although the grounds of the impeachment proceedings later brought against Chase in-

cluded his conduct in Fries's trial, those charges focused solely on Chase's alleged expulsion of counsel from the trial. What Chase said about Fries's former trial was never alluded to in the impeachment charges.[58] Perhaps late
eighteenth-century proprieties about reference to former trials were not as
strict as ours. Accordingly, although one juror in the first trial had been found
to be prejudiced, the judge and second jury could still regard the earlier verdict
as a useful precedent.

The most unbelievable event connected with the *Fries* trial happened after
Fries was convicted, however, and after President Adams pardoned Fries.
Shortly after his release from custody, Fries reportedly journeyed to Baltimore
and personally thanked Chase for the "fair and impartial trial."[59] This event
may be apocryphal—only one account of it exists—but it is consistent with
Richard Peters's later account of Chase's conduct at the trial. There may have
been grounds for Fries's conclusion that Chase bore him no malice, and, to an
observer present, it may have appeared that the overall conduct of the trial
demonstrated Chase's concern for the prisoner as well as for the government.
Most importantly for us, Fries's attitude that Chase bore him no malice may
illuminate one of the most important characteristics of Chase's jurisprudence,
one that he may well have shared with many other early Federalist judges. This
was the essentially religious character of his conservative criminal jurisprudence, following the same strain in that of contemporary England.[60]

The best evidence of this religious character is Chase's speech to Fries before
condemning him to the gallows, following the second jury's return of a guilty
verdict on the capital crime of treason.[61] In the course of his comments, Chase
identified the evil in Fries's deeds as rising against his country at a moment
when it was desperate for the cooperation of its citizens. Referring to the formally undeclared, but very real conflict then occurring, Chase explained that
America was at war with France, and badly needed the revenue from the taxes
against which Fries rebelled. Chase tried to explain his views of the responsibilities of citizens in a republic, and the required practice of public virtue, the
sacrifices they were called upon to make in the national and collective interest.

Even in this awful moment of contemplating his own looming death, Fries
was probably receptive to Chase's comments. Fries had behaved, even in the
course of the rebellion, with some sense of responsibility. For example, Fries
made sure that his rebels did not physically harm at least one tax collector.
Perhaps Chase simply convinced Fries that the conception of popular sovereignty that resulted in direct action was the wrong one. In other words, Chase
may have persuaded Fries that their political ideals were ultimately the same
because they both believed in the people as the ultimate legitimate authority.
Chase's articulation of this principle, however, as we have seen, required more
deference to the established government. The odd fact that Fries was a Federalist, and a nominal supporter of the current administration, may have furnished a basis for this mutual understanding of Fries's political errors.[62]

It might seem incredible that Fries would repent at the eleventh hour, during the sentencing at his own trial, especially because legitimate grievances against congressional policies still unevenly affected some parts of the country. Moreover, whether the Federalists really implemented popular sovereignty is dubious. Nevertheless, the religious rather than the political aspect of Chase's remarks to Fries does suggest precisely such an epiphany for Fries and underscores the ephemeral nature of temporal partisan politics in the early American Republic. This may also help explain why Chase was able to move from being an ardent opponent of the Constitution to being an even more ardent Federalist with relative ease.

"I suppose you are a Christian," Chase said as he prepared to pass sentence on Fries, indicating the deeper basis than politics for spiritual kinship between the prisoner and the supposedly brutal judge. Chase then laid out something like a program of spiritual aerobics which Fries might and ought to perform in order to save his everlasting soul:

> Be assured, my guilty and unhappy fellow-citizen, that without serious repentance of all your sins, you cannot expect happiness in the world to come. . . . Your *day* of *life* is almost spent; and the *night* of *death* fast approaches. Look up to the Father of mercies and God of comfort. You have a great and immense work to perform, and but little time in which you must finish it. There is no repentance in the grave, for after death comes judgment, and as you die, so you must be judged. . . . If you will sincerely repent and believe, God has pronounced his forgiveness; and there is no crime too great for his mercy and pardon.[63]

Chase informed Fries, in short, that American law recognized Fries's Christianity, and in its generosity would allow him to "converse and commune with ministers of the gospel" before his execution. Chase strongly recommended such consultation so that Fries might prepare himself for everlasting life in the world to come. Chase noted his belief in a God who was merciful, and that even Fries, who had committed one of the worst sins any Christian could commit—forcibly opposing the God-given government of his country—might still repent, and gain God's forgiveness, so that his soul might gain everlasting peace. As we have seen, Chase believed that given the magnitude of the sin, the work required for Fries's repentance would be very demanding, but with the help of religious professionals, he might still succeed. There is no record of Fries's contradicting Chase on this point, so it seems safe to assume that Fries was a Christian. In our secular era it is difficult to recapture the public nature of late eighteenth-century American Christianity, but, just as limned by Chase in the *Fries* trial, it is the conclusion of American religious historians that the pervasive essence of eighteenth-century American Christianity was a belief in the salvation of souls through faith in Christ and repentance for sins.[64]

Viewing the events of the late eighteenth century from the great distance current American mores impose, it is important to bear in mind the conclusion of one of the most perceptive students of late eighteenth-century New England, that "political rhetoric in New England grew more secular in the eighteenth century only in the sense that it no longer stressed the doctrines of a specific theology."[65] This conclusion about New England may not be strictly applicable to Pennsylvania, and Samuel Chase may not have realized that much of Pennsylvania may have been more interested in democracy than Christianity at the time he gave his comments to Fries. Nevertheless the views of New England were probably the same as those of Chase's home state. It bears remembering that even after the Anglican church was disestablished in 1776, the Maryland government remained "positively religious and specifically Christian."[66]

Whatever the general feelings in Pennsylvania, with Fries Chase may have struck a sympathetic chord. Fries must have felt the real compassion of the "American Jeffreys." There is every reason to believe[67] that Chase's Christianity and his sympathy for Fries were sincere, and that Chase's religion was the principal guiding force in his life and in his politics. Chase's religious orientation, as well as his beliefs about the nature of the jury's law-finding task, then, allows us to put in better perspective the impeachment charges that Chase was guilty of "high crimes and misdemeanors" in the conduct of the *Fries* trial. In particular, we can now view with some perspective the first charge in the articles of impeachment later brought against Chase, that by his conduct he deprived Fries of counsel.

As we have seen, it was Chase's conception of the proper roles of judge and jury with regard to legal determinations that prompted Fries's counsel, of their own volition, to resign from the case. They did this, really, not because of Chase's alleged misconduct, but in order to maximize the chances that public opinion could be manipulated against Chase and thus create pressure to secure a presidential pardon for their client. Moreover, we have seen that by what might have been indicated by Fries's own postpardon conduct, by the standards of the day, and particularly by the standards of English conservative jurisprudence, it could be argued that Fries had not been deprived of counsel at all. Samuel Chase managed to act not only as Fries's legal, but also as his spiritual, counselor. Still, Chase's hair-trigger temper, his stubbornness, and, above all, his sense of his own Christian conservative judicial prerogatives, borrowed in large part from England, led him to rush precipitously into a confrontation on a sensitive jurisprudential point for which he had little support in Pennsylvania.

The debate over the province of judge and jury in legal determinations, as American conservative and opposition notions began violently to clash, had just begun in earnest, and the statement of conservative views like those of Chase, in Pennsylvania, was bound to cause trouble. The Pennsylvania Jeffersonian Republican press, at the time of the *Fries* trial, was quick to pounce on

Chase. Until about this time, press criticism of the federal courts had been somewhat muted. But with the election of 1800 fast approaching, the campaign of the Jeffersonian Democratic-Republican press to discredit the federal courts, and particularly Justice Chase, began in earnest.[68]

Why, then, in the *Fries* trial, did Chase proceed in such a steamrolling manner, when he was warned by Peters[69] and when he must have known that he would be subjected to intense popular criticism? In his defense at his impeachment trial, years later, although Chase did not overtly invoke the religious basis of his conduct, it might be implicit in several of the reasons he gave for limiting the arguments to the jury in the *Fries* case. First, he said, he felt a strong duty to adhere to the legal precedent clearly established in the earlier cases. Second, he believed that the large backlog of civil cases in the circuit court made it incumbent on him to keep the criminal trials as short as possible. Third, he stated that *he* knew what the constitutional definition of treason was, and he did not think it worth spending much time on. Fourth, because of his certainty as to the law of treason, he felt it his strong judicial duty to prevent the jury from getting the wrong impression as to the law.[70]

All of this, however, has something of the quality of after-the-fact rationalizations. Probably as important for Chase at the time was his political, but also religious, feeling that the conduct of the *Fries* insurgents represented a real threat to the continued peace and political stability of the country. What God had beneficently allowed to come to pass in North America, the establishment of a republic based on principles of deference, decorum, law, and order, Chase believed, should not be allowed to be put asunder by men who failed to grasp the bounty that they had received. Three years later, for example, in the jury charge that ultimately triggered his impeachment, Chase was to rail against the excesses of Jeffersonian opposition democracy and to acknowledge that there was a grave risk that "our Republican Constitution will sink into a mobocracy. . . . "[71]

It was in the context of his religiously sermonic remarks to Fries, when, as he condemned Fries to death and advised him on the measures necessary to save his soul, Chase explained to his "guilty and unhappy fellow citizen" that if obedience to laws could not be compelled, "there must soon be an end to all government in this country." In Chase's mind, in short, there was a close linkage between fidelity to God's laws and those of man. But whether or not the religious basis of Chase's jurisprudence was paramount in his actions in the late eighteenth century, the importance of his fear of American anarchy could not have been clearer in his remarks to Fries and in subsequent trials.

Fries was told that "the time you chose to rise up in arms to oppose the laws of your country, was when it stood in a very critical situation with regard to France, and on the eve of a rupture with that country." Because the crippling expenses involved in quelling the two Pennsylvania insurrections that had already occurred were putting a critical strain on the administration's ability to meet the needs of national defense, future rebellions had to be prevented. So Chase concluded that "the end of all punishment is example; and the enormity of your crime requires that a severe example should be made to deter others from the commission of like crimes in the future."[72]

The need to prevent further uprisings from destroying the national defense and weakening the blessed foundations of American government, in short, led to Chase's zeal in seeking the conviction of Fries. That sincere and religious concern for the safety of what he believed to be the true principles of the American Republic, and not a brutal bias against the American people, was Chase's real motivation in his conduct at the *Fries* trial is also strongly suggested by his behavior in a closely contemporary trial on the Pennsylvania circuit, to which we now turn.

The Trial of Thomas Cooper

Even before Chase had ignited the fires of criticism in the second *Fries* trial, he had already provided the Republicans with a welcome target two weeks earlier in his presiding over the trial of Thomas Cooper. Cooper, before he emigrated to America in the 1790s, had been one of the most prominent of the English opposition theorists. He was a radical critic of the monarchy and of inequality. He was a pacifist and a pamphleteer against Burke's *Reflections*.[73] Driven from England for his views, by 1800 Cooper had managed to ally himself strongly with Thomas Jefferson, and to be prosecuted, in America, for his criticism of the Federalist Adams administration. Cooper had been indicted for violations of the Federalists' Alien and Sedition Acts of 1798.[74] These acts have been excoriated from the time of their passage, principally by Jeffersonians and their latter-day sympathizers. Before coming to the actual events of Cooper's trial, it is worthwhile to spend some time in a brief reconsideration of these acts, viewing them principally from the perspective of the Federalists instead of the Jeffersonians.[75]

Section 2 of the Alien and Sedition Acts of 1798 imposed a penalty for publishing "false" and "scandalous" materials creating distrust of the federal government—the crime of seditious libel. The usual American scholars' opinion of these acts and the period of their implementation is that they reflected a "reign of terror" on the part of the ruling Federalist party of John Adams. There have been occasional attempts, however, to portray these acts and other Federalist activities at this time as merely the "natural reaction" of a government seriously concerned about the country's chances for survival as an independent republic, and seriously concerned about a well-orchestrated and "extremely indecent campaign of public mendacity."[76]

Given the evidence presented here from the trials in the Pennsylvania federal courts, and given what we have learned about American and English conservative legal theory, what happened during this period may be easily portrayed, especially in hindsight, as an "overreaction" on the part of the Federalists in all three branches of government. However, it will be argued here that placed in the context of the Federalists' ideas about law, religion, and government, it was a reasonable, perhaps even an inevitable, reaction.[77]

The examination of the context of these Federalist measures must, in order to put them in proper perspective, include an examination of the effects of contemporary events not only in America, but also in Europe, where the threat of sedition was often perceived as even more dangerous than in America. In England, during these years, a law was passed making it possible to speak or write as well as to act treasonably. The same acts that might have resulted in relatively mild fine or imprisonment under the Federalists' Alien and Sedition laws, then, could result in capital punishment in England. The same fear of treason caused the Hungarians to put to death a man who translated the Marseillaise, the French revolutionary anthem, into Magyar. Similarly, the governments of Austria, Rumania, and Russia, during this period, regularly meted out to dissidents sentences of death, sixty years in chains, exposure in the stocks, and confiscation of property. In light of this contemporary European experience, it is difficult to regard the feeble efforts of the Federalists—a few sentences for fines of a few thousand dollars, and no more than a few months in prison imposed as punishment for seditious libel—as a "reign of terror."[78]

In the 1790s, to the Europeans and to the Federalists, it looked as though France, following the revolution of 1789, had embarked on a widespread program of subversion of liberty, property, and good order, and that the governments of European nations were slowly falling like so many dominoes. The Federalists were greatly concerned with the vulnerability of free governments to what they perceived as well-organized and demogogic tyranny, such as what they believed to exist in revolutionary France. Moreover, they thought they could discern a pattern of French incursions which began with friendly overtures, included the formation of native pro-French "democratic" societies, and ended with submission to French-style military dictatorship. This was the theory propounded even by the relatively liberal Justice Iredell in his charge to the grand jury that indicted the *Fries* rebels.[79]

Observers could see the beginning of this pattern of subversion in America with the activities of the French ambassador, Citizen Genet, who encouraged the American "democratic societies" to become pro-French. Some of the participants in the Fries Rebellion were reported to have worn the French tricolor and to have declared that "it should soon be in this country as it was in France,"[80] and so there was a linkage in America, as late as 1799, with what was happening to the traditonal order in Europe. As well as holding somewhat

sophisticated fears based on the inevitable cycle of decay of republics, as fore-
told by classical and Renaissance scholars,[81] some of the Federalists seem to
have been prepared to surrender themselves completely to more vulgar conspiracy theorists.

In a manner that eerily foreshadows American fears of a "communist conspiracy" in the 1950s, many of the Federalists in the 1790s could discern dark
and terrible doings on the part of supposed American branches of the "United
Irishmen," who were given credit for the Whiskey Rebellion.[82] Even more fan-
tastically, otherwise sensible Federalists believed that they could see evidence
of American machinations of the "Society of the Illuminati," an allegedly
worldwide secret organization dedicated to the destruction of all religious es-
tablishments and existing governments. The society was said to have been responsible for the French Revolution itself, the contemporary slave uprising in
Santo Domingo, and the Fries Rebellion.[83] In what might have been described
as a Federalist best-seller of the time,[84] the doctrines of the Illuminati were
described as "so abominably wicked as to be thought by some persons to exceed belief."

Thus, the residual Federalist fears of mob violence were exacerbated by the
added threat of Francophilic and other subversion and produced widespread
political reaction, culminating in the Alien and Sedition Acts, the *Fries* treason
trial, and the Alien and Sedition Acts trials. In order to understand the causes
of the magnitude of this political reaction, then, it is necessary to read the
times as the judges of the Pennsylvania federal courts did. Each of the events
of recent American history—the Whiskey Rebellion, the Democratic Societies, the Fries Rebellion, and Republican criticism of Federalist policies—were
viewed as fitting into a pattern that threatened to destroy the constitutionally
constituted American government and to substitute a Jacobinic dictatorship.

Even though at these Pennsylvania trials the judges (and particularly Justice
Chase) were portrayed as stepping out of bounds, as will be demonstrated,
this is not necessarily the case, and, moreover, at the legislative level the Federalist reaction was not without some restraint. As Professor Crosskey pointed
out, though the Federalist fears resulted in federal legislation to punish seditious libel, the legislation was a liberalization of the common law.[85] As we saw
in chapter 6, at the time of the Alien and Sedition Acts, the prevailing judicial
opinion was that there was a federal common law of crimes which was used
at least once to begin a prosecution for seditious libel in a federal court in
Pennsylvania,[86] and which could theoretically have continued to be used to
prosecute other persons for that crime in the federal courts.

The Federalist legislators seemed to feel, however, that they needed to demonstrate that they were not out to silence all political criticism, but merely
dangerous falsehoods.[87] The statute they passed was thus designed to alter the
law of seditious libel. First, while truth of a libel was no defense to the crime

at common law, it became one in the Alien and Sedition Acts.[88] Second, while at common law in England the jury had frequently been barred from making the determination of the seditious or provocative nature of a particular libel, in America under the Sedition Act the jury was to determine both "the law and the fact, under the direction of the court, as in other cases."[89] This provision must be read as an attempt to ensure that the still-prevailing American trend of greater jury discretion would be reflected in seditious libel cases and that unlike the practice under the common law in England, juries here would not be restricted to passing merely on the factual question of publication.[90]

Because of the Federalist desire to accommodate prevailing opinions regarding the liberalization of the common law even in the face of what was perceived as a grave threat to American stability, one might have expected that the Federalist cause would have had great popular support. For some months after the passage of the Sedition Act this was apparently the case. Unfortunately, the promise of accommodating this popular opinion, which seems to have been made in the Sedition Act (as it was originally made in the Constitutional Convention), was able to be portrayed as broken through the conduct of Samuel Chase.

In 1800, when the transplanted English radical Thomas Cooper came before Chase on the Pennsylvania circuit,[91] Cooper was charged with publishing a document accusing President Adams of incompetence, borrowing money at a usurious rate of interest "during peacetime," maintaining a standing army and navy contrary to the dictates of the Constitution, and releasing an American seaman to the British for impressment.[92] In retrospect these charges may not seem extremely dangerous, but at the height of the Federalist Francophobia of November 1799 when the charges were published, they may well have seemed seditious to strong supporters of President Adams. In the spring of 1800, they certainly seemed so to the Federalist prosecutor, William Rawle. Rawle noted in his arguments to the jury that it was "false" charges like those of Cooper that had incited the Whiskey Rebellion of 1794 and the Fries Rebellion of 1799. It was now time to put a stop to this conduct, he urged, before it again plunged the state and the nation into chaos and disorder.[93]

In his opinion to the jury that was to pass on Cooper's case, Chase stated that the charges, if true, would have rendered President Adams odious and unfit for office. Chase explained, however, that because the national welfare depended on respect for the executive, and because the president could not perform his duties without the national deference and cooperation which comes from that respect, the judiciary had to guard carefully against anything that would wrongly damage the president's reputation.[94] Chase implied that if the charges were true, then there was no legal impediment to making them, because a virtuous American population should be informed about the deeds of such a reprehensible chief executive, from whom his people would have been duty bound to withdraw their cooperation and respect. As Chase explained, however, there was a great danger of misleading the public through the dissemination of incorrect information. Because the incompetency of legitimately selected public officials was not to be presumed, Chase declared, the defendant had the burden of proving the truth of his charges "beyond a marrow."[95]

As Chase interpreted the federal statute, the falsity of the charges of misconduct was presumed. The government, not the defendant, began the seditious libel prosecution with an advantage. This sort of criminal procedure runs counter to basic American notions of fairness, but those notions—which put the burden of proof of all elements of criminality on the prosecution— may be a fairly modern evolution. They may not have existed when the government did not possess the superior resources and physical force which it now does, and which allow us the luxury of such adversarial prosecutions.[96] On the other hand, in two other seditious libel cases a contemporary Federalist judge suggested that the government had the usual burden of proving guilt "beyond a reasonable doubt."[97]

By requiring "proof beyond a marrow," Chase created a rigorous standard of proof for the affirmative defenses of truth in a criminal libel trial. It was theoretically possible, however, for Chase to have maintained, as apparently other American judges did, that the defendant should simply have the burden of raising a "reasonable doubt" that his assertions were true. Where then, did Chase get the standards he used? Curiously, there was a body of law, the English civil law of libel, which applied standards more or less the same as those Chase employed. The rule in English civil law cases was that a plea of truth as a defense to a suit for libel was bad "unless it establishes that the statement which was allegedly libelous 'was true as a whole and in every material point thereof.' "[98] Further, according to the English rules, if the defendant's evidence "showed the truth of nine of the charges made by him against the plaintiff, but did not prove the tenth, his plea [of truth] was not proved."[99] Apparently Chase read the English civil law of libel, which did place such a strict standard on defendants, into the American criminal law.

Chase's apparently proprosecution stance in *Cooper* did much to inspire the series of charges, in the Jeffersonian press, that Chase was a fiercely Federalist partisan judge.[100] It seems particularly necessary, then, to determine the philosophical and jurisprudential underpinning of this supposed partisanship, and in particular why Chase applied an English civil standard in an American criminal libel case. This confusion may have stemmed from the difficulty in eighteenth-century Anglo-American law in drawing distinctions between civil and criminal wrongs. In the early days of the common law, of course, every wrong tried in the king's courts was literally a crime against the king.

Only gradually did different standards and doctrines apply to private wrongs against subjects and to wrongs against the throne. One of the hallmarks of modern American jurisprudence is its ability to differentiate—for good or ill—between public and private spheres. Chase probably did not quite recognize this differentiation; nor did many of his contemporaries in America and England. Indeed, it was not until the nineteenth century that American law successfully "create[d] a clear separation between constitutional, criminal, and regulatory law—public law—and the law of private transactions— torts, contracts, property and commercial law."[101] If, as seems to be the case, Chase believed that his private gain redounded to the public good,[102] perhaps he was equally unable to draw strict lines between what standards ought to apply when libel against the president was publicly or privately prosecuted. In any event, the standard Chase applied resulted in Cooper's conviction.

In his defense, Cooper had a number of persuasive arguments. For example, there had been no formal congressional declaration of war with France, which meant that America was technically at peace. Accordingly, one could have said that Adams's payment of a high rate of interest on federal loans was too high for peacetime. Chase explained to the Cooper jury, however, that American involvement in undeclared war against France was notorious. This meant, said Chase, that no responsible person could believe that peace existed, and thus only the worst motives could be premised in Cooper's case. Similarly, Chase explained to the jury that there were no standing armies in the sense that Congress had not made appropriations for periods greater than the constitutionally mandated two-year period. On the other hand, Cooper had been quite correct that the government had continuously maintained the army and the navy for the last few years. In reality, if not in funding, there was a standing army and navy in America. Finally, Chase acknowledged that Cooper was correct that Adams had turned over an "American" seaman, Jonathan Robbins, to the British. This transfer occurred, apparently, only after an American court determined that Robbins was actually a British subject who was probably guilty of murder aboard a British ship and that an Anglo-American treaty required that Robbins be returned to the British.[103]

All of Cooper's charges, in other words, contained elements of truth, and their veracity, in the final analysis, might have turned on questions of judgment or opinion. By placing the burden of proof "beyond a marrow" on the defendant, however, Chase assured the defendant's conviction, because by definition one could not prove beyond a marrow a matter of judgment or of debatable opinion.

Chase became convinced, probably during the trial but conceivably earlier, that Cooper's charges were maliciously motivated. Chase attributed Cooper's statements to Cooper's failure to gain an office that he believed Adams had promised him.[104] By the end of the trial, Chase also believed or suspected that Cooper had sold his literary services to a political faction, the Jeffersonians, that would subsidize any fine levied against Cooper. Chase sought to find out if this was true by asking Cooper himself, before he was sentenced.[105] Chase indicated that, if Cooper had partisan financial backing, he would impose the maximum fine the law allowed. Cooper denied that he wrote for a "party" save the "great party of mankind," and while he admitted that "friends" had offered to help him meet his expenses if he was fined, he would pay as much of it as he could afford himself.[106]

United States District Court Judge Richard Peters, Chase's more politically adept colleague on the circuit bench, stated that the identity of the person who would pay the fine, as well as the existence of any political parties in America, were irrelevant to the decision of what sentence to mete out to Cooper. Chase, on the other hand, apparently believed it his moral and judicial duty to repress the faction for whom Cooper might be speaking. Peters understood that such an approach, at least in highly politicized Philadelphia, might be counterproductive.[107] Chase and Peters deliberated, as they did in the *Worrall* case when they disagreed,[108] and ultimately agreed upon a fine. Having duly punished Cooper, Chase proceeded to the dramatic capital case left over from 1799, *United States v. Fries*, and immersed himself in the trouble we have already observed. It remains for us to try to understand more of the background and the nature of Pennsylvania indigenous jurisprudence, how Chase could misread it so badly, and how the Pennsylvanians could be so rigorously stirred up against Chase.

Misreading Commerce: Chase's Mistake in *Fries*

The feature of Pennsylvania jurisprudence and politics which emphasized commerce, as discussed in chapter 5, probably misled Chase and caused him to make the blunder that would eventually and directly lead to his impeachment by the Jeffersonians in 1805. When Chase arrived to preside on circuit in 1800, as we have seen, he discovered a great backlog of commercial cases, which he believed had been created during the very lengthy deliberations at the first treason trial of John Fries.

Since Chase's aim in this second *Fries* trial was to ease the circuit court's backlog of commercial disputes, he was probably doing what he thought would win general approval. This was to become an element in the impeachment charges later brought against him, however, because some of the radical Jeffersonian Pennsylvanians would argue that by restricting the arguments of his lawyers, Chase was unconstitutionally depriving Fries of the assistance of counsel. As we have seen, capitalizing on Chase's circumscription of them, Fries's counsel withdrew from the case, claiming they were useless to Fries. Apparently the two of them recognized that they had a sure loser on the facts if they could not argue law, and they refused to return to Fries's defense, even after Chase appeared to soften his stand on permitting them to argue law to the jury. The enemies of the federalism Chase represented were thus able to present his conduct, which he mistakenly believed to have a basis in popular opinion favoring commerce, as the unfeeling deprivation of counsel to a prisoner charged in a capital crime.

Chase's mistake is understandable because it does appear that commercial prosperity was a popular concern in Philadelphia, with even some of the more radical or anti-Federalist publications recognizing the benefits to all the working people of Philadelphia of increased commerce.[109] Indeed, while Chase's conduct in the *Fries* trial was used against him when the Jeffersonians took power, at the time it did not create a substantial stir. On leaving Philadelphia, Chase appeared to go with the respect and something like affection of the leaders of the bar, which he reciprocated. It is not clear whether most of the Philadelphia bar approved of Chase because of his concern with Pennsylvania commerce or whether they simply acknowledged his legal talent and even though there were some rocky moments in his circuit experience there, his detractors appear to have been in the minority. In 1800, then, particularly because of his attention to Pennsylvania commerce, Chase must not have been fully aware of what a personal disaster he was creating.

The True Character of Pennsylvania Popular Jurisprudence

In late eighteenth-century Pennsylvania, boiling below the surface and probably unapparent to Chase, there seems to have been some ambivalence about commerce, or at least some debate over how commerce and law ought to be controlled by democracy. In the early years of the Republic, at least, that ambivalence resulted in the jury's discretion in implementing equitable solutions to commercial disputes.[110] Indeed, great scope for juries in making and implementing law in all types of cases appears to have been the feature of Pennsylvania jurisprudence which Chase understood least, although Pennsylvania natives and adepts, such as United States District Court Judge Richard Peters, could perceive and appear to defer to it.[111] Philadelphia counsel William Lewis and Alexander James Dallas, Fries's lawyers, also had a better understanding of the Pennsylvania tradition of jury activism, and, perhaps, the practice of jury nullification, and they were able to turn this against Chase, as suggested earlier, in a manner that ultimately resulted in the first article of the impeachment charges against him.[112]

What happened to Chase because of his rulings in the *Fries* case was simply part of a larger failure on Chase's part to grasp the contours of Pennsylvania jurisprudence and its intimate connection with late eighteenth-century Pennsylvania politics. When Chase sat on circuit in Philadelphia in 1800 and when he sought to rule in the *Cooper* case based on his personal political predilections, he was walking into a political maelstrom. He then created more of a sensation in Jeffersonian quarters with his presiding over Fries's prosecutions. Probably as significant as anything Chase himself did, however, was his value as a symbolic counter to be used by both sides (the opposition democratic Republicans and the more conservative Federalists) in the political battles that were being waged over control of the branches of the Pennsylvania state government.

Philadelphia's artisan radicals, at the time Chase arrived in 1800, had begun agitating for a new code of law, shorn of the Latin phrases and the technical terms of the English common law, to simplify court procedures, to replace much litigation by arbitration, and to create a judiciary more responsive to the legislature.[113]

Alexander James Dallas and the Attacks on the Judiciary

Alexander James Dallas, as noted earlier, was one of the two counsel to Fries and helped in the shrewd manipulation of Chase that resulted in driving the hapless prisoner's lawyers from the case, thus making Fries appear defenseless before a supposedly brutal and prejudiced Federalist judiciary.[114] Dallas was also one of the leaders in several struggles to implement a very democratic version of republicanism in Pennsylvania, and to reduce the influence of the purported remnants of aristocracy, such as Federalist judges.

In the course of what amounted to a warm-up for the Chase impeachment, Dallas, as prosecutor before the Pennsylvania senate, spearheaded a successful effort in 1803 to remove from the bench one Alexander Addison, a Federalist state supreme court judge who had been outspoken in his criticism of the Pennsylvania Democrats, of whom Dallas was then the most prominent. In particular, Dallas and his fellows were irked because Addison had made clear his belief that the Pennsylvania Democrats were wrong to praise the principles of the Virginia and Kentucky resolutions, the two late eighteenth-century documents which expressed dismay at the Federalists' policy of prosecuting for seditious libel in particular and operating a strong central government in general.[115] As noted earlier, the Virginia and Kentucky resolutions set forth the erroneous "compact" theory of the federal Constitution, which suggested that the federal government was simply a contract among the states and that this meant that any of the contracting parties had the right to refuse to abide by activities which it believed to have been outside the scope of the original compact. Addison and his fellow Federalists believed that the theory of the Virginia and Kentucky resolutions would lead, if implemented, to anarchy, chaos, and mobocracy.[116]

Dallas himself, when he became more secure in his own personal political power and forged an alliance with the moderate Pennsylvania governor,

Thomas McKean, appears to have rapidly backed off from the flirtation with opposition political extremism which his manipulation of Chase and his prosecution of Addison suggest. When some still-radical Pennsylvania Republicans sought to transform their impeachment victory against Addison into a complete purge of the Pennsylvania Supreme Court, Dallas switched sides and joined in the defense of the remaining supreme court judges. The remaining Pennsylvania radicals, whose chief prosecutor in the Pennsylvania senate, Caesar A. Rodney, would soon help manage the United States Senate trial of Chase, had charged that the Pennsylvania supreme court judges, in their use of the contempt power, were behaving in an arbitrary manner which constituted a "high misdemeanor" and thus an impeachable offense. Dallas's successful defense of the judges was premised on the fact that Pennsylvania judges were entitled to exercise the contempt power of English judges, since it had never expressly been prohibited and was a part of the common law incorporated by statute into Pennsylvania jurisprudence.

For the Pennsylvania radicals, however, the exercise of the contempt power, and the principle of judicial independence on which it was based, were fundamentally inconsistent with what they believed to be the needs of American democracy or republicanism, which they believed required legislative hegemony. As William Duane wrote in the radicals' principal organ, the *Aurora*, on March 31, 1803:

> The frequent abuse of power by [Pennsylvania's] judges . . . will one day render a total revision of the received maxims concerning the tenure of judicial office necessary. . . . It will one day be a subject of enquiry, why judges and justices of the peace should be more independent of the control of a free people, than those who have the formation and the execution of the laws entrusted to them. It will become a subject of enquiry, whether there is any analogy between what is called the independence of the judges in England, and the independence of the judges in America—and whether making the former independent of the king justified the making of the latter independent of the people.[117]

No doubt it was such thinking on the part of the Pennsylvania radicals that led the Pennsylvania Federalist, United States District Court Judge Richard Peters, in one of his more important admiralty opinions, to question the very wisdom of new, popular legislative enactments, suggesting that the maxims of the English common law much more often proved superior to legislative innovation.[118] In any event, by 1805, when the Federalists threw their support to Pennsylvania's Governor McKean in a contest with a radical who had the express endorsement of Thomas Paine, men such as Dallas could see that the Pennsylvania radicals were going too far, and Dallas joined with McKean in defeating the radicals' proposals for reform of the common law and the judiciary.

The arguments of the radicals, as explained by Richard Ellis in his seminal study of the early nineteenth-century Pennsylvania political and judicial imbroglio, were that "Judges had to be brought under the direct control of the people. Lawyers as a group were innately depraved and dishonest, and had an unnatural and exaggerated influence in the running of government. . . . [T]he common law, that product of aristocratic deviousness, was incompatible with the plain republicanism of the American people," and should be replaced with a system of "legislative" rather than "lawyers' law."[119]

The Pennsylvania radicals, such as Jesse Higgins and the transplanted English opposition theorist Thomas Paine, argued that venal and crown-pleasing English judges and lawyers had corrupted the purity of the democratically based original Saxon common law. Its purity could only be restored in America, they argued, by placing full power to control the judiciary in the people's immediate agents, the legislature, by implementing popular arbitration, and by restoring the purportedly ancient Saxon discretion to give rulings on law and fact to the jury.[120]

Chase's Federalist Reaction and the Similar Spirit of Dallas's Recantation

Each and every one of the Pennsylvania radicals' propositions, propositions undoubtedly borrowed from English radical or opposition thought, had by 1800 become anathema to Chase. When he rode on circuit in Pennsylvania and was confronted with the demagogical Paineite rhetoric of Thomas Cooper, who had been one of the most prominent English radical proponents of the theory of aristocratic corruption of the English common law, he reacted strongly, and tried to punish both Cooper *and* his party. When Chase watched Dallas's antics in the *Fries* trial, he reacted similarly. Chase must have linked Dallas's behavior to radical political sentiments and to the popular agitation that had resulted in the Whiskey Rebellion and the Fries Rebellion, and probably also with the writing and actions of France's radicals and undoubtedly with Cooper and Paine's radical writing in England.

His aggressive spirit triggered, Chase then sought mightily, earnestly, and roughly to demonstrate the error of the Pennsylvanian radicals' ways. In the *Fries* and *Cooper* trials, Chase tried to show, as did the conservative judges in England when he was there in 1784, that deference was owed to the prosecuting government and that popular control of the law, even in America, ought to be strictly limited. The only methods by which the people could change the law, Chase maintained, were the legislative action of the people's representatives, by the means set forth for constitutional amendment or by the election of representatives committed to legal or constitutional change.[121] Until and unless these measures were taken, said Chase, the jury was bound by the legal directions of the judges. Since the jury could not reject the law as laid down by the judges, then, it followed that the jury could not hear arguments critical of the Sedition Act under which Cooper was prosecuted, or critical of the settled interpretation of the treason doctrine under which Fries was prosecuted.

Similar sentiments, at least in spirit, were expressed in 1805 by Dallas himself and the Pennsylvania Federalists, to the effect that the Pennsylvania radicals' calls for "pure democracy" were simply inappropriate in a "populous country" such as America, and that to succumb to their pleas for the overthrow of the common law would be to surrender to "barbarism."

Dallas, by then making the case for the moderates or conservatives, composed a defense of the Pennsylvania common law as modified by the acts of the general assembly, and as stripped of its more feudal trappings by Pennsylvania judges. Echoing some of the points made by the archconservative Federalist Richard Peters several years before,[122] Dallas suggested that the Pennsylvania common law, as administered by the judges, was much more comprehensive than any scheme of legislation could be, and therefore better protected "rights, titles, persons, and liberty," and better guaranteed the historic rights of the American people, including trial by jury.[123]

Dallas's move across the ideological spectrum, a move which actually vindicated the positions taken by Chase in 1800, shows how jurisprudential debates could be influenced by the varying political fortunes of individuals and offers an intriguing parallel to the similar move on the part of Chase (and Burke) from left to right. In any event, Dallas's trimming and the backing of the Federalists enabled McKean to win reelection as governor of Pennsylvania in 1805, and thus to frustrate the radicals' ambitions in Pennsylvania. Nevertheless, the ideological battles and their attendant attitudes toward legal institutions would still be fought for several years in Pennsylvania, and, whatever Dallas's change of heart, radical resentment against Chase in Pennsylvania, spawned by his ideologically based conduct in the *Fries* and *Cooper* trials, would soon reappear in the United States Congress as Rodney and others sought to implement their ideology at the federal level and crush that of Chase.

A fuller understanding of the competing ideologies which resulted in the Chase impeachment, suggested by the political and judicial conflicts in Pennsylvania, is provided by a consideration of the manifestations of these radical or oppositionist beliefs, which we have now seen in context in England and in one state, Pennsylvania, by moving to a second state, Virginia. We have seen how these beliefs could be transplanted to Pennsylvania from England by individuals who traveled the Atlantic, such as Thomas Paine and Thomas Cooper. We will probably also come to understand that such thoughts could also be transmitted by letter and through personal friendships, as the Pennsylvania radicals corresponded with their Virginia political brethren.[124]

8

Confronting the Virginians: Part One
The Trial of James Thomson Callender and Chase's Activist Jurisprudence

Introduction

Samuel Chase's principal activity in Virginia, which brought him to the attention of the opposition lawyers and theorists in Jefferson's home state, was his presiding over a case for seditious libel, in a manner somewhat similar to that he employed in Pennsylvania in Thomas Cooper's trial. The defendant, like Cooper, was another radical immigrant writer, this time a Scotsman. Chase's adventures in the course of this trial are of interest to us not only for the political and legal issues, which are complex and important, but also because some connection probably existed between Chase's religiosity and his extreme re-action—later an important element in his impeachment—to the defendant, one James Thomson Callender. The *Callender* trial has usually been pointed to as the worst of Chase's excesses,[1] and even modern commentators have been at a loss to understand how Chase could have conducted himself in the manner he did. It will be argued here that modern commentators have failed to understand the legal and political issues involved in the trial, and have also failed to grasp how Chase's firm personal and religious morality propelled him into the actions he took.

It has been common to portray James Thomson Callender as a helpless victim of Chase's ire, but more careful students of the Alien and Sedition Acts era have also made clear to us that Callender was, without doubt, one of the most scurrilous and slimy publicists who ever wrote. One of the leading historians of the Federalist era, John C. Miller, not without some charity, describes Callender as "a little reptile."[2] Miller duly notes that Callender was once "turned out of Congress for being covered with lice and filth." There is no doubt that Thomas Jefferson personally encouraged Callender's publications and helped pay the fine Chase's court imposed on him. The Federalists must have had their revenge, however, when an ungrateful Callender later turned on Jefferson with "the same venom he had once directed against Adams and Hamilton," by accusing the sage of Monticello of fathering most of his plantation's many mulattos.[3] In the late 1790s, in any event, Callender was still exercising his awesome invective abilities in serving the Virginia Republicans in their struggle against the Adams administration.

Callender's rather loathsome and fantastic book, *The Prospect Before Us*,[4] published at the height of the presidential campaign in 1800, predicted the direst of consequences if the incumbent administration continued. John Adams was portrayed as, among other things, an aristocrat who had no real interest in the American people. He was a "hoary headed incendiary" bent on squeezing the last bit of solace out of an already gloomy and damned temporal existence, described as "the dark and despicable farce of life."[5] This depiction must have upset Chase, not only because of his increasingly firm loyalty to Adams and his policies, but also because Chase's theology included a much richer view of this world, and one's duties and obligations in it. Unlike those who belonged to the Hamiltonian wing of the Federalists, Chase remained a firm supporter of John Adams, even after Adams alienated Hamilton by attempting a rapprochement with France and by pardoning the leaders of the Fries Rebellion. The best evidence of Chase's continuing loyalty is probably his manuscript Jury Charge Book,[6] where, in a charge delivered in 1800, he called Adams "our illustrious and patriotic beloved President, the determined foe of vice, the uniform friend of Religion and piety, morality and virtue."[7]

Callender's pessimistic and perverted brand of eschatology apparently held out virtually no hope of happiness in this world, at least if Thomas Jefferson was not elected. Moreover, Callender's otherworldliness was at odds with Chase's belief that happiness could best be found in this life if men bent their wills to the service of their country and their God by exercising virtue, performing civic duties, and avoiding abstract, hedonistic, and atheistic democracy. If views like Callender's prevailed, and were accepted by an uninformed public, Chase believed, the Spirit of '76 might be forever extinguished. The labors of the revolutionary generation would, then, have been hideously in vain.[8]

There is strong evidence that Chase received a copy of Callender's book before leaving for the Virginia circuit where Callender was tried.[9] Chase probably concluded that Callender, because of his obvious attempt to impugn the character and motives of President Adams, had published a seditious document. It remained to be seen, however, whether Callender could prove the truth of the charges in his book. While Chase was probably convinced that Callender could not make such proof, he was prepared to allow Callender to try. Accordingly, there is no credible evidence to support the frequently leveled charges that Chase sought to pack the jury, or that he told the federal marshal in Richmond that he wanted "none of those creatures or people called Democrats" on the jury.

Those who charge Chase with an intention to pack the jury appear to be relying on the testimony, at Chase's impeachment trial, of one John Heath, a member of the bar of the Richmond circuit, who "swore that he heard Judge [sic] Chase issue the instructions [about excluding Democrats from the jury] to the federal Marshall, David M. Randolph."[10] At the same Senate impeachment trial, however, Mr. Randolph "swore that he had never received such instructions from the judge." In light of this circumstance and evidence that testimony at the impeachment trial revealed that Heath was never present in Chase's company with Randolph, the testimony of Randolph himself seems more credible, and Albert Beveridge's overlooked conclusion that Chase never attempted to pack the jury seems correct.[11]

Whether or not Chase attempted to pack the *Callender* jury, however, it seems clear that the trial itself was stacked against Chase, as suggested by the machinations of Callender's defense counsel.

The Rules of Evidence and Callender's Critique of Adams

Callender's counsel were three of the leaders of the Virginia Republicans, William Wirt, George Hay, and Philip Nicholas. As was true for John Fries's attorneys, the defense strategy of these men apparently departed sharply from the logic of the law according to Chase.[12] The first important point of disagreement was a difficult matter involving the rules of evidence to be applied in a criminal trial, a point on which Chase clearly had the better of Callender's counsel. This was probably of very little moment to those counsel, however, since their motivation had little to do with law and a lot to do with partisan politics.

Wirt, Hay, and Nicholas ostensibly tried to prove the truth of the statements referred to in one of the nineteen charges of seditious libel which had been brought against their client. However, they made little serious effort to gather evidence to prove the truth of the other eighteen statements. Given the nature of the charge the attorneys sought to prove true, their tactics, and their assertion of the alleged unconstitutionality of the seditious libel law, it seems that they were far more concerned about scoring political points against the Adams administration than they were with actually defending Callender. The conclusion drawn on these points by John Marshall's biographer, Albert Beveridge, as early as 1919, has withstood the test of time, although it has been too often neglected by those sympathetic to Jefferson and thus antagonistic to Chase. Of Callender's lawyers, Beveridge wrote that they "had not acted in his interest and had cared nothing about him; they had wished only 'to hold up the prosecution as oppressive' in order to 'excite public indignation against the court and the government. . . . ' "[13]

It appears, at last, as if modern American historians may be on the verge of returning to Beveridge's conclusion. In a recent excellent book on the American law of libel, Norman L. Rosenberg appears to have conceded that it is incorrect, as so many American historians have done, to portray the Callender trial "as a classic example of judicial bias against a defendant and in favor of the state."[14] Rosenberg noted the confession at Chase's impeachment trial of Callender's counsel, George Hay, that "the defense team intended to 'render a service, not to the man, but to the cause,' "[15] and appears to share the conclusion of William Wirt's nineteenth-century biographer that Wirt, Hay, and Nicholas "deliberately baited the easily irascible Chase; anticipated his explosive response; and planned from the outset to walk out of the courtroom and leave Callender to his fate."[16] The obviously political aims of Callender's counsel, their unwillingness to build a full legal defense for their client, and their plans to humiliate and use Chase may explain both his extraordinary condescension to them and his pointed humor at their expense.[17]

As indicated, Callender's counsel did attempt to prove the truth of only one of the nineteen allegedly libelous statements. This assertion was made in two important clauses, separated by a semicolon, to wit, that "*John Adams was a professed aristocrat; he had proved faithful and serviceable to the British interest.*"[18] The only proof of the truth of this statement offered by Callender's counsel was the testimony of Col. John Taylor, a leading Virginia Jeffersonian Republican, and a notorious professed foe of aristocracy.[19] Apparently the defense's theory was that Col. Taylor knew well his enemy[20] and could best testify about the enemy's characteristics.

Col. Taylor was prepared to explain that, on the basis of Adams's writing, it was clear Adams thought aristocracies and monarchies were the best forms of government, and the British constitution the best model. Col. Taylor was also prepared to testify that, as vice-president, Adams had voted in the Senate against the Sequestration Act, which, if it had passed, would have approved American confiscation of British property. This was the defense's way of proving that Adams was serviceable to the British, who, of course, opposed the sequestration law. Thus, on the surface at least, if Col. Taylor had been allowed to testify, Callender's counsel may have been able to prove the truth of both elements of the statement referred to in the charge. As indicated, Taylor could have testified to prove the truth of both clauses: that Adams was an aristocrat and that he was serviceable to the British.

Chase ruled, however, that Col. Taylor's testimony could not be introduced. Apparently suspecting something when he saw Col. Taylor asked to the stand, Chase proceeded to determine the content of Taylor's proposed testimony by

requiring that the questions for direct examination of Taylor be first reduced
to writing. This was done, and Chase proceeded to rule Col. Taylor's testimony inadmissible. Chase's ruling is at first difficult to understand because
Col. Taylor seemingly offered the very proof of truth demanded of the defense.
Nevertheless, Chase explained that the gravamen of the offense charged in this
count of the indictment was not simply the suggestion that Adams was an aristocrat, or the assertion that Adams had proved serviceable to the British interest. Either or both of these, if true, would not have constituted questionable
behavior, Chase explained, and the making of such statements could not support prosecution for seditious libel. Seditious libel could only occur when one
had cast unwarranted assumptions on the government or its leaders. It was no
crime to be an aristocrat, and it was not wrong to prove serviceable to the
British interest, so long as one did not betray American interests. To accuse
anyone of either of those two attributes, then, would not impugn them in a
libelous manner.

Nevertheless, according to Chase, the form of the statement in two phrases
separated by the semicolon had to be interpreted as implying that, because of
his aristocratic beliefs, Adams had consciously acted in a manner to the det-
riment of his country. Chase therefore asserted that the real nature of Callender's offense, made by the two phrases as he published them, was to accuse
Adams of acting with treasonous motives. In other words, Chase explained
that Callender's alleged offense had been to assert that Adams, as a professed
aristocrat, was an enemy to the republican government of the United States.
Adams's enmity, Callender had suggested, was manifested in his voting against
the Sequestration Act, to favor the British interests at the expense of the interests of the American people. In short, the statement was seditiously libelous
because it accused the president of having consciously acted against the interests of his country.

The testimony of Col. Taylor as outlined above was all Callender's counsel
had to offer. Neither Col. Taylor nor any other defense witnesses could demonstrate such disloyalty on Adams's part. Because no one could demonstrate
this treasonous, or at least extremely unpatriotic, motive for Adams's vote
against the Sequestration Act, Chase ruled that the evidence, which, according
to his construction only partially established the truth of the charge, could not
be admitted, lest the jury be influenced into believing that the defense had submitted evidence on the truth of the whole charge.

Chase's ruling is quite narrowly technical, perhaps even overnice; not surprisingly, commentators on the *Callender* trial or Chase's impeachment have
failed to defend it. Indeed, no one who has written on the case appears to have
actually understood the legal basis for Chase's ruling. Nevertheless, Chase did
rule in accordance with the philosophy of the common law rules of evidence,
which, while still in a rudimentary stage in those years, did operate to exclude

prejudicial testimony. Although most commentators have raised questions about the correctness of Chase's ruling,[21] if one construes Callender's language as Chase did, his ruling was legally correct, and perhaps inescapable.

In excluding Col. Taylor's testimony, Chase appeared to follow a general principle enunciated by Lord Mansfield twenty-five years earlier, in an anonymous case in 1775. Lord Mansfield stated that it was better not to let the jury weigh misleading evidence, but to exclude it altogether, since "it was not for courts of law 'to consider how far the minds of men may be capable of resisting temptation, but to take the most anxious care that they shall not be exposed to any temptation at all. . . . ' "[22] The assertions of Chase's critics which might seem to indicate the contrary notwithstanding, the practice of having the judge pass on whether evidence was of a character sufficient to go to the jury was well established in America by Chase's time.[23]

An examination of the debates over the federal sedition law, which Chase was ruling on, indicates that the act was drafted so as to preserve the judge's power of passing on the sufficiency of evidence.[24] Indeed, even the radical English Wilkites of the late eighteenth century, the inspiration for many acts of the similarly opposition Jeffersonians, apparently believed that it was acceptable for the judge to ensure that only "lawful" evidence was admitted.[25] There seems very little doubt, then, that Chase had the law on his side in his ruling.

Moreover, even if Chase had allowed the evidence on this charge, he would still have been obliged to inform the jury that they would be legally required to bring in a guilty verdict, since Callender's counsel offered no evidence to rebut the prosecution's charges on the other eighteen counts of the indictment. Of some significance in testing Chase's good faith in his legal rulings on Callender's proffered evidence from Col. Taylor was his willingness at the trial, even though he knew it to be contrary to the rules of evidence, to proceed to admit the testimony, even if prejudicial, simply to pacify the defendant's counsel. Chase asked the prosecutor in the case if he would allow him to offer this testimony to the jury, but when the prosecutor stood on the rules of evidence and refused to agree to Chase's proposal for its admission, Chase felt he had to follow his sworn judicial duty and exclude the testimony.[26]

The Virginia Syllogism

Failing in their attempt to offer their limited evidence of truth, and thereby to tarnish John Adams's reputation, Callender's counsel switched to their other major aim in Callender's defense, a direct attack on the constitutionality of the sedition law. This argument of Wirt, Hay, and Nicholas, known thereafter as the "Virginia Syllogism," was designed to get the Virginia jury to decide the constitutionality of the sedition law. Defense counsel probably believed a jury would be more sympathetic to invalidating the sedition law than would the Federalist judges.

The legal argument of Callender's counsel ran roughly as follows:

> 1. The Federal courts are required by the Judiciary Act of 1789 to follow state procedures.
> 2. According to Virginia court procedures the jury is the finder of both fact and law.
> 3. The United States Constitution was the law, indeed the supreme law, of the land.
> 4. Therefore, the jury could decide whether a statute exceeded the bounds authorized by the United States Constitution, because this was simply a finding about law.

Chase, upon hearing this argument, stopped Callender's counsel with the pronouncement "A *non sequitur*, Sir."[27] This ruffled the feathers of the Virginians who, suspiciously like Fries's counsel a few weeks before, folded their briefs and withdrew from the case. It is likely that their withdrawal had been planned to embarrass Chase, but it is also likely, in retrospect, that their conduct and Chase's also tell us something significant about the difference between Chase's conception of the role of juries and that held by the Jeffersonian Virginians, the Jeffersonian Pennsylvanians, and several other contemporary American legal theorists. The Jeffersonians were clearly flirting with a much more democratic conception of the juror's role than Chase would allow. As Chase had shown in the *Fries* case by giving a pretrial opinion on the law, he again demonstrated in Callender's trial that he believed the jury's task was to do no more than apply the legal rules as given to them by the judge. Their job was *not* to create their own legal rules for the particular case.

In other words, Chase believed the jurors were supposed to be "law finders," applying the guidelines given to them by the court, and not "law makers." This was easy to see in the materials regarding Fries's case,[28] but Chase's theories took on an even more emphatic dimension when the legal issue involved was one of constitutional law, and the review of a federal statute. It was Chase's belief that determining the constitutionality of the sedition law, or even interpreting the sedition law, was a matter exclusively for the judge, not the jury.

Chase's view on this legal point was certainly not his alone. He agreed, for example, with his colleague, Associate Justice William Paterson, who had previously decided in another seditious libel case in Vermont that the jury should not pass on the constitutionality of the federal statute.[29] Chase believed that if the jury determined the applicable rules of law in each case, rather than simply applying the rules, trial results would be arbitrary, and the cherished concept of the rule of law would evaporate. In other words, Chase believed that in all cases the jury must take from the judge the ruler used in measuring out the result. The jurors must take the legal standard, the ruler, as the judge gave it to them, apply it to the facts as they found them, and announce their "measurement" of law to the court. They were not permitted to tell the court that the standard was impermissible; they were not permitted to protest that their ruler was faulty. Nor were they allowed to protest that they were not dealing with a law, but with something else, something that could not validly be construed to be law.

Chase's behavior in these cases probably seemed very sensible to his fellow conservatives, the Federalists, but his attitudes toward the jury must equally have seemed odd to many Americans, particularly the Jeffersonian oppositionists, because the notion that the jury should have a broad lawmaking role was often seen by them to have been established in Anglo-American jurisprudence. This attitude may have stemmed from the popular memory of such cases as the *Seven Bishops* trial in England,[30] the *Zenger* trial in colonial America,[31] the *Writs of Assistance Case* or the *Parsons' Cause* in the prerevolutionary era,[32] or, most recently, the acquittal of Gideon Henfield.

Chase, however, had support in solid English conservative doctrines, doctrines even older than the English opposition ones suggesting great jury discretion. Chase could point, with some justification, to the work of one of the champions of English conservative jurisprudence, Sir Edward Coke, to apply the essentially English notion that determining rules of law was not a matter for laymen, not even for the "excellent reason" of a king.[33] The law to be applied in a given case, according to Coke, was the "artificial reason" of the judges. This "artificial reason" could be gained only by long study of the reports and statutes, and was a matter for legal professionals. A layman could find fact and apply the legal rule to it, but could not, and should not, determine the legal rule itself.

Given Chase's belief that the times were dangerous and called for strict and clear rules of law, he not surprisingly differed from those who took a more democratic view of the jury's task. Those who differed with him, the Jeffersonians like Wirt, Hay, and Nicholas, were more concerned with their particularized notions of local equity than they were with national uniformity. Just as was true for Pennsylvania, however, the particular events in Callender's trial hint at a richness of local Virginia opposition jurisprudence, a "richness" that must be explored in order to speak confidently about the nature of judging in the early Republic.

The Meaning of the "Virginia Syllogism"

Those who sought to impeach Chase, and thus to embarrass the Federalists and remove their influence on the judiciary, concentrated their criticisms of Chase's activities on his 1800 circuit sittings in Pennsylvania and Virginia. We have already seen how Pennsylvania's politics contributed to an environment in which an outsider like Chase could find himself overwhelmed by the force of local struggles. The same is true for Virginia, although the variety of "democratic republicanism" which confronted Chase on the Richmond circuit in 1800, when he tried the seditious libel case of James Thomson Callender, was subtly different from that of Pennsylvania.

Undoubtedly, this was not apparent to Chase, who must have simply responded adversely to the surface similarities in the resistance he encountered to his restrictive views on the ambit of jury discretion which he enunciated in both *Fries* and *Callender*. The Virginia lawyers, as did Dallas and Lewis in Pennsylvania, broadly maintained the notion that discretion ought to be given to juries to make law, which proposition was at the heart of their "Virginia Syllogism."[34] The Virginia Syllogism, however, was not accepted by any of the judges of the United States Supreme Court. Indeed, as Chase called to the Virginians' attention in the course of the *Callender* trial, referring to the Virginia Supreme Court's opinion in *Kamper v. Hawkins* (1792), even such a Jeffersonian Republican as St. George Tucker[35] appears to have conceded that testing constitutionality was a matter for courts, and, implicitly, not juries.[36]

It may thus be that Wirt, Hay, and Nicholas were overstating the democratic elements in Virginia jurisprudence, and it is likely that Chase did not understand the culture out of which their views emerged. Unlike the case in Pennsylvania, for example, the Virginia theorists of the jury in the late eighteenth and early nineteenth centuries did not seem to have been prompted by pressures from below, that is, by strictly democratic feelings.

While the language used to sustain the claim for a great role for the jury in passing on the law may have been democratic in nature, the tradition in Virginia was undoubtedly more aristocratic, with the jury acting as a sort of buffer between the royal government and the powerful planters, as it did, for example, in the immediately postrevolutionary period, in the *Parsons' Cause*.[37]

By the late eighteenth century, however, the Virginia tradition of opposition to crown authority through juries, and Patrick Henry's natural rights theory of jurisprudence used in the course of the *Parsons' Cause*, which he articulated to get a jury, in effect, to nullify the king's disallowance of a colonial law, had subtly altered. The basis of Virginia jurisprudence had remained the consent of the people of the state, which was still thought to be best articulated by the state legislature, but the villainy against which the people of Virginia had to be on their guard was not the arbitrary power of a corrupt king, but the perceived arbitrary power of an indigenous corrupt magistry or aristocracy.

A. G. Roeber, in his splendid study of Virginia legal culture, has demonstrated that at the close of the eighteenth century a newly professionalized cadre of lawyers, of which Wirt, Hay, and Nicholas were apparently members,[38] but which was more conspicuously led by St. George Tucker, George Wythe, Spencer Roane, and Thomas Jefferson,[39] had begun to use English opposition, or as Roeber calls it, Republican "country" rhetoric, to argue that legislative reform was necessary to curb the jurisdiction of antirepublican justices of the peace, and to place control over legal disputes, instead, in the hands of a professional judiciary, aided by juries. This was, as Roeber has shown, part of a very complex transfer of political and legal power from a traditionally minded, and anticommercial set of great planters to a more diverse, though probably equally elitist, set of lawyers, judges, and merchants.

Chase's Alarm at and Overreaction to Virginia Legal Rhetoric

Unfortunately, the same rhetoric used to attack the hegemony of the old Virginia planter aristocracy could easily be employed in questioning the Federalist-controlled central government. The Virginia and Kentucky resolutions of 1798–99, key documents of this emerging Virginia opposition or country Republican movement, and drafted respectively by the Virginians Madison and Jefferson, excoriated the Federalists for their theories of the existence of a federal common law of crimes, which the Federalists were accused of relying on as a basis for the Alien and Sedition laws. These resolutions and the compact theory of the federal Constitution on which they were based went so far as to claim that the states or their legislatures possessed the power to nullify federal legislation based on the common law of crimes, or legislation premised on any other foundation allegedly not expressly permitted by the federal Constitution.[40]

As a newly converted firm Federalist, Chase could see the Virginia and Kentucky resolutions as a threat to the union of the United States, which he believed necessary to prevent foreign-inspired intrigue, chaos, and disorder, but it is likely that he was also painfully aware of the fact that much of the philosophy expressed in those resolves had once been his. In the jurisprudence expressed in the Virginia and Kentucky resolutions, Madison and Jefferson appear to have been engaging in an application of the sort of country Republican theory made most famous by Bolingbroke, and to which Chase himself probably once subscribed.[41]

The essence of this form of American opposition or country Republican theory was the perception that a strong central government would inevitably become corrupt. So the thrust of Madison and Jefferson's arguments was that the federal government had succumbed to such corruption and now seemed bent on enslaving the states. The evidence of such corruption were the judicial excesses such as the asserted jurisdiction over a federal common law of crimes[42] and the legislative excesses of the Alien and Sedition laws, as manifested in the prosecution of Callender. Worse still, in the minds of many Virginians such as Col. Taylor, were the executive excesses of Hamilton, abetted by the federal legislation, in his creation of the traditional "court" theory bogeymen of central institutions favoring a financial oligarchy, like a central bank and federal subsidies to encourage the establishment of large-scale commerce and manufacturing.[43] These Jeffersonian perceptions of "excess" on the part of the Federalist government, of course, have something of the character of Chase's jurisprudence of "restraint," but this fact was not significant to Chase.

This was because by this time in the late eighteenth century, the Virginians' theories seemed to him to diverge from his, because, as suggested by his remarks to Fries and Cooper,[44] Chase had become convinced that the danger to the Republic lay not in corruption at the center, but in licentiousness at the periphery. Further, by the late 1790s, if not before, Chase's brand of country republicanism had apparently come to embrace commercial prosperity, and had recognized the need for a strong central government to secure it.[45] In order better to understand the contrast between Chase and the Virginians on this point, it is instructive to pause and consider a roughly contemporaneous demonstration of the essential principles of Chase's jurisprudence, to be found in his Jury Charge Book. This consideration also illuminates one of the most puzzling aspects of Chase's behavior in 1800, more perplexing really than his conduct in the *Fries*, *Cooper*, and *Callender* trials, his actively campaigning for John Adams.[46]

Chase's Grand Jury Charge Book: Chase on the Active Virtues of Judging

Chase's excitement at Callender's trial was owing in no small part to the fact that Samuel Chase was deeply distressed at the possibility that Wirt, Hay, and Nicholas's fellow Virginian, Thomas Jefferson, might become president in 1800. As indicated in the preface, the Jeffersonian press criticized Chase's public appearances to support Adams's reelection as demeaning to the judiciary.[47] The press even charged, wrongly, that Chase's campaigning caused the Supreme Court to cancel some sessions because he was unable to attend. Actually Chase was present for all court sittings during this period, except when incapacitated by illness.[48] Nevertheless, Chase's presidential campaigning activity strikes the modern observer, mired in the idea of judicial political neutrality, as indefensible. Once again, Chase likely felt that as a professional preserver of the Constitution, his job was to help assure that the men whom he believed to be its sworn enemies, the atheistic and Francophilic Jeffersonian Republicans, did not have the opportunity to subvert the Constitution.

When the principal atheist and Francophile himself was elected president in 1800, Chase was despondent. Consistently with his essentially Machiavellian, and hence cyclical,[49] view of history, Chase concluded that the American experimentation in republicanism was likely to fail soon. The people, by electing the Jeffersonians and permitting their legislative excesses, had finally failed to exercise the virtue necessary for citizens in a republic in picking their leaders. Although Chase may have believed, at least from 1800 to 1803, that the struggle had been lost, he was too much of a fighter, too much of a proselytizing Calvinist to give up the battle. Thus, through his jury charges during those years he made one last attempt to ignite the virtue of the people. Perhaps he knew that what he had to say would be widely disseminated and hoped against all probability that he might still arrest and reverse the decline of civic virtue in America.

Chase Rejected the Idea of Judicial Neutrality

In a survey of late eighteenth-century federal grand jury charges, Ralph Lerner concluded that American judges usually saw their task as one of instructing jurors on the basic principles of politics—to function as "Republican schoolmasters."[50] Nevertheless, Lerner concluded that judges took as their text the existing law, and saw as their task simply explaining how the American balanced constitutional system worked and interpreting the meaning of legislation. Lerner went as far as suggesting that it was obviously improper for a judge to criticize congressional statutes.[51]

Lerner's model does not fit the work of Chase. Chase believed that a judge's duties included the obligation, in jury charges, to test federal or state statutes for compliance with the requirements of the United States Constitution, even if no action challenging their constitutionality had yet been brought. Moreover, some of the constitutional tests, in Chase's mind at least, appeared to be implicit, rather than explicit, in the federal Constitution. These requirements, which scholars have frequently referred to as the "Unwritten Constitution,"[52] were the great principles of justice to which Chase had alluded in *Calder v. Bull*.[53] Some of these principles are clearly reflected in the Constitution, such as the principle of the independence of the judiciary. Others which were of equal, or even paramount, importance to Chase could only be inferred by applying political or religious principles derived from other sources. Two examples are the inviolability of private property and person, which Chase explicitly mentioned in *Calder*, and the necessity of religion to secure virtue in a republic, as Chase mentioned in his jury charges.

Lerner praises the federal judges who refrained from criticizing the law and remained content with explaining it, perhaps because he believes they anticipated modern "process" theories of jurisprudence. Under this modern approach the judge's task is, supposedly, simply to help ensure the smooth functioning of the political process, and to apply legal and constitutional rules neutrally, objectively, and generally.[54] This modern aspirational jurisprudence is predicated on the idea that legislative and constitutional decisions reflect a choice between subjectively weighted alternative values. Such choices are said to be for legislators in our system of government, and judges should implement the lawmakers' subjective choice, not substitute one of their own.[55]

It is not at all clear whether such an objective process-oriented philosophy of judging can ever exist, but even if it could, such was not Chase's brand of jurisprudence, nor was judicial neutrality or passivity the practice in contemporary England. The English required judges actively to exercise discretion to ensure the people's respect for and compliance with the law. Moreover, late eighteenth-century English scholars understood that "political ideology and the law as ideology were intertwined, and that legal bodies and processes (many of which had an overt political function anyway) were frequently the foci of political expression and political conflict."[56]

Paradoxically, in implementing discretion, Chase, like the English, did not think he was behaving in a partisan manner of any kind. For eighteenth-century American conservatives, then, as Morton Horwitz has recently described the "republican" character of their thought, they "proceeded from an objective conception of the public interest and a state that could legitimately promote virtue."[57] Chase did not, then, consider himself a partisan who implemented a particular faction's view. Chase was convinced that his study of the law, and his understanding of the nature of man and of legal philosophy, enabled him to apply certain and objective standards to evaluate legislation. Moreover, he believed, he was compelled to apply those standards if the purposes of legislation and constitution-making—securing human liberty and freedom—were ever to be accomplished.[58]

The Political Philosophy of the Baltimore Grand Jury Charge

Chase's notions of the judges' task in passing on law and his views on the nature of law and man receive their fullest treatment in his fifty-page manuscript Jury Charge Book,[59] a source that has infrequently been consulted by modern American legal historians, due partly, no doubt, to what Julius Goebel correctly called Chase's "execrable handwriting."[60] The charge book is now preserved in the Maryland Historical Society and includes revised charges delivered to grand juries in 1799, 1800, 1803, and 1806. Several portions of the charge book are identical to the Baltimore grand jury charge of 1803 which led to his impeachment, and it thus seems fair to take that charge, which is better known than the others, as a typical manifestation of Chase's mature ideas on society, politics, law, and religion. As a whole, then, what we might call the tone of the charge book does not differ from that of the grand jury charge, although after his 1805 acquittal on the impeachment charges the text seems to reflect a calmer, or a somewhat chastened, attitude.

In the 1803 Baltimore grand jury charge, Chase tells the grand jury that he believes that "liberty" is essential in society. True liberty, however, Chase explained, in a critical reference to the work of English and American opposition theorists and their French mentors, is neither the abstract goddess of the theorists of the "rights of man" nor, strictly speaking, merely a by-product of democracy. Moving well beyond the normal categories of republican thought, Chase explained that "a monarchy may be freer than a republic," and a "republic" may be a "tyranny" if it fails properly to protect property and person. America and Maryland, he warned in 1803, were in grave danger of passing from a free society, one in which liberty was secured by protecting person and property, to the worst of all tyrannies, a mobocracy, where property and person would not be safe.

Addressing himself first to the current problems of his native state, Chase cited as the most prominent Maryland dangers the establishment of universal male suffrage and the abolition of one of the state's supreme courts. Moving to the federal level, he referred to Jefferson's congressional allies' repeal of the Federalists' 1801 Judiciary Act, thereby abolishing the offices of the new federal circuit judges.

Chase's reaction to Maryland's political evolution in the late 1790s indicates how far he had come from the days when he was a firebrand, a revolutionary "son of liberty" with "a mob constantly at his heels."[61] It seems likely that Chase realized at a late stage in his life that democracy was a young person's game. With age, he concluded that higher values existed than simply implementing the ephemeral mayfly wishes of the people. Chase told the 1803 Baltimore grand jury that by implementing universal suffrage, the sons of the Maryland fathers who had woven the magnificent fabric of the 1776 Maryland Constitution were destroying their patrimony. Chase had been a major framer of that constitution, which carefully balanced the privileges of property with some broadening of the base of political power. Chase warned that to grant universal suffrage, as Maryland had done, was to go too far, was to upset the delicate balance between property and popularity, and would bring into the political process men with no real attachment to, or interest in, the community. Those men, he believed, would inevitably become the playthings of power-mad demagogues or unscrupulous, avaricious adventurers.[62]

Chase's views of property and its relationship to the community illustrate what we might call his essentially "classical," Aristotelian, or Platonic view of an organic, rather than an individualistic, community,[63] in which ownership of land linked one with the rest of the community. According to this theory, the property owner felt a common interest in the community, and was more inclined to subscribe to the correct legal and constitutional choices to preserve the community interests. Most American political thinkers of the time, as we are just beginning to realize,[64] adhered to what was variously labeled the "civic," "classical," or "Aristotelian" conception of property. I have called this dominant perspective in early America the "conservative" perspective, and this aspect of the conservative's theory suggested that the franchise should be limited to those with enough property so that their favor could not be bought. The classic defender of the limited franchise in England[65] was Blackstone,[66] and it is striking how many of our Constitution's framers demonstrably held these Blackstonian views. For example, this was a clear qualification to the supposedly "democratic" thinking of James Wilson.[67] Similarly, Chase and his conservative American contemporaries in the 1790s thought that the independence which wealth provided was an essential guarantee of the honesty and objectivity of both voters and legislators.[68]

Moreover, for Chase, as for his fellow American conservatives, property ownership carried with it a sense of duty to the community. Property ownership was not for Chase what it was already becoming for many Americans, including, as will be argued, John Marshall: a means of furthering individual, increasingly atomistic, enterprise. Moreover, it was certainly not the competitive vehicle it eventually became in the hands of the Jacksonian entrepreneurs and their champion, Roger Taney.[69] Whatever property meant to Chase, however, with the election of Jefferson in 1800, and the conduct of his administration and the Congress he controlled from 1800 to 1803, Chase thought that property was in grave danger and that universal male suffrage might lead to its utter demise.

Chase still believed in the early nineteenth century that a vigilant conservative judiciary might be able to salvage liberty, property, and the Republic from the ravages of opposition Jeffersonians. The state and federal actions of the Jeffersonians to abolish part of the judiciary jeopardized this possibility, however, and threatened the judiciary's independence, if not its very existence. By 1803, then, Chase understood, appreciated, and embraced the classical theories of a balanced polity. These theories included an enhanced role for the judiciary as articulated by Alexander Hamilton in *Federalist* 78, 79, and 80.[70] Nevertheless, Chase believed, the role of the judiciary could only be preserved if the American people realized its importance. Ultimately, then, even Chase's conservative philosophy had to have a base of faith in the people, what we might describe as its very real "popular" dimension. Accordingly, Chase believed it his obligation to instruct his grand jurors in their duties, and Chase explained to them, in 1803 and in prior charges, that the only hope for avoiding an American slide into mobocracy was if Americans exercised the virtue classically necessary to preserve a republic. The implication of these jury charges is that the American people could exercise this necessary virtue by choosing representatives who would repeal the odious state and federal acts endangering both property and the independence of the judiciary.

It was at this point in the Baltimore grand jury charge, the statement of juror's duties, that Chase injected the religious dimension of his jurisprudence, which I have argued was so important to him, and crucial to a true understanding of his verison of conservative or republican judicial theory. Indeed, it might be concluded, from a review of Chase's writing and actions, that the entire edifice of classical or republican theory was really of much less moment than late eighteenth-century American and English notions of proper "Christian" conduct.[71] At any rate, in Chase's case, and that of many of his eighteenth-century conservative contemporaries in England and America, it is probably impossible to disentangle the two threads of political conservatism and Christianity. To encourage implementation of true republican virtue, Chase reminded his grand jurors that true liberty could not exist without morality, and that morality could not exist without religion. With what we have seen so far, particularly in Pennsylvania and Virginia, we are now ready to present the outlines of Chase's internal religious feeling, which dictated what he told the grand jurors in 1803, which prompted what he did in the *Fries* trial, which must have been operative as well in his reaction to the defendant at the *Callender* trial, and which sustained him throughout all his tribulations.

Religious Elements in Chase's Politics and Jurisprudence

Chase's God.   An initial understanding of Chase's religious views can be achieved by pointing out how they both resembled and differed from those of the first of the great modern political thinkers, Thomas Hobbes. The religious or eschatological basis of Hobbes's thought, although virtually unknown to modern political scientists, was probably of great moment to Hobbes, and was one of the essential engines which drove his theories.[72] This was also true for Chase, because without the force of his religion, if his own testimony and the clear evidence of his conduct is to be believed, he could not have done what he did. Unlike Hobbes's God, however, Chase's God did not resemble the modern radical theologians' *deus ahsconditus*, a God who seems to have absconded from our midst, whose only temporal activities, while of great moment and continuing importance, were in the biblical past and an eschatological future.[73]

Instead, Chase's God was an omnipresent very personal lord and master, to whom he spoke everyday, who presumably listened carefully, and who had particular plans for Samuel Chase and his family. This God, Chase believed, went so far as to see personally that he survived dangerous missions intact, and, on at least one occasion, dramatically saved Chase from drowning.[74] His belief in a God who was constantly present and often directly intervened in the present world clearly differed from his deist Republican contemporaries, as Jefferson is usually characterized. The Deists, like Hobbes, may have believed in a God with a master plan for the human race, but not one who had as direct an effect on individuals as Chase's God. With such a personal deity, it is no wonder Chase had the passion to carry out particularized service to his God, and the tireless energy to devote to the task.

Scholars have suggested that Chase was a "strange inconsistent man," but one of the essential features of Chase's intellectual orientation was his particular sense of a divinely inspired personal mission, which seems to have been with him throughout his life. This consistent aspect of Chase's pattern of personal belief and action, his version of republicanism or of conservative political theory was based on personal philosophical notions about religion, human nature, and the nature of the social order.

The Religious Basis of Chase's Republicanism.   One can understand Chase's brand of republicanism by bearing in mind that, whatever the philosophy of the ancients, Chase saw a modern republic as inevitably a Christian social order. Chase put the demands of religion over the demands of the temporal polity in both his life and work.[75] The current common perception is that a judge's views on the law depend on, or at least are influenced by, his or her views on other matters, particularly politics.[76] If one can accept at face value his explicit language in his opinions and jury charges, this is certainly true of Chase.

Moreover, Chase's politics had an explicitly eschatological dimension.[77] He saw man's task on earth as a challenge by an omnipresent and personally relevant God. Compliance with the rigors of that task would have inevitable results in a world to come. For Chase, the temporal order frequently paled into insignificance when he contemplated an individual's future in the next world, after God's judgment.[78]

Republicanism and the Imperfectibility of Man.   Chase frequently described the ideal American government as "republican,"[79] but it has been a major theme in this book that Chase's republicanism was an essentially conservative, religious variant. In his early days Chase may have believed, like Jefferson, that the best government was that in which the people governed most. By the time he became a federal judge in 1796, however, Chase had concluded that there was a profound difference between a democracy and a Christian republican balanced government. The sources of this conservatism, as we have seen, are probably various, and undoubtedly include the influence of his Anglican minister father and his favorable impression of English conservatives.[80]

It seems most likely, however, that, as we saw in chapter 7, seeing democracy in action in the French Revolution pushed Chase toward the right.

Taking precedence in Chase's republicanism, as distinguished from the more deist democratic variant of Jeffersonian republicanism,[81] was the realization that people were imperfect and imperfectible beings. Men and women must realize the limits of their own understanding, Chase believed, and ultimately be guided by faith. Accordingly, one's purpose on the planet, and the only manner in which one could assure oneself of a rich and meaningful existence, was to glorify the creator by selflessly fulfilling the duties that the creator required. In response, one could expect to be judged, in a life to come, on the basis of how well one had succeeded in meeting the Creator's requirements.[82]

Chase's Burkean Conservative Jurisprudence.   For Chase, unlike many earlier American Puritans or Calvinists, God was a merciful being, a great searcher of souls, and not a deity who conferred salvation simply as a matter of unmerited grace.[83] Further, for Chase, compliance with what he believed to be the popularly sanctioned federal Constitution seemed to be an instance of obedience to the will of God.[84] To this extent, and to the extent he saw a necessary role for the American people in exercising their virtue in their choice of representatives, Chase favored popular sovereignty and believed in a religious basis for the principle that the people ought to rule.

As Chase sought to implement this ethical philosophy by condemning further rebellion against the supposedly popularly established federal constitutional government, however, his operational jurisprudence was little different from Burkean conservatism.[85] Because, as Chase put it in his now infamous 1803 Baltimore grand jury Charge, "the bulk of mankind"[86] was easily swayed by passion, and not governed by reason in the face of temptations, it was the judiciary's job to restrain democratic tendencies in the populace, lest the nation degenerate into "mobocracy, the worst of all possible governments."[87]

Probably reflecting his reading of Burke, Chase observed in his 1803 charge that the concept of the "rights of man" existing in a state of nature was a dangerous fiction of visionaries.[88] Moreover, paraphrasing Hobbes or perhaps some intermediary like Allan Ramsey,[89] Chase noted that no society ever existed except when the weak submitted to the strong to secure minimal protection of property and person.[90] Chase's notion that governments came not from the popular idea of a social contract among equals, but from the weak inevitably seeking the protection of the strong, is also an element of the Scottish common-sense philosophy of men like David Hume, Adam Smith, and Adam Ferguson, a philosophy that is increasingly being recognized as influential in the early years of our republic.[91]

This all suggests that Chase was well in the mainstream of late eighteenth-century American republican thought, and not, as he is often made out to be, some deranged reactionary. In any event, most important to Chase in 1803 was the notion, usually associated in the late eighteenth century with Burke, that no limits could be set on the visionary rights of man, and thus, for Chase, the only means of preventing mobocracy was for Americans to resist pressures for universal suffrage or legislative interference with the judiciary. Instead, Americans should exercise "Republican virtue" by structuring the franchise to ensure that only those with enough wealth to secure independence of mind and only those with interests consistent with that of the community could vote.[92]

Conservative Jurisprudences
Passing in the Night

So it was, then, that Chase's republicanism made the transition from the Tory "country" conservatism of Bolingbroke to the Rockingham Whig conservatism of Burke.[93] Chase's beliefs moved from being closest to what most historians call the "country" theorists of England to a position where he embraced a political program much closer to that of the English ministry of the 1790s. Unfortunately, just as Chase, when he presided over the *Callender* trial, viewed the Virginians as adhering to the same dangerous radicalism as did his critics in Pennsylvania, in the ideologically tinted glasses through which the Virginians viewed the champions of the Adams administration, Chase's English-inspired move to the right could only be interpreted as "court" corruption.

Moreover, though it was true that the Virginians were actually invoking a theory of jurisprudence based on deference and religion, and thus exhibiting elements in common with Chase, there were certainly aspects of Virginia jurisprudential philosophy aired in the *Callender* trial which Chase would have found revolting at best, and revolutionary or anarchic at worst. It was, after all, the aim of Wirt, Hay, and Nicholas in the course of their arguments at Callender's trial, an aim much more important than their client's defense, to condemn the Federalist candidate for president, the incumbent, John Adams, as a traitor and enemy of the American people.[94]

Callender's counsel sought, as we have seen, publicly and officially to excoriate Adams by presenting the all but irrelevant testimony of John Taylor of Caroline, then one of the most radical sounding of Virginia Republicans. Col. Taylor was a sometime friend of Jefferson, but his utterances and writings were more in line with the thought of the "*tertium quids*," the radical Virginians like the mercurial John Randolph of Roanoke. These men eventually were to bolt from the Jefferson administration because of their beliefs that the federal government under Jefferson was infringing too much on state sovereignty.[95]

Even apart from Chase's sensitivity to slights on Adams, there was much in Taylor's philosophy which would have disturbed Chase, and of which Chase was likely to have been informed before Col. Taylor actually appeared in his court. It was Taylor, after all, who, like some of the Pennsylvanians whom we have mentioned, "explicitly repudiated the notion that the judiciary ought to be independent."[96] Thus, Chase would have perceived Taylor, like the Pennsylvania radicals, as seeking to undermine one of the central principles on which Chase's late career was based, and which were clearly stated in the Baltimore grand jury charge of 1803.[97] Though he might not have quite worked it all out as early as 1800, Taylor was soon to rail magnificently against the whole emerging Federalist and even Jeffersonian structure of bankers, merchants, and lawyers, whom he believed to be a corps of miscreants working fiendishly to transform the agrarian early Republic.[98]

When in 1798 Chase pronounced his *Worrall* opinion on the nonexistence of a federal common law of crimes, contemporaries seem to have believed that he had fallen under the spell of the "Virginia metaphysicians," presumably Jefferson and Madison.[99] This theory would have been consistent with the suggestion that Washington's purpose in appointing Chase was to represent Southern views on the Court, and, in some respects, Chase's early Supreme Court opinions are consistent with basic Southern jurisprudential tenets such as the need for circumscription of the executive and for the maintenance of supraconstitutional principles. Chase's opinion in *Calder v. Bull*, his strongest such jurisprudential statement, bears a marked similarity to Virginia philosophical and legal expressions such as those articulated by Patrick Henry in the *Parsons' Cause*, or Thomas Jefferson in the Declaration of Independence, or Virginia Justice Spencer Roane in his opinion in *Currie's Administrators*.[100]

By 1800, however, Chase had irretrievably broken faith with this strand of opposition Southern jurisprudence. One is tempted to speculate on the irony, of which Chase might have been aware, that one of the thorns in his side in the *Callender* case, defense counsel Wirt, had begun his career as a lawyer in Maryland, where Chase himself eventually honed his deferential brand of jurisprudence, and where the early Wirt appears to have been a champion of the great conservative Tory judge, Mansfield.[101] Wirt's move from right to left, so to speak, like Dallas's move from left to right, presents further proof of the elusive character of jurisprudential loyalties in the late eighteenth century. In any event, the extent to which Chase moved away from the Virginians' country jurisprudence, and the nature of the difference in views between Chase and the Virginia lawyers with whom he battled in *Callender*, can best be gauged by moving on to compare Chase's views in the late 1790s and early 1800s with those of the leader of the Virginia Jeffersonians himself.

9

Confronting the Virginians: Part Two
Samuel Chase, Thomas Jefferson, and John Marshall

Thomas Jefferson's Jurisprudence

Was Thomas Jefferson a "Moderate"?

By the mid-twentieth century in America, it had become the conventional wisdom to perceive Thomas Jefferson as a moderate, as firmly within an "American political tradition," which eschewed extremism of either the left or right.[1] It is a matter of no small irony, since the two cordially despised each other, but this making a moderate of Jefferson probably has much in common with the prevalent apotheosis of John Marshall as the founder of an American *judicial* tradition.[2] Both historiographical assessments may result from the desire common to many modern scholars to legitimate, by supplying a long historical pedigree, twentieth-century democratic liberalism as practiced either by the Federal legislature (the New Deal) or the United States Supreme Court (the Warren and Burger years).

If one takes seriously many of Jefferson's political pronouncements, however, and particularly those which concerned the judiciary, it is impossible to picture Jefferson accurately as a moderate.[3] Jefferson's well-known concern that the judicial branch of government always represented the greatest threat to liberty or to democracy must be an indication of immoderation, given the usual American consensus that the judiciary is the best guardian of liberty.[4] Daniel Boorstin, in his perceptive *The Lost World of Thomas Jefferson* (1948), may have put it best when he observed:

The contempt for the judiciary which Jefferson expressed freely and repeatedly had been occasioned by immediate political irritations, but it did betray his inability to feel respect for law. When judges crossed Jefferson's political aims, they became "the corps of sappers and miners" working to undermine the independence of the states and to consolidate political power. He could not imagine that in the long run a strong and independent judiciary might fortify the restraints on political power; he had not wholly purged himself of that desire for power of which he accuses his "monocratic enemies." In his own thinking, Jefferson had made political and legal questions indistinguishable.[5]

Jefferson's views on the judiciary, in short, look a lot like those of the Pennsylvania radicals studied in chapter 7, and bear a strong resemblance to the thought of Col. John Taylor in Virginia, which we examined in chapter 8.

Jefferson's distrust of the judiciary, as Boorstin implies, ostensibly stemmed from his belief that the notion of an independent judiciary with life tenure was contrary to the republican principles of government, because the judges could end up aristocratically unresponsive to the people.[6] It is likely, of course, that such a view of the judiciary owed much to Jefferson's observation of the conservative English jurists, whose work was reviewed in chapter 4, such as Blackstone, Mansfield, or Buller.

Throughout at least the latter part of his career, then, Jefferson's vision of republicanism was far more democratic than that of Chase or of most of Jefferson's American contemporaries and seemed to have a lot in common with the English opposition thought examined in chapter 4. For example, explaining his views to Col. John Taylor some time after the period we are examining, and perhaps to justify them to his, in some ways, more radical fellow Virginian, Jefferson wrote that,

> [O]f the term *republic*, instead of saying, as has been said, "that it may mean anything or nothing," we may say with truth and meaning, that governments are more or less republican, as they have more or less of the element of popular election and control in their composition; and believing as I do, that the mass of the citizens is the safest depository of their own rights and especially, that the evils flowing from the duperies of the people, are less injurious than those from the egoism of their agents, I am a friend to that composition of government which has in it the most of this ingredient.[7]

Unlike Chase or Hamilton, who appear to have believed that the essence of, in Chase's phrase, "free republican government" was the representation of the people by those above them in wisdom and wealth, Jefferson seems to have believed that to have a republic was to seek to come as close as possible to direct democracy.[8]

Although occasionally, as we have seen, some of Jefferson's actions appear to have been too far to the right for *tertium quids* such as Randolph or Taylor, it seems to me that Jefferson has pretty solid credentials as a radical, or at least as someone who could honestly be perceived as having imbibed the opposition or democratic thought from the English radicals as did the Pennsylvanians and the Virginians discussed in chapters 7 and 8. Jefferson, after all, seems to have been sincere when, much earlier than his letter to Col. Taylor, he wrote a famous letter to his colleague Madison in 1787 in which he said that "I hold it that a little rebellion now and then is a good thing, and as necessary in the political world as storms in the physical. Unsuccessful rebellions indeed generally establish the encroachments on the rights of the people which produced them."[9]

Jefferson goes even further toward the radical position with his suggestions in another famous 1787 letter to one Col. Smith in which the future third president writes "God forbid we should ever be twenty years without such a rebellion [as that of 1776]. . . . What signify a few lives lost in a century or two? The tree of liberty must be refreshed from time to time with the blood of patriots and tyrants. It is its natural manure."[10] Finally, it bears remembering that shortly after the 1792 September Massacres in France, in January 3, 1793, Jefferson wrote William Short that the loss of life in France in the cause of liberty, while a source of some sadness, was hardly regrettable. For such a cause, Jefferson explained, "I would have seen half the earth desolated. Were there but an Adam and an Eve left in every country, and left free, it would be better than as it now is."[11] This last strangely foreshadows the attitude of the American troops in south Vietnam, who piously destroyed villages in order to "save" them from the Viet Cong. If this is moderation, to paraphrase H. L. Mencken, then moderation is not what it was when I was young.[12]

It should come as no surprise that the views of Jefferson, and the adherents to his thinking in Pennsylvania and Virginia, disturbed Samuel Chase a great deal. He made clear, in the trial of Thomas Cooper in 1800, that he believed that the presence of Jefferson's challenge to Adams, insofar as it had resulted in the creation of a political party hostile to the incumbent Adams administration, posed a great danger to the American Republic. This is implicit in his comments, before he sentenced Cooper, that he, Chase, was aware of the notorious fact that the country now had two political parties, one of them hostile to the government. This was exceedingly dangerous, Chase appears to have believed, because Jefferson's party had the potential to underwrite the fines incurred by those "party writers" in his employ convicted of seditious libel for falsely, scandalously, and maliciously attacking the character of those serving the Adams administration.[13]

Given the easy excitability of public opinion, and that the public was thus prey to the kind of designing demagogues Chase probably believed Jefferson, Dallas, Wirt, Hay, and Nicholas to be, Chase believed that the United States needed the law of seditious libel to protect its own people from their enemies, and to shield the characters of virtuous public servants like Adams from unfair attacks. Chase's belief in the need for a law of seditious libel and his mistrust of public opinion is in sharp contrast to Jefferson's faith in public opinion and democracy generally. Chase's fears of the public, of course, are what lay behind his frequent efforts to circumscribe the scope of juries, and his concomitant struggle to implement what he believed to be the rule of law. On this issue, as well, Jefferson appears to have been poles apart from Chase.

Jefferson and Chase on Law and Religion

While Chase was ultimately prepared to submit to a rather strict notion of the rule of law, with either the Constitution or statutes as limits on his discretion, pursuant to his conception of a jurisprudence of restraint limned earlier (chapter 3), Thomas Jefferson was not. Jefferson seems fervently to have believed that in the service of his ultimate democratic ends, or his particular conception of the "salvation of the people," it was permissible to ignore inconvenient legal limits, such as the Constitution, the rules of property, or the federal law of criminal procedure. Some of Jefferson's decidedly immoderate views on this question are set forth in his letter to John B. Colvin, editor of the *Republican Advocate* of Fredericktown, Maryland, written on September 10, 1810. Jefferson there tells Colvin that his views on the question of the rule of law are "for your own eye only," and on Colvin's assurance that "they will not get into the hands of newswriters." In that letter Jefferson makes clear his views that "a strict observance of the written laws is doubtless *one* of the high duties of a good citizen, but it is not the *highest*. The laws of necessity, of self-preservation, of saving our country when in danger, are of higher obligation. To lose our country by a scrupulous adherence to written law, would be to lose the law itself, with life, liberty, property and all those who are enjoying them with us; thus absurdly sacrificing the end to the means."[14]

Jefferson's suggestion in this letter, that one might depart from the rule of law in order to save the country itself, makes a certain amount of sense, but Jefferson goes on in the letter to explain how this principle justifies ignoring the rules of private property in wartime, to justify piracy on the grounds of self-preservation, to justify his Louisiana purchase when he lacked official authorization, and to justify his agents' ignoring of the niceties of federal law in the prosecution of his archenemy Aaron Burr. This last, says Jefferson, was necessary because of "the danger of [the Burr conspirators'] rescue, of their continuing their machinations, the tardiness and weakness of the law, apathy of the judges, active patronage of the whole tribe of lawyers, unknown disposition of the juries, an hourly expectation of the enemy, salvation of the city [New Orleans], and of the Union itself, which would have been convulsed to its centre, had that conspiracy succeeded; all these constituted a law of necessity and self preservation, and rendered the *salus populi* supreme over the written law."[15] Given Jefferson's myriad definitions for fatal dangers to the Republic, it is difficult to understand how the rule of law could function as a barrier to executive misconduct, and to understand how Jefferson could so easily be characterized as a true champion of individual liberty.[16]

Jefferson's implied arbitrariness, concealed in this letter to Colvin, was not, of course, known to Chase and his fellow Federalists in 1800. It does seem that Jefferson's apparently well-known encouragement of party writers like Cooper and Callender,[17] and his affinity to the agitation by the Pennsylvanians and Virginians, suggest irresponsibility on his part. Equally alarming as far as Federalists like Chase were concerned,[18] Jefferson was known to have maintained that Christianity was not a part of the common law. Indeed, Jefferson seems to have believed in a maximum of tolerance and a minimum of religious influence on the law, for his time a fairly radical position, one that echoed that of the English opposition thinkers. Jefferson believed that religious freedom ought to be extended not only to Christians, but to "the Jew and the Gentile, the Christian and Mohametan, the Hindoo, and Infidel of every denomination. . . ."[19]

Samuel Chase, on the other hand, the son of an Anglican minister, was more conservative in legal/religious matters, as were most Anglican lawyers of his time, even some of Jefferson's fellow Virginians, such as Edmund Pendleton, or Jefferson's sometime ally George Mason. Chase, Pendleton, and Mason believed fervently that religion, and particularly its Christian eschatology with its preoccupation with salvation and another world, was an indispensable foundation for the law.[20] In Chase's case, at least, this seemed to extend to both federal and state law.

As we saw in the *Fries* case in chapter 7, Chase, like his conservative fellows in contemporary England, had no hesitation in invoking his Christianity as a legal tool to remind miscreants of their obligation to conform to the strictures and the virtues demanded by his deferential brand of politics.[21] Chase, as was true for even some Jeffersonian Virginians, claimed that his deferential notions were the essence of republicanism,[22] but when Chase voiced them, they seemed, to his Virginia and Pennsylvania critics, to have a lot more in common with English monarchy and aristocracy.[23]

Jefferson and Chase on Trusting the Public

On all of these issues the principal difference between Jefferson and Chase is probably in the amount of faith each was willing to place in the general population to exercise the virtue necessary in order to support a republic.[24] As clearly indicated in his Baltimore grand jury charge of 1803, Chase was convinced that in late eighteenth-century America the people's virtue was insufficient, and had to be supplemented and protected by the restraints imposed either internally through Christian religious dictates of conscience or externally by a divinely inspired crusading federal judiciary. The early Jefferson may have believed in a structured society with limited social mobility and an educational system which discouraged ambition,[25] but the Jefferson who relied on popular favor in the 1800 and 1804 elections apparently came to believe that it was appropriate not to articulate such restraints on the people. While Chase followed the usual pattern of becoming more conservative with age, in this respect Jefferson seems to have gone against the grain, and in a manner that terrified Chase.

Indeed, perhaps it does not go too far to suggest that Jefferson's views on the judiciary, and the danger to liberty there posed, were molded in large part by what he perceived to be the requirements of conforming to public opinion. His writings, as is true with regard to the theories of his political colleagues who defended Callender, do not articulate a theory of judicial review as a means of implementing popular sovereignty. Jefferson's visceral fear of judges, and the aristocratic danger he believed they posed, appears to have prevented him from giving much thought to how they could be used positively in a republic.

Perhaps until the Federalist judges zealously implemented the federal common law of crimes and the Alien and Sedition Acts against Jeffersonians, Jefferson had not paid too much attention to the workings of the judicial branch, but from then on, as the issue became embroiled in popular fears, he appears to have embraced the spirit of the radical efforts in Pennsylvania and Virginia to rein in the independence of judges.

Jefferson's Impeachment Move against Chase

After Jefferson took office, when he became aware that Associate Justice Samuel Chase, a sitting federal judge, was actively criticizing the legislation of the Jeffersonian majorities in the federal legislature and in Maryland, Jefferson reacted strongly and swiftly, and ordered Chase's impeachment. Jefferson hedged his bets, however, warning his hatchet man to make sure that his own name was not linked to the effort.[26] It soon became clear to Jefferson, however, that Chase's legal defense was much more formidable than the prosecution being conducted by his impeachment managers, such as his fiery but ineffectual and disorganized cousin John Randolph.

Some of the arguments which Chase used at his impeachment trial have already been mentioned—his defense of his ruling on the admissibility of Col. Taylor's testimony, his rejection of the Virginia syllogism, and the explanation of why he issued an opinion on the elements of treason prior to Fries's second trial.[27] In the context of Chase's confrontation with Jeffersonian thought, however, the most notable element of his defense against the impeachment charges concerns the most nebulous charge against him. This charge, clearly prompted by the young Virginia radicals such as Wirt, Hay, and Nicholas, referred to Callender's trial and accused Chase of engaging in unjudicial behavior through "the use of unusual, rude and contemptuous expressions towards the prisoner's counsel. . . . In repeated and vexatious interruptions of the said counsel . . . [and by manifesting] an indecent solicitude . . . for the conviction of the accused."[28]

To combat this charge Chase brilliantly decided to use the Jeffersonian Republicans' argument against the common law of crimes, adopted from his own opinion in the *Worrall* case. Chase argued, in his defense, that prosecuting conduct defined so vaguely as "rude and contemptuous," "vexatious," or "indecent" betrayed the fundamental principles of American jurisprudence. In his formal answer to the impeachment charges, Chase stated that he felt it "his duty" to "enter his solemn protest against the introduction in this country, of those arbitrary principles, at once the offspring and the instruments of despotism, which would make 'high crimes and misdemeanors' to consist in 'rude and contemptuous expressions,' in 'vexatious interruptions of counsel,' and in the manifestation of 'indecent solicitude' for the conviction of a most notorious offender."[29] Expressing the notion he had articulated in *Worrall*, Chase acknowledged that:

> [s]uch conduct is no doubt improper and unbecoming in any person, and much more so in a judge: but, it is too vague, too uncertain, and too susceptible of forced interpretations, according to the impulse of passion or the views of policy, to be admitted into the class of punishable offences, under a system of law whose certainty and precision in the definition of crimes, is its greatest glory, and the greatest privilege of those who live under its sway.[30]

In short, as Chase suggested in his answer to the impeachment charges, the only permissible criminal prosecution in America, including the impeachable offenses of "high crimes and misdemeanors," was pursuant to a statute or constitutional provision that clearly defined the crime committed and the punishment imposed. Chase thus twisted into the Jeffersonians the very knife their president had used to slash against the Federalists in the Virginia and Kentucky resolutions.

Eventually Jefferson perceived that Chase was successfully using his own jurisprudential philosophy against the president's allies in the House. He also had observed that his impeachment manager, Randolph, was falling out of political favor, because of his uncompromising stand in the highly devisive Yazoo land controversy.[31] Jefferson appears to have sensed that moderation on the Chase impeachment could win him a more solid base of support, even among some of the Federalists.

Accordingly, Jefferson left Randolph twisting slowly in the wind and watched the Chase impeachment effort fail. The Randolph wing of Jefferson's party, the *tertium quids*, isolated itself and lost political influence, and Jefferson went on to implement his Embargo Act and other measures for which he felt he needed the widest political support.[32] As the *tertium quids* realized, even if he had democratic pretensions, Jefferson found himself forced to act in a centralizing manner which even made him disguise his distaste for the views of the Federalists and Chase, in an effort to appear to be the president of all the people.

Jefferson's moderate pretensions did not appear to have won over the New England Federalists, who did all they could to block the embargo, enlisting in their efforts even the young Jeffersonian Joseph Story, who for the rest of his life questioned the wisdom of Jefferson's democratic conception of republicanism.[33] As far as Chase himself was concerned, once he was acquitted by the Senate and, shortly thereafter, came into a great deal of wealth as a result of the settlement of Maryland's claims on England, his old ideological fire appears to have cooled, and he seems not to have been terribly disturbed when his beloved daughter married a Jeffersonian.[34] All of this calls into question, to some extent, the influence of ideology on Jefferson and Chase, or at least its influence on their actions following the cooling of the emotionally charged atmosphere of the late 1790s and early 1800s. Or, more to the point of this chapter, all of this suggests that what appeared to Chase and Jefferson as wildly inconsistent political positions may have had more of a common core than either of them could or would admit.

The Conservative Alliance that Never Was: Chase, Jefferson, Taylor, and Randolph

Jefferson on Social Station

Perhaps Chase, in the flush of wealth and having enjoyed a form of public exoneration following his acquittal on impeachment charges before the Senate, was at last able to reflect on the fact that ultimately he and Jefferson did share some political and social premises. As indicated earlier, at one time Jefferson appears to have believed in the need for a hierarchical society and for an educational system fit for an individual's particular abilities and his particular "condition," the economic and social class into which he had been born.[35] Jefferson, at least when he wrote his *Notes on Virginia* (1781), believed that men should be educated to understand that true happiness depended not on rising to a social station superior to that of one's family, but rather that it depended on making the best of one's abilities within the station in society to which one had been born.

In those *Notes* Jefferson indicated a willingness to see some men advanced in social or class standing through education, a process which he tellingly called "geniuses raked from the rubbish." This advancement was not solely for the good of the individual, but was to serve the ends of the whole society, by having the fittest characters possess the fullest education. Most of the population, Jefferson appears to have believed, was entitled to enough education to learn to read and write, and presumably to cast a ballot for their educational and social superiors, but most of the population should also be content to exist as yeoman farmers, living a simple life, free from the taints of excessive luxury fostered by commerce.[36] This was not exactly Chase's vision of American utopia, but the utopia Jefferson expressed in the *Notes* had in common with Chase's view a reliance on the politics of deference, and a sense of the organic nature of American society.

In any event, Jefferson's demagoguery in 1796 and 1800 led Chase and his Federalist colleagues, such as President John Adams, astray, and convinced him and them that there was an enormous difference between the elitism boldly expressed by Adams[37] and the professed democracy of Jefferson, although at the time this may have been much more apparent than real.[38] This led Chase, at least in those years, into dangerous moves to control Jeffersonian influence on popular institutions like the jury and to criticize universal suffrage, since it could lead to a demogogically inspired "mobocracy." All of this, of course, led Jefferson to set in motion Chase's impeachment.

It seems quite possible, though, that Adams, Jefferson, and Chase in 1800 were really not very far apart on certain fundamental political premises, such as the need for an ordered society, the need for the lower orders to stay in their places, and the need for the mass of voters to pick their leaders from the class above them. In any event, when Chase, who had once been a demagogue (although a demagogue who was careful to erect constitutional restraints against popular excess) became frightened by events in Europe and America in the late 1790s, he turned decisively away from democracy and its current Jeffersonian and Madisonian language of states rights, as expressed in the Virginia and Kentucky resolutions.

In rejecting these Jeffersonian and Madisonian popular ideas as they were expressed in the Virginia and Kentucky resolutions, Chase appears to have been making the only response an English-style true conservative could. The elitism that Chase and the Jefferson who wrote the *Notes on Virginia*, at least, wanted to conserve failed to endure in an atmosphere which encouraged popular measures such as hostility to the federal judiciary, or universal manhood suffrage.

Elitism and Fear of Commerce: Jefferson, John Taylor, and John Randolph

As he grew older, Jefferson seems to have increasingly felt that democracy could be trusted to act wisely, but other Virginians who unwittingly embraced the ostensibly democratic philosophy of the Virginia and Kentucky resolutions probably came to regret it. If Jefferson continued to favor the government that encouraged the most direct participation of the people, he came to differ from his friend John Taylor of Caroline, whom we observed at odds with Samuel Chase in chapter 8. Unlike Taylor, Jefferson seems not to have understood that with a truer democracy might eventually come a preference for commerce and manufacturing over agriculture, and the corruption of all American classes by luxury. Jefferson seems to have been unaware that with such democracy could come a proliferation of acquisitive urges and ambition for social mobility that he himself had once condemned.

Chase's conservative position was also somewhat ironic, since his advocacy of commercial expansion may have carried with it democratizing tendencies. When wealth from manufacturing and commerce could become available to persons without grounding in deferential politics, the classical virtue of deference in an organic, hierarchically organized state that Chase favored would be neglected by a new ideology of individual acquisition and democratic commercial expansion.

Finally, and most ironically, whatever they may have concluded in 1800 and in 1804 about Jefferson, Chase and many of the other Federalists failed to grasp the common conservative basis they shared with the aristocratic philosophy of some other Virginians. These men, such as Col. Taylor and John Randolph,[39] maintained throughout their careers the same elitist views as the early Jefferson. The Federalists probably failed to see this, either because the Virginians did not share the Federalists' commitment to commerce and manufacturing, or, equally likely, because the Federalists viewed the Virginians through tinted ideological glasses, and were distracted by other elements of Randolph's and Taylor's political or judicial philosophies. These other elements, particularly Randolph's and Taylor's condemnation of judicial independence, looked too much like the really dangerous Pennsylvania urban radicalism which did present a real threat to American elitist government.

Like the Pennsylvanians, Randolph and Taylor put great stock in jury discretion, and in a view of the federal constitution which limited the executive and judicial power of the federal government.[40] Whatever the pretensions of some Virginians, such as the later Thomas Jefferson, "outside agitators" like the transplanted Scotsman Callender, or the "young gentlemen" for Callender's defense, who might have had a vision of life in Virginia which bore a strong resemblance to that of some of the Pennsylvanians, those were not the ultimate desires of Randolph or Taylor. Those two might have shared in 1799 and 1800 "radical" Jeffersonian views on the federal judiciary, but they were decidedly undemocratic in their conceptions of what life should be like in Virginia.

How the Elitists Defeated Themselves

Had Chase not been perceived as an unprincipled apostate to the original "antifederalist" cause by those Virginians, and had he been able to perceive distinctions among the Virginians, perhaps a common conservative cause could have been made, and the late 1790s would have turned out differently. Instead, Chase's zealous campaigning for Adams, and his sincere and not inappropriate fears of Pennsylvania and Virginia Jacobinism, led him to create a reaction against himself on the part of the Virginians who should have been his natural allies. When those Virginians, blinded by their version of country hostility to a powerful fiscally adept central government,[41] joined forces with the Pennsylvania radicals in 1800 and in 1804, they ensured Jefferson's triumph. By doing that, they also legitimized and encouraged forces of democracy in the North which would eventually undermine the Southern aristocracy they cherished. This undermining was eventually facilitated by the jurisprudential synthesis of John Marshall, which made possible the triumph of Northern economic individualism and thus "Northern-style" democracy, and it is to that synthesis we now move.

Samuel Chase and John Marshall

John Marshall's Jurisprudence of Synthesis

The synthesis of Chase's beliefs in the need for deference and stability in the law and in the nobility of commerce, and of Jefferson's faith in the wisdom of the masses and in the ability of man's reason through democratic-republican institutions to solve political problems, came with the jurisprudence of John Marshall. Marshall accepted (indeed, may have borrowed) Chase's ideology of the expression of popular sovereignty in the Constitution and the institution of judicial review,[42] and he accepted Chase's belief that the nation could not flourish without the protection of the rights of those engaged in contracting and commerce. But to a greater extent than Chase did, Marshall also seems to have needed to acknowledge not only the ultimate sovereignty of the people as expressed in the Constitution, but, at least for most practical purposes, the sovereignty of the people as expressed in the ongoing work of the legislature. As a result, Marshall gained great fame as the man who took the Supreme Court out of politics, and who left "political questions" to the legislature.[43]

This traditional apotheosis of Marshall as the father of an American judicial tradition of judges above legislative politics, however, misses much of the meaning of what he did, and obscures the sources of his synthetic views. When

Marshall sought to move away from expressing the ideological version of elitist views that Chase and his Federalist fellow judges had exhibited in the late 1790s, he was, in effect, abandoning the conception that the Constitution of 1787 was a document with fixed historical conservative meaning.

The "Original Understanding" as Manifested by Chase and His Fellows

The basis of the actions of Chase and his fellow federal judges in the 1790s was probably very different from Marshall's secular, pragmatic, and modern notions. As has been maintained here (chapters 3 through 8), those pre-Marshallian Federalists adhered to jurisprudential principles similar to those relied on by Coke, Hale, and Burke, when they sought to interpret England's Ancient Constitution.[44] Chase and his brethren were like the great English common lawyers who believed in the hegemony of the "artificial reason" of the common law, the series of customs and practices which had grown up out of the experience of many men, and which embodied the wisdom of the ages, wisdom that could only be tapped by those who had long studied it.[45] Their school of American common-law constitutional interpretation, a school which it now appears reflected the original understanding of the original intent of the Constitution's framers, believed, as did their English ideological mentors, in a jurisprudence of deference, one which had a positive duty to restrain popular and unwise excesses, whether on the part of the public, the legislature, or the executive.[46]

Chase and his Federalist colleagues believed, then, that the citizens of the late 1790s needed to be told by those who had special expertise what the true meaning of the Constitution was, and how it was dependent on a particular vision of deferential republican virtue in the citizenry. They were, of course, different from their English predecessors, since the Federalist judges' expertise may have accrued more immediately from their actual American Whig revolutionary experience rather than from their intimate familiarity with the generations-old tradition expressed in the volumes of English common law books.[47] Nevertheless, as scholars such as John Reid are beginning to show, whether or not the Americans' understanding of the rights of Englishmen were altered by their own experience, their conceptions of constitutional law probably owed more to the historic rights of Englishmen, as expressed by the great English common lawyers and judges, than to any other source.[48]

Marshall's Failure to Adhere to the Original Understanding of Original Intent

This points up a most profound difference between Chase, his colleagues in the 1790s, and Marshall. At the time of the Chase impeachment efforts, when the Jeffersonians controlled the executive and legislative branches of the federal government, instead of keeping the judiciary as the custodians of the Constitution's meaning, John Marshall, the man usually credited with doing the most to preserve judicial review in America, *actually maintained that it might be wisest to lodge the power of ultimate constitutional interpretation in the federal legislature.*[49] While Marshall seems to have retreated eventually from that particular position, his failure in the first years of Jefferson's administration to acknowledge the blatant unconstitutionality of the Jeffersonian-controlled federal legislature's repeal of the 1801 Judiciary Act and his failure effectively to protest the Jeffersonian's sacking of the Federalist "midnight judges" appear to be a shirking of the responsibility for fidelity to the Constitution on the part of the judiciary. In these instances Marshall appears to have rejected the concept of the judiciary's ultimate interpretive responsibility embodied in *Federalist* 78 and in Chase's opinion in the *Callender* case.[50]

Marshall did make a contemporary ritual incantation of the principles of *Federalist* 78 in the *Marbury* case in 1803, but evaluating it in context, it is difficult to regard *Marbury* as the luminous polar star of judicial review and judicial independence which we have so often made it. The result in *Marbury* was for the Court, on a somewhat dubious basis,[51] to declare itself without jurisdiction to provide a remedy for admittedly unconstitutional action on the part of the popular Jefferson administration.

Perhaps Marshall believed that Jefferson's democracy ought to be permitted to flex its muscles, at least insofar as he permitted great leeway to the acts of the federal legislature. Finally in 1819, of course, Marshall did demonstrate that when fundamental commercial concerns were attacked he would play a conservative role in preserving the meaning of the 1787 document, but this appears to have been only to the extent of checking the unconstitutional activity of state legislatures.[52] In 1802, appalled and irate over the Jeffersonian Congress's repeal of the 1801 Judiciary Act, Chase wrote Marshall, urging that the Supreme Court check what Chase believed to be the unconstitutional actions of the Jeffersonian majority.[53] Marshall's habitual avoidance of direct confrontation prevailed, however; the Supreme Court only obliquely criticized the unconstitutional actions of the Jeffersonians in *Marbury*, and Chase was apparently alone in his wishes for the Court to take a firm stand that the 1802 repeal of the 1801 Judiciary Act was unconstitutional.

Perhaps the somewhat more secular Marshall, freed from the hag-ridden religiosity of Chase, did not quite see the same need for the preservation of virtue in all political spheres. Moreover, as indicated, Marshall saw the possibility of combining democracy with commercial prosperity in a way that neither Chase or Jefferson ever did. Marshall's flexible constitution, tailored to expand the sphere of both federal legislative action and commercial certainty, may not have been the document the essentially aristocratic framers envisioned, but could win wide popular acceptance until aristocracy made its last, doomed stand over the rights of property in slaves.

Moreover, the spirit of Marshall's expansionist Constitution, poured into the new bottles of late New Deal social legislation and Warren court civil rights jurisprudence, was savored and won popular acceptance among most lawyers and academics, if not the general population, until very recently.[54]

"Preinstrumentalism" and "Instrumentalism," the Temporal World and Eternity

How then was it that Marshall in 1802 differed so dramatically from Chase on the necessity to keep the federal legislature in line, and what was the meaning of the eventual synthesis of federal jurisprudence, as outlined in the preceding section? One explanation for the differences regarding opinions on the appropriate judicial role between Marshall and Samuel Chase (and perhaps an explanation of the perception of a difference of opinion between Chase and Thomas Jefferson as well) was that Marshall (like Jefferson, in his way) seems to have demonstrated the essentially secular nineteenth-century faith in progress and manifest destiny of the young United States.[55]

In Marshall's conception of the temporal world, unlike that of Samuel Chase, the task of worldly man was to expand his commercial horizons, and to absorb himself in the affairs of his polity. For Chase, however, man's task was more to reflect the glory of his creator, and the eventual object of what Chase conceived of as American Christian Republican virtue was to prepare one's soul for the coming day of judgment, when one was brought once again before one's Creator.[56]

At some level, of course, Chase too must have sensed the possibilities for temporal growth and magnificence on the American continent, and he was certainly aware of the possibility that a less corrupt social order might be built in America than in Europe. Still, it seems likely that Chase's preoccupation with his and others' salvation, and his sense of otherworldliness, predisposed him to share with the anti-Federalists of the 1780s the belief that Americans would eventually suffer the fate of many republics before them, and that, when their virtue was found wanting, the caprices of fortune would ravage their civilization.

Chase's view of history, like that of most of his contemporaries, was not the view of the nineteenth-century English Whig historians like Macaulay, or his American contemporary Bancroft, who believed in an ever-expanding providentially directed progress for Anglo-Saxon peoples, although this might well have been the view of Marshall. Chase was of an earlier generation, and for him the future was not a theater of temporal progress, but an eternity of spiritual salvation or damnation.

The difference between the jurisprudence of men of the time of Chase and that of the next generation, men like John Marshall and his colleague Joseph Story, or their contemporary James Kent, has been described by Morton Horwitz as the difference between a "natural law" or "preinstrumental" and an "instrumental" style of jurisprudence. According to Horwitz, before about 1790 the view was nearly universal among Americans that judges "discovered" law and did not make it up as they went along.

The task of a judge, as conceived by most of the judges of Chase's generation, says Horwitz, was simply to apply the eternal and divinely inspired principles of the common law, principles which they supposed to have existed in essentially the same form since the folkmoots in the Teutonic forests. With the American Revolution, Horwitz suggests, came a realization for many American lawyers that the basis of law was not eternal verities, but rather the will of the temporal sovereign, and this realization eventually led judges, as the nineteenth century wore on, more or less self-consciously, to mold at least the private law doctrines of the common law to fit their particular conceptions of social policy.[57]

As Horwitz himself appears implicitly to concede, one can find instrumentalist or preinstrumentalist approaches to jurisprudence on either side of Horwitz's dividing lines,[58] and a move from natural law to instrumentalist jurisprudence may not thus be all that was going on in the period of jurisprudential change Horwitz discusses. In any event, there does seem to be plenty of evidence to support Horwitz's broader claim that nineteenth-century jurisprudence differed from eighteenth-century styles of judicial reasoning,[59] and that the nineteenth-century judges were proceeding according to a conception of law that favored its use to foster economic progress and individual acquisitive behavior. Chase seems uneasily poised between the two styles, embracing something of an instrumentalist style when he issued his *Worrall* opinion, holding that there was no common law of crimes, but evincing the preinstrumentalist set of beliefs when he wrote his famous opinion in *Calder v. Bull*, which relied on the existence of more or less eternal supraconstitutional principles.

At the end of the eighteenth century, when Chase made his speech on preparation for salvation to Fries,[60] and when he lectured to his Baltimore grand jury,[61] he seemed to be telling them again about transcendent values in the law, and sounded very much like one of Horwitz's preinstrumental judges. Still, when he helped to formulate his impeachment trial defense, Chase returned to instrumentalist arguments, the same ones he had used in the *Worrall* case, to suggest that he could not be impeached on vague notions of inappropriate judicial behavior, suggesting thereby that there was no preexisting natural law standard which one could access to pass on judicial transgressions. Instead, his defense suggested that even in an impeachment proceeding it was necessary for the legislature first to formulate and then for the judicial tribunal to employ clear standards. Such clear standards, Chase and his lawyers argued, could only be found in the Constitution and criminal statutes, the only valid statements of American criminal law, none of which, Chase noted, had he transgressed.[62]

Chase's switching back and forth from instrumentalist to preinstrumentalist and then to instrumentalist again suggests either that styles of judicial reasoning were simply political tools (a not unreasonable assumption, given the highly politicized nature of the late 1790s) or the more fascinating conclusion that Chase unconsciously embraced both. When he believed that the fundamental interests of the Republic were at stake, he expressed his concern in the language of natural law, in the traditions of the common law as interpreted by Hale, Blackstone, and Burke. When he understood that what was at stake was the rights of an individual offender like Robert Worrall (or perhaps even like himself in the impeachment trial), or an important experiment in governmental policy, as was true in *Hylton v. United States*,[63] a case in which Chase broadly construed the taxation power of the federal government, as well as in *Ware v. Hylton*,[64] where Chase upheld the national government's power to overturn acts of state legislatures, he took a different view. In those cases of individual rights or experiments in state policy, Chase seems to have instrumentally viewed the law as primarily the preserve of the legislature, and as a means to implement a choice made on social policies which might differ in different republics.

John Marshall, too, could speak both a language that sounded like natural law, as he did in the *Dartmouth College* and *Fletcher v. Peck* cases, where he interpreted vested rights to the ownership of property as fundamental necessities in an ordered republic. More often than not, however, Marshall's jurisprudence was that of a flexible instrumentalist. The key example is *McCulloch v. Maryland*, when Marshall made the great statement that if the end in view by the federal legislature was legitimate under the Constitution then "all means which are plainly adapted to that end, which are not prohibited, but consist with the letter and spirit of the constitution, are constitutional," or his reminder that the judiciary must never forget that it is a "constitution" it is expounding, or, perhaps, expanding.[65]

By the end of Marshall's life, with the accession to the chief justiceship of Roger Taney, Marshall's instrumentalist, legislatively permissive style of constitutional adjudication had permeated even the vested-rights area. Taney in effect decided, in the *Charles River Bridge* case, that state legislatures could sport merrily with the contracts they entered into, so long as they justified it on "public interest" grounds. All of this activity of Marshall and Taney was justified on the grounds of promoting such higher public purposes, and particularly in the service of economic expansion, the principal legal aim of the nineteenth century. This particular means of economic expansion, the undercutting of previous state contracts or grants, seems not to have been favored by the framers, who had drafted the Constitution's "contract clause," at least in part, to prevent it.[66]

Beyond Instrumentalism: The Purpose of Republics

Taking what happened in the first half of the nineteenth century into account, as well as the jurisprudential synthesis as suggested here, it seems prudent that we take care that Horwitz's perceived instrumentalist/preinstrumentalist dichotomy not be allowed to mask a deeper division among jurists in the late eighteenth and early nineteenth centuries, a division over the very purposes of republics.

The Marshall who decided *McCulloch* and his successor, Taney, who wrote for the majority in *Charles River Bridge*, had both concluded that the purpose of the American Republic was to encourage the temporal economic growth of the country through the facilitation of competitive, atomistic enterprise.[67] In contrast, throughout most of his life, Samuel Chase believed that the purpose of a republic was to further the individual exercise of religion and moral service to God.

While economic expansion in the late nineteenth century became atomistic in form, and fostered what has been called "possessive individualism," Chase seems to have hoped for a more organic community, in which individuals were engaged ultimately not in competitive, but in cooperative, enterprise. Any other course, Chase and his fellow anti-Federalists of the late 1780s believed, would lead to the weakening of virtue, and accelerate what might in any event be the inevitable ravagement of the Republic by fortune.

The Federalists' Core Beliefs and the "Original Misunderstanding"

The Federalists who promoted the Constitution of 1787 may have been men of somewhat more faith who believed that commercial expansion's facilitation through individual enterprise would not lead to a decline in virtue, but even they seemed to have believed that they were erecting a structure which only the amendment process could alter. This seems to be Hamilton's claim in *Federalist* 78, that judges would merely be following the express dictates of the Constitution when they interpreted it, unless Hamilton was engaging in an exercise of the most blatant hypocrisy.[68]

It is argued here that Samuel Chase eventually came to abandon his early antifederalism to the extent of concluding that there were express and implied clear constitutional principles, which he could interpret and apply, in the interests of a strong central government, objectively as a federal judge. This view, however, is not the same as Marshall's view of a flexible constitution, as modern commentators have begun to explore. It has been repeatedly argued that the notion of a flexible constitution, if it differs from the "original understanding," is a notion that illegitimately usurps popular power.[69]

Probably Chase convinced himself, when he accepted appointment as a federal judge, that he could avoid the problem of illegitimacy by sticking in his interpretation to the clear principles he saw, and his steadfast religious faith helped him to give substance to these virtue-preserving constitutional principles. The eventual jurisprudence of Marshall and Taney employed much of the same language Chase used about popular sovereignty and about the process of interpretation. Once the concession was made to a flexible constitution, however, something different came to pass. There had been, we might say, "an original misunderstanding," and constitutional and private law became less concerned with the original republican ideals in America of civic virtue, and more concerned with a new ideal of individualistic commercialism.

When the country was expanding and Americans seemed untroubled by the idea of insular minorities suffering or destroyed through this expansionism, a constitutional and private law jurisprudence which facilitated economic expansionism had wide popular support. Its chief exponents, Marshall and eventually Taney, became great figures of the law, and they were said to be the progenitors of an American judicial tradition. Now that the idea of possessive individualism is more frequently seen to have unacceptable consequences for the community, now that the plight of insular minorities evokes more sympathy, now that society struggles more coherently toward a new organic conception of American republicanism,[70] perhaps it is time to recognize that there was such an original misunderstanding by Marshall and his followers about the meaning of the American Constitution.

Toward an Organic Jurisprudence

Without exactly raising the frequently discredited idea of turning back the clock,[71] perhaps there is still something to be gained by considering the values of the organic, religious, and ultimately fulfilling controversial jurisprudence of Samuel Chase. That jurisprudence, as discussed in chapter 3, was clear at the center, in its core of extraworldly doctrine and the linkage of liberty, morality, and religion. At the periphery, however, it was a mass of obfuscatory contradiction. Chase seems neither to have been exclusively an instrumentalist prepared to allow choice between a range of social policies nor a preinstrumentalist believer in constant fundamental principles.

Chase appeared at various points in his life to embrace the commercialism, but not the democracy, of Pennsylvania. To a certain extent, however, his essentially elitist conceptions of government, and his belief in the importance of the deference of most of the people toward their leaders, appeared to be similar to the notions of the Virginia aristocracy. Still, Chase clearly rejected the Virginians' anticommercialism and much of their "democratic" jurisprudence. That jurisprudence, insofar as it gave juries a large lawmaking role, did appear to have the effect of facilitating the hegemony of the slave-owning planter class, but Chase disapproved of the fact that it also allowed for conceptions such as the Virginia Syllogism, or more broadly "jury nullification," which seemed to Chase to render the law unbearably uncertain.

We may come to realize, however, that some of Chase's contradictions may be inevitable in the jurisprudence of any nation simultaneously committed, as our Republic is, to the maintenance of the rule of law as a restraint on arbitrary power, the protection of the rights of private property, and the ideal of popular sovereignty. Chase, like the greatest of the modern English conservatives, Edmund Burke, was not really very worried about theoretical inconsistencies in his jurisprudential scheme, and seems to have believed that he could reconcile these contradictory imperatives through his great religious faith, and through his articulation of constitutional principles he thought fundamental.

The effort took its toll on Chase, as such effort always does, but the engagement of the man, in the end, seems to have often and ultimately been a source of deep satisfaction for him. In a time when disengagement is what we most fear, when alienation has become a principal bugbear of academics, at least, Chase's example might still offer some inspiration.

The contemporary unpopularity of Chase's views, that is, his rejection by the Jeffersonians, causes most American historians sympathetic to the democratic ideas of the Jeffersonians to dismiss Chase as unimportant at least and brutal and insensitive at worst. To the ideological victors often belong the spoils of writing history. Because of the ideological victories of his enemies, Chase's views seem atavistic in contrast to those of some of his contemporaries, particularly the Jeffersonian Republicans, but also one Federalist in particular, John Marshall. As we have seen, Marshall learned from Chase and borrowed some of his judicial perspectives, but was able to synthesize the views of Chase and Chase's antagonists. Marshall thus moved the jurisprudential dialectic into a phase from which it only now may be emerging.

Over one hundred and fifty years ago, in his wildly adulatory *Biography of the Signers of the Declaration of Independence*, John Sanderson wrote that Samuel Chase "was one of the most extraordinary men of his age, and exerted perhaps as potent and extensive influence over the minds of others, as any one of the distinguished personages who assisted in the establishment of this great and growing empire."[72] Of Chase, Sanderson concluded that he "was gifted with 'a soul of fire.' "[73] Wild adulation among legal historians is now reserved for "progressive" and creative liberal nationalists like John Marshall or Earl Warren. Perhaps as we come to realize the limits of their atomistic, impersonal, secular, and individualistic federal jurisprudence, we might better try to rekindle among us the fire of the soul of Samuel Chase.

10

Conclusion:
The Machiavellian Moment of
Federalism

The Great Men before Agamemnon

According to the conventional wisdom among American historians, until John Marshall graced the United States Supreme Court, it was of decidedly secondary institutional importance in America. For the most part, scholars continue to believe that the earliest Supreme Court justices either bordered on the incompetent or were simply marking time in their professional careers until something better came along.[1] Occasionally we have been reminded that "there were great men before Agamemnon"[2] or that the justices of the Supreme Court before Marshall performed an important task as "Republican Schoolmasters."[3] Still, the accomplishments of the early Supreme Court were advanced almost in mitigation, as if it were faintly miraculous that anything good occurred in the barbaric period before the Great Chief. Nevertheless, an examination of the Court's early years such as that in which we have been engaged here demonstrates that most of the characteristics of the Court's institutional role that Marshall and his colleagues later developed were initially articulated by the earliest Supreme Court justices, well before Marshall's appointment. Much of this articulation, however, took place when the Supreme Court justices rode circuits and delivered opinions or charges in the lower federal courts.

For example, in the trial of James Thomson Callender for seditious libel—while John Marshall sat in the audience, absorbing the lesson for later use—Justice Samuel Chase eloquently elaborated the doctrine that the national judiciary had the exclusive tasks of determining the constitutionality of congressional legislation, and invalidating any acts which failed to conform with that national charter.[4] It might even be said that what Chase did in *Callender* required much more political courage, or political daring, than Marshall's later statement of the doctrine of judicial review in *Marbury v. Madison*,[5] because Chase was performing before a hostile audience in Virginia and before lawyers committed to the proposition that the jury, not the bench, ought to determine the constitutionality of legislation.[6] Indeed, part of the effect of Chase's decision in *Callender* was that the House of Representatives brought impeachment charges against Chase. In contrast, Marshall's decision in *Marbury*, although it reminded the Jefferson administration of the ultimate power of the Supreme Court, actually had no immediate effect. Similarly, in the lower federal court decision *Van Horn's Lessee v. Dorrance*,[7] Justice Paterson established the sanctity or ascendancy of vested property interests under the federal Constitution in a manner which clearly anticipated Marshall's famous opinion in *Fletcher v. Peck*.[8]

Why then, does Marshall still receive virtually all the credit for creating an independent and significant federal judiciary? As hinted in chapter 9, the deepest cause of American legal scholars' failure to appreciate the significance and accomplishments of the pre-Marshall justices may have been these scholars' need to use John Marshall's supposed greatness to legitimize United States Supreme Court actions since the "Constitutional Revolution" of 1937. "Liberal" court critics since the early 1920s and 1930s had argued that the Supreme Court's job was to accommodate the Constitution to the changing economic and social needs of the country.[9] It seems more than coincidental that at about the time the courts were frustrating implementation of New Deal legislation, scholars began lavishly to praise John Marshall for his famous decisions.

They declared that decisions such as *McCulloch v. Maryland*[10] and *Gibbons v. Ogden*[11] expansively interpreted the powers of the national government to regulate and promote the economy.[12] Similarly, when liberal academics praised the Warren Court's expansive interpretation of the Bill of Rights and the Fourteenth Amendment to protect the victims of educational, political, and economic discrimination,[13] more volumes appeared apotheosizing Marshall.[14]

Using Marshall to legitimize recent court decisions is a striking instance of a legal phenomenon noted by J. G. A. Pocock, a scholar of early modern English and American politics and law. He explained how both the Royalist and Parliamentary parties in the seventeenth century sought to implement their ideas about the appropriate allocation of power in England by referring to an "Ancient Constitution" which had supposedly existed from time immemorial.[15] The Royalists thought that they could find in the Ancient Constitution an expansive ambit for the king's prerogative. The advocates of Parliament were equally certain they could find prescriptive rights to circumscribe the king. These arguments became unsatisfactory when it became widely known that English scholars had discovered a feudal system with concrete social and political arrangements which belied the existence of both such "Ancient Constitutions."[16]

Legal historians have recently begun to make discoveries in American history which threaten similarly cherished assumptions. This book has attempted to explore some of their ramifications with respect to the early American judiciary. Like seventeenth-century English scholars, lawyers, and politicians, we must now recognize the need to examine our apotheosis of particular American legal historical actors and theories, and our attempts to legitimize present policies through reference to an imagined stable past.

Since the 1959 publication of Caroline Robbins's seminal *The Eighteenth-Century Commonwealthman* and the 1968 publication of Bernard Bailyn's *The Ideological Origins of the American Revolution*, American historians have paid more attention to the influence in early American life of preliberal classical ideas about the nature of men in a political system. The ideology that evolved from an application of these classical ideas in English radical thought in the seventeenth century is now understood to have become the dominant "republican" ideology of civic virtue in eighteenth-century America. Described by English contemporaries and American historians in varying manners, these notions included "court" and "country" ideologies, as well as their American amalgams and variants, such as "republicanism" or "federalism."[17] They continued to play a prominent part in influencing events in America well into the nineteenth century.[18] Similarly, scholars are beginning to better understand that American ideas about the young Republic's special religious significance influenced and shaped the activities of prominent Americans.[19]

With the increased understanding of the psychological, comparative, religious, and ideological strains in the American revolutionary and early national periods has come an appreciation that the late eighteenth century in America was not dominated simply by Lockean rationalism or liberalism of the type espoused by John Marshall and his successors. Instead, ancient and modern political writers' ideas and theories about the political development of societies exerted a profound effect on Americans of the revolutionary generation. What the ancient and modern theorists taught Americans about the inevitable pattern of historical change, given certain widely shared assumptions about the nature of man in society, determined the nature of American politics and law in the late eighteenth century. The recent scholarship exploring this ideology in early America has yet to be extensively applied to legal thought in the early Republic,[20] and this study has accordingly undertaken such an application, in the course of questioning the conventional wisdom regarding the pre-Marshall Court.

Those who seek to relegate the pre-Marshall Court to obscurity usually argue that the Court was so mired in partisan politics that it could not engage in independent and objective action. In the course of telling the story of Chase and his fellows, however, and in the course of explaining the accomplishments of the earliest federal judges, it is argued here that the assumption that Associate Justice Samuel Chase and his Federalist fellows were inferior jurists because they were "zealous partisans" is open to question.

By reexamining the issue of partisanship in Chase's case, the effort here has been to show that our contemporary ideas about judicial objectivity cannot serve as useful standards for evaluating the jurisprudence of the late eighteenth century. The argument advanced here is beginning, at last, slowly to percolate within the community of American legal scholars.[21] It is, simply stated, that what most contemporary American historians, in the far too prevalent presentist mode of thought,[22] are prone to dismiss as judicial partisanship was an attempt at a creative and objective form of jurisprudence, based solidly in Anglo-American traditions. To put this in the currently popular Kuhnian vernacular,[23] Samuel Chase and his less flamboyant judicial colleagues did not believe that their jurisprudence was a product of partisan politics[24] because their jurisprudential "paradigms" convinced them that their interpretation of the law was objective, and not manipulation for factional political ends.

This judicial paradigm, unlike the paradigm of "liberalism" which eventually prevailed in American law, incorporated a value system which did not permit multiple ends to be sought legitimately through political discourse. For Chase and his colleagues, only one end—achieving what is once again being called "republican" or "civic" virtue—was a legitimate end of government or of law. Moreover, because government and law had only one legitimate end, there was no need to separate law from politics. At the most fundamental levels, at least as applied to the early federal judges, the concept of a partisan use of law simply made no sense.[25]

The idea of the influence of republicanism on early American politics has now become a commonplace among historians of the early Republic, but much work still remains to be done in order to explain what political, moral, and religious ideas lay concealed within the loosely used word "republican."[26] A study of Samuel Chase's jurisprudence is useful in this endeavor, because for Samuel Chase it was much more important that America adopt correct political, moral, and religious principles than it was that it be classifiable, strictly speaking, as a republic.

Law, Politics, and Morality

Our consideration of the application of theories of jurisprudence in America in the late eighteenth and early nineteenth century leads to the conclusion that Samuel Chase was caught in the antinomies and paradoxes of early American republican theory. Like his contemporaries, the Jeffersonians, he believed in the people as the only legitimate source of sovereignty in America, but like his ultimate political allies, the Hamiltonian and the Adams Federalists, he had grave doubts about the American people's capacity for the possession of the virtue necessary to preserve a republic. Like the Federalists, he saw the erection of a firm commercial and financial structure as a safeguard against internal political weakness, but like the Republicans, he probably understood that the pursuit of individual gain at the expense of community solidarity could lead to chaos. In the early 1800s Chase thought that the country was on the brink of such chaos, as did the other high Federalists, and he seemed prepared to jettison most democratic principles in order to preserve the existence of the Republic and the law on which he believed that Republic depended. Jefferson, as we have seen,[27] was prepared to dispense with law to preserve democracy, but Chase preferred the rule of law over the rule of the mob.

After Chase's defense in his impeachment trial was successful, however, and following personal financial success when he was finally paid for his negotiation for the payment of English monies owed to Maryland, he seems to have achieved a kind of personal peace with the world. Unlike Adams or Jefferson in their last years, Chase appears not to have been alienated by an America transforming itself through the machinations of commerce and finance.[28] He seems to have understood that commerce itself was a calling not without honor, and that professions in finance presented a means for men of humble birth with great talents to rise to a station in which they could best contribute to the leadership of their society.[29] Because Chase had used the commercial route to gain his own position, however, he may not have fully understood that the ideology of commerce and the pursuit of financial success could undermine his most cherished foundation of society, the belief in the primacy of religion and morality.

Chase's own jurisprudence was permeated with notions of equity, and his opinions presupposed the existence even of supraconstitutional principles of divinely inspired right. Chase's morality was such that it dictated a public infusion of religious principles, and an ethical content to legal rules. For him there was no separation between the *is* and the *ought* of the law. Law *was* morality.

As American legal theorists began seriously to work through the implications of a market system, however, this primacy of morals was lost to American law, and it became more and more common for contemporary Mansfieldian English principles of commercial law to win ascendancy in America.[30] This strain of jurisprudence gave primacy to certainty in commercial dealing, and limited the reach of equitable forces, for example, in the discretion of juries to reevaluate commercial transactions. Chase appears to have believed that "there could be no liberty without morality," but American conceptions of liberty were beginning to articulate a notion that it was the job of the law to liberate the individual from the moral dictates of the community.[31] When this transformation of American law was complete, the foundation was laid for the modern American industrial and commercial economy, but the early American spirit of community, and the public morality of which Chase was an exponent, had been lost.

What seems to have happened, in short, is that following the failure of excessively democratic state legislatures to promote commercial certainty in the 1780s and 1790s, the conservative aspects of Chase and his contemporaries, for example, the deferential judicial politics which Chase promoted, and which had been inspired through the example of English judges, eventually established ascendance in American law. The reaction to "democratic" excesses eventually led to an abandonment of the essentially popular or "country" notion that the legal system ought to maintain and reflect the equitable sense, the moral aspirations of the people. Contrary to the thought of Chase, however, along with this rise of deferential commercial law jurisprudence came the ascendance of the notion that there ought to be a radical separation between the law and politics.[32]

Chase's wish to lay under the law a firm moral foundation, and to ensure that that foundation also supported politics, is thus an impressive contrast to the legacy of John Marshall. The record shows that Chase had far more personal courage, or at least was an individual who flinched from public battle much less, than Marshall. Marshall seems to have been willing, at the crucial moment, to jettison the Supreme Court's role as the ultimate arbiter of constitutional law; he sidestepped most of the severe controversy over the constitutionality of the Judiciary Act of 1802, and seems to have been quite careful, at least until the very end of his career, only to make statements of such judicial supremacy when their application did not actually conflict with the policies of the current administration. In a sense, of course, Marshall was making sure that constitutional law took politics into account, and safely skirted it, but the doctrine which he fathered of "avoiding political questions" hypocritically masked the inevitable connection of the law with politics.

Chase offered an alternative vision of the Court and politics. Chase did not see the need for the Court to avoid difficult political questions. In his early Supreme Court opinions he did show a tendency to defer to the more popular branch, the legislature,[33] but in the political crisis of the late 1790s and early 1800s he seems to have stopped that deference. He appears to have then concluded that it was the job of the federal judges to instruct the legislatures and juries on the finer points of politics, and to explain how there was a necessary connection between political and religious morality, between the preservation of certain governmental forms and the maintenance of morality; between the realities of the condition of human weakness and the wise principles of the federal Constitution, especially the guarantees of independence of the judiciary. Chase was restrained by Marshall, by Peters, and probably by others of his colleagues, but he did not shrink from a fight, and, alone among Supreme Court justices, he wanted to render a decision clearly declaring what he took to be the usurpations of the Jeffersonians unconstitutional.

Contemporary American constitutional law scholarship has now virtually unanimously come to acknowledge that law *is* politics,[34] and the most advanced thinking is beginning to search for a firm basis for declaring that there ought to be some objective morality to serve as a basis for such politics.[35] So far, however, the current debate over constitutional and legal morality has too often failed to acknowledge that a similar battle over the nature of law took place here two centuries ago. Surely, if we now need to extricate ourselves from a dilemma, it is useful to study how we originally plunged ourselves into it.

The writing of individual judicial biography in this country has tended toward hagiography, but it is occasionally understood that the multiple forces which shape an individual's jurisprudence could bear study for what they might contribute to our understanding of the true complexity and subtlety of judicial behavior.[36] Such an understanding, we have seen, can be furthered by examining the context in which Samuel Chase judged. An appreciation of the complexity and multileveled nature of early American federal jurisprudence is revealed when it is realized that one judge could decide both *Calder v. Bull*, a case that restated the notion of supraconstitutional principles of law, and *United States v. Worrall*, a case which dismissed the possibility of a federal common law of crimes.

The lesson to be learned about Chase's brand of early American jurisprudence is that there was no core conception of American law as "instrumental" or "noninstrumental," but rather that jurisprudence continually reflected coexisting and antagonistic conceptions underlying the law, and that those conceptions were themselves based on political, social, or religious premises. It would appear, then, that the meaning of Chase's jurisprudence is that historians of the early American legal system cannot rest with conclusions about hermetically sealed conceptions of the nature of the law, but must realize that such an inquiry leads inevitably to an examination of conceptions of the nature of man's relationship to his God and to his fellow citizens in the polity.

Partisanship and Ideology: Chase v. Marshall

Such a realization ought to result, at the very least, in an abandonment of the still prevalent notion that Chase and his fellows on the pre-Marshall Court were somehow unique and inappropriate because they were judicial "partisans." Even many of those who understand that the characteristic mode of jurisprudence from colonial days through the ascendance of the Jeffersonian Republicans was to integrate law with politics seem to cling to the belief that with John Marshall, suddenly, the law became less political, and Republicans were able to join Federalists on the bench in an orgy or an apotheosis of objective jurisprudence. For example, reviewing a recent work on the Supreme Court, Francis N. Stites, the author of a fine short biography of John Marshall,[37] notes with approval what he calls the author's conclusion that there was a

> sharp contrast between this diminished political role for the Court [in the early nineteenth century] and the patterns of the 1790's. The earlier Court . . . had simply adhered to a colonial tradition in which judicial activity was in many respects merely the continuation of political controversy by other methods. Nonpartisan judicial behavior was the exception. Even the Republicans in 1801 were concerned less about partisan behavior than anti-administration partisanship. The ensuing struggle over the limits and extent of judicial power was really a struggle to separate the traditional union of law and politics. Moderates in all camps found room for adjustment, and Marshall's knowledge of Republicans gave him "a better perspective and greater faith in their integrity, if not their politics" [citation omitted]. This thesis certainly helps explain the growing impartiality of the Court as new Republican justices replaced old traditional partisans like Chase.[38]

What actually happened, as we now are beginning more clearly to understand,[39] is that both the Marshall and the pre-Marshall Courts adhered to ideologies that can equally well be described, as ultimately can all ideologies, as either attempts to create objectively valid systems of belief, or as "partisan."

If Samuel Chase is typical, in accordance with the case that has been made in this book, and there are increasing signs that he was,[40] the pre-Marshall Court adhered to an ideology where it was the duty of judges explicitly to call the citizenry or the legislature to account when there was a failure on the part of the people to adhere to what these judges believed to be the wisest American republican norms of political deference to established authority. These norms included ancient English practices such as the limitation of the franchise to those with substantial property interests, or more recently established normative principles, such as the maintenance of the judiciary's independence.[41]

The Marshall Court adhered to an ideology that surrendered overt supervision of some "political" acts of redistribution, including the democratization of the franchise, but eventually drew the line at some infringements of vested rights, particularly those ostensibly guaranteed by the contracts clause.

One convenient explanation for the move to a more apparently apolitical constitutional jurisprudence is John Marshall's fear that any power in the judiciary would be taken away if it too often interfered with the legislature.[42] There is surely some truth to this, but there is somewhat more to be said. A more subtle development of the explanation is that Marshall understood that in an expansionist, individualist economy of the type that he could see beginning in America, it was only necessary to protect individualistic rights such as those of property and contract. It seems likely that the extremely pragmatic Marshall came to believe that it was no longer required, and, indeed, counterproductive, to enforce an essentially precommercial, communitarian deferential standard of political values.[43]

The point of the comparison between Marshall and Chase, then, is that it seems wrong simply to view Samuel Chase as an "old traditional partisan."[44] He was old and traditional, but the tradition he represented was organic, statist, nonindividualistic, and deeply religious, a tradition or an ideology rather different from that represented by John Marshall. More, while Chase understood that the country had come to be divided into two ideological camps, as he noted in the *Cooper* case, it is doubtful that Chase believed that he, himself, was partisan. Chase believed that the party he truly represented was, in Cooper's grand Enlightenment phrase, "the party of humanity." Chase's religiously-inspired republican convictions led him firmly to believe that if his objectively sensible views did not prevail, the Republic was doomed to collapse for lack of the citizenry's virtue.

What Marshall might have been able to see better than Chase was that Chase's ideas about the importance of commerce could be cut loose from their moorings in a collectivist republican ideology of virtue, and be made to serve an emerging American republican ideal of acquisitive individualism.[45] For this ideology to win judicial ascendance, however, it was necessary for the constitutional system of adjudication to take on the character of an objective market-enforcement mechanism, so that the differences in the distribution of wealth and talent which an expanding economy of acquisitive individualism produced or reinforced would seem natural and immutable. This was what Marshall and his contemporaries accomplished, and only recently has the entire structure he and his nineteenth-century colleagues erected been subjected to the scrutiny suggested by viewing it simply as one in a number of possible judicial ideologies.[46]

If, as suggested here, Chase represented an authentic American strand of jurisprudence which had some claim to objectivity, why then have so many historians tended so flippantly to dismiss him as a partisan, and failed to understand the subtleties of his thinking and the profoundly religious, almost late medieval, character of his jurisprudence?[47] Much of our neglect of Chase seems to have come from an obsession with the superficial oddities of the man, his overbearing nature with lawyers and with juries, his apparently distasteful bombastic style, his unwillingness to suffer fools, and his failure late in life to indulge in the kind of Jeffersonian demagoguery that brought him into prominence initially.[48]

Where Chase's attempts to implement his version of traditional jurisprudence clashed with other traditions, for example, the practices of jury discretion in Virginia and Pennsylvania, he seems to have been doubly damned by history. His views about the appropriate circumscription of juries were eventually to prevail because the market demanded it. Nevertheless, Chase gets none of the credit for the development because he was trying to implement judicial certainty in the service of a now discredited deferential politics which the new market-oriented jurisprudence ostensibly disclaimed.

Chase thought that such deference was essential because he feared that the anarchy that he believed had become manifest in Europe could easily be transplanted to America. In retrospect Chase's attitude seems fantastic and paranoid, but at the time, with French agents publicly seeking to recruit Americans to their cause and with whole counties in armed rebellion, it may have been a most reasonable reaction. More important, perhaps there is something to be said for the idea that a legal system which enforces only deference to those who accumulate wealth and power through the market will be enforcing, on one level, a kind of amoral anarchy and chaos.

The Legacy of the Eighteenth Century

Pushing the analysis to a somewhat different level, Chase's career not only reveals some important heuristic contrasts with the aims and ideology of his fellow judges, it also underscores some of the complexities and contrasts which have remained as the legacy of the late eighteenth century in American life. Chase was a man of the people, or at least of the petty bourgeoisie, but he never lost his admiration for what an enlightened aristocracy could do to promote the virtue of the citizenry. In Chase's early career his hostility to privilege often won out over his sense of the possibilities for aristocratic restraints, but by the end of his days he seems to have been amused by this youthful folly. Like most Americans of his generation and since, however, he believed that whatever enlightened leadership an American aristocracy might provide, it could not be based on hereditary position. Accordingly, like his fellow Federalist Hamilton and like his successor, John Marshall, Chase probably sought to use the developing commercial market as a means of creating and maintaining a class of wise leaders. This effort may have led him, as it has led so many since, to rationalize his desire for personal acquisition and financial power by maintaining that he was merely putting himself in a position to be most useful to his fellows. He would, as we have come to say, do good by doing well.

After two centuries of living with an American market system, it is now increasingly common to recognize that a competitive market divides us from each other, even if it furnishes a new class of leaders. As indicated here several times, there was a strain in English "country" politics, articulated most forcefully by Bolingbroke and embraced in America by Jefferson, Randolph, and Taylor,[49] that commerce would lead inevitably not to enlightened leadership but to corruption. This was a message that seems to have been warmly embraced by members of the eighteenth-century American and English landed gentry who could use it as a bulwark to buttress the hegemony of their own ideology, which stressed the primacy of landed wealth. For those like Samuel Chase and Alexander Hamilton who had not been impressed by the quality of leadership provided by the American landed gentry, who had not been born to that class, and who saw commerce as the route to personal and community rewards, this aspect of Bolingbrokian politics was soon forgotten.

Nevertheless, Chase's simultaneous ability to engage in what appear to be monstrously self-serving pecuniary adventures, and still believe he was serving his fellow man, calls for a deeper explanation than the mere rejection of a hereditary landed aristocracy. In Chase's case the deepest underlying cause of his behavior may well have been his deep and abiding religious conviction that whatever he did sprung from the wishes of a benevolent and omnipotent God.

Because we in late twentieth-century America usually profess ourselves to be a secular and rational society, those of us who study the workings of that society tend too frequently to assume secular and rational explanations for historical and contemporary phenomena. We tend too often to forget that there was, and continues to be, a strong undercurrent of faith and mysticism in America. Since Max Weber and R. H. Tawney, it has been a commonplace to notice the coincidence between industrial capitalism and Protestantism, but the latter must not be dismissed because of its coincidence with the former. The source of much of Chase's virtually superhuman tenacity, his willingness to risk life and limb in a revolutionary adventure in his early life, and his willingness to suffer personal scorn and humiliation, to endure long absences from his beloved family, and even subject himself to grave physical danger to preserve the rule of law,[50] was his solace in his belief that he had a role to perform in this world for which he would be rewarded in the next.

One can, as Marx did, dismiss religion as the opiate of the masses, but its primary force in American society may be as such a solace and stimulant for the elite. Any attempt to furnish an alternative ideology to classical market-oriented liberalism must therefore recognize the paradox of the power of religion in an ostensibly secular society, and there are real signs that this is happening.[51] The life of Samuel Chase is a case study in the manner in which spiritual faith can buttress and shape secular behavior.

The Limits of Chase's Conservative Jurisprudence

There are limits to the usefulness for human beings of secularization and rationalization, or at least this was the belief of Chase and his contemporaries. With Burke, Chase seems to have understood that to abandon traditional religion in order to find deeper truth in abstract theories such as "the rights of man" was a prescription for anarchy at best and for tyranny at worst. Chase's means of avoiding these undesirables, late in life, was to seek to forge an American constitutional jurisprudence which assumed that men needed the restraints of judicial institutions to limit their discretion, and particularly the discretion of those without the ownership of sufficient property which Chase, with Blackstone, believed necessary to guarantee that the actions of the citizen would correlate with the needs of the community.[52]

Chase never spelled out exactly how ownership of property would lead to altruistic acts, however, nor could he without exposing that this conception was borrowed from a time when the characteristic wealth, land, dictated the organization of the community. Chase seems to have failed to recognize that the change from landed wealth to commercial pursuits as major concerns of the law might well have political and moral implications inconsistent with the deferential legal doctrines of the eighteenth century which he sought to embrace. Small wonder that when, at least on the eastern seaboard, commercial, entrepreneurial, and manufacturing interests tended to preoccupy the lawyers and judges, they were able to turn Chase's theories about restraining jury discretion and curbing democratic excesses into an effective framework for an atomistic, secular society that he would never have recognized or approved of.

One of the tragedies, or at least the ironies, of legal and all human actors, as recent scholarship has stressed, is that the presumptions of youth, when manifested in later life, have consequences and implications that the actors themselves cannot understand.[53]

To a certain extent, then, Chase's story is that of any man or woman. There are limits to the human condition. These limits must be faced, and where reason fails to explain, mysticism will be resorted to because it is the nature of man, even legal man, to search for the repose and certainty mysticism and religion provide, even if "certainty is an illusion, and repose is not the destiny of man."[54] The nature of this search, and the accommodation one is able to make between the urge to fashion rationalist theories and the need for mystical solace, Chase's career teaches us, varies over time.

Even Chase, when young, seems to have embraced democracy as an ultimate principle, and to have borrowed, temporarily, a Wilkite or Paineite fervor for emancipation from corrupt aristocratic leadership in late colonial Maryland. With more experience, however, and with several reversals of personal fortune, Chase became more circumspect and seems to have lost faith in the power of democracy to achieve good ends, even while his faith in the power of God to dictate just solutions increased. There is an inevitable tension in society between the rationalists and the rationalist theoreticians, like John Locke on one side, and the traditionalists and the traditionalist theoreticians, like Burke or Matthew Hale on the other. Chase seems to be a classic example of the appeal of the former in youth and the reassurance provided by the latter in maturity.[55]

Revising the History of the Federalists, Inspired by J. G. A. Pocock

The study of individuals such as Samuel Chase, and of how their views altered over time, used to be the traditional occupation of biography. In recent years, this sort of literature has been frequently discredited as an elitist, and all but irrelevant, style of writing history.[56] Nevertheless, it does seem that only by this close scrutiny of an individual and his or her views as they evolve over time can we grasp the richness of individual lives and the effect of context on personality. Such scrutiny, as Gerald Stourzh has shown in his biography of Alexander Hamilton[57] and as Linda Kerber has demonstrated in her work on several individual Federalists,[58] can save us from the vulgar neo-Jeffersonian error of believing that the Federalists were simply power-mad "monarchists" or "aristocrats," with utter contempt for the common people and with thoroughly avaricious desires for self-aggrandizement. Instead, we can come to understand that at least some of the Federalists shared with the young Jefferson an organic conception of the state with a clearly defined social hierarchy, and an understanding that individuals owed a duty to their society greater than that they owed to themselves.

The sort of close study of the parameters of an individual's thought that I have offered here seems to be becoming more frequent, and is resulting in a new melding of the disciplines of biography, political science, and intellectual history. The principal master of this new discipline is J. G. A. Pocock, and what he achieved in his *The Ancient Constitution and the Feudal Law* has served as a model for this study of Chase. Pocock's study climaxed in an interpretation of the thought of James Harrington, who represented for Pocock a great leap of the imagination in late Renaissance England.

When Pocock analyzes the achievement of Harrington's *Oceana*,[59] Pocock says that it was Harrington's great feat of historical scholarship to break away from the brilliant Italian Renaissance political theoretician Machiavelli, whose work had originally inspired Harrington. For Machiavelli, Pocock explains, historical developments were intimately involved with the wheel of fortune and with inevitable consequences of inescapable human frailties. Machiavelli could find no satisfactory means of explaining historical developments as a result of temporal causes, perhaps because, like the ancient Greek political theoreticians who served as his masters, he lived in a city-state, where the cultural institutions were somewhat similar to those of the ancients.

Machiavelli thus simply adopted the classic Aristotelian notion of the inevitable cycle of change and decay of governmental institutions. Harrington, however, impressed by the force exerted by the ownership of land in the more rural society of England, moved issues of land ownership to the center of his political theory, and explained the nature of change in his society and legal system, and its difficulties, as a result of the maldistribution of land in late imperial Rome and in contemporary England.

Machiavelli, according to Pocock, could see that temporal events were cyclical, and that political rule moved from the one to the few to the many, but he offered no explanation for why the process should take place, and no way to break out of the inevitable circle of repetition and decay, other than the temporary fortuitous manifestation of an extraordinary quantity of virtue in particular peoples during particular eras. For Harrington, though, it became possible to theorize that a society could break out of this inevitable cycle by an equitable distribution of land. Such a distribution, Harrington believed, could make possible a stable form of republicanism, which Machiavelli had apparently not been able to guarantee in his theories.

In his later work Pocock has continued to treat this problem of "breaking out of the circle of decay," and has suggested that it became not only a problem in seventeenth-century English politics, but was also the central problem of late eighteenth-century American republicanism.[60] Pocock calls the confrontation of such a problem a "Machiavellian moment," to evoke Machiavelli's recognition of the problem of temporal permanence of republics.

Recapitulation

I have tried to suggest that the problem of breaking the cycle of Republican corruption and decay troubled Chase and his Jeffersonian antagonists, and thus this entire essay might also been called "A Machiavellian Moment in American Law." Chase and the Jeffersonians articulated, however, some quite different theories for dealing with the problem. The late Federalist thesis, which maintained the necessity for a hierarchical distribution of commercial and political power to counter people's inherent tendency to neglect their virtue, contrasted dramatically with the contemporary Jeffersonian antithesis, which postulated the ability of the people (or at least the white Virginians) to maintain the virtue necessary for a republic if a maximum of democracy and a minimum of luxury, commerce, and hierarchy existed in the country.

To the surprise of both camps, as indicated by the poignant correspondence in the third decade of the nineteenth century between Adams and Jefferson, the late eighteenth-century philosophies were replaced by a synthesis that abandoned the organic concept of the virtue of the people, and replaced it with an atomistic market model of individualistic economics. The synthesis embraced the centrality of commerce and manufacturing from the Federalists, but sought also to achieve the democracy of the Jeffersonian Pennsylvanians and Virginians, not only by the wide distribution of land, but also through economic development which offered what most believed to be the greatest promise of social mobility.

In this manner the Jacksonian entrepreneurs, the heirs of both the Federalists and the Jeffersonians, successfully added individual wealth maximization to the already existing American core legal values of the restraint of arbitrary power and the promotion of popular sovereignty. Harrington's insight about how to preserve a republic had been transformed, and participation in a market economy through agriculture, commerce, and manufacturing was to furnish the stability Harrington had sought simply through the equitable distribution of land. This has come to seem natural and inevitable to us because of the prevalence of evolutionary theories of law on the left and right. Perhaps the seeming naturalness of these prevailing economic theories has obscured for too long the actual nature of what the late nineteenth century pre-Marshall justices were up to.

If we restate the argument of thesis, antithesis, and synthesis in early American jurisprudence, we can then use this restatement to summarize how late eighteenth-century judicial practice differed from what was to come, and how the theories of recent American legal historians might be modified in light of a closer examination of Chase.

Pursuant to the organic, Christian, conservative jurisprudence of Samuel Chase, influenced probably by the example of contemporary England and by what he saw happening in Pennsylvania and Virginia, the jury, for example, would be expected to follow the law laid down by the judge; pursuant to its antithesis, which flourished in Virginia and occasionally in Pennsylvania—the oppositionist jurisprudence of Col. Taylor, John Randolph, and defendants' counsel at the *Fries* and *Callender* trials—the content of the law itself was subject to jury revision at each trial.

The synthesis of these two strands of jurisprudence was produced in the work of early nineteenth-century thinkers such as John Marshall, Theodore Sedgwick,[61] or, perhaps most interestingly and provocatively, by the later Samuel Chase himself, in a case he decided some time after the impeachment trial, when he declared that in America—implying that it was different in England—the judge had as his simple task the declaration of the law as it had been given to him in a written constitution or statute.[62] In this new victorious synthetic jurisprudence, which manifested itself as a governing force in the procedure not only of criminal, but also of civil, trials, the jury lost the right (though not the power) to make the law, but the judge gave up the right to declare his view on the application of the evidence to the law.[63]

Probably this new allocation of responsibilities came to be recognized as consonant with the new role the law was required to play in an economy more interested in the promotion of commerce and manufacturing than in the stability of a deferential land-based society. The character of the mid-eighteenth century organic Anglo-American polity, which could paradoxically support both jury discretion on the law in Virginia and judicial commentary on the evidence in England, gave way, in all of America, to an individualistic, atomistic, and market-oriented model.

To some extent then, the Federalists like Hamilton and Chase prevailed in their passion for commerce, and the anticommercialists like Jefferson, Randolph, and Taylor lost, but Hamilton and Chase, in effect, were made to surrender their aim to preserve deferential politics. This surrender includes, too, the eclipse of some of the views expressed by Jefferson in his *Notes on Virginia*, most particularly the idea that people's happiness does not depend on social mobility. Economic progress and social mobility became the culture's recognized goals, and the law was changed to accommodate them. American culture (and, we might add, the legal system) no longer gives primary deference to virtue in the individual citizen in the service of an organic republic, instead deference is more frequently granted to the possessors of economic power in the market.

Because our Supreme Court works virtually exclusively at an appellate level, and because Supreme Court justices no longer are required to ride circuit, we have perhaps not been inclined to consider how different jurisprudential practice was in the late eighteenth century when the highest judges in the land were demonstrating their jurisprudence in the trial courts. Samuel Chase worked at a time when the ideology of the Supreme Court justices had a more direct impact on the lower courts, and when his ideology could be seen to clash fundamentally with that of the lawyers who appeared before him. These ideological clashes, revealed in the jury charges and in the other aspects of trial practice, are the most important developments in jurisprudence in the late eighteenth century, and were, in effect, the battles which forged modern American jurisprudence. Because our legal historians are not familiar with this earlier style of judicial behavior we have tended to dismiss the pre-Marshall Court, but perhaps the early American judges can now more clearly be seen for what they were, and for what they did.

In the course of the matters that have been here presented, it has been observed that early American judicial practice did not have as its ideal the ideologically neutral, remote, or objective judge. This has not been entirely concealed from us, and previous scholars have noted that the earliest federal judges understood their task as that of "Republican schoolmasters."[64] What needs to be emphasized more than it has been in the past, however, is the variety within "Old Republican" theory, and how partisans of various strains of old republicanism, Federalists and Jeffersonians, could conceive the judicial task differently, and yet both believe that they were acting objectively.

Nevertheless, it also seems important to stress that while the "Old Republicans" could conclude that they were acting objectively, it is probably erroneous to suggest that their behavior, and that of those who followed them, results from the emergence of an "instrumental" theory of common law judging. What the behavior of Chase and his fellows demonstrates, rather, is that the contrast between an oracular and an instrumental theory of judging, once made much of by Professor Horwitz,[65] is essentially illusory.

There may really be no dichotomy between the two views, or at least it may be usual for the same judge to implement aspects of both instrumental and preinstrumental jurisprudence. It may be more correct to suggest that all through American legal history, judges have tried to explain that they were "applying" (not really "finding") the law, rather than making it, yet judges have felt constrained to acknowledge that there is some limited discretion in their role.[66]

Chase knew that there was some uncertainty in the process, just as all human existence is uncertain—he trusted in God and his own abilities to discover and apply the correct law. He did believe that the ultimate source of this law was God, not man, but he appears to have recognized that it was the job of men, legislators, and judges to declare and implement God's will, and that this gave them a certain freedom to do so. It somewhat oversimplifies to suggest, as Horwitz does, that what happened was a transition from a dominant natural law theory to a will theory of law, although there may have been some aspects of jurisprudential change which do suggest such an analysis.

In the late eighteenth and early nineteenth century in America, then, what occurred was not primarily a major rethinking of the sources of law, as Horwitz's theory suggests, although this may indeed have happened. More important perhaps was the dialectical struggle which resulted in an altered sense of the law's job in the community. The task of jurisprudence changed from that of maintaining a land-based hierarchy, to that of creating a market favorable to commercial exchange and social mobility. This is not the place to elaborate the details, most of which have been brilliantly spelled out by Horwitz, William Nelson, Maxwell Bloomfield, Kent Newmyer, and others, but it appears that lawyers and judges grew to conclude that for the economically free market to govern, the law needed a certain flexibility that it had not possessed in prerevolutionary America, although Mansfield's work in England had already brought such a commercially viable jurisprudence to Britain. The transition, in America at least, was thus not from natural law to instrumentalism, but from organic politics and religion to individualist economics, or to the jurisprudential expression of MacPherson's "possessive individualism."[67]

In the conclusion to an essay such as this one it is inevitable to seek to reach some kind of Santayanian epiphany. The work of Chase studied here does carry with it some relevance for the present, since we are at a moment in history when a number of legal thinkers, proceeding under the rubric of the critical legal studies movement, seek to remove the fetters which bind American law to the market system. Many of the critical legal studies scholars, as did

Samuel Chase, seek to fashion a means of imposing an equitable jurisprudence on American law, and, again like Chase, to derive a single vision of the good to prevail in American society. As their master theoretician, Roberto Unger, has urged, they hope, perhaps through divine inspiration, to articulate a means of leaving behind the inevitable antinomies and inconsistencies of modern pluralistic liberal political theory.

Chase's attempt to implement a republican justice based on a unitary vision of religion, morality, and liberty ended with the means he created to implement his vision—circumscription of juries, legitimation of commercial doctrines—used by his successors, most notably John Marshall and Roger Taney, to create a society premised on values he abhorred. The aims of nineteenth-century jurisprudence, instead of retaining the self-conscious promotion of deferential politics, political hierarchies, and the encouragement of virtue in the individual citizen, became the ostensibly passive promotion of democracy, unlimited social mobility, and virtually unregulated economic progress. Chase's republican virtue somehow was transformed into nineteenth-century rugged individualism, as the impersonal regulator of the market replaced the personal direction of enlightened judges.

It appears, then, that the ultimate irony of Chase's judicial philosophy, which sought to implement an "Old Republican" ideology of an organic deferential state, is that it somehow appears to have carried within itself carcinogenic cells that led to its own demise. Chase wanted to save what he believed to be a republican form of government sanctified by God, but he acted in a manner that resulted in the abandonment of most of the premises he thought worth living or dying for. The true nature of Chase's Machiavellian moment in American jurisprudence is the revelation of the fragility of purposeful ideologies when faced with the imperfections and multiple purposes or misunderstandings of human beings.

As Homer knew, and the critical legal studies scholars remind us, the human condition itself seems to have within it contradictory imperatives, and there are inevitable conflicts between the striving to accomplish personal goals and the striving to fulfill one's societal duties; without the society individual life seems meaningless, but without individual excellence and accomplishment participation in the society seems unfulfilling.[68] Perhaps a system based on a single imperative, or a single set of them, as Chase tried to construct in response to the French Revolution, is doomed to failure. Chase's mistake may be the same mistake of some of the critical legal studies scholars and their fellow travelers, such as Michael Perry, who are engaged in an elusive search for an objective natural morality. And yet, what Chase's life also teaches us is that a sublimer irony or tragedy of the human condition is that one of the enterprises that seems to make the judicial life most worth living, most fulfilling, is the struggle to articulate a single morality, a single imperative, that we somehow cannot cease to call with the singly objective terms "truth" or "justice."

Robert Bork, exploring that judicial perspective, the articulation of which eventually cost him his seat on the Supreme Court, in a review of the late Alexander Bickel's *Morality of Consent*, suggested that Bickel was engaged in the challenging and desperately needed task of formulating a modern conservative American legal philosophy, which could draw on the insight of Edmund Burke, which could present the multiple aspect of human strivings as interconnectable, which could point the way toward a brotherhood of mankind, and which could thus offer some comfort in the modern age.[69] This essay has been offered in this same spirit, in the hope that by resurrecting a lost conservative jurisprudence of late eighteenth-century America, we might gain some insight into how to inform and implement one for the present.

The rule of law, as Morton Horwitz has reminded us,[70] is inevitably a conservative concept, and if we are serious about maintaining the rule of law, even though Horwitz and his fellow critical legal studies thinkers might advise against it, we ought to recognize our responsibility to buttress the rule of law with a proper conservative philosophy. Such a philosophy ought to seek to do what Chase tried, to provide a theory that can link our enterprise with that of the classical thinkers of the past, the Greeks, the Romans, and the progenitors of our own "classical tradition," the eighteenth-century English and American philosopher-statesmen.

In our attempt to forge links with the past, though, we might well be able to move on from the philosophies of Chase, or even the conservative aspects of Jefferson.[71] In the end, for both Chase and Jefferson, the maintenance of the Republic was a fragile and difficult enterprise. For both Thomas Jefferson and Samuel Chase, the great jurisprudential ideological antagonists, pursuant to their once shared belief in the Bolingbrokian English "country" ideology, real human freedom was hoped for in the future, but was believed to have existed in reality only in a distant, uncorrupted past. At some level, both may have believed that real human liberty could only be achieved for virtuous humans in the next world. The great accomplishment of Marx and Engels, in the middle of the nineteenth century, was to place human freedom in an inevitably occurring temporal future, and thus, for a half-century, their ideology appears to have been able to enrapture or enslave half the world.

This book has been offered to meet the challenge for our time: to recapture and develop the philosophy of our eighteenth-century ancestors, republican thinkers like Samuel Chase, and conservative thinkers like Edmund Burke,[72] so that we might eventually realize a world in which human freedom and spiritual reward exist in the present.

Notes

INTRODUCTION

1. For the most part, this book will follow the usage of such works as R. Buel, Jr., *Securing the Revolution: Ideology in American Politics 1789–1815* (1972) and H. Tinkcom, *The Republicans and Federalists in Pennsylvania 1790–1801* (1950), insofar as the adherents to the views of the principal spokesmen for the Washington and Adams administrations (usually Alexander Hamilton and John Adams) will be called "Federalists," and the adherents to the views of Thomas Jefferson (and occasionally James Madison) will be called "Republicans." This may be the source of some confusion, because, as will become evident later, I will also be exploring some broader implications of the term "republican," insofar as it expressed notions of appropriate civic ideology held in common by both Federalists and Jeffersonians. Further, this sort of classification by political party with party labels risks falling into an historicist fallacy, or into some Cartesian dualistic trap, since only late in the period here under review were two firm political party alignments clearly recognizable.

2. 25 F. Cas. 239; F. Wharton, ed., *State Trials of the United States During the Administrations of Washington and Adams*, 688 (C.C.D. Va. 1800) (No. 14,709) (1849).

3. On Chase's determination to correct what he believed to be a political wrong by punishing the abusive Virginians, see, e.g., J. Smith, *Freedom's Fetters: The Alien and Sedition Laws and American Civil Liberties*, 342–45 (1956).

4. For good accounts of the political machinations surrounding the Chase impeachment effort, see, e.g., R. Ellis, *The Jeffersonian Crisis*, 78, 81–82 (1971), and P. Hofer and N. Hull, *Impeachment in America, 1635–1805*, 228–38 (1984).

5. Quoted in C. Warren, *The Supreme Court in United States History*, vol. 1, at 156, n. 1 (rev. ed. 1947).

6. *Philadelphia Aurora*, January 15, 1801.

7. D. Stewart, *The Opposition Press of the Federalist Period*, 543 (1969), quoting *Philadelphia Aurora*, August 8, 1800.

8. For some typical Jeffersonian press commentary on Chase and the Federalist judges, see D. Stewart, supra note 7, at 533–35, nn. 138 and 141–43.

9. See C. Warren, supra note 5, at 168.

10. See id. at 273, concluding that "of all the judges, no one was more hated than Chase," and see *State Trials*, supra note 2, at 42, where Chase is given credit for nearly destroying the federal judiciary.

11. An act to provide for the more convenient organization of the courts of the United States, 2 Stat. 89 (1801).

12. See, e.g., F. Frankfurter and J. Landis, *The Business of the Supreme Court*, 21–25 (1928); Turner, "The Midnight Judges," 109 *U. Pa. L. Rev.* 494, 495, 521–23 (1961).

13. R. Ellis, supra note 4, at 15–16, 36–52.

14. See generally F. Frankfurter and J. Landis, supra note 12, at 14, 21–29, 35–37. The Federalist desires for an effective system for the administration of justice by the lower federal courts finally came about in the act of 1869 "which drastically curtailed circuit riding" and the act of 1875 "which vastly extended the domain of the federal courts." Id. at 30.

15. See, e.g., R. Bork, "Tradition and Morality in Constitutional Law" (Am. Enter. Inst., 1984); Bork, "Neutral Principles and Some First Amendment Problems," 47 *Ind. L. J.* 1 (1971); and, most recently, his *The Tempting of America: The Political Seduction of the Law* (1990).

16. See, e.g., Meese, "Towards a Jurisprudence of Original Intention," 2 *Benchmark* 1 (1986); Address at the meeting of the American Bar Association House of Delegates 15–17 (July 9, 1985); Meese, "The Battle for the Constitution: The Attorney General Replies to His Critics," 35 *Policy Review* 32, 34 (1985), reprinted in 19 *U.C. Davis L. Rev.* 22, 26 (1985) ("Where there is a demonstrable consensus among the framers and ratifiers as to a principle stated or implied by the Constitution, it should be followed").

17. See, e.g., *Wallace v. Jaffree*, 472 U.S. 38, 91–114, 105 S. Ct. 2479, 2508-20 (Rehnquist, J., dissenting).

18. See, e.g., Tepker, "The Defects of Better Motives: Reflections on Mr. Meese's Jurisprudence of Original Intention," 39 *Okla. L. Rev.* 23, 26 (1986) ("Neither the text nor the cryptic evidence of the Framers' original intentions provide a meaningful, conclusive guide for decision of a present-day constitutional case.")

19. For one of the most notable assertions regarding the obscurity of the framers' intentions given the passage of two hundred years and the possible multiple intentions of framers and ratifiers, see the speech delivered, implicitly critical of Attorney General Meese's views, by Associate Justice William Brennan, "The Constitution of the United States: Contemporary Ratification," Text and Teaching Symposium, Georgetown University, Washington, D.C., October 12, 1985, at 4, reprinted at 19 *U.C. Davis L. Rev.* 2 (1985).

20. See, e.g., Brennan, supra note 19, at 7–8, J. Ely, *Democracy and Distrust*, 11–41 (1980).

21. Powell, "The Original Understanding of Original Intent," 98 *Harv. L. Rev.* 885 (1985).

22. See, e.g., Hamilton's famous defense of judicial review in *Federalist* No. 78, where he claims that judicial interpretation can only be of the "manifest tenor" of the Constitution, and suggests further that there need be no rational fears of judicial usurpation since the judges who interpret the Constitution will be regulating their decisions by the "fundamental law" in the Constitution, which embodies the sovereign "power of the people," a power said to be superior to both the legislative and the judicial power. It strikes me that Hamilton's defense of judicial review, that it merely implements the will of the people, makes no sense unless one assumes that the will of the people exists objectively for the judges to find. In other words, *Federalist* 78 is bottomed on the proposition that judges do not *make*, instead they *find*, constitutional law. For *Federalist* 78 see, e.g., "Publius [Alexander Hamilton]," *The Federalist Papers*, 464–71 (Clinton Rossiter, ed., 1961).

23. Cf. Powell, supra note 21, at 888 ("This original 'original intent,' was determined not by historical inquiry into the expectations of the individuals involved in framing and ratifying the Constitution, but by consideration of what rights and powers sovereign polities could delegate to a common agent without destroying their own essential autonomy. Thus the original intentionalism was in fact a form of structural interpretation [footnote omitted]").

24. Cf. Kurland, "Judicial Review Revisited: 'Original Intent' and 'The Common Will,' " 55 *Cinc. L. Rev.* 733, 738 ("Constitutional law consists not only of the text but of fundamental principles inherent in that document").

25. See the provocative article by Morton Horwitz, "Republicanism and Liberalism in American Constitutional Thought," 29 *Wm. & Mary L. Rev.* 57 (1987), and sources there cited.

26. See, e.g., Horwitz, supra note 25, at 69; Robert Gordon, *The Politics of Legal History and the Search for a Usable Past*, 4 *Benchmark* 269 (1990), and R. Kent Newmyer, *Supreme Court Justice Joseph Story: Statesman of the Old Republic* (1985).

27. Lance Banning, "Quid Transit? Paradigms and Process in the Transformation of Republican Ideas," *Reviews in American History*/June 1989, 199–204, at 200.

28. See, e.g., J. Blum, E. Morgan, et. al., *The National Experience*, vol. 1, at 170 (5th ed., 1981); R. Current, T. Williams, and F. Freidel, *American History: A Survey*, vol. 1, at 192 (5th ed., 1979).

29. See, for a comprehensive treatment of the work of the earliest federal judges, Julius Goebel, Jr., *The Oliver Wendell Holmes Devise History of the Supreme Court of the United States: Antecedents and Beginnings to 1801*, vol. 1 (1971). Chase's opinions and jury charges as noted by Goebel do not appear to have differed significantly from that of most of his brethren on the Supreme Court, save for his ill-fated stand on the federal common law of crimes, discussed infra.

30. For a similar effort at demonstrating some of the reactionary, aristocratic, and deferential thought which went into the making of the Constitution of 1787, see Gordon S. Wood, *The Creation of the American Republic 1776–1787* (1969). A recent succinct summary of the argument in Wood's book is presented in Wood, "The Political Ideology of the Founders," in Neil L. York, ed., *Toward A More Perfect Union: Six Essays on the Constitution*, 6–27 (1988). By suggesting that American jurisprudence had about it something of the deference characteristic of the law in the realm of the British monarch in the late eighteenth century, I want to revise, somewhat, the impression among many American and English historians that the United States Constitution incorporates many of the devices dear to English radicals, at least insofar as that impression might suggest that the Constitution was more characteristic of English radical thought than it was of mainstream or conservative English legal beliefs. For the assertion about the incorporation of English radical thought, see C. Robbins, *The Eighteenth-Century Commonwealthman*, at 385–86 (1959).

31. See generally J. G. A. Pocock, *The Ancient Constitution and the Feudal Law*, (Norton, ed., 1967).

CHAPTER 1

1. Letter from Richard Peters to Timothy Pickering, quoted in C. Warren, *The Supreme Court in United States History*, vol. 1, at 281 (rev. ed., 1947).

2. Letter from Richard Peters to Timothy Pickering (Jan. 24, 1804), 10 Peters Papers 91 (Manuscript Collection, Historical Society of Pennsylvania, Philadelphia).

3. Id.

4. F. Wharton, ed., *State Trials of the United States During the Administrations of Washington and Adams*, 41 (1849).

5. Binney, "The Leaders of the Old Bar of Philadelphia," 14 *Pa. Mag. Hist. & Biog.* 1, 19, 20 (1859).

6. See, e.g., Letter from Richard Peters to Timothy Pickering (Jan. 24, 1804), supra note 2, where Peters observes that Chase was baffled that he should run into trouble in Philadelphia merely because he was following a practice done "every day" in England.

7. Binney, supra note 5, at 20.

8. Letter from Timothy Pickering to Richard Peters (Jan. 6, 1803). Pickering wrote: "The object is to remove Chase, to get rid of a troublesome judge, and to make room for one of the orthodox set no doubt of the *same state* with Chase . . . I conclude they mean not seriously to attack you." Pickering's reference to a Republican replacement for Chase must have been to Congressman Joseph H. Nicholson. See A. Beveridge, *The Life of John Marshall*, vol. 3, at 170–71 (1916).

9. For this summary of the committee's findings, see *Richard Peters, His Ancestors and Descendants 1810–1889*, 79–80 (N. Black, ed., 1904).

10. For Peters's own admission that he acquiesced in these rulings, see Letter from Richard Peters to Timothy Pickering (Jan. 24, 1804), supra note 2. Peters there wrote that Chase often spoke as if he represented "the court," and that though he (Peters) did not "authorize" Chase in such conduct, his habit of avoiding controversies which could result in "great injury of parties and delay of justice" made him let "many occurances & positions pass *sub silentio*." Id. Equally suggestive is the fact that Chase also sat with another judge, Judge Griffin, in the *Callender* case in Virginia, and Griffin was not prosecuted along with Chase, though the Virginia proceedings represented perhaps the most serious charges against Chase. Chase suggested to a correspondent that Griffin had managed to make his own personal political peace with the Jeffersonians, and so he was spared.

11. Id. This is one of the better examples of Peters's celebrated wit. As a punster, he was said to be "unrivalled in this country," although his fabulous sense of humor seems to lose something with the passage of almost two centuries. For an example, this gem appears in "A Collection of Puns and Witticism of Judge Richard Peters," 25 *Pa. Mag. Hist & Biog.* 366, 367 (1901) (copied from the manuscript of Samuel Breck): "The judge had an uncommon sharp nose and chin, and as he grew old they became more prominent and approached each other. A friend observed to him one day that his nose and chin were getting so near they would quarrel. 'Very likely,' he replied, 'for hard words often pass between them.' "

12. See supra note 11.

13. For a sample of this attitude, see the stiff and formal letter from Samuel Chase to Richard Peters (Jan. 22, 1804), in 10 Peters Papers, supra note 2, at 90, requesting Pe-

ters to undertake some investigations which might have proved helpful to Chase's defense.

14. Presser, "A Tale of Two Judges: Richard Peters, Samuel Chase, and the Broken Promise of Federalist Jurisprudence," 73 *Nw. U.L. Rev.* 26, 39–40 (1978).

15. J. Haw, F. Beirne, R. Beirne, and R. Jett, *Stormy Patriot: The Life of Samuel Chase*, 7 (1980).

16. See, e.g., John Adams to Abigail Adams (Feb. 6, 1796), warning about Chase at the time of his appointment by George Washington. "Mr. Chase is a new Judge, but although a good 1774 Man his Character has a Mist about it of suspicion and Impurity which gives occasion to the Enemy to censure. He has been a warm Party Man, and has made many Enemies. His Corpulency which has increased very much since I saw him lately in England, is against his riding Circuit very long." Reproduced in *The Documentary History of the Supreme Court of the United States: Appointments and Proceedings*, vol. 1, at 835 (Marcus, Perry, et al., eds, 1985).

17. Chase is ranked second behind Daniel Dulaney, but in front of Luther Martin, William Pinckney, William Wirt, and even Roger B. Taney. La Trobe, "Biographical Sketch of Daniel Dulaney," 3 *Pa. Mag. Hist. & Biog.* 1 (1879).

18. Riddell, "Benjamin Franklin's Mission to Canada and the Causes of Its Failure," 48 *Pa. Mag. Hist. & Biog.* 111, 149 n. 59 (1924).

19. J. Sanderson, *Biography of the Signers to the Declaration of Independence*, vol. 9, at 233 (1827).

20. Id. at 230.

21. *State Trials*, supra note 4, at 46.

22. *Penn's Lessees v. Pennington* (New Castle Circuit Court for Delaware, June 5, 1804), quoted in Rodney, "The End of the Penns' Claims to Delaware 1789–1814," 61 *Pa. Mag. Hist. & Biog.* 182, 196 (1937).

23. See infra chapter 7.

24. See infra chapter 7.

25. Id.

26. Letter from Richard Peters to R. Stratham (Dec. 2, 1793), 10 Peters Papers, supra note 2, at 21. See also, for an expression of similar sentiments, Letter from Richard Peters to Ralph Peters (Dec. 2, 1793), 10 Peters Papers, supra note 2, at 22.

27. Letter from Timothy Pickering to Richard Peters (Aug. 18, 1798), 10 Peters Papers, supra note 2, at 53.

28. *Case of Fries*, 9 Fed. Cas. 826, 874 (C.C.D. Pa. 1799) (No. 5, 126).

29. See infra chapter 2, text accompanying notes 68–71.

30. Letters from Richard Peters to Timothy Pickering (Aug. 24, Aug. 30, 1798), quoted in J. Miller, *The Federalist Era*, 137 (1960).

31. *Van Horne's Lessee v. Dorrance*, 28 F. Cas. 1012 (C.C.D. Pa. 1795) (No. 16,857).

32. Id. at 1015

33. See infra chapter 7.

34. See infra chapter 7.

35. Id.

36. *Case of Fries*, 9 F. Cas. 841.

37. Id.

38. See, e.g., J. Miller, supra note 30, where he discusses a Senate plan to pass a bill for settling disputed federal elections by using a closed-door tribunal composed of seven senators and six representatives.

39. J. Miller, *Alexander Hamilton and the Growth of the New Nation*, 513–14 (Torchbook, ed., 1959).

40. Id. We will see that this notion, that the rule of law itself might have to give way to preserve the society was shared not only by Hamilton's fellow Federalist Richard Peters (see infra chapter 7) but by their enemy Jefferson (infra chapter 9).

41. See Miller, supra note 39, at 520-25.

42. For general statements of this Federalist political philosophy, see R. Buel, Jr., *Securing the Revolution: Ideology in American Politics 1789–1815*, 231 (1972); J. Miller, supra note 30, at 276; and J. Smith, *Freedom's Fetters: The Alien and Sedition Laws and American Civil Liberties*, 332 (1956).

43. R. Buel, Jr., supra note 42, at 231; J. Miller, supra note 30, at 276.

44. See infra chapter 7.

45. Id.

46. See, e.g., *Philadelphia General Advertiser*, November 2, 1790, which reprints an Irish story from Mr. Brown's *Gazette*, about a bold jury that brought in a "not guilty" verdict against the wishes of the court because the jurors felt

> that we are appointed . . . by the law and the constitution—not only as an impartial tribunal to judge between the King and his subjects . . . but that by the favour of that Constitution we act in a situation of a still greater consequence; for we serve as a jury the barrier of the people against the possible influence, prejudice, passion or corruption of the bench!

47. See infra chapter 7.

48. See infra chapters 7 and 8.

49. See G. Stourzh, *Alexander Hamilton and the Idea of Republican Government*, 87–90 (1970), for Hamilton's views to this effect. As we will see infra chapters 8 and 9, even Jefferson and some of his fellow Republicans, such as Randolph and Taylor, partook to a certain extent of these eighteenth-century elitist views, although, in Jefferson's case at least, he may have eventually convinced himself to abandon them, at least in public, in favor of more democratic pretensions.

50. Id. at 97. On the fear of other American "republican" theorists, following the work of the Florentine "republican" theorists such as Machiavelli, that all republics were inevitably subject to disorder and decay if the proper virtue of the citizenry were not maintained, see also J. G. A. Pocock, *The Machiavellian Moment*, 526–42 (1975).

51. J. Miller, *Alexander Hamilton*, supra note 39, at 541–42.

52. Letter from Samuel Chase to John F. Mercer (Mar. 6, 1803), reprinted in 29 *Pa. Mag. Hist & Biog.* 205–6 (1905).

53. The quote is Crane Brinton's description of Robespierre's political philosophy, which Robespierre based on Rousseau. It applies in this context equally well to Chase. C. Brinton, *A Decade of Revolution*, 160 (Torchbook, ed., 1963).

54. C. Warren, supra note 1, at 292-95.

55. Id. at 292-93.

56. See, e.g., R. Ellis, *The Jeffersonian Crisis: Courts and Politics in the New Republic*, 60–61 (1971).

57. G. White, *The American Judicial Tradition*, 1–2 (1976).

CHAPTER 2

1. J. Smith, *Freedom's Fetters: The Alien and Sedition Laws and American Civil Liberties*, 248 (1956).

2. J. Miller, *The Federalist Era 1789–1801*, at 235 (1960).

3. R. Ellis, *The Jeffersonian Crisis*, 79 (1971).

4. Letter from Alexander Contee Hanson to Unknown Person (July 25, 1790) in Chase Papers MS 1235, Maryland Historical Society, Baltimore (quoted in J. Haw, F. Beirne, R. Beirne and R. Jett, *Stormy Patriot: The Life of Samuel Chase* (1980) [hereafter cited as *Stormy Patriot*], at 2).

5. *Stormy Patriot*, supra note 4.

6. M. Horwitz, *Transformation of American Law 1780–1860*, (1977).

7. M. Horwitz, supra note 6, at 11–12.

8. W.W. Crosskey, *Politics and the Constitution*, vol. 1, at 1322–23, n. 35 (1953). For the currently accepted notion that the views in *Politics and the Constitution* extend "beyond reasonable limits of history," see Katz, "Introductory Note" to Hart and Wechsler, *The Federal Courts and the Federal System*, 1, n. 1 (2d ed., 1973). But see Murrin, Book Review, 58 *N.Y.U.L. Rev.* 1254 (1983) (makes a powerful case for taking Crosskey's research and scholarship seriously).

9. Id.

10. Id.

11. On the later Federalists and their program, see generally J. Miller, supra note 2; M. Dauer, *The Adams Federalists* (1953); L. Kerber, *Federalists in Dissent* (1970).

12. Proceedings in the Circuit Court of the United States Held in Philadelphia, April 11, 1800, at 58–59 (T. Cooper, ed., Philadelphia, 1800). Pamphlet in the collection of the Historical Society of Pennsylvania. (Letter from Thomas Cooper to Samuel Chase, chronicling Chase's differences from the practices or views of his brethren.)

13. Id.

14. A good summary of Chase's career is to be found in the short biography by Edward S. Corwin, 4 *Dictionary of American Biography* 34 (1935). An earlier, but still useful, treatment is in J. Sanderson, *Biography of the Signers to the Declaration of Independence*, vol. 9, at 233 (1827). A more brilliant and detailed analysis of Chase's activities as a postwar Maryland politician is in F. MacDonald, *E. Pluribus Unum*, 89–99 (1965). Two full-length biographies of Chase have recently appeared. They are J. Haw, F. Beirne, et al., *Stormy Patriot: The Life of Samuel Chase* (1980), and J. Elsmere, *Justice Samuel Chase* (1980). Both go some distance toward dispelling the conventional caricature of Chase, though neither has much to say about his jurisprudence or its relation to other constitutional thought of the period.

15. See, in addition to sources cited in the preceding note, Dillard, "Samuel Chase," in *The Justices of the Supreme Court*, vol. 1, at 185 (L. Friedman and F. Israel, eds., 1969).

16. F. MacDonald, supra note 14. The most famous of Chase's pecadillos along these lines is his notorious speculation in flour futures as a result of his acquiring information when he served in the Continental Congress. See infra text accompanying notes 30–31. For this he was roundly denounced by Alexander Hamilton in the "Publius" essays he wrote in 1778. Hamilton wrote that Chase had "the peculiar privilege of being universally despised." *The Works of Alexander Hamilton*, vol. 1, at 203 (H. C. Lodge, ed., 1971).

17. Kenyon, "Men of Little Faith: The Anti-Federalists on the Nature of Representative Government," 12 *Wm. & Mary Q.* (3d ser.) (1955). See also H. Storing, *What the Anti-Federalists Were For: The Political Thought of the Opponents of the Constitution* (1981).

18. See generally, for the clearest statement of Chase's anti Federalist views, his "Objections to the Federal Government," probably written in 1788, as reprinted, introduced, and annotated in Haw, "Samuel Chase's 'Objections to the Federal Government,' " 76 *Md. Hist. Mag.* 272 (1981).

19. Cf. ibid.

20. For Chase's favorable opinion on commerce, see Chase's Manuscript Letter to His Children (Feb. 8, 1784), Ettings Jurists Collection, at 37 (Historical Society of Pennsylvania), where he implies that the business of a merchant is an honorable profession, second only to that of the law. For the best discussion of the Jeffersonian ambivalence toward commerce, see D. McCoy, *The Elusive Republic: Political Economy in Jeffersonian America*, 76–104 (1980).

21. This was a report that Alexander Hamilton submitted to Congress in 1791, in which he surveyed American manufacturing and laid out the steps he believed necessary to make manufacturing cement the bonds of tbe American union by making America independent of foreign powers. J. Miller, *Alexander Hamilton and the Growth of the New Nation*, 280–90 (1959).

22. See *Stormy Patriot*, supra note 4, at 17–30.

23. See generally Chase's comments on government in his Jury Charge Book, for the years 1798–1800, 1802–03, and 1805–06, an unpublished manuscript in the Vertical File of the Manuscript Division of the Maryland Historical Society, Baltimore, passim.

24. For the idea that what the American revolutionaries were seeking was simply a return to a previously achieved (though mythical) pristine English past, see generally B. Bailyn, *The Ideological Origins of the American Revolution*, passim (1967), and B. Bailyn, *The Origins of American Politics*, passim (1968).

25. For this classical influence see generally G. Wood, *The Creation of the American Republic 1776–1787*, 52–53 (1969). See also Chase's Letter to His Children, supra note 20 (for his listing of and praise of important classical Roman authors, presumably for their demonstration of selfless civic virtue).

26. These ideas are implicit in the Chase Jury Charge Book, supra note 23. For Chase's disparaging comments on the Maryland reform of universal suffrage, see id. at 40–41.

27. *Stormy Patriot*, supra note 4, at 125.

28. *Stormy Patriot*, supra note 4, at 174.

29. In a letter from Samuel Chase to George Washington (Sept. 3, 1789, Gratz Collection, Box 19, Case 1, Historical Society of Pennsylvania), Chase asked for an appoint-

ment as a Supreme Court justice, and promised that if nominated he would "exert [himself] to execute so honourable and important a station with integrity, fidelity, and diligence." Chase added: "I flatter myself that you will never have the occasion to regret the confidences bestowed in me." The two most important later letters assuring Washington of Chase's loyalty to Federalist principles are the Letter from Samuel Chase to George Washington (July 19, 1794, Library of Congress), and the Letter from James McHenry to George Washington (June 14, 1795), quoted in C. Warren, *The Supreme Court in United States History*, vol. 1, at 125–26 (rev. ed., 1947). For discussion of Chase's desire in 1793 to "quit the state service and to be employed by the General Government," where he promises to "render it every support, that office and duty may require," see Letter from Samuel Chase to Tench Coxe (Apr. 2, 1793, Tench Coxe Papers, Historical Society of Pennsylvania).

30. *Stormy Patriot*, supra note 4, at 108.

31. One can find the Hamilton "Publius" letters in *The Papers of Alexander Hamilton*, vol. 1, at 580 (H. Syrett, ed., 1961). See also supra note 16.

32. *Stormy Patriot*, supra note 4, at 108–9.

33. For Story's belief that he could perform these roles simultaneously and thus better serve the public interest, see generally R. Kent Newmyer, *Supreme Court Justice Joseph Story: Statesman of the Old Republic* (1985).

34. For Marshall's intriguing refusal to recuse himself in Supreme Court cases in which he had a financial interest, see M. Tachau, *Federal Courts in the Early Republic*, 186–89 (1978). For a recent statement of how Marshall "took advantage of the greatness of the nation to enrich himself and at the same time improve his community," see Brisbin, "John Marshall on History, Virtue, and Legality," in T. Shevory, ed., *John Marshall's Achievement: Law, Politics, and Constitutional Interpretations*, 101 (1989).

35. All of this could have been rationalized as within the parameters of the civic republican notion that only those with the means to make them independent in judgment could serve the public, or exercise the franchise. For recent discussions of this aspect of late eighteenth-century political theory, particularly as demonstrated by the Federalists, see generally Brisbin, supra note 34; Howe, "Anti-Federalist/Federalist Dialogue and Its Implications for Constitutional Understanding," 84 *Nw. U.L. Rev.* 1 (1989); and McWilliams, "The Anti-Federalists, Representation, and Party," 84 *NW. U.L. Rev.* 12 (1989).

36. See, e.g., Letter from Oliver Wolcott to an Unidentified Correspondent (Feb. 1, 1796), reprinted in *Memoirs of the Administrations of George Washington and John Adams*, vol. 1, at 300 (G. Gibbs, ed., 1846); see also vol. 1, C. Warren, supra note 29, at 143–44.

37. The quote is the conclusion of W. Brown, *The Life of Oliver Ellsworth*, 240–41 (1905).

38. Brown, supra note 37, characterizes Rutledge, who accepted a position on the Supreme Court in 1795, as "one of the very foremost characters in the whole country," and Ellsworth, who became chief justice, had a career of very great distinction in the Senate. Id. For correspondence suggesting that the Ellsworth appointment was regarded as important to Ellsworth, Connecticut, and the Union, see *Memoirs*, supra note 36, vol. 1, at 306, 320, 324.

39. For the correspondence of a high Federalist urging the appointment of Chase because of his recent conformity to Federalist principles, which also praises Chase's "professional knowledge" and his "very valuable stock of political science and information," see Letter from James McHenry to George Washington (June 14, 1795), quoted in C. Warren, supra note 29, vol. 1, at 125–26; B. Steiner, *The Life and Correspondence of James McHenry*, 159, 160n (1907); *Stormy Patriot*, supra note 4, at 175.

40. Regarding Washington's preference to keep his own counsel and remain inscrutable about his motives in appointments, see Letter from John Jay to Matthew Ridley (Oct. 8, 1789) (copy in Ridley Papers, Mass. Hist. Society), quoted in *Stormy Patriot*, supra note 4, at 166. For the suggestion that Washington was a "genius" in the use of political power, see E. Morgan, *The Genius of George Washington* (1980).

41. For the opinion that the Chase appointment was part of a strategy to remedy the "lack of Southerners" in the national government, see J. Flexner, *George Washington: Anguish and Farewell 1793–1799*, at 250–51 (Samuel Chase erroneously referred to as "Thomas" Chase).

42. Chase was born April 17, 1741. A few years before his death in 1811 Chase was to tell his son-in-law, a Jeffersonian who married his beautiful and beloved daugher: "[Y]ou are a democrat and you are right to be one, for you are a young man; but an old man . . . would be a fool to be a Democrat." J. Sanderson, *Biography of the Signers to the Declaration of Independence*, vol. 9, at 234 (1827). This is reminiscent of the modern aphorism: "A man who, at twenty, is not a socialist has no heart, but a man who remains a socialist at thirty has no head."

43. In some ways Samuel Chase, like the English governor of Massachusetts Thomas Hutchinson a generation before, may have been a prisoner of his times, trapped into acting in a manner which now seems arbitrary, but may have made good sense then. Compare the attitude taken toward the loyalists, the "losers" of the American Revolution, in B. Bailyn, *The Ordeal of Thomas Hutchinson*, ix–xii (1974).

44. See G. Wood, supra note 25, at 77 (1969). The American view of the British constitution, with the Americans' emphasis on the right of the people to actual representation in the national legislature, was not the current understanding in England and represented a somewhat atavistic "Republican Commonwealth" strain of thought. See generally B. Bailyn, *The Origins of American Politics*, 11–12, 131–36 (1967), and B. Bailyn, *The Ideological Origins of the American Revolution*, 34–54, 162–75 (1967) [hereafter cited as *Ideological Origins*]. Nevertheless, for several generations, this constitutional theory had taken strong root in America and became such a widely shared and unquestionable article of faith that its adherents were willing to bring the country to war because of it. On the particular relevance and the meaning of the concept of "liberty" to the Whigs, see John Philip Reid, *The Concept of Liberty in the Age of the American Revolution* (1988).

45. For a description of the effect of these forces on substantive law generally, see W. Nelson, *The Americanization of the Common Law*, 67–68, 89–144 (1975).

46. John Adams wanted to see America recreate what he believed to be the British distribution of national power. He apparently toyed with the idea of an American hereditary chief executive and Senate, and wanted thus to preserve a balance between

monarch, aristocracy, and people in America. J. Adams, "Defense of the Constitutions of Government of the United States," in *Works of John Adams*, vol. 4, at 379, 392, 397 (for the theory of a balanced constitution); letters from John Adams to Benjamin Rush (Feb. 8, June 19, July 5, and July 24, 1789), quoted in G. Wood, supra note 25, at 587–88. For a general discussion of Adams's mature political thought, and its anomaly in late eighteenth-century America, see G. Wood, supra note 25, at 567.

47. Some of the thought of these Pennsylvanians is discussed in Henderson, "Some Aspects of Sectionalism in Pennsylvania, 1790–1812," 61 *Pa. Mag. Hist. & Biog.* 113 (1937), and a more recent treatment of Duane, emphasizing his mature political views, is Phillips, "William Duane, Philadelphia's Democratic Republicans, and the Origins of Modern Politics," 101 *Pa. Mag. Hist. & Biog.* 365 (1977). See also H. Tinkcom, *The Republicans and Federalists in Pennsylvania 1790–1801*, 71, 77 (1950), G. Wood, supra note 25, at 85–90. The classic statements of the democratic views of these Pennsylvanians, as they applied to the law, is to be found in B. Austin, *Observations on the Pernicious Practice of the Law, as Published Occasionally in the Independent Chronicle, in the Year 1786* (1819), reprinted in 13 *Am. J. Legal Hist.* 244 (1969), and J. Higgins, *Sampson Against the Philistines or the Reformation of Lawsuits* (2d ed., 1805).

48. H. Tinkcom, supra note 47, at 1–3.

49. G. Wood, supra note 25, at 403–9.

50. The classic exposition of Federalist thought is, of course, A. Hamilton, J. Madison, and J. Jay, *The Federalist* (first published 1787–88; all page cites which follow are to the New American Library Paperback ed., 1961) [hereafter cited as *The Federalist*]. *The Federalist*'s position on the separation of power issue is set forth by James Madison in Nos. 47–51, at 300–325. As indicated, the theory, which borrowed, as we now know, from ancient theories, beginning probably with Aristotle, about the wisdom of mixed constitutions, arose in America in the 1780s in response to desires to reign in the state legislatures, particularly the lower houses. This was to be done by creating stronger executives, stronger upper houses, and a more independent judiciary than the first wave of state constitutions had provided. Finally, all branches of government were to circumscribe their activities pursuant to the directives of written constitutions, which were to become "fundamental law." The concept of the constitutions as "fundamental law" is discussed in G. Wood, supra note 25, at 260–82, and in Nelson, "Changing Conceptions of Judicial Review in the States 1790–1860," 120 *U. Pa. L. Rev.* 1166 (1972).

51. See G. Wood, supra note 25, at 446–49, and sources there cited.

52. *The Federalist* No. 78, at 464 (A. Hamilton) (famous statement of the principle of judicial review).

53. Id. No. 79, at 472 (A. Hamilton; discussions of judicial independence and accountability in general); No. 81, at 481 (A. Hamilton; discussions of the Supreme Court in particular). In the early years there seems to have been a popular assumption that judges, like other governmental officials, should be elected. See, e.g., *Philadelphia General Advertiser*, November 8, 1790, at 3, col. 1 (editorial suggesting that in a republic it is better to elect rather than to appoint judges).

54. *The Federalist* No. 78, at 467–69 (A. Hamilton). For a general discussion of Federalist views of the judiciary, see G. Wood, supra note 25, at 453–63.

55. *The Federalist* No. 79, at 474 (A. Hamilton).

56. On Hamilton's efforts, sec generally J. Miller, *Alexander Hamilton and the Growth of the New Nation*, 219–310, 537 (Torchbook, ed., 1959).

57. G. Wood, supra note 25, at 453–63.

58. H. Tinkcom, supra note 47, at 12–17.

59. In September 1791 the tax had been decried in a Pittsburgh town meeting as "similar to the action of monarchical countries" and discouraging to agriculture. In August 1792 there were antitax riots in western Pennsylvania which included break-ins at the revenue collection office. There was relatively little outright resistance until the summer of 1794. See generally, on the Whiskey Rebellion, H. Tinkcom, supra note 47, at 92–95, and L. Baldwin, *Whiskey Rebels: The Story of a Frontier Uprising* (rev. ed., 1968).

60. The entire economy of western Pennsylvania seems to have been heavily dependent on the manufacture of whisky as the best means of preserving the grain crop. The tax struck particularly hard in the west because the excise was figured on the basis of quantity and the price of whisky was less in the west. See, e.g., H. Tinkcom, supra note 47, at 92, and J. Miller, supra note 2, at 155–56 (1960).

61. H. Tinkcom, supra note 47, at 101, quoting Report of the United States Commissioners to E. Randolph, reprinted in 4 *Pennsylvania Archives* 164 (2d ser.)

62. See, e.g., *United States v. Insurgents*, 26 F. Cas. 499, 506–7 (C.C.D. Pa. 1795) (No. 15,443), for the suggestion that this number was as high as 7000.

63. Id. at 507–11; H. Tinkcom, supra note 47, at 104–5.

64. See generally Eastman, *The Fries Rebellion* (1922), and H. Tinkcom, supra note 47, at 215–19.

65. Miller, supra note 2, at 233, n. 15.

66. See, e.g., *Philadelphia Aurora* April 11, May 15, May 16, and May 24, 1799. See generally J. Smith, *Freedom's Fetters: The Alien and Sedition Laws and American Civil Liberties*, 277–306 (1956).

67. See, e.g., J. Miller, supra note 2, at 138–39 (Whiskey Rebellion), 247–50 (Fries Rebellion).

68. H. Tinkcom. supra note 47, at 96. William Findley, no great friend to the Federalists and himself a man of western Pennsylvania, apparently believed that a show of federal force was indispensable to maintain the authority of the federal government in western Pennsylvania. Id.

69. J. Miller, supra note 2, at 158, refers to the fear that the resistance might spread to Maryland, Georgia, and the Carolinas.

70. See, e.g., H. Tinkcom, supra note 47, at 216, (Tinkcom calls Eastman "The historian of the Fries Rebellion"); D. Stewart, *The Opposition Press of the Federalist Period*, 141 (1969) (citing Eastman and Tinkcom).

71. See generally G. Wood, supra note 25, at 319–23.

72. Id. at 323–28.

73. Reid, "In a Defensive Rage: The Uses of the Mob, the Justification in Law, and the Coming of the American Revolution," 49 *N.Y.U.L. Rev.* 1043 (1974).

74. G. Wood, supra note 25, at 326–27.

75. J. Sanderson, supra note 42, vol. 9, at 190–91.

76. See, e.g., J. Miller, supra note 2, at 247, for the suggestion that the participants in the Fries Rebellion had been led to believe "President Adams, among other enormities,

planned to marry his daughter to the son of King George of England and to establish an American dynasty."

The position of the Pennsylvania farmers that one essential component of American liberty was freedom from taxation was, admittedly, not as farfetched as it might now seem. For several years after the Revolution, the state of Pennsylvania had been able to secure adequate revenues principally through the sale of public land and had not imposed direct taxes. H. Tinkcom, supra note 47, at 273. It should have been only natural for those opposing taxation by the state similarly to reason that if the federal government needed to raise funds, it should do it by, for example, disposition of public lands, and not through raiding the pockets of its citizens.

77. C. Brinton, *A Decade of Revolution*, 90, 117 (Torchbook, ed., 1963).

78. See generally id. at 167–74.

79. R. Buel, Jr., *Securing the Revolution: Ideology in American Politics 1789–1815*, 128–29 (1972).

80. Id. at 129–30.

81. C. Brinton, supra note 77, at 55, referring to the November 19, 1792, declaration of the French convention.

82. Id. at 230.

83. R. Buel, Jr., supra note 79, at 137–38.

84. Id. at 171, 176.

85. C. Brinton, supra note 77, at 218.

86. F. Wharton, ed., *State Trials of the United States During the Administrations of Washington and Adams*, 9 (1849).

87. Id., at 5, note.

88. See, e.g., Reid, "Lawless Law and Lawful Mobs," 23 *NYU Law* 32 (1977).

89. See G. Nash, *The Urban Crucible* (1979), and E. Foner, *Tom Paine and Revolutionary America* (1976). For the eventual alienation of even Adams and Jefferson, from the new order, see M. Peterson, *Adams and Jefferson: A Revolutionary Dialogue*, 104–28 (1976).

90. For the events which led to passage of the English Reform Bill of 1832, see generally W. Wilcox, *The Age of Aristocracy*, 271–79 (1976).

91. See generally the discussions of the implementation of popular sovereignty through the state and federal constitutions in G. Wood, supra note 25.

92. Cf. Shalhope, "Republicanism and Early American Historiography," 39 *Wm. & Mary Q.* (3d ser.) 334, 341–44, 345–50 (1982).

93. For the transformation see M. Horwitz, *The Transformation of American Law: 1790–1860* (1977).

CHAPTER 3

1. For some general definitions of republicanism, and "court" and "country" ideologies in their legal context, see A. G. Roeber, *Faithful Magistrates and Republican Lawyers: Creators of a Virginia Legal Culture, 1680–1810*, xvii–xviii (1981). For what has become something of a classic discussion of court and country ideologies in England and America in the eighteenth century, see J. G. A. Pocock, *The Machiavellian*

Moment: Florentine Political Thought and the Atlantic Republican Tradition, 462–552 (1975).

On American "republicanism" generally there is a wealth of material. The most frequently cited pieces seem to be Pocock, supra; J. Appleby, *Capitalism and a New Social Order: The Republican Vision of the 1790's* (1978); B. Bailyn, *The Ideological Origins of the American Revolution* (1967); J. Diggins, *The Lost Soul of American Politics: Virtue, Self-Interest, and the Foundations of Liberalism* (1986); and G. Wood, *The Creation of the American Republic 1776–1787* (1969). Two indispensable articles for mastering the burgeoning scholarship on republicanism are Shalhope, "Toward a Republican Synthesis: The Emergence of an Understanding of Republicanism in American Historiography," 29 *Wm. & Mary Q.* (3d ser.) 49 (1972), and Shalhope, "Republicanism and Early American Historiography," 39 *Wm. & Mary Q.* (3d ser.) 334 (1982).

For the suggestion that there is now a "general agreement (not unanimous, of course) that both ("modern liberal" and "classical republican" traditions) were present in the new Republic (as were other modes of thought), that both of them were vastly influential, and that neither should be seen as having exercised an undisputed primacy during the 1780s or 1790s," see Lance Banning, "Quid Transit? Paradigms and Process in the Transformation of Republican Ideas," *Reviews in American History*, June 1989, 199–204, at 199. Banning cites in support of this assertion the following important recent works: Lance Banning, "Jeffersonian Ideology Revisited: Liberal and Classical Ideas in the New American Republic," 63 *William & Mary Q.* (3d ser.) 3–19 (1986); Joyce Appleby, "Republicanism in Old and New Contexts," ibid., 30–34; James T. Kloppenberg, "The Virtues of Liberalism: Christianity, Republicanism, and Ethics in Early American Political Discourse," 74 *Journal of American History* 9–33 (1987); Isaac Kramnick, "The 'Great National Discussion': The Discourse of Politics in 1787," 45 *William & Mary Q.* (3d ser.) 3–32 (1988); and the letters of J.G.A. Pocock and Isaac Kramnick, ibid., 817-18.

At this point it might also be useful for me to define the term "ideology" as it is here used. I am using the term in one of the senses defined by Roger Scruton, as "Any systematic and all-embracing political doctrine, which claims to give a complete and universally applicable theory of man and society, and to derive therefrom a programme of political action." R. Scruton, *A Dictionary of Political Thought*, 213 (1982). For another definition, which seems to have been fairly frequently relied on by American historians of republicanism, see Geertz, "Ideology as a Cultural System," in *Ideology and Discontent*, 47 (D. Apter, ed., 1964) (defining ideology as a cultural system that is itself ideologically charged and that "names the structure of situations in such a way that the attitude contained toward them is one of commitment").

2. For a summary of the reasons the consensus regarding the origination of American jurisprudence with John Marshall is in error see, in addition to the arguments presented here, Presser, "Resurrecting the Conservative Tradition in American Legal History," 13 *Reviews in American History* 526 (1985).

3. In developing this dialectical model, I do not mean to embrace all of the tenets of Marxist dialectical materialism. I seek only to suggest that with regard to early American constitutional jurisprudence "change [took] place through the meeting of two op-

posing forces (thesis and antithesis); [and] their opposition [was] resolved by a com-
bination produced by a higher force (synthesis)." *The New Columbia Encyclopedia*,
757 (W. Harris and J. Levey, eds., 1975) (entry for "dialectical materialism").

4. Richard Hofstadter has described our moderate political tradition as creating a
"consensus" school of American history. R. Hofstadter, *The American Political Tradition and the Men Who Made It*, xxvii–xxix (1974). According to Hofstadter, the main
tenet of the consensus school of history is that despite deep divisions in American society over other issues, there is a remarkable amount of agreement on "the sanctity of
private property, the right of the individual to dispose of and invest it, the value of opportunity, and the natural evolution of self-interest and self-assertion, within broad legal limits, into a beneficent social order." Id. at xxxvii. This is what the suggestion in
the text about our "moderate" political tradition refers to. For an expression of the
view that this moderate tradition yielded general agreement on the basic principles governing American jurisprudence, see generally G. E. White, *The American Judicial Tradition: Profiles of Leading American Judges* (1976) (leading American judges agreed
on certain moderate and self-limiting principles).

5. This point, about the suppression and ignorance of extremism in American history, is similar in spirit to the one made by Karl Klare in his fine study of the Wagner
Act. See generally Klare, "Judicial Deradicalization of the Wagner Act and the Origins
of Modern Legal Consciousness, 1937–1941," 62 *Minn. L. Rev.* 265 (1978).

6. The charge is recorded in Chase's hand in his Jury Charge Book, a manuscript
which is unpublished but can be found in the Vertical File of the Manuscript Division
of the Maryland Historical Society, Baltimore (hereafter Chase Jury Charge Book),
which includes charges Chase gave to grand juries in 1798–1800, 1802–03, and 1805–
06. The 1803 charge, widely reprinted at the time, is also to be found in S. Presser &
J. Zainaldin, *Law and Jurisprudence in American History*, 223–25 (2d ed., 1989).

7. For further discussion of the Midnight Judges' Act see Turner, "The Midnight
Judges," 109 *U. Pa. L. Rev.* 494 (1961).

8. For a summary of the statement of these ideas by Thomas Paine and others, see
Rabban, "The Ahistorical Historian: Leonard Levy on Freedom of Expression in Early
American History," 37 *Stan. L. Rev.* 795, 837–40 (1985), and sources there cited.

9. This is clearly spelled out in Chase's comments to John Fries, following his sentence of death, when Chase explained that Fries was soon to face the Day of Judgment
and had better put his conscience and earthly affairs in order. *United States v. Fries*, 9
F. Cas. 924, 932–34 (C.C.D. Pa. 1800) (No. 5,127). It is also explicit in Chase's personal daily prayer, where Chase noted that he himself would eventually appear to be
judged by his Maker. Manuscript Prayer of the Hon. Samuel Chase, Associate Justice
of the United States Supreme Court, Haverford College Quaker Collection, No. 715
(n.p.,n.d.).

10. For assessments of the thought of Chase's great Federalist successor, Joseph Story,
which stress similar religious strains in that justice's thought, see J. McClellan, *Joseph
Story and the American Constitution: A Study in Political and Legal Thought with
Selected Writings* (1971), and R. K. Newmyer, *Supreme Court Justice Joseph Story:
Statesman of the Old Republic* (1985).

11. See *Hylton v. United States*, 3 U.S. (3 Dall.) 171, 173–75 (1796).

12. For the anti-Federalist hostility to the executive, see H. Storing, *What the Anti-Federalists Were For*, 49–50 (1981).

13. *Murray v. The Charming Betsey*, 6 U.S. (2 Cranch) 64 (1804).

14. *United States v. Worrall*, 2 U.S. (2 Dall.) 384 (1798) (Chase was sitting as circuit justice in the Circuit Court for the Pennsylvania District). It appears, however, that, at least in this case, Chase reversed himself on this issue, most probably when reminded that his new Federalist colleagues disagreed with him. See infra chapter 6.

15. For the country party strain in early American political thought, see the two articles by Shalhope, supra note 1. See also Pocock, "Introduction," in *Three British Revolutions, 1640, 1688, 1776*, at 3–17 (J. Pocock, ed., 1980).

16. 3 U.S. (3 Dall.) 386 (1798).

17. Id., at 388.

18. See, e.g., Grey, "Do We Have an Unwritten Constitution?," 27 *Stan. L. Rev.* 703, 708, n. 21 (1975). For one of the most provocative attempts to articulate the "unwritten Constitution" along "religious" lines, see M. Perry, *The Constitution, the Court, and Human Rights* (1982).

19. See, e.g., Roane's opinion in *Currie's Administrators v. The Mutual Assurance Society*, 14 Va. (4 Hen. & M.) 315 (1809).

20. Peters's views on the common law of crimes are set forth in his opinion in *United States v. Worrall*, 2 U.S. (2 Dall.) 384, 395 (1798), considered in some detail infra chapter 6.

21. The religious base of Chase's jurisprudence can be examined in the Chase Jury Charge Book, supra note 6, at 41–46. Jefferson's reference to "Nature and nature's God" is in the opening to the Declaration of Independence.

22. See, e.g., Chase Jury Charge Book, supra note 6, at 41–46.

23. For the argument that Chase consistently maintained this position, see Preyer, "Jurisdiction to Punish: Federal Authority, Federalism and the Common Law of Crimes in the Early Republic," 4 *Law and History Review* 223, 230–36, 239–42 (1986) (Chase against common law crimes in 1798, 1805, and 1806). For Chase's 1804 statement that it is the duty of American courts to follow the law as laid down by legislatures, see *Penn's Lessees v. Pennington* (New Castle Circuit Court for Delaware, June 5, 1804), quoted in Rodney, "The End of the Penn's Claims to Delaware, 1789–1814," 61 *Pa. Mag. Hist. & Biog.* 182, 195–96 (1937).

24. The report of the trial of the "Seven Bishops" in 1688 is found at 12 Howell's State Trials 183. The most famous account of the trial and the events leading up to it, as the seven Anglican bishops challenged the authority of the Catholic James II, is by the great Whig historian, Thomas Babington Macaulay, and is probably most accessible in *Macaulay's History of England from the Accession of James II*, vol. 2, at 82–175 (Everyman's Library ed., 1906). Macaulay's account is excerpted and placed in its American context in S. Presser and J. Zainaldin, *Law and Jurisprudence in American History*, 10–27 (2d ed. 1989).

25. *U.S. v. John Fries*, 9 Fed. Cas. 826 (C.C.D. Pa. 1800).

26. *U.S. v. James Thomson Callender*, 25 F. Cas. 239 (C.C.D. Va. 1800).

27. See Presser and Hurley, "Saving God's Republic: The Jurisprudence of Samuel Chase," 1984 *U. Ill. L. Rev.* 771, 811–12, and sources there cited.

28. It must be admitted that this "supraconstitutional" jurisprudence, which I do believe to have been approved of by most of the early Federalist judges, was questioned by at least one of them. See, e.g., the opinion in *Calder v. Bull* by North Carolinian Justice Iredell, who questioned the value of judging according to any principles not express in the Constitution itself.

29. For the Virginia legal culture, see Roeber, supra note 1, for Pennsylvania see R. Ellis, *The Jeffersonian Crisis: Courts and Politics in the Young Republic*, 157–84 (1971), and for Massachusetts see G. Gawalt, *The Promise of Power: The Emergence of the Legal Profession in Massachusetts, 1760–1840* (1979).

30. For the elaboration of the theory that Marshall's views and those of eighteenth-century Massachusetts jurisprudence were based on "communitarian" notions, see W. Nelson, *The Americanization of the Common Law* (1975), and Nelson, "The Eighteenth Century Background of the Jurisprudence of John Marshall," 76 *Mich. L. Rev.* 893 (1978).

31. For one excellent example of an American constitutional historian who has shown what can be done by studying the English sources of American thought, see the provocative Review Essay by David M. Rabban, "The Ahistorical Historian: Leonard Levy on Freedom of Expression in Early American History," 37 *Stan. L. Rev.* 795 (1985). For some of the pioneering work by more general American historians relating English radical thought to the American experience, cited by Rabban, see, e.g., A. Lincoln, *Some Political & Social Ideas of English Dissent, 1763–1800* (1938 and photo. reprint 1971); E. Link, *Democratic-Republican Societies, 1790–1800* (1942); R. R. Palmer, *The Age of the Democratic Revolution* (2 vols., 1959, 1964) B. Bailyn, *The Ideological Origins of the American Revolution* (1967) and G. Wood, *The Creation of the American Republic 1776–1787* (1969), discussed by Rabban at 822. None of these works, however, analyzes the thought of the American judges in the 1790s in the context of the experience in England in the late eighteenth century, the project that is attempted here. Furthermore, while I think the Rabban essay is a splendid piece of work and a model of integrating English and American thought, I think that Mr. Rabban too quickly concludes that the theory of popular sovereignty of the English radicals enjoyed hegemony in America and was fully reflected in the American Constitution of 1787. See, e.g., Rabban, supra, at 841. To restate a main theme, I am trying to show in this essay that there were bastions of American conservative thought where popular sovereignty, if it was the dominant ideology, came freighted with baggage that set limits on what the people could do, and included ideas about deference, hierarchy, morals, and religion that were closer to the thought of the English conservatives than the English radicals. To be fair to Mr. Rabban, he recognizes that the Federalists in the 1790s believed that there ought to be some restraints on "simple democracy," and that the ideology of the American "Democratic-Republican" societies went too far. See, e.g., Rabban, at 846–47, quoting R. Buel, *Securing the Revolution*, at 99–101 (1972), a study of Republicans and Federalists in Pennsylvania. See also Rabban, supra, at 849, where Rabban notes the borrowing from English political suppression of dissent by the American Federalists. Nevertheless, I think Rabban somewhat overstates the influence of English radical thought in America, and fails adequately to limn the influence of English conservative thought here, particularly on members of the American judiciary.

Moreover, Rabban, at 850, following earlier work by Buel, supra, and J. Smith, *Freedom's Fetters: The Alien and Sedition Laws and American Civil Liberties* (1956), asserts that the Federalists in the late 1790s, in their defense of the Alien and Sedition Acts, were inventing new theories of government, borrowed from the English, to restrain American popular sovereignty. It seems equally likely to me that many of the Constitution's framers, and Americans in close touch with English thought, such as the judicial figures Richard Peters and Samuel Chase, and other American politicians such as the Federalists Hamilton and Adams, could well have imbibed English conservative notions in the period *before* the American Constitution. I find it difficult to believe, in other words, as Rabban apparently does not, that the Jeffersonian Republicans had cornered the market in "true" American republican ideology.

CHAPTER 4

1. J. Haw, F. Beirne, R. Beirne, and R. Jett, *Stormy Patriot: The Life of Samuel Chase*, 125 (1980).

2. For a description of Achilles's Shield, see XVIII:468–607 of Homer's Iliad, e.g., *The Illiad of Homer*, 387–391 (R. Lattimore, trans., 1951).

3. Quoted in J. Plumb, *England in the Eighteenth Century*, 75 (1963 ed.).

4. "I have seen the future, and it works," said Lincoln Steffans (1866–1936), after visiting Moscow in 1919. *The Oxford Dictionary of Quotations*, 518 (3d ed., 1979).

5. The best examination of this British "radicalism" that I have found is A. Goodwin, *The Friends of Liberty: The English Democratic Movement in the Age of the French Revolution* (1979).

6. On the matters in this paragraph, see generally A. Goodwin, supra note 5.

7. For a recent treatment of Thomas Erskine's theories of freedom of the press, the heart of his opposition thought, see L. Levy, *Emergence of a Free Press*, 282–91 (1985).

8. It is certainly true that the English political opposition to the court interests invoked much of the thought of the country thinkers such as Harrington and Bolingbroke, but since the chief oppositionist theorists in the late eighteenth century were, more often than not, urban radicals, it seems misleading to call their philosophy "country" thought.

9. See, e.g., J. G. A. Pocock, *The Ancient Constitution and the Feudal Law*, 229–51 (Norton, ed., 1967), and particularly his comments on the thought of Edmund Burke. For a primary source, drawn from the world of the law which stresses the importance of the "glorious revolution," see, e.g., Mr. Justice Barrington's opinion in the *Dean of St. Asaph's* case, where he indicated that the only relevant authorities for determining the law of seditious libel are those "since the time of the Revolution [of 1688]." *King v. Jones*, 21 State Trials 847, 872 (1783).

10. For a discussion of the English conservatives' constitutional trinity, see J. G. A. Pocock, *The Ancient Constitution and the Feudal Law*, 229–51 (Norton, ed., 1967). Pocock's comments on the thought of Edmund Burke, id. at 242–43, are particularly supportive of the analysis presented here. For the theories of balancing orders in society which came from the classical models of government, supplied by such thinkers as Ar-

istotle and Polybius, see generally J. G. A. Pocock, *The Machiavellian Moment: Florentine Political Thought and the Atlantic Republican Tradition*, 361–67 (1975).

11. On the "bloody assizes," findings of guilt, and carrying out death sentences for four hundred peasants who participated in the rebellion against James II staged by Charles II's illegitimate son, The Duke of Monmouth, see L. B. Smith, *This Realm of England 1399 to 1688*, 292 (3d ed., 1976).

12. For Lord Macaulay's praise of Powell's opinion, in terms that seem to track the philosophy of the late eighteenth-century conservatives, who saw themselves as custodians of the glorious revolution, see the excerpt in S. Presser and J. Zainaldin, *Law and Jurisprudence in American History*, 22 (2d ed., 1989).

13. See, e.g., *The Whole Proceeding on the King's Commission of the Peace, Oyer and Terminer and Gaol Delivery for the City of London and also the Gaol Delivery for the County of Middlesex held at Justice Hall in the Old Baily taken in short hand by E. Hodgson, on Wednesday the 19th of December, 1783, and on the following Days* ... no. I, pt. I [hereafter cited as OBSP] ("Old Baily Sessions Papers"), at 4–5 (presiding judge informs jury about the practices of "these kind of men," referring to the criminal classes).

14. For a thorough review of this English jury tradition, see T. Green, *Verdict According to Conscience: Perspectives on the English Criminal Trial Jury 1200–1800* (1985).

15. W. Blackstone, 4 *Commentaries on the Laws of England* 343, 354, 355 (quoting Hale at 355, Blackstone remarked "for if the judge's opinion must rule the verdict, the trial by jury would be useless").

16. Id. at 354.

17. T. Hutchinson, "A Dialogue Between an American and a European Englishman," printed in 4 *Perspectives in American History* 343, 399 (B. Bailyn, ed., 1975) (original manuscript dates from 1768).

18. Id. at 408.

19. See, e.g., Lord Kenyon's opinion in the *Dean of St. Asaph's* trial for seditious libel, where he notes that "human nature, in the state of corruption in which we find it, always is prompt to transgress all the bounds that common and ordinary rules can prescribe," and therefore juries need the careful guidance of judges. *King v. Jones*, 21 *State Trials* 847, 871 (1783).

20. See, e.g., Document 19(e), Harrowby Mss., Notes on a "Speech to the Grand Jury (1755)" by Sir Dudley Ryder, in the Dudley Ryder notebook manuscripts, Lincoln's Inn, where he advises a grand jury that the English laws against "popery" are not "laws against conscience," but serve an important temporal purpose because "long and melancholy experience has taught us [that Popery] is constantly attended with principles of a temporal kind, absolutely inconsistent with our civil interests. Their [the Catholics'] first principle is blind submission to a foreign power." Similarly in Document 19(f), Ryder records having exhorted a special jury to "steadiness in attachment" to their religion against the popish enemy. In Document 19(g), Notes on a Ryder Speech to Grand Jury delivered in August 1754, he stresses English citizens' obligation to "promote the sense of the divine supreme being of God, and Worship of God," and notes that the king, through his chancellor, had recently proclaimed and commanded that his judges inculcate such behavior, and, in particular, "spread amongst the people a proper

respect for God and the Christian religion, and a sense of love of their country." The Ryder manuscripts further note that the chancellor stated that the king was particularly disturbed by neglect of religion in the realm. After stressing that the "peace and order" of His Majesty's government depended on his subjects' understanding that the Deity "knows, examines, and will one day call all of us to account," and that judges should make sure offenders understand that they are in danger not only in "this world, but in the next which is to come," the chancellor concluded, in words much like those Chase would use in his 1803 Baltimore grand jury charge that "Religion respects both worlds. It is the cement of civil society and the great security of governments in this, as well as the sole foundation of rational hopes in the next. Without it, no government ever did or can subsist, and the Protestant religion is in a peculiar manner the solid basis of our present happy establishment." Id.

21. OBSP, supra note 16, pt. II, at 5, 22 (Old Baily judges advising capitally convicted defendants to apply to ordinaries in order to correct their "malignant tempers" before the dates of their executions, in order that they might procure divine mercy, and thus save their everlasting souls).

22. See, e.g., the comments of the prosecutor's counsel, Mr. Bearcroft, in the trial of the Dean of St. Asaph's, in August 1784, to the effect that "farmers" should leave matters of politics, which they should not be expected to comprehend, to "the King and Parliament." The text of such farmers, said Mr. Bearcroft, ought to be "Fear God and honour the King," because England "would be in a tumult if every man of 21 voted with a musket at this side." In words which could have applied equally to the trial of Fries, over which Chase would preside sixteen years later, Bearcroft concluded, "if any man advises a set of men to bear arms, to make an alteration in the state and government that obtains in this country, and shall so far succeed as to persuade these men to take arms and banners, declaring that such is their object, both he and they in point of law, as has been solemnly determined, are guilty of the crime of high treason." *King v. Jones*, 21 *State Trials* 847, 888–89 (1784).

23. In the Dudley Ryder Notebooks, supra note 20, Document 19(i), a charge Ryder gave to a grand jury in Chelmsford, he calls the Revolution of 1688 the "greatest and most happy event this nation ever experienced," and says that it was "the fruit of those strong convulsions the nation underwent for many years before, and which, by the overruling goodness of God has ended in an entire settlement of the liberties of the nation upon the truest foundation."

24. For the suggestion that Blackstone, the leading legal writer of the conservatives, clearly put absolute sovereignty in a parliament beyond the control of the people, see Rabban, "The Ahistorical Historian: Leonard Levy on Freedom of Expression in Early American History," 37 *Stan. L. Rev.* 795, 826–27 (1985).

25. Quoted in Goodwin, supra note 5, at 87, and Rabban, supra note 24, at 836, n. 192.

26. See generally on Wilkes, G. Rude, *Wilkes and Liberty* (1983 ed.); J. Brewer, *Party Ideology and Popular Politics at the Accession of George III* (1976); and Ian R. Christie, *Wilkes, Wyville, and Reform* (1962).

27. For some sources and thoughts on the emergence of the late eighteenth-century English theory of popular sovereignty, see Rabban, supra note 24, at 823–24.

28. For the most influential contemporary statements of this theory of the Ancient Constitution, and its modern reformist implications, see O. Hulme, *Historical Essay on the English Constitution* (1771), and J. Burgh, *Political Disquisitions* (3 vols., 1774– 75). For Thomas Paine's use of Burgh in *Common Sense*, see T. Paine, *Common Sense* 111n. (I. Kramick, ed., 1976).

29. See, e.g., Wilkes's famous suggestion in No. 45 of the *North Briton*, his oppositionist journal, that "the King is only the first magistrate of this country . . . responsible to his people for the due exercise of the royal functions in the choice of ministers," quoted in Plumb, supra note 3, at 120.

30. The implications of these theories would also be worked out in American politics and constitution-making after the Revolution of 1776. See generally G. Wood, *The Creation of the American Republic 1776–1787* (1969).

31. For a discussion of the tract-circulating acitivities of the London Revolutionary Society and the Society for Constitutional Information, see A. Goodwin, supra note 5, at 65–98.

32. These eighteenth-century tracts on the jury are discussed in T. Green, *Verdict According to Conscience: Perspectives on the English Criminal Trial Jury, 1200–1800*, at 346–49 (1985).

33. *King v. Jones*, 21 *State Trials* 847, 851, 854, 864 (1783).

34. See, e.g., ibid., at 871 (Lord Kenyon) and 872 (Justice Barrington).

35. Id., at 847, 851, 854, 864.

36. W. Forsyth, *History of Trial by Jury*, 278 (1852) (Fox's Libel Act simply placed "trials for libel on the same footing as trials for other offenses; and it in no respect absolves a jury from the duty of obeying the direction of the judge as to the legal character of the writing which is the subject of the inquiry").

37. Goodwin, supra note 5, at 65–98.

38. For the most comprehensive treatment of all of these strands of thought, see A. Goodwin, supra note 5, at 65–98, for a discussion of the religious and philosophical ideas behind the British radical movement. For the case that one of the most important radicals, Thomas Paine, made for Christian religious liberty, see T. Paine, supra note 28, at 108–9.

39. For a discussion of Wilkes's denial that he himself was a "Wilkite," see A. Goodwin, supra note 5, at 44.

CHAPTER 5

1. Quoted in J. Miller, *The Federalist Era 1789–1801*, 255 (1960).

2. For the case which outlawed union organization, see *Commonwealth v. Pullis*, mayor's court of Philadelphia, 1806, J. Commons et al., *A Documentary History of American Industrial Society*, vol. 3, at 60 (1910), edited with commentary in S. Presser and J. Zainaldin, *Law and Jurisprudence in American History*, 600–619 (2d ed., 1989). For portraits of late eighteenth-century Philadelphia, see E. Foner, *Tom Paine and Revolutionary America*, 19–69 (1976), and G. Nash, *The Urban Crucible* (1979).

3. R. Harper, "A letter . . . to his constituents" (1801), reprinted in *Selected Works of Robert Goodloe Harper*, vol. 1, at 325 (1814), quoted in R. Buel, Jr., *Securing the Revolution: Ideology in American Politics 1789–1815*, 241 (1972).

4. Biographical data on Peters can be found in *Richard Peters, His Ancestors and Descendants 1810–1889*, 68 (N. Black, ed., 1904) [hereafter cited as N. Black]. For a brief treatment, see the entry for Richard Peters by Edward S. Corwin, in 14 *Dictionary of American Biography* 509 (1934).

5. U.S. Const., art. III, sec. 2, gave the federal courts admiralty jurisdiction, and the Judiciary Act of 1789 gave this jurisdiction to the district court. Peters wrote nineteen of the twenty-four published opinions during the period 1789 to 1801, the period most relevant to our review here. All of the published opinions dealt with matters of admiralty law.

6. *Willings v. Blight*, 30 F. Cas. 50, 52 (D. Pa. 1900) (No. 17,765).

7. See, e.g., B. Bailyn, *The Ideological Origins of the American Revolution*, 30–31 (1967).

8. See, e.g., L. Friedman, *A History of American Law*, 96–97 (1973).

9. See generally G. Gilmore and C. Black, *Admiralty* (1975).

10. For Hopkinson's references to "law and reason," see *Rice v. The Polly and Kitty*, 20 F. Cas. 666 (1789) (D. Pa. No. 11,754). For the "rights of humanity," see *Dixon v. The Cyrus*, 7 F. Cas. 755 (1789) (D. Pa. No. 3,930). Both cases held that ships' captains have certain obligations to their seamen, whether or not there is an express contract. Among these were said to be "seaworthiness" of the vessel, sufficient meat and drink, and humane treatment.

11. See generally Stein, "The Attraction of the Civil Law in Post-Revolutionary America," 52 *Va. L. Rev.* 403, 407–9 (1966).

12. 13 F. Cas. 540, 542 (D. Pa. 1792) (No. 7,281).

13. See also *Hart v. The Littlejohn*, 11 F. Cas. 687, 688 (D. Pa. 1789) (No. 6,153) (American admiralty court not bound by English common law, but by rules of the "civil and maritime" law).

14. 29 F. Cas. 215 (D. Pa. 1792) (No. 17,165).

15. Id. at 217.

16. *Brevoor v. The Fair American*, 4 F. Cas. 71 (D. Pa. 1800) (No. 1,847).

17. On the "actuarial consciousness" of American judges, see M. Horwitz, *The Transformation of American Law, 1790–1860*, at 226–37 (1977).

18. 23 F. Cas. 1028 (D. Pa. 1795) (No. 13,949).

19. Id. at 1029.

20. Ibid.

21. 12 F. Cas. 348 (D. Pa. 1795) (No. 6,612).

22. Id. at 351. Peters's practice here is similar to the law court practices of using special or "struck" juries in commerical matters, discussed in M. Horwitz, supra note 17, at 155–59.

23. 23 F. Cas. 560 (D. Pa. 1799) (No. 13,697).

24. 19 F. Cas. 945 (D. Pa. 1799) (No. 11,234).

25. Id. at 946.

26. 30 F. Cas. 50 (D. Pa. 1800) (No. 17,765).

27. See generally M. Horwitz, supra note 17, passim.

28. M. Horwitz, supra note 17, at 211–12. But see Presser, Book Review, 52 *N.Y.U.L. Rev.* 700 (1977) (suggesting that there may have been no great division between the

majority of the people and those favoring commerce). For a recent work on republican-ism in late eighteenth-century America, which finds great ambivalence among the American people and among their political theorists over the value of commerce, see D. McCoy, *The Elusive Republic: Political Economy in Jeffersonian America*, 100–104 (1980).

29. The most eloquent statement of these views is probably Jefferson, "Notes on Vir-ginia," in, e.g., *The Life and Selected Writings of Thomas Jefferson*, 279–80 (A. Koch and W. Peden, eds., 1944).

30. R. Buel, Jr., supra note 3, at x.

31. See, e.g., the popular organ, the *Philadelphia General Advertiser*, November 27, 1790, at 3, col. 3 (stressing importance of agriculture but also commerce and manu-facturing); November 28, 1790, at 3, col. 2 (importance of carrying trade).

32. The New Jersey federal admiralty court, by contrast, operated with a jury, pre-sumably because of popular approval of juries, and hostility to the example of English admiralty courts, which had none. See D. Henderson, *Courts for a New Nation*, 56 (1971).

33. See R. Buel, Jr., supra note 3, at 40–42.

34. *Findley v. The William*, 9 F. Cas. 57 (D. Pa. 1793) (No. 4,790); *Moxon v. The Fanny*, 17 F. Cas. 942 (D. Pa. 1793) (No. 9,873).

35. These details regarding Peters and agriculture are given in an address by Samuel Breck to the Blakely and Merion Agricultural Society (Sept. 20, 1828), in 5 *Farmers Library* (1845), reprinted in N. Black, supra note 4, at 68.

36. Letter from George Washington to Richard Peters, January 21, 1797, 10 Historical Society of Pennsylvania, Peters Papers 46 (hereafter cited as Peters Papers); Letter from George Washington to Richard Peters (Mar. 4, 1796), 10 Peters Papers, supra, at 40.

37. Letter from Alexander Hamilton to Richard Peters (Aug. 13, 1791), 9 Peters Papers, supra note 36, at 121.

38. N. Black, supra note 4, at 8.

39. N. Black, supra note 4, at 67, 78, 79.

40. See, e.g., Letter from Timothy Pickering to Richard Peters (Apr. 9, 1790), 9 Peters Papers, supra note 36, at 108; Letter from Timothy Pickering to Richard Peters (Sept. 28, 1797), 10 Peters Papers, supra note 36, at 51; Letter from Timothy Pickering to Richard Peters (Aug. 28, 1798), 10 Peters Papers, supra note 36, at 53.

41. Letter from Thomas Jefferson to Richard Peters (June 13, 1790), 9 Peters Papers, supra note 36, at 109; Letter from Thomas Jefferson to Richard Peters (June 30, 1791), id. at 119.

42. See, e.g., R. K. Newmyer, *Supreme Court Justice Joseph Story: Statesman of the Old Republic*, 93, 104–5 (1985). Newmyer's recent brilliant book on Story (now the definitive biography of that great justice) unfortunately follows the usual practice of giving Story credit for innovation in doctrine when he was simply following the paths already laid down by Richard Peters.

43. W. W. Story, *Life and Letters of Joseph Story*, vol. 1, at 540 (1851).

44. On the practice of federal judges "riding circuit," see F. Frankfurter and J. Landes, *The Business of the Supreme Court*, 11, 14–20 (1928).

45. See G. White, *The American Judicial Tradition* (1976). White suggested that be-ginning with Justice John Marshall there was an American judicial tradition character-

ized by "a tension between independence and accountability," "a delicate and unique relation to politics," and "a ... trade-off between ... powers and freedoms in the individual judge, and constraints on the institution." Id. at 2. Based on what is presented in this book, it is easy to understand how the pre-Marshall federal judges' failure to maintain what later scholars have felt to be an appropriate distance from political controversy impedes scholars such as White from recognizing them as progentors of an American judicial tradition. There is some merit to this view, of course, but I think it smacks a bit too much of presentism. The effort undertaken here is to show, as recognized by a few scholars such as Paul Freund, that "there were brave men before Agamemnon." "Editor's Introduction," to J. Goebel, Jr., *A History of the Supreme Court: Antecedents and Beginnings to 1801*, vol. 1, at xiv. Unfortunately these "brave men before Agamemnon" had some tragic flaws, none more grievous than those of Samuel Chase, which substantially prevented later recognition of their greatness.

46. 2 U.S. (2 Dall.) 409 (1792).

47. Act of March 23, 1792, ch. 1, 1 Stat. 324, sec. 2–4.

48. Id. at sec. 2.

49. Id. at sec. 3.

50. Id. at sec. 4.

51. The letter is reprinted in 2 U.S. (2 Dall.) 411 (1792). For a discussion of *Hayburn* in particular and "extrajudicial activities" of the pre-Marshall Supreme Court in general, see Wheeler, "Extra-Judicial Activities of the Early Supreme Court," 1973 *Sup. Ct. Rev.* 123, 135–39. For a recent suggestion, however, that the Supreme Court's actions in *Hayburn* should not be taken as precedent for a "case in controversy" requirement, and thus may not be a valid example of "judicial restraint," see Marcus and Teir, "Hayburn's Case: A Misinterpretation of Precedent," 1988 *Wis. L. Rev.* 527.

52. Act of February 28, 1793, ch. 1, Stat. 324, but see Wheeler, supra note 51, at 138–39, for the assertion that Congress set up the new scheme, not because of the separation of powers problem, but because those judges who were participating as "commissioners" were too "sympathetic" in granting pensions. It seems that Wheeler's authorities may show congressional parsimony as a main motive for the passage of the 1793 statute. Nevertheless, the fact that no one was prepared to act as a "commissioner" in the Pennsylvania circuit must have equally influenced Congress. This difficulty in Pennsylvania, of course, was solely owing to thc principled stand on judicial independence taken by the judges of the Pennsylvania circuit.

53. See, e.g., *National Gazette*, April 12, 1792, quoted in C. Warren, *The Supreme Court in United States History*, vol. 1, at 70 n. 1 (rev. ed., 1947), also quoted in H. Hart and H. Wechsler, *The Federal Courts and the Federal System*, 87 (2d ed. 1973):

> Our poor, starving invalids have at length some provision made for them by Congress; and as the distresses of many of them are urgent in the extreme, it is to be hoped that not a moment's delay will be made by the public officers who are directed to settle their accounts. ... If through unavoidable delay any of those unfortunate men should starve before their pittance is paid, then it is to be hoped their widows and orphans will on the first application receive it, that they may at least have something to purchase coffins for the deceased.

54. This activity of the Pennsylvania troops was part of general army dissatisfaction with the Continental Congress which led in March 1783 to the "Newburgh Ad-

dresses," pleas by veterans recommending, in the interests of justice, the establishment of a military dictatorship for the new nation. See generally J. Alden, *The American Revolution*, 265–67 (1954).

55. The Pennsylvania federal judges were criticized for this refusal in a "Letter from Camden," published in the *Philadelphia General Advertiser (Aurora)*, later the leading Republican party newspaper, on April 21, 1792, cited in Wheeler, supra note 51, at 138, n. 73.

56. See Ritz, *United States v. Yale Todd*, 15 *Wash. & Lee L. Rev.* 220 (1958). But see J. Goebel, Jr., supra note 45, vol. 1, at 564 n. 37.

57. 54 U.S. (13 How.) 40, 53 n (1851). Chief Justice Taney summarizes the result in the case of *United States v. Todd* (Feb. 17, 1794), in which the Supreme Court declared that Mr. Todd had to refund his pension, which he was granted by some "Judge-commissioners." The ruling is apparently construed by Taney as an acknowledgment that those judges who *did* act as commissioners acted illegally and that their actions were therefore void. Indeed, Taney believed that the decision in the *Todd* case was unanimous, and that therefore "Chief Justice Jay and Justice Cushing (who had acted as commissioners) became satisfied, on further reflection, that the power given in the act of 1792 to the circuit court as a court, could not be construed to give it to the judges out of court as 'Commissioners.' " Id. at 53. Taney appears to have taken the reversal on the part of Jay and Cushing as an indication that they belatedly perceived the separation of powers problems. But see Wheeler, supra note 51, at 139, and n. 77, for the assertion that Jay and Cushing had merely come to the realization that "judges do not make good administrative officers," that "judge-commissioners were not qualified to determine the pension claims, and that as a consequence, many undeserving applicants had been placed on the pension list."

58. 28 F. Cas. 1012 (C.C.D. Pa. 1795) (No. 16,857).

59. Act of March 28, 1787, 1787 Pa. Laws 770.

60. 5 U.S. (1 Cranch) 137 (1803). For a discussion of *Marbury*, giving a good statement of the traditional view of the case's importance, see G. White, supra note 45, at 22–24.

61. 28 F. Cas. 1014.

62. 28 F. Cas. 1018.

63. Id. at 1019.

64. See, e.g., *Fletcher v. Peck*, 10 U.S. (6 Cranch) 87, 139 (1810). Cf. Grey, "Do We Have an Unwritten Constitution?," 27 *Stan. L. Rev.* 703. 708 (1975) (suggests that Marshall's views on property rights were not supported by constitutional text).

65. *Searight v. Calbraith*, 21 F. Cas. 927 (C.C.D. Pa. 1796) (No. 12,585).

66. *Wilkinson v. Nicklin*, 29 F. Cas. 1263 (C.C.D. Pa. 1798) (No. 17,673).

67. See, e.g., *Livingston v. Swanwick*, 15 F. Cas. 696 (C.C.D. Pa. 1793) (No. 8,419); *Parassell v. Gautier*, 18 F. Cas. 1089 (C.C.D. Pa. 1795) (No. 10,709); *Wharton v. Lowrey*, 29 F. Cas. 855 (C.C.D. Pa. 1796) (No. 17,481).

68. *Searight v. Calbraith*, 21 F. Cas. 927 (C.C.D. Pa. 1796) (No. 12,585).

69. Id. at 928–29.

70. Ibid.

71. W. Nelson, *The Americanization of the Common Law: The Impact of Legal Change on Massachusetts Society, 1760–1830*, 54–63 (1975); M. Horwitz, *The Transformation of American Law 1780–1860*, 166–67 (1979).

72. *Van Horne's Lessee v. Dorrance*, 28 F. Cas. at 1013, 1015.
73. See, e.g., the views of the Massachusetts judge Theodore Sedgwick, described in R. Ellis, *The Jeffersonian Crisis: Courts and Politics in the Young Republic*, 190 (1971).

CHAPTER 6

1. 11 F. Cas. 1099 (C.C.D. Pa. 1793) (No. 6,360).
2. See *National Gazette*, August 3, 1793; *Philadelphia General Advertiser*, August 3, 1793.
3. *Works of Thomas Jefferson*, vol. 9, at 73 (P. Ford, ed., 1904), quoted in A. Beveridge, *The Life of John Marshall*, vol. 2, at 29 (1916).
4. A. Beveridge, supra note 3, vol. 3, at 23.
5. *Compare*, e.g., Warren, "New Light on the History of the Federal Judiciary Act of 1789," 37 *Harv. L. Rev.* 49, 73 (1923), with J. Goebel, Jr., *A History of the Supreme Court: Antecedents and Beginnings to 1801*, vol. 1, at 229–30, 626–27 (1971), and *Compare* Preyer, "Jurisdiction to Punish: Federal Authority, Federalism and the Common Law of Crimes in the Early Republic," 4 *Law and History Review* 223 (1986), and Palmer, "The Federal Common Law of Crime," 4 *Law and History Review* 267 (1986), with Jay, "Origins of the Federal Common Law: Part One," 133 *U. Pa. L. Rev.* 1003 (1985), L. Levy, *Emergence of a Free Press*, 275–79, 298 (1985), and Presser, "The Supra-Constitution, the Courts, and the Federal Common Law of Crimes: Some Comments on Palmer and Preyer," 4 *Law and History Review* 325 (1986).
6. An act to establish the judicial courts of the United States, ch. 20, 1 Stat. 73 sec. 11 (1789).
7. Jay's charge was apparently delivered May 4, 1790. The quotations in the following paragraphs are taken from *Independent Chronicle*, May 27, 1790, at 2. Jay's 1790 charge was published at the request of the grand jury and was thus widely circulated. If Jay's conception of what constituted a federal crime was incorrect, since his charge was so close in time to the passage of the Judiciary Act itself, one might have expected to find some contemporary criticism of it. My research has, so far, not turned up any.
8. Id.
9. Id. This change of Jay's appears nearly identical to the one he delivered April 12, 1790, in New York, recently reprinted in *The Documentary History of the Supreme Court of the United States, 1789–1800*, vol. 2, at 25–30 (Marcus, ed., 1988).
10. *Henfield's Case*, 11 F. Cas. 1099, 1100–01 (C.C.D. Pa. 1793) (No. 6,360); *State Trials of the United States During the Administrations of Washington and Adams*, 50, 52 (F. Wharton, ed., 1949) (hereafter cited as *State Trials*). This change delivered to the grand jury of the Circuit Court for the District of Virginia appears in a fuller version in *Documentary History*, supra note 9, vol. 2, at 380–91.
11. For a concise discussion of the split of public opinion and the political background of the "Neutrality Proclamation," see J. Miller, *The Federalist Era 1789–1801*, 363–69 (1960).
12. 11 F. Cas. 1102; *State Trials*, supra note 10, at 53.
13. 11 F. Cas. 1103; *State Trials*, supra note 10, at 54.
14. See generally Lerner, "The Supreme Court as Republican Schoolmaster," 1967 *Sup. Ct. Rev.*, 127, 129–55.

15. 11 F. Cas. 1106; *State Trials*, supra note 10, at 61. Wilson's charge is reprinted in *Documentary History*, supra note 9, vol. 2, at 414–23.

16. Id. at 1106; *State Trials*, supra note 10, at 61, 65. This accords with Thomas Jefferson's views on the Saxons and the Normans. See Waterman, "Thomas Jefferson and Blackstone's Commentaries," 27 *Ill. L. Rev.* 629, 643–45 (1933).

17. 11 F. Cas. at 1107; *State Trials*, supra note 10, at 61.

18. Id. at 1107; *State Trials*, supra note 10, at 61–62.

19. Id. at 1107; *State Trials*, supra note 10, at 62.

20. Ibid.

21. Id. at 1108; *State Trials*, supra note 10, at 63.

22. Id.

23. The indictment is reproduced in id. at 1109, 1115; *State Trials*, supra note 10, at 66, 76–77.

24. Other counts of the indictment charged Henfield with specific violations of particular treaties. In the excerpt quoted, however, the offense charged was said to exist simply by virtue of "the law of nations." Id.

25. The points made by Rawle are reported in id. at 1116–17, *State Trials*, supra note 10, at 78–79 (emphasis in the original). As authority for this last proposition, Rawle cited W. Blackstone, *Commentaries*, vol. 4, at 69.

26. 11 F. Cas. 1117; *State Trials*, supra note 10, at 79–80 (emphasis in original).

27. Id. at 1119; *State Trials*, supra note 10, at 83.

28. Id. at 1120; *State Trials*, supra note 10, at 84.

29. No defense was based on the facts, and Wilson in his charge to the petit jury stressed that the relevant facts had been "clearly established" or "explicitly acknowledged." No commentators on the case have disagreed with this assessment.

30. See R. Buel, Jr., *Securing the Revolution: Ideology in American Politics 1789–1815*, at 25 (1972).

31. *National Gazette* of Philadelphia, August 3, 1793, quoted in R. Buel, Jr., supra note 30, at 25.

32. This same article, under the title of "From a correspondent," appeared word for word in the *Philadelphia General Advertiser*, August 3, 1793, although one word in the last paragraph was erroneously typeset.

33. *National Gazette* of Philadelphia, supra note 31.

34. The seven bishops were being prosecuted under the notorious seditious libel doctrine of the Stuarts: the greater the truth of the libel, the greater the crime. The jury apparently rejected this doctrine, in a holding which seemed to indicate that they regarded truth as a defense to the crime of seditious libel, and the bishops were acquitted. The trial was on June 29, 1688, and is reported in *A Complete Collection of State Trials*, vol. 4, at 300–392 (2d ed., 1730). The most famous account of the trial is T. Macaulay, *History of England*, vol. 2, at 990–1039 (1858). The trial of the seven bishops was frequently cited as precedent by counsel for John Peter Zenger in his celebrated 1735 New York trial for seditious libel. Americans (and English opposition theorists, and probably even some conservatives) regarded the verdict of acquittal in the *Seven Bishops* case as a great triumph for the liberty of the subject against the arbitrary persecution of the sovereign. See generally J. Alexander, *A Brief Narrative of the Case and Trial of John Peter Zenger*, 28, 72–73, 85 (S. Katz, ed., 1963).

35. J. Marshall, *Life of George Washington*, vol. 2, at 273–74 (1807), quoted in A. Beveridge, supra note 3, vol. 3, at 26, also quoted in C. Warren, *The Supreme Court in United States History*,vol. 1, at 113 (rev. ed., 1947).
36. *Massachusetts Mercury*, August 9, 1793, at 2, col. 3.
37. Letter from Thomas Jefferson to Robert Morris (1793), reprinted in *State Trials*, supra note 10, at 89 note.
38. Id.
39. See J. Marshall, supra note 35.
40. *United States v. Ravara*, 27 F. Cas. 714; *State Trials*, supra note 10, at 90 (C.C.D. Pa. 1794) (No. 16,122).
41. 27 F. Cas. 714; *State Trials*, supra note 10, at 90. There was some skirmishing over whether or not the circuit court could take jurisdiction over the case, since the consti-tutional provision giving the Supreme Court original jurisdiction "in all cases affecting ambassadors, other public ministers, and consuls" might well have been intended to vest exclusive jurisdiction in the Supreme Court. U.S. Const., art. III, sec. 2. Justice Wilson and Judge Peters agreed that the provision of the Judiciary Act giving jurisdic-tion to the circuit courts for "all crimes and offenses, cognizable under the authority of the United States" gave the circuit courts concurrent jurisdiction. Ravara's motion to quash the indictment was thus denied, and he pleaded not guilty. His trial was post-poned until the next term by agreement.

Some latter-day critics of the common law crimes jurisdiction have distinguished *Ra-vara* from other true "common law" cases, such as *Worrall*, infra, on the grounds that since the Constitution explicitly granted the federal courts jurisdiction over cases in-volving "consuls," or "law of nations" jurisdiction, it was not a usurpation to accept such jurisdiction in *Ravara*, though it might have been in *Worrall*. This ignores the fact that Peters, Wilson, and probably most Federalists did not make fine distinctions among matters involving consuls, the law of nations, or the common law, viewing them all as aspects of the same problem, the government's need to prosecute some crimes even before statutes (or treaties) had been passed making them crimes. Such an argu-ment also ignores the fact that while the Constitution may have given the Supreme Court jurisdiction involving consuls, no statute explicitly gave it to the lower federal courts, nor did any statute explictly make extortion on the part of consuls a crime.
42. 27 F. Cas. 714; *State Trials*, supra note 10, at 91.
43. See supra note 15, and accompanying text. This also makes it rather difficult to use *Ravara* as a case to support an argument that late eighteenth-century Americans believed in a limited jurisdiction for federal common law crimes.
44. 27 F. Cas. 714; *State Trials*, supra note 10, at 92.
45. Id.
46. C. Warren, supra note 35, vol. 1, at 114–15.
47. *United States v. Guinet*, 26 F. Cas. 53; *State Trials*, supra note 10, at 93, 101 (C.C.D. Pa. 1795) (No. 15,270).
48. See R. Buel, Jr., supra note 30, at 126–29.
49. C. Warren, supra note 35, vol. 1, at 114.
50. J. Goebel, Jr., supra note 5, vol. 1, at 629–30.
51. 28 F. Cas. 774; *State Trials*, supra note 10, at 189 (C.C.D. Pa. 1798) (No. 16,766).

52. Id. at 776, 777; *State Trials*, supra note 10, at 192, 194. To demonstrate that an attempted bribe was indictable at common law, the prosecutor, William Rawle, cited English authority, 4 Burr. 2494 (*Rex v. Vaughan*, 98 Eng. Rep. 308 (1769)), and Ld. Raym. vol. 1, at 1377.

53. One of the counsel for the defense, Mr. M. Levy, observed that the offense "must be legally defined," but there is no suggestion from the report that this was expanded before the jury into an argument against the indictment of crimes without statutes. Most of the argument before the jury seems to have been over the legal question of whether or not the court sitting in Philadelphia could take jurisdiction, since the letter in which the bribe was originally offered, though written in Pennsylvania, was delivered to Mr. Coxe in New Jersey. The court ruled that writing and delivering the letter to the post office in Pennsylvania was sufficient to confer jurisdiction over the crime. Id. at 776; *State Trials*, supra note 10, at 192.

54. R. Buel, Jr., supra note 30, at 166–83.

55. 28 F. Cas. 776-77; *State Trials*, supra note 10, at 193.

56. Id. at 777; *State Trials*, supra note 10, at 194.

57. Id.

58. Id. at 777; *State Trials*, supra note 10, at 195. The report has Dallas referring to "the twelfth article of the amendment," but the text he quotes is that which we now refer to as the Tenth Amendment: "the powers not delegated to the United States by the Constitution, nor prohibited by it to the States, are reserved to the States respectively, or to the people." U.S. Const., Tenth Amendment (1791).

59. U.S. Const., art. I, sec. 8, cl. 6.

60. Id. cl. 18.

61. 28 F. Cas. at 778; *State Trials*, supra note 10, at 195. But see supra note 43 for the suggestion that there are flaws in Dallas's argument. A quarter of a century later Peter S. DuPonceau, in *A Dissertation on the Nature and Extent of the Jurisdiction of the Courts of the United States*, 18 (1824), retooled Dallas's argument, and suggested that where the United States Constitution gave the federal courts explicit jurisdiction over broad subject matters (as it did with admiralty, for example) the federal government could use the common law to support prosecutions. Where there was no such broad grant (for example, in bribery cases), DuPonceau maintained, the common law could furnish no basis for prosecution. This approach, which is intellectually very sophisticated, to me at least reflects a level of abstraction which may go beyond the framers' intentions, as will be developed in greater detail, infra. In any event, this view is not the view of either Chase or Peters as stated in the *Worrall* case.

One further precedent cited by Dallas on the question of jurisdiction over crimes at common law should be noted in passing. In *Respublica v. Shaeffer*, the mayor's court of Philadelphia had permitted a prosecution by the state of Pennsylvania against persons accused of forging claims to United States land warrants issuable under the resolutions of Congress. Since by virtue of the 1799 Judiciary Act, jurisdiction over crimes and offenses against the United States was exclusively vested in the federal courts, counsel for the defense in Shaeffer moved in arrest of judgment on the grounds that the offense was a federal crime and therefore not punishable in a state court. Since there was no federal statute making the counterfeiting of these warrants a federal crime, the defense motion amounted to a claim that there was exclusive federal common law jurisdiction. The recorder of the mayor's court overruled the motion. Thus Dallas cited the case as support for the proposition that there was no federal common law.

Rawle attempted to suggest that the *Shaeffer* ruling did not go to the existence or nonexistence of a federal common law, that the crime in question was a state crime, defrauding of citizens in Pennsylvania, and thus the case was simply concerned with "forgery," an offense punishable at state law. 28 F. Cas. at 778; *State Trials*, supra note 10, at 196.

62. 28 F. Cas. 778; *State Trials*, supra note 10, at 196. In the report in *State Trials* there is an obvious error in the substitution of the word "distinguishable" for "indistinguishable" in the fifteenth line of page 196.

If one examines the initial pleadings in each case, one does get the impression that they were framed, by the prosecution, and probably by Rawle himself, with the understanding that they were indictments at common law, indictments which presumed a power in the federal courts to punish crimes even if no statute had defined an offense and prescribed a penalty.

63. See text accompanying notes 6–22, *supra*.

64. See also the pleadings of *Ravara* in the case, which seem to admit the common law jurisdiction. Supra note 42.

65. 28 F. Cas. at 779; *State Trials*, supra note 10, at 197.

66. Id. at 779; *State Trials*, supra note 10, at 197–98.

67. Id. at 779–80; *State Trials*, supra note 10, at 198.

68. For an account see J. Smith, *Freedom's Fetters: The Alien and Sedition Laws and American Civil Liberties*, 131–35 (1956).

69. See note 3, supra (Jefferson's letter calumnizing the Federalists for the suggestion that there was a federal common law of crimes).

70. See, e.g., the Virginia and Kentucky resolutions, which were designed principally to argue against the existence of a federal common law of crimes, discussed in J. Miller, *Crisis In Freedom: The Alien and Sedition Acts*, 169–80 (1951).

71. J. Goebel, Jr., supra note 5, vol. 1, at 658–59.

72. See id. at 229–30.

73. Id. at 654. The speech is reported at 8 *Annals of Cong.* 2145 (1804).

74. Id.

75. J. Goebel, Jr., supra note 5, vol. 1, at 296.

76. Id.

77. See, e.g., Jefferson's fiery letter on the matter, supra note 3.

78. K. Preyer, supra note 5, at 237, quoting from Marshall to St. George Tucker, November 27, 1800. Marshall Papers. Ac. 2354, Library of Congress.

79. See, e.g., those of Henfield, Ravarra, Worrall; the aborted prosecution of Benjamin Bache for seditious libel; the prosecution of Isaac Williams; and several other cases noted by Preyer, supra note 5, at 230.

80. See Preyer, supra note 5, and Palmer, supra note 5.

81. See text accompanying notes 6–22, *supra*, for Jay and Wilson. For Ellsworth, see *U.S. v. Isaac Williams*, 29 F. Cas. 1330, and *State Trials*, supra note 10, at 652 (Case No. 17,170, C.C.D. Conn. 1799).

82. Preyer, supra note 5, at 228.

83. Professor Preyer's quotes are from a grand jury charge of June 1, 1794, recorded in J. McRee, ed., *Life and Correspondence of James Iredell*, vol. 2, 423 (New York, 1949). The date should probably have been June 2, 1794, and the charge appears to have been the same as the one Iredell delivered May 12, 1794, in Columbia, South Carolina, reprinted in *Documentary History*, supra note 9, vol. 2, at 454–70.

84. Id., quoting from McRee, supra note 83, vol. 2, at 467–74.

85. 4 Dall. 426, 429.

86. Professor Preyer concedes in a footnote that "it is entirely possible that Bushrod Washington should be included" with the group favoring common law crimes jurisdiction, though she is unwilling to so place him because she views the evidence as indirect. Preyer, supra note 5, at 231, n. 31. The evidence may be indirect, but Washington's words from the *McGill* case are very clear in their import.

87. J. O'Conner, *William Paterson: Lawyer and Statesman 1745–1806*, 330 (1979).

88. Jay, supra note 5, at 1084–85. Stewart Jay's thorough treatment of the early federal common law advances an interpretation that is similar to that attempted in this chapter.

89. Charles Warren, *The Supreme Court in United States History*, vol. 1, at 433 (rev. ed., 1926). As far as I am aware no scholar has disputed this claim of Warren's.

90. W. W. Story, ed., *Life and Letters of Joseph Story*, 299 (1851), quoted in C. Warren, supra note 35, at 434n. For Story's unsuccessful efforts at saving some federal common law of crimes jurisdiction, see R. Newmyer, *Supreme Court Justice Joseph Story: Statesman of the Old Republic*, 100–104 (1985).

91. Jay, supra note 5, at 1016, and sources there cited.

92. *United States v. Worrall*, 28 F. Cas. 774, 799; *State Trials*, supra note 10, at 189, 198 (C.C.D. Pa. 1798) (No. 16,766).

93. Id. at 800; *State Trials*, supra note 10, at 198.

94. Warren, "New Light on the History of the Federal Judiciary Act of 1789," 37 *Harv. L. Rev.*, 49, 73 (1923) (emphasis added by Warren).

95. Id. at 77.

96. See text accompanying notes 6–22, *supra*. Section B, supra.

97. J. Goebel, Jr., supra note 5, vol. 1, at 493.

98. Id.

99. I refer to this as Warren's "celebrated" argument because it was cited with approval by the Supreme Court in overruling *Swift* in *Erie v. Tompkins*, decided in 1934. Some irony is intended, because I think Warren was wrong about *Swift v. Tyson*, and Story, the author of that opinion, was right. On Swift and Story see generally Newmyer, supra note 90, at 332–43.

100. Warren, supra note 5, at 85.

101. Id. at 73.

102. 304 U.S. 64 (1938).

103. See text accompanying note 58, supra.

104. See, e.g., A. Kelly and W. Harbison, *The American Constitution*, 134–37 (5th ed., 1976) for a short summary of the delegates' actions and views on the locus of sovereignty under the proposed constitution. It should be noted that there is an excellent

new edition of the Kelly and Harbison classic, which adds Herman Belz as a third author. Professor Belz has done a substantial editing job, and reoriented the text toward an interpretation of constitutional history in the early republic which stresses the shared assumptions and philosophy of the Constitution's framers. My citation of the earlier edition, which focused more on differences between the framers, should not be taken as disparaging what I regard as a much more sophisticated, modern, and politically astute sixth edition, which contains, among its other features, one of the best annotated bibliographies on constitutional history available. See A. Kelly, W. Harbison, and H. Belz, *The American Constitution: Its Origins and Development* (6th ed., 1983).

105. C. Warren, supra note 35, vol. 1, at 67–69.

106. Even the Bill of Rights suffered from this kind of compromised ambiguity. See, for example, Richard Henry Lee's comment on the Senate's redrafting of the House proposals, much of which redrafting was to be enacted into the Bill of Rights: "The English language has been carefully culled to find words feeble in their nature or doubtful in their meaning." Letter from Richard H. Lee to _____ (Sept. 27, 1789), reprinted in *Letters of Richard Henry Lee*, 504 (J. Ballagh, ed., 1914), quoted in J. Goebel, Jr., supra note 5, vol. 1 at 447.

107. A. Kelly and W. Harbison (5th ed.), supra note 104, at 165. One of the "attempts" in question was Elbridge Gerry's motion to insert the word "expressly" before the word "delegated" in the draft of what became the Tenth Amendment, which was defeated in the House. See J. Goebel, Jr., supra note 5, vol. 1, at 441–42.

108. See text accompanying notes 52–71, *supra.*

109. See chapters 5 and 7. This is also indicated by the fact that in the congressional debates over such measures as the Bill of Rights, Peters was in close correspondence with the arch-Federalists in both the House and Senate. See, e.g., Letter from George Clymer to Richard Peters (June 8(?), 1789), 9 Peters Papers, Historical Society of Pennsylvania, at 96 (Representative Clymer's ideas about James Madison's motives in presenting a Bill of Rights to Congress), quoted in J. Goebel, Jr., supra note 5, vol. 1, at 432–33, and Letter from Robert Morris to Richard Peters (Aug. 24, 1798), 9 Peters Papers, supra, at 99 (Senator Morris's irritation over wasting the time of the Senate on the proposed Bill of Rights), quoted in 1 J. Goebel, Jr., supra note 5, vol. 1, at 446.

110. M. Horwitz, *The Transformation of American Law 1780–1860*, 11–12 (1977).

111. This might, then, be an instance of a Federalist enunciating the new American rhetoric of popular sovereignty, or, put another way, might as easily be taken as an expression of Chase's jurisprudence of restraint limned in chapter 3.

112. This would certainly seem to be the view, for instance, of Justice Wilson. See text accompanying notes 14 to 22, supra.

113. M. Horwitz, supra note 110, at 11–12, 16–30.

114. Ibid.

115. See supra chapter 5.

116. *Calder v. Bull*, 3 U.S. (3 Dall.) 386 (1798). For a discussion of Chase's views as an antecedent of substantive due process, see G. Gunther, *Constitutional Law*, 550–52 (9th ed., 1975).

117. See supra note 61.

118. Palmer, supra note 5.

119. As in the case of Bache, or the other cases cited by Preyer, supra note 5, at 230, or *Hudson* and *Goodwin*, 11 U.S. (7 Crunch) 32, L. Ed. 259 (1812).

120. This is basically a more sophisticated elaboration of the argument put forward by DuPonceau in 1824, supra note 61, which itself is simply an attempt to provide a more cogent technical support to the arguments of Dallas and Chase based on the Tenth Amendment.

121. Supra chapter 5.

122. Richard Peters, in *Thompson et al. v. The Catherina*, 23 F. Cas. 1028, n. 8, reproduced in an edited version in S. Presser and J. Zainaldin, *Law and Jurisprudence in American History*, 145–49, n. 8 (2d ed., 1989).

123. Ibid.

124. On Wilson's views see his *Henfield* grand jury charge, discussed supra, and well analyzed in Jay, supra note 5, at 1054–55.

125. Emmerich de Vattel, *The Law of Nations, or, Principles of the Law of Nature, Applied to the Conduct and Affairs of Nations and Sovereigns*, lviii (London, English translation, 1797).

126. Id. at lv.

127. For Vattel, see id. at lviii, as well as the title of his book. For Wilson, see supra.

128. Vattel, supra, at lviii, Christian Wolff, *Jus Gentium Methodo Scientifica Petractactum*, 10 (trans. by Joseph H. Drake, vol. 2, at 1764 ed., 1934) (referring to Grotius's conception of an internal law of nations).

129. Vattel, supra note 125, at 4, 5.

130. Id. at 292, 399. Samuel Pufendorf, *De Jure Naturae et Gentium Libri Octo*, vol. 2, at 1299 (trans. by C.H. and W.A. Oldfather, 1688 ed., 1934).

131. This charge of Ellsworth's is reported in the *Independent Chronicle* (Boston), June 10–13, 1799, and is discussed by Preyer, supra note 5, at 229.

132. See supra chapter 5.

133. T. Hobbes, *The Elements of Law*, 189–90 (originally published 1640, modern 2d ed., Tonnies, ed., 1969).

134. Id. at 190.

135. Preyer, supra note 5.

136. See text accompanying note 3.

137. Supra, text accompanying note 78.

138. See generally chapter 4, supra.

139. Supra, text accompanying note 122.

140. On the Jeffersonian departure from "original understanding," see Jefferson Powell's article, Powell, "The Original Understanding of Original Intent," 98 *Harv. L. Rev.* 885 (1985).

141. *United States v. Worrall*, 28 F. Cas. 774, 780; *State Trials*, supra note 10, at 189, 198 (C.C.D. Pa. 1798) (No. 16,766).

142. Id. at 780; *State Trials*, supra note 10, at 198–99.

143. *State Trials*, supra note 10, at 199n.

144. Id. See the opinion of Justice Ellsworth in Isaac Williams's Case, 29 F. Cas. 1330; *State Trials*, supra note 10, at 652 (C.C.D. Conn. 1799).

145. See L. Levy, *Freedom of Speech and Press in Early American History: Legacy of Suppression*, xv–xvi (Torchbook, ed., 1963). Levy discovered *United States v. Sylvester* in volume I of the manuscript Final Record of the United States Circuit Courts of Massachusetts, 1790–1799, at page 303, at the Federal Records Center, Dorchester, Mass. The case is unreported.

146. J. Smith, *Freedom's Fetters: The Alien and Sedition Laws and American Civil Liberties*, 188–92 (1956).

147. There is a report of Bache's arrest and appearance before Judge Peters in his paper, the *Philadelphia Aurora*, June 27, 1798, and June 30, 1798. The case is briefly discussed in J. Goebel, Jr., supra note 5, vol. 1, at 632.

148. Letters from James McHenry to George Washington (Jan. 24 and 31, 1796), cited in C. Warren, supra note 35, vol. 1, at 142. McHenry was reporting Chase's attitude to Washington. McHenry, Washington's close friend, had recommended Chase to Washington and had written that Chase's "political or other errors . . . exist no longer." Letter from James McHenry to George Washington (June 14, 1795), cited in C. Warren, supra note 35, vol. 1, at 125–26.

149. 29 F. Cas. 1330; *State Trials*, supra note 10, at 652 (C.C.D. Conn. 1799) (No. 17,708).

150. See, e.g., J. Goebel, Jr., supra note 5, vol. 1, at 631.

151. Id. at 630.

152. See J. Goebel, Jr., supra note 5, vol. 1, at 631, n. 83.

153. For the suggestion that Ellsworth was the "leading projector" of the Judiciary Act, see Letter from Paine Wingate to Timothy Pickering (Apr. 27, 1789), quoted in C. Warren, supra note 5, vol. 1, at 59. Warren himself reported that the handwriting of the draft of the Senate bill was in the hands of William Paterson, Oliver Ellsworth, Caleb Strong, and a recording clerk. Id. at 50.

154. Julius Goebel seems to have suggested that the jury charge in 1799 represented a "change" for Ellsworth, but Goebel furnishes no direct evidence that Ellsworth ever believed there was no federal common law. J. Goebel, Jr., supra note 5, vol. 1, at 630–31.

155. See supra.

156. 11 U.S. (7 Cranch) 32 (1812).

157. Id. at 33–34. Cf. *United States v. Worrall*, 28 F. Cas. 774, 779; *State Trials*, supra note 10, at 189, 197 (C.C.D. Pa. 1798) (No. 16,766) ("[I]t appears to my mind, to be as essential that congress should define the offenses to be tried, and apportion the punishments to be indicted, as that they should erect courts to try the criminal, or to pronounce a sentence on conviction").

158. For a similar opinion on the importance of Justice Chase in this regard, see *State Trials*, supra note 10, at 41–42.

159. Id. at 42.

CHAPTER 7

1. There is a brief description of the Whiskey Rebellion in H. Tinkcom, *The Republicans and the Federalists in Pennsylvania 1790–1801*, 91–111 (1950). Details are to be found in the official report of the trials, *United States v. Insurgents*, 26 F. Cas. 499

(C.C.D. Pa. 1795) (No. 15,443). The standard secondary source, until recently, was L. Baldwin, *Whiskey Rebels: The Story of a Frontier Uprising* (originally published 1939, rev. ed., 1968). This should now be supplemented with T. Slaughter, *The Whiskey Rebellion: Frontier Epilogue to the American Revolution* (1986), and the collection of essays, S. Boyd, ed., *The Whiskey Rebellion: Past and Present Perspectives* (1985).

2. See, e.g., J. Marshall, *Life of George Washington*, vol. 2, at 346 (1807), quoted in F. Wharton, ed., *State Trials of the United States During the Administrations of Washington and Adams*, 145–56 (1849).

3. See supra note 1.

4. There has been, however, a fine recent piece that finds in the trials of the whiskey rebels a delicate working-out of the balance between state and federal jurisdiction in the early Republic, as the nation began its experiment in federalism. R. Ifft, "Treason in the Early Republic: The Federal Courts, Popular Protest, and Federalism During the Whiskey Insurrection," in Boyd, ed., supra note 1, at 165–82.

5. For the characterization of this interpretation of the law of treason as "constructive," see Attorney General William Bradford to George Washington, August 2, 1794, in George Washington Papers, Library of Congress, quoted in Ifft, supra note 1, at 171–72. For the characterization of Justice Paterson's ruling in the trials of the whiskey rebels as acceptance of the doctrine of "constructive levying of war," see Ifft, supra note 1, at 174. Cf. U.S. Const., Art. III, Sec. 3: "Treason against the United States, shall consist only in levying war against them, or in adhering to their Enemies, giving them Aid and Comfort."

6. Article III, Section 3, of the United States Constitution provides in pertinent part that "treason against the United States, shall consist only in levying War against them, or, in adhering to their Enemies, giving them Aid and Comfort."

7. *United States v. Mitchell*, 26 F. Cas. 1277, 1278 (C.C.D. Pa. 1795) (No. 15,778) (argument of Mr. Rawle).

8. Rawle cited Douglas's English King's Bench Reports, 570. Id. The inference in the text seems justified from Paterson's statement in his charge to the jury that if the object of the insurrection "was to suppress the excise offices, and to prevent the execution of an act of congress, by force and intimidation, the offense, in legal estimation is high treason; it is an usurpation of the authority of government; it is high treason by levying of war." 26 F. Cas. at 1281.

9. *United States v. Insurgents*, 26 F. Cas. 499, 511–12 (C.C.D. Pa. 1795) (No. 15,443).

10. Id. at 513–14.

11. For Peters's low opinion of statutes, in which he suggests that they rarely improve upon the common law, see footnote 8 of his opinion in *Thompson et al. v. The Catherina*, 23 F. Cas. 1028 (1795), reported in S. Presser and J. Zainaldin, *Law and Jurisprudence in American History*, 148 (2d ed., 1989).

12. 28 F. Cas. 376 (C.C.D. Pa. 1795) (No. 16,621).

13. Id. at 377.

14. 26 F. Cas. 1277 (C.C.D. Pa. 1795) (No. 15,788).

15. Id. at 1281–82.

16. T. Slaughter, supra note 1, at 220.

17. See, e.g., Green, "The Jury and the English Law of Homicide 1200–1600," 74 *Mich. L. Rev.* 413, 489–92, 499 (1976), and sources cited therein. The author of this piece, Professor Thomas Green of Michigan, is probably the leading American expert on the history of the English jury, and has written an exhaustive book-length treatment of the subject. He notes that while it was a long-standing complaint against English judges that they might "coerce," either by browbeating jurors or denying them food and drink until a verdict was reached, this ought to be distinguished from "the judge's unquestioned right to make his views known to the jury." T. Green, *Verdict According to Conscience: Perspectives on the English Criminal Trial Jury 1200–1800,* 140 (1985). For Green's comments on English developments in the late eighteenth century, tracking much of the period here discussed, see id. at 318–55.

18. See discussion of the *Henfield* case, supra chapter 6.

19. See, e.g., *Case of Fries*, 9 F. Cas. 826, 838 (C.C.D. Pa. 1799) (No. 5,126) (charge to grand jury of Justice Iredell).

20. A fine account of the Fries Rebellion, although it probably treats it as less serious than it was, is Elsmere, "The Trials of John Fries," 103 *Pa. Mag. Hist. & Biog.* 432 (1979).

21. See supra text accompanying notes 5 to 6.

22. An act to establish the judicial courts of the United States, ch. 20, 1 Stat. 73 (1789).

23. 9 F. Cas. 846.

24. Id.

25. Letter ftom Richard Peters to Timothy Pickering (Jan. 24, 1804), 10 Peters Papers, Historical Society of Pennsylvania, 91.

26. Id.

27. Id.

28. Id.

29. For the account of these trial tactics, see the testimony of the prosecutor, William Rawle, given at the impeachment trial of Justice Chase, and reproduced in the report of Fries's trial. 9 F. Cas. 941, note.

30. *Case of Fries,* 9 F. Cas. 895, 899.

31. Id. at 897.

32. Id. at 908.

33. Id. at 910.

34. See supra text accompanying notes 12–14.

35. 9 F. Cas. at 916.

36. Id. at 918.

37. Letter from James Iredell to Mrs. James Iredell (May 16, 1799), quoted in D. Henderson, *Courts for a New Nation,* 129 (1971).

38. 9 F. Cas. 923.

39. Letter from Richard Peters to Timothy Pickering (Jan. 24, 1804), supra note 25.

40. See, e.g., Letter from Timothy Pickering to Richard Peters (Jan. 6. 1803), 10 Peters Papers, supra note 25, at 82.

41. Letter from Richard Peters to Timothy Pickering (Jan. 24, 1804), supra note 25. Several of Fries's companions had also been tried with him in 1799. Two of these were

convicted along with Fries, and were later pardoned when he was. At least one of Fries's companions was acquitted through a successful factual defense. Id.

42. This account of Chase's thinking is taken from Richard Peters to Timothy Pickering, ibid., as are the quotations in the following paragraphs. Peters's letter has something of a self-defensive tone to it, but there is no reason to doubt the substantial accuracy of the facts as he recounts them. Julius Goebel has called this the most "circumstantial" account of the second *Fries* trial. J. Goebel, Jr., *A History of the Supreme Court: Antecedents and Beginnings to 1801*, vol. I, at 658, n. 171 (1971).

43. See supra text accompanying note 29. The avoidance of citations to these two cases was the motive attributed to Chase by prosecutor Rawle in his testimony at Chase's trial for impeachment. 9 F. Cas. 942 n. This also seems to be the inference from Peters's letter of January 24, 1804, where he writes that Chase "mentioned some of the cases" from Fries's earlier trial and "reprobated them." In the same letter, Peters mentions the yeoman's and innkeeper's cases as two examples of the "abominable and reprobated" cases of constructive treason. Letter from Richard Peters to Timothy Pickering (Jan. 24, 1804), supra note 25.

44. 9 F. Cas. 937.

45. 9 F. Cas. 943–44 (emphasis added).

46. Letter from Richard Peters to Timothy Pickering (Jan. 24, 1804), supra note 25.

47. This was Dallas's testimony before the Senate in Chase's impeachment trial. The testimony is reproduced following the text of the report of the *Fries* trial, 9 F. Cas. 941. It may well be subject to some skepticism, however, since it seems clear that by then Lewis and Dallas had decided Chase's behavior offered them a fine opportunity to walk away from the case, and that only by leaving the case, and thus conveying the impression that the repressive Chase had forced them off, leaving Fries defenseless, could they save their client.

48. See supra text accompanying notes 44 to 45.

49. Letter from Richard Peters to Timothy Pickering, supra note 25.

50. This was acknowledged by Dallas in his testimony at the Chase impeachment trial. See 9 F. Cas. 941. It is thus incorrect to have believed, as Julius Goebel did, that the withdrawal of Lewis and Dallas from the *Fries* defense was because "the honor of the bar evidently weigh[ed] more with them than their duty to their client." J. Goebel, Jr., supra note 42, vol. 1, at 658, n. 171. Their idea was to free their client, and, by pulling the strings of popular opinion and a popularity-seeking president, they succeeded.

51. 9 F. Cas. 942.

52. Letter from Richard Peters to Timothy Pickering (Jan. 24, 1804), supra note 25.

53. W. Blackstone, *Commentaries on the Law of England*, vol. 4, at 349 (1769, University of Chicago Press Reprint, 1979).

54. Ibid. It should be noted that while no counsel was legally permitted in felony cases, there was an exception made for treason which worked corruption of the blood, by 7 Will. 3, ch. 3 (1695). By the end of the eighteenth century, the appearance of defense counsel in felony cases was becoming increasingly common. Nevertheless, the law against such appearances was not repealed until 1836, in the Trials for Felony Act, 6 and 7 Will. 4, ch. 114. For recent examinations of criminal procedure in the precounsel days, which were useful in formulating this part of the book, see Baker, "Criminal

Courts and Procedure at Common Law 1550–1800," in *Crime in England 1550–1880*, at 15 (J. Cockburn, ed., 1977); Oldham, "The Origins of the Special Jury," 50 *U. Chi. L. Rev.*, 137 (1983); Langbein, "Shaping the Eighteenth Century Criminal Trial: A View from the Ryder Sources," 50 *U. Chi. L. Rev* 1 (1983); and Langbein, "The Criminal Trial Before the Lawyers," 45 *U. Chi. L. Rev.* 263 (1978).

55. J. Goebel, Jr., supra note 42, at 658, n. 171.

56. *Calder v. Bull*, 3 U.S. (3 Dall.) 386 (1798).

57. I strongly differ with the conclusion of the two Chase biographies (see J. Haw, F. Beirne, R. Beirne, and R. Jett, *Stormy Patriot: The Life of Samuel Chase*, 202 (1980), and J. Ellesmere, *Justice Samuel Chase*, 110 (1980), that once Chase took over from Lewis and Dallas, so to speak, the rest of the second *Fries* trial proceeded smoothly, impartially, and without incident. The incidents referred to in the text seem quite significant to me, and, indeed, the most exciting drama in the trial, at least as far as Chase's incantation of his religiously based jurisprudence was concerned, came at the end, at the sentencing, well after defense counsel had fled.

58. For the full text of the impeachment charges, see *Trial of Samuel Chase, An Associate Justice of the Supreme Court of the United States*, vol. 1, at 5–8 (S. Smith and T. Lloyd, eds., 1805) [hereafter cited as *Trial of Samuel Chase*].

59. J. Sanderson, *Biography of the Signers to the Declaration of Independence*, vol. 9, at 230 (1827).

60. See supra chapter 4.

61. This account of Chase's comments to Fries is drawn from the excerpts of Chase's closing statements to be found reproduced in S. Presser and J. Zainaldin, *Law and Jurisprudence in American History*, 174–77 (2d ed., 1989).

62. See Ellsmere, supra note 57, at 98.

63. Presser and Zainaldin, supra note 61, at 177.

64. This is the essence of the thought of the "new divinity" school, contemporary with Chase, that laid the intellectual foundation for the second great awakening in America. See S. Ahlstrom, *A Religious History of the American People*, 404–14 (1972).

65. T. Breen, *The Character of the Good Ruler*, 202 (1970).

66. T. Hanley, *The American Revolution and Religion: Maryland 1770–1800*, at 51–52 (1971).

67. See supra chapter 3.

68. See Preface, supra.

69. See supra notes 42–43 and accompanying text.

70. See generally the materials on the impeachment trial reproduced in 9 F. Cas., 934–40.

71. Charge to the federal grand jury in Baltimore (May 2, 1803), reprinted, inter alia, in 8 *Annals of Cong.* 673, 675 (1804).

72. 9 F. Cas., 933–34.

73. On Cooper's career as a leading English radical in the 1780s and 1790s, see generally A. Goodwin, *The Friends of Liberty: The English Democratic Movement in the Age of the French Revolution*, 146, 202, 229, 262–63, 268, 487, 491 (1979), and see generally D. Malone, *The Public Life of Thomas Cooper, 1783–1839* (rev. ed., 1961).

74. This statute is commonly referred to as the "Alien and Sedition Acts." Its official title was "An act in addition to the act, entitled 'Act for the punishment of certain crimes against the United States,' " ch. 74, 1 Stat. 596 (1798).

75. For good (although, alas, too Jeffersonian) treatments of the Alien and Sedition Acts, see J. Miller, *Crisis in Freedom: The Alien and Sedition Acts* (1951), and J. Smith, *Freedom's Fetters: The Alien and Sedition Laws and American Civil Liberties* (1956).

76. Compare J. Miller, supra note 75, and J. Smith, supra note 75 ("reign of terror" advocates), with W. W. Crosskey, *Politics and the Constitution*, vol. 2, at 767 (1953) (Sedition Act a "natural reaction" to "extremely indecent campaign of public mendacity") and J. Goebel, Jr., *A History of the Supreme Court: Antecedents and Beginnings to 1801*, vol. 1, at 633 (1971) (a similarly dry-eyed discussion of the prosecutions).

77. To the same effect, see W. W. Crosskey, supra note 76, and J. Goebel, Jr., supra note 76.

78. For the details of the European events, see C. Brinton, *A Decade of Revolution*, 173, 179 (Torchbook, ed., 1963).

79. 297 9 F. Cas. 833.

80. 9 F. Cas. 859 (report that some of Fries's men were adorned with "large three coloured French cockades") 849 (quote about making what happened in France happen here). But see 9 F. Cas. 885 for Judge Peters's report that he believed the Fries insurgents were anti-French.

81. For a recent treatment of this Federalist fear, see Brisbin, "John Marshall on History, Virtue, and Legality," in T. Shevory, ed., *John Marshall's Achievement: Law, Politics, and Constitutional Interpretation*, 96 (1989).

82. J. Smith, supra note 75, at 45.

83. Id. at 145.

84. "Dr. Robinson's Proofs of a Conspiracy," quoted in J. Miller, supra note 75, at 146.

85. W. W. Crosskey, supra note 76, at 767.

86. See supra chapter 6, (prosecution of Benjamin Franklin Bache).

87. See W. W. Crosskey, supra note 76, at 767.

88. An act in addition to the act entitled "Act for the punishment of certain crimes against the United States," ch. 74, 1 Stat. 596, secs. 2, 3 (1798).

89. Id. sec 3.

90. On these American developments see Howe, "Juries as Judges of Criminal Law," 52 *Harv. L. Rev.* 582, 586–88 (1939). Cf. Henderson, "The Background of the Seventh Amendment," 80 *Harv. L. Rev.* 289, 326–27, 328–30, 335–36 (1966) (English juries had discretion to acquit). It should be noted also that Fox's Libel Act, a British measure passed in 1792 that imposed these two reforms, the use of truth as a defense and the ability of the jury to pass on the seditious character of the utterance, on English common law as well.

91. *United States v. Cooper*, 25 F. Cas. 631 (C.C.D. Pa. 1800) (No. 14,865).

92. Id. at 640–41. The first two charges could arguably have been seen to have been true, but the third was a clear fabrication. "In the cold light of history," writes Cooper's American biographer Dumas Malone, "the action of Adams [in the Jonathan Robbins matter, to which this third charge referred] seems to have been entirely justifiable, and Cooper's invective appears to have been a bit of sheer demagoguery, but his position was in full accord with that of the most distinguished Republicans." Malone, supra note 73, at 121.

93. 25 F. Cas. at 634.

94. Id. at 641.

95. Id. at 642.

96. Scholarship on the origins of the Anglo-American adversarial system is only now beginning in earnest. For one of the best of these efforts, with citations to others, see Landsman, "The Decline of the Adversary System: How the Rhetoric of Swift and Certain Justice Has Affected Adjudication in American Courts," 29 *Buffalo L. Rev.* 487 (1981); Landsman, "A Brief Survey of the Development of the Adversary System," 44 *Ohio St. L. J.* 713 (1984).

97. *United States v. Lyon*, 15 F. Cas. 1183, 1185 (C.C.D. Vt. 1798) (No. 8,646); *United States v. Haswell*, 26 F. Cas. 218, 219 (C.C.D. Vt. 1800) (No. 15,324).

98. W. Holdsworth, *A History of English Law*, vol. 7, at 375–76 (7th ed., 1956), quoting F. Pollock, *Torts*, 261 (12th ed., 1923). See also *Fleming v. Dollar*, [1889], 33 Q.B. 388, 392, quoting an opinion by Lord Campbell, C.J., in *Regina v. Newman*, I E & B 558 to the effect that "the plea of justification is one and entire, and raises only one issue, and that unless the whole plea is proved, that issue must be found for the plaintiff. . . . " Id. at 577.

99. Ibid.

100. For a summary of these charges, with citations, see D. Stewart, *The Opposition Press of the Federalist Period*, 480–84, 543 (1969).

101. For the evolution of the public-private distinction in American jurisprudence, see Horwitz, "The History of the Public/Private Distinction," 130 *U. Pa. L. Rev.* 1423, 1424 (1982). Id. at 1424.

102. See supra chapter 2, supra, text accompanying notes 31–35.

103. *United States v. Cooper*, 25 F. Cas. 634–43.

104. See generally *United States v. Cooper*, 25 F. Cas. 631, and the report of the case with comments by Cooper himself, in *Proceedings in the Circuit Court of the United States Held in Philadelphia, April 11, 1800*, 58–59 (T. Cooper, ed., Philadelphia) (Pamphlet in the Collection of the Historical Society of Pennsylvania). For a full description of Cooper's newspaper publishing activities including President Adams's opinion that Cooper's behavior was caused by Adams's refusal to give him a federal office, see J. Smith, supra note 75, at 311–14. Cooper's biographer, Dumas Malone, appears to dissent mildly from this charge against Cooper, writing, supra note 73, at 129, that "it seems safe to say that Cooper was never in a primary sense a place-hunting politician, and that he belonged to a higher order than such Republican writers as Callender and Duane. He never entirely lost his youthful ideal of truth and the betterment of humanity."

105. 25 F. Cas. 643.

106. Id. at 644–45.

107. Letter from Richard Peters to Timothy Pickering (Jan. 24, 1804), 10 Peters Papers 91 (Historical Society of Pennsylvania).

108. Supra chapter 6.

109. See, e.g., supra chapter 5.

110. *Searight v. Calbraith*, 21 Fed. Cas. 927 (C.C.D.Pa. 1796), discussed supra chapter 5.

111. For Richard Peters's better reading of the political climate in Philadelphia, see, e.g., supra text accompanying notes 42–43.
112. For the politics of the Chase impeachment see Ellis, "The Impeachment of Samuel Chase" in M. Belknap, ed., *American Political Trials*, 55 (1981).
113. Ellis, *The Jeffersonian Crisis: Courts and Politics in the Young Republic*, 158–62 (1971).
114. See supra note 47.
115. See supra chapter 6.
116. For the error of the "compact" theory of the federal Constitution, see Powell, "The Original Understanding of Original Intent," 98 *Harv. L. Rev.* 885 (1985).
117. Quoted in Ellis, supra note 113, at 167.
118. *Thompson et al. v. The Catherina*, 23 F. Cas. 1028 (D. C. Pa., 1795) n 8.
119. Ellis, supra note 113, at 176, citing J. Higgins, *Sampson Against the Philistines, or the Reformation of Lawsuits, and Justice made Cheap, Speedy, and Brought Home to Every Man's Door: Agreeably to the Principles of the Ancient Trial by Jury, Before the Same Was Innovated by Judges, and Lawyers*, 2d ed., Philadelphia, 1805.
120. Higgins, supra note 119, and Ellis, supra note 113, at 175–76 (Paine's views).
121. For these beliefs of Chase, see his comments to John Fries prior to his sentencing, reproduced in S. Presser and J. Zainaldin, supra note 11, at 175.
122. Supra note 118.
123. Ellis, supra note 113, at 179–80.
124. A hint as to how the trading back and forth of ideological arguments must have worked is provided by the letter from J. Dawson of Fredericksburg, Virginia, to Alexander James Dallas, September 28, 1800. Dallas Papers, Historical Society of Pennsylvania. Dawson wrote to Dallas asking for Dallas's arguments which he used in the submission to John Adams seeking the pardon of Fries. Dawson told Dallas that he was writing on behalf of St. George Tucker, who later was to publish an edition of Blackstone annotated with suitable Virginia Republican comments. "[J]udge Tucker as a man of worth, and a good republican," Dawson wrote, "who as professor of law in the University of William and Mary is about to deliver a lecture on treason, in opposition to the doctrine which has been supported by our federal judges—he has requested me to apply to you for a copy of the opinion which you and Lewis sent to the president in the case of Fries. . . . " For Tucker's admiration for the American democratic societies, for Thomas Paine, and for sweeping American theories of popular sovereignty, see Rabban, "The Ahistorical Historian: Leonard Levy on Freedom of Expression in Early American History," 37 *Stan. L. Rev.*, 795, 851–52 (1985), and sources there cited.

CHAPTER 8

1. See, e.g., R. Berger, *Impeachment: The Constitutional Problems*, 224–51 (1973).
2. J. Miller, *Crisis in Freedom: The Alien and Sedition Acts*, 211–20 (1951).
3. Id. at 215, 220.
4. J. Callender, *The Prospect Before Us* (1800).
5. Quoted in *United States v. Callender*, 25 F. Cas. 239 (C.C.D. Va. 1800) (No. 14,709).

6. Chase's Manuscript Jury Charge Book is in the Vertical File of the Manuscript Division of the Maryland Historical Society, Baltimore. The Jury Charge Book records charges which Chase gave to grand juries in 1798–1800, 1802–03, and 1805–06 [hereafter cited as Chase Jury Charge Book].

7. Chase Jury Charge Book, supra note 6, at 21. See also J. Haw, F. Beirne, R. Beirne, and R. Jett, *Stormy Patriot: The Life of Samuel Chase*, 207–8 (1980). For the hostility of Hamilton to Adams, see, e.g., F. McDonald, *Alexander Hamilton*, 346–52 (1982). For the notorious document which Hamilton circulated to Federalist leaders chronicling his problems with Adams, see Letter from Alexander Hamilton, and the introductory note in 25 The Papers of Alexander Hamilton, 169–234 (H. Syrett, ed., 1977).

8. For Chase's most powerful Burkean statements of the nature of man's gullibility to abstract theories, and his belief that men could be too easily swayed by designing evildoers who might play upon their passions, see the Chase Jury Charge Book, supra note 6, at 22, 35, 38–46, 51–53.

9. For the several assertions that Chase was given Callender's book by his friend Luther Martin, and that he concluded, before the trial, that it was seditious and that its author ought to be punished, see *Trial of Samuel Chase An Associate Justice of the Supreme Court of the United States*, vol. 1, at 193 (testimony of John Thomas Mason), 232–33 (Luther Martin's admission that he gave Chase the book as he was on his way to the Virginia circuit), 234 (testimony of James Winchester) (S. Smith and T. Lloyd, eds., 1805).

10. See, e.g., J. Smith, *Freedom's Fetters: The Alien and Sedition Laws and American Civil Liberties*, 348, n. 50 (1956), quoting C. Evans, *Report of the Trial of the Hon. Samuel Chase*, 43–44 (1805).

11. See A. Beveridge, *The Life of John Marshall*, vol. 3, at 191–92 (1919).

12. *United States v. Callender*, 25 F. Cas. 239.

13. See A. Beveridge, supra note 11, and the argument of Luther Martin (from which the internal quotes were taken) at Chase's trial, *Trial of Samuel Chase,* supra note 9, vol. 2, at 216–17 (Callender's counsel Hay was interested more in politics than in his client). See also id. at 296–97, 301 (argument of Chase's counsel Robert G. Harper that Callender's counsel used delaying tactics because they knew "Callender to be incapable of defence, on any other ground than the unconstitutionality of the sedition law. . . . ").

14. N. Rosenberg, *Protecting the Best Men: An Interpretive History of the Law of Libel*, 295, n. 29 (1986). Rosenberg does conclude, however, that Chase's conduct "was hardly exemplary." Id. Regrettably, even Rosenberg appears not to have understood exactly what Chase was up to in *Callender*, concluding simply that "Chase refused to allow the defendant's lawyer to question John Taylor of Caroline about the truth of specific facts at issue." Id. at 88. As demonstrated in the text, the problem, for Chase, was that Taylor was not actually offering evidence as to the truth of the relevant issue, Adams's motivation in opposing the sequestration act.

15. Id. at 295, quoting *Chase Trial* supra note 9, vol. 1, at 169 (testimony of George Hay).

16. Rosenberg, supra note 14, at 296, n. 29, quoting John P. Kennedy, *Memoirs of the Life of William Wirt*, vol. 1, at 81–84 (1849, reprint 1973).

17. For a list of the instances in which Chase offended the Virginia counsel by suggesting sardonically that their arguments were illogical or the product of youthful enthusiasm rather than rigorous legal analysis, see A. Beveridge, supra note 11, at 36–41, 189–91.

18. For these and the other phrases taken from *The Prospect Before Us* and reproduced in the indictment against Callender, see 25 F. Cas. 239–40.

19. For the career of Taylor, and for his elaborate, passionate, and brilliant brand of republicanism, see R. Shalhope, *John Taylor of Caroline: Pastoral Republican* (1980).

20. Taylor later wrote a sophisticated intellectual defense of antiaristocratic Jeffersonian Republicanism, directed primarily at the writings of John Adams. J. Taylor, *An Inquiry into the Principles and Policy of the Government of the United States* (photo. reprint 1950).

21. For the suggestion that Chase's ruling was incorrect and for an example of an otherwise careful scholar who has misunderstood Chase's ruling, see J. Smith, supra note 10, at 353.

22. Quoted in Baker, "Criminal Courts and Procedure at Common Law, 1550–1800," in Crime in England 1550–1800, 15, 39 (J. Cockburn, ed., 1977).

23. See Howe, "Juries as Judges of Criminal Law," 52 *Harv. L. Rev.* 582, 588 (1939).

24. See 8 *Annals of Congress* 2135 (1798), cited id. at 586.

25. Brewer, "The Wilkites and the Law 1763–74," in *An Ungovernable People: The English and Their Law in the Seventeenth and Eighteenth Centuries*, 128, 157 (1980).

26. *United States v. Callender*, 25 F. Cas. 252.

27. Id. at 253.

28. Supra Chapter 7.

29. *United States v. Lyon*, 15 F. Cas. 1183 (C.C.D. Vt. 1798) (No. 8,646).

30. For the most famous account of the *Seven Bishops* trial, which presents it, somewhat too facilely, as a great and good defeat for Stuart despotism, see T. Macaulay, *History of England*, vol. 2, at 990–1039 (1858). The official report is at 12 Howell's *State Trials* 183 (1688).

31. J. Alexander, *A Brief Narrative of the Case and Trial of John Peter Zenger*, [1735], Printer of the *New York Weekly Journal* (S. Katz, ed., 1963).

32. See generally M. Smith, *The Writs of Assistance Case* (1978), and J. Smith, *Appeals to the Privy Council from the American Plantations*, 607–26 (1950) (*Parsons' Cause*). Defense Counsel William Wirt would have been particularly prone to imbibe the philosophy of the *Parsons' Cause* because he was the son-in-law and proud biographer of *Parsons' Cause* defense counsel Patrick Henry.

33. For the best dramatic treatment of Sir Edward Coke's explanation to James I that even though his majesty was endowed with "excellent reason," this was not enough to penetrate the artificial reason of the law, see C. Bowen, *The Lion and the Throne*, 302–5 (1957).

34. On the trial of Callender, see Presser and Hurley, "Saving God's Republic: The Jurisprudence of Samuel Chase," 1984 *Ill. L. Rev.* 771, 808–14 (1984).

35. On Tucker see supra chapter 7, note 124, supra.

36. Discussed by A. G. Roeber, *Faithful Magistrates and Republican Lawyers: Creators of a Virginia Legal Culture, 1680–1810*, at 218 (1981). It is noteworthy also that

as late as four years after this case, defendant's counsel in *Ware v. Hylton*, none other than the fabulous radical Republican Col. Taylor, also maintained the necessity for judicial review. J. Goebel, *A History of the United States Supreme Court: Antecedents and Beginnings to 1801*, vol. 1, at 590–91 (1971). Chase, who wrote the Court's opinion in *Ware v. Hylton*, must have been somewhat chagrined to find Taylor in cahoots with Virginia Republicans who were seeking in *Callender* to question the hegemony of judicial review. Julius Goebel's assessment was that the Virginians reversed themselves "for political reasons," in order to contend "that the function of deciding upon an issue of constitutionality was one to be exercised by a trial jury." Id. at 591.

37. For discussions of the *Parsons' Cause*, placing the case in its political context, see Roeber, supra note 36, at 148, and J. Smith, *Appeals to the Privy Council from the American Plantations*, 620–21 (1950).

38. For the information on Wirt, at least, see Roeber, supra note 36, at 241–46.

39. Id. at 234–36.

40. On the "compact theory" and its illegitmacy, see generally Powell, "The Original Understanding of Original Intent," 98 *Harv. L. Rev.* 885, 924–35 (1985).

41. For Chase's regard for Bolingbroke, see his Letter to His Children, Historical Society of Pennsylvania, Ettings Jurists Collection, vol. 1, at 37 (Feb. 8, 1784). For the anti-Federalist reliance on Bolingbroke, see Kenyon, "Men of Little Faith: The Antifederalists, on the Nature of Representative Government," reprinted in *The Formation and Ratification of the Constitution: Major Historical Interpretations*, 348 (K. Hall, ed., 1987).

42. See supra chapter 6, and sources there cited.

43. For the Virginians' hostility to British centralized financial institutions, see D. McCoy, *The Elusive Republic: Political Economy in Jeffersonian America*, 185–86 (1980).

44. See supra chapter 7.

45. For Chase's comments on the virtues of the profession of merchants, which he ranked by 1784 as second only to those of lawyers, see His Letter to his Children, supra note 41. For his growing belief that a strong central government was needed, see Presser, "A Tale of Two Judges: Richard Peters, Samuel Chase, and the Broken Promise of Federalist Jurisprudence," 73 *Nw. U.L. Rev.* 26, 73 (1978), and "Saving God's Republic," supra note 34, at 778–80, 781–82, 814–19.

46. For the particulars of Chase's campaign activities on behalf of Adams, see *Stormy Patriot*, supra note 7, at 207–8.

47. See Preface, text accompanying note 5. Compare the recent mini-flap in connection with the nomination by President George Bush in July 1990 of David Souter to the Supreme Court, when sitting Supreme Court Justice Thurgood Marshall indicated that he had never heard of Souter, and was critical of George Bush, whom Marshall indicated he would not vote for. Marshall had also indicated his disapproval of Bush's predecessor, Ronald Reagan.

48. M. Marcus, J. Perry, J. Buchanan, and S. Tull, *"It is my wish as well as my Duty to attend the court": Cases of Absenteeism from the Supreme Court of the United States 1790–1800*, at 14–15 (prepublication draft, 1984).

49. On Federalist adherence to cyclical views of the decline of republics, see generally Brisbin, "John Marshall on History, Virtue and Legality," in T. Shevory, ed., *John Marshall's Achievement: Law, Politics, and Constitutional Interpretations*, 95 (1989).

50. Lerner, "The Supreme Court as Republican Schoolmaster," 1967 *Sup. Ct. Rev.* 127.

51. Id. at 155.

52. See, e.g., Grey, "Do We Have an Unwritten Constitution," 27 *Stan. L. Rev.* 703 (1975).

53. 3 U.S. (3 Dall.) 386 (1798).

54. For statements of the modern orthodox "process" theory of law, see, e.g., Green-awalt, "The Enduring Significance of Neutral Principles," 78 *Col. L. Rev.* 982 (1978). For trenchant critiques of that theory from the left, and the far left, respectively, see Wright, "Professor Bickel, the Scholarly Tradition, and the Supreme Court," 84 *Harv. L. Rev.* 769 (1971), and D. Kairys, ed., *The Politics of Law* (1982).

55. For statements recommending such a judicial role, see generally the following books by the late Alexander Bickel, the most gifted, perhaps, of the modern process theorists: *The Morality of Consent* (1975), *The Least Dangerous Branch* (1962), and *The Supreme Court and the Idea of Progress* (1970).

56. Brewer, "The Wilkites and the Law 1763–74," in *An Ungovernable People: The English and Their Law in the Seventeenth and Eighteenth Centuries*, 128, 133, 135, 221 (1980).

57. Horwitz, "Republicanism and Liberalism in American Constitutional Thought," 29 *Wm. & Mary L. Rev.* 57, 67 (1987).

58. This seems to be the inescapable implication of the judicial philosophy limned in the Chase Jury Charge Book, supra note 6.

59. See supra note 6. The subsequent discussion in the rest of this chapter on Chase's jury charges in general, and, in particular, on his infamous Baltimore grand jury charge of 1803 is derived from that manuscript Chase Jury Charge Book.

60. J. Goebel, supra note 36, at 493n.

61. For a concise account of Chase's relatively radical views in those early years, see *Stormy Patriot*, supra note 7, at 42–57.

62. Compare Chase Jury Charge Book, supra note 6, at 42–46 (Chase's orthodox conservative or Tory remarks), with B. Bailyn, *The Ordeal of Thomas Hutchinson*, 70–108 (1974) (views of Governor Thomas Hutchinson on the American radicals of the 1760s and 1770s). Both Chase and Hutchinson feared the same twin evils—the demagogues and the avaricious.

63. For an elaborate description of the classical view of property as contrasted with modern "juristic" or individualistic views of property, see Pocock, "The Mobility of Property, and the Rise of Eighteenth-Century Sociology," in *Theories of Property: Aristotle to the Present*, 140–64 (1979).

64. For calls that American historians take account of the difference manifested in early America between the "classical," "organic," or "Aristotelian" theories of "republicanism," and the newer "republican" or "liberal" philosophy of individualism, see, e.g., Horwitz, "Republicanism and Liberalism in American Constitutional Thought," 29 *Wm. & Mary L. Rev.* 57 (1987), and Horwitz, "History and Theory," 96 *Yale L.J.* 1825 (1987). For work on theories of property that illustrate the dichotomy, see Hendrik Hartog, *Public Property and Private Power: The Corporation of the City of New York in American Law 1730–1870* (1983), and Jennifer Nedelsky, *Private Property and the Limits of American Constitutionalism* (1990).

65. For a thorough study of the importance of opposing notions of liberty and property in eighteenth-century England, see H. Dickenson, *Liberty and Property: Political Ideology in Eighteenth-Century Britain* (1977).

66. See W. Blackstone, *Commentaries*, vol. 1, at 165 (1765, and photo. reprint, 1979).

67. See G. Seed, *James Wilson*, 23 (1978), quoting *The Works of James Wilson*, 406–7 (1967).

68. For the relevant discussions of Chase's belief in the wisdom of government by those possessing substantial landed and personal property, a belief which closely tracks late eighteenth-century conservative English political ideology as elaborated by H. Dickenson, supra note 65, at 270–318, see Chase Jury Charge Book, supra note 6, at 10–11, 40–41, 43–46.

69. Chief Justice Roger Taney might be said to have completed the transformation of American property, begun by Marshall or Story, from a "civic" to a "juristic" conception, as the terms are used in Pocock, supra note 63. The apotheosis of Taney's view of property as an element in individualistic competition is usually thought to be *Proprietors of Charles River Bridge v. Proprietors of Warren Bridge*, 36 U.S. (11 Pet.) 420 (1837). One could argue, however, that individualistic or "juristic" notions of property are actually carried to their fullest, if only for white persons, in Taney's *Dred Scott* opinion, where the Southern slaveholder's individual property right in slaves seems so inviolable that it is not subject to congressional manipulation in the interests of national unity. *Dred Scott v. Sandford*, 60 U.S. (19 How.) 393 (1856).

70. As will be suggested, infra, by embracing Hamilton's views on the separation of governmental powers as a guarantee against corruption, instead of the more ancient English constitution's separation of orders in society, Chase may have undermined his own cherished belief in an ultimately deferential society. On the American transition in political theory from the separation of orders to the separation of powers, with its attendant collapse of deferential politics, see G. Wood, *The Creation of the American Republic 1776–1787*, at 150–61, 449–52 (1969).

71. For a similar conclusion on late eighteenth-century American political discourse, see Kloppenberg, "The Virtues of Liberalism: Christianity, Republicanism, and Ethics in Early American Political Discourse," 74 *J. Am. Hist.* 9 (1987).

72. On Hobbes's political, religious and eschatological thought, a good starting point is the essay on Hobbes by J. G. A. Pocock in *Politics, Language, and Time*, 148 (1973).

73. Id. at 184.

74. Probably the clearest statement of the manner in which Chase believed his maker to be watching over him and constantly affecting his destiny is a letter from him to Hannah Chase dated February 4, 1800 (misdated as 1/4/1800), from the Dreer Collection of the Signers of the Declaration of Independence, Historical Society of Pennsylvania, where Chase reports divine intervention to save his life. In addition, see Chase's personal prayer, which appears to be his daily morning conversation with God, in which he expresses his sensitivity to the inevitable appearance to be made at the bar of Heaven on the Day of Judgment. He also thanks God for preserving him "from all the Dangers of the Past Night and for bringing me in Health and Safety to the Beginning of this day." Prayer of the Hon. Samuel Chase, Associate Justice of the United States Supreme Court, Haverford College Quaker Collection, No. 715 (n.p., n.d.) [hereafter cited as Prayer of the Hon. Samuel Chase].

75. For perhaps the best general introduction to the religious or eschatological basis of early American political theory, see J. G. A. Pocock, *The Machiavellian Moment*, 32–34, 43–46 (1975). For a discussion of the importance of religion to the theories of the anti-Federalists, the political group to which Chase belonged in his early years, see H. Storing, *What the Anti Federalists Were For*, 22–23 (1982). For further reading on the religious basis of English conservatism in the late eighteenth century, which is very close to Chase's religious ideas, and which undoubtedly exerted an influence on him when he was in England, see H. Dickenson, *Liberty and Property: Political Ideology in Eighteenth-Century Britain*, 294–96, 302–6, 313–15 (1977). Chase fully outlined the relationship between morality, politics, and religion in his manuscript, Chase Jury Charge Book, supra note 6. For further evidence of the importance of religion in his life and work, see the Letter to His Children, supra note 41, and his daily prayer, supra note 74. For the manner in which he integrated his Christian belief in a day of judgment and an afterlife, see his comments to John Fries, infra note 78.

76. But see G. Haskins and H. Johnson, *History of the Supreme Court of the United States: Foundations of Power*, vol. 2, at 7, 396–97 (1981) (for the now rather remarkable suggestion that John Marshall got the Supreme Court out of politics). For trenchant criticism of Haskins and Johnson on this point, see Nedelsky, "Confining Democratic Politics: Anti-Federalists, Federalists, and the Constitution" (*Book Review*), 96 *Harv. L. Rev.* 340, 350–60 (1982). For the more current conventional wisdom, see Sanford Levinson's review of *The Politics of Law* (D. Kairys, ed., 1982). There Levinson essentially suggests that all law is inevitably politics. Levinson, "Escaping Liberalism: Easier Said than Done" (*Book Review*), 96 *Harv. L. Rev.* 1466 (1983).

77. Regarding Hobbes's eschatology, see *Politics*, supra note 72, at 148.

78. For Chase's powerful statements about the world to come, the need to put one's affairs in order before embarking on the journey there, and his personal prayers for one convicted of a capital crime, see his comments to John Fries following Fries's conviction for treason in *United States v. Fries*, 9 F. Cas. 924, 932-34 (C.C.D. Pa. 1800) (No. 5,127), discussed supra chapter 7.

79. As he did, for example, thoughout his Jury Charge Book.

80. See supra chapter 3. For further evidence on the English aspects of Chase's views, see also Chase's Letter to His Children, supra note 41 (he urges them to pay particular attention to several English and classical authors, including the great Tory thinker Bolingbroke).

81. Perhaps it is more accurate to call Jefferson's brand of religion, "Thomas Paine's Religion of Humanity," rather than deism. On Jefferson's religious beliefs, see, e.g., D. Boorstin, *The Lost World of Thomas Jefferson*, 151–66 (1948). See also infra chapter 9.

82. See Prayer of the Hon. Samuel Chase, supra note 74.

83. See his remarks to Fries in *United States v. Fries*, 9 F. Cas. 932–34.

84. Id.

85. The most famous statement of what is here called "Burkean conservatism" is E. Burke, *Reflections on the Revolution in France* (1790). A very accessible introduction to the thought of Burke is R. Kirk, *The Conservative Mind from Burke to Eliot* (6th rev. ed., 1978).

86. The phrase "bulk of mankind" seems to be Burke's, used to suggest the somewhat unthinking character of most men, particularly in a horde. For its use in Burke's speech to the electors of Bristol, see E. Burke, *The Works of the Right Honourable Edmund Burke*, vol. 3, at 186 (London, 1826), excerpted in R. Kirk, The Portable Conservative Reader, 6 (1982). It seems likely, given Chase's acquaintance with Burke, that Chase borrowed the phrase, and perhaps the sentiments behind it, from its English author. For Chase's use of the phrase, see Chase Jury Charge Book, supra note 6, at 38.

87. Chase Jury Charge Book, supra note 6, at 40–41.

88. Id. at 35, 41–43.

89. See [A. Ramsey], *Thoughts on the Origin and Nature of Government Occasioned by the Late Dispute Between Great Britain and Her American Colonies*, 8, 9, 10, 12, 15, 29, passim, 53, 55, 59 (1769) (written in 1766). Bernard Bailyn described Ramsey's work, citing those pages, as a "handbook of applied Hobbesianism, cold, harsh, and disillusioned." B. Bailyn, *The Ordeal of Thomas Hutchinson*, 77 (1974). The ideas of Chase noted here could have come from a variety of sources, however, because they were clearly widespread in the eighteenth century. For a concise introduction to the thought, society, and institutions of the eighteenth century, and recent scholarship, see Stone, "The New Eighteenth Century," 31 *N.Y. Rev. Books* 42 (Mar. 29, 1984); R. Porter, *English Society in the Eighteenth Century* (1982).

90. Chase Jury Charge Book, supra note 6, at 41–43.

91. For a discussion of these authors and citations to their works, see H. Dickenson, supra note 75, at 132–40, 297–98. See also G. Wills, *Inventing America: Jefferson's Declaration of Independence* (1978), and *Explaining America: The Federalist* (1981) (influence of Scottish enlightenment on American political thought), and Horwitz, "Republicanism and Liberalism in American Constitutional Thought," 29 *Wm. & Mary L. Rev.* 57, 65 (Scottish enlightenment philosopher Adam Smith's philosophy in the great republican tradition; Smith's lectures underline late eighteenth-century republican theory of law as constitutive and creative of political culture).

92. Chase Jury Charge Book, supra note 6, at 40–44.

93. For the differences between these two "conservative" approaches, both based on conceptions of the "Ancient Constitution," see J. G. A. Pocock, *The Ancient Constitution and the Feudal Law*, 229–251 (Norton, ed., 1967), and *Politics Language and Time*, supra note 72, at 202–32.

94. See supra, text accompanying notes 14–18.

95. "Asking a state to surrender part of its sovereignty is like asking a lady to surrender part of her chastity," Randolph once explained. H. Butterfield, *The American Past: A History of the United States from Concord to Hiroshima, 1775–1945*, at 37 (1947). On Col. Taylor see R. Shalhope, *John Taylor of Caroline: Pastoral Republican* (1980).

96. Roeber, supra note 36, at 235.

97. See supra, text accompanying note 70.

98. For Taylor's magisterial indictments, in particular of John Adams and John Marshall, see J. Taylor, *An Inquiry into the Principles and Policy of the Government of the United States* (R. P. Nichols, ed., 1950), and J. Taylor, *Construction Construed, and Constitutions Vindicated* (1820).

99. See supra chapter 6.

100. *Currie's Administrators v. The Mutual Assurance Society*, 4 Hen. & M. (14 Va.) 315 (1809).
101. R. Ellis, *The Jeffersonian Crisis: Courts and Politics in the Young Republic*, 78 (1971), and Roeber, supra note 36, at 231–32.

CHAPTER 9

1. For the argument that Jefferson was a moderate, within the American political mainstream, see R. Hofstadter, *The American Political Tradition and the Men Who Made It*, 22–55 (Vintage Books, ed., 1973, originally published 1948).
2. For this characterization of John Marshall, see G. White, *The American Judicial Tradition: Profiles of Leading American Judges*, 7–34 (1976).
3. For recent works emphasizing the radical cast of Jeffersonian political thought, see R. Matthews, *The Radical Politics of Thomas Jefferson* (1984), and Matthews, "Beyond 'Sanctimonious Reverence' for a 'Sacred' Law," in T. Shevory, ed., *John Marshall's Achievement: Law Politics and Constitutional Interpretation* (1989).
4. For Jefferson's fear of the judiciary, and what is said to be his countervailing attempt to erect an elite corps of Virginia lawyers trained in the non-Christian old-Saxon uncorrupted common law, see A. G. Roeber, *Faithful Magistrates and Republican Lawyers: Creators of a Virginia Legal Culture 1680–1810*, 224 (1981).
5. D. Boorstin, *The Lost World of Thomas Jefferson*, 202–3 (1948).
6. See, e.g., Thomas Jefferson to Col. John Taylor, May 28, 1816, reproduced in J. Somerville and R. Santori, eds., *Social and Political Philosophy*, 251, 253, 254 (1963), where Jefferson observes that the Virginia judiciary is "seriously anti-republican, because for life," and where he notes implicitly that the national judiciary cannot be republican because it is "independent of the nation, their coercion by impeachment [presumably referring to the failed Chase removal effort] being found nugatory."
7. Id. at 254.
8. Again quoting from the letter to John Taylor of May 28, 1816, Jefferson says that if he were to define the term "republic" it would mean "a government by its citizens in mass, acting directly and personally, according to rules established by the majority, and that every other government is more or less republican, in proportion as it has in its composition more or less of this ingredient of the direct action of the citizens." Id. at 252.
9. The letter to Madison is from Paris, January 30, 1787, and is reproduced in Somerville and Santori, supra note 6, at 258, 259.
10. Jefferson to Colonel Smith, from Paris, November 13, 1787, id. at 259, 260.
11. Reproduced id. at 260–61.
12. Cf. Mr. Mencken's comments on Mr. Justice Holmes, suggesting that Holmes's admirers, who characterized him as a liberal, were mistaken. "He believed that lawmaking bodies should be free to experiment almost *ad libitum*, that the courts should not call a halt upon them until they clearly passed the uttermost bounds of reason, that everything should be sacrificed to their autonomy, including, apparently, even the Bill of Rights. If this is liberalism, then all I can say is that Liberalism is not what it was when I was young." H. Mencken, *The Vintage Mencken*, 190 (gathered by A. Cooke, 1955).

13. See, e.g., the report of the trial of Thomas Cooper, from 25 Fed. Cas. 631 (C.C.D. Pa. 1800), excerpted in Presser and Zainaldin, *Law and Jurisprudence in American History*, 203–10 (2d. ed., 1989). Chase's cooler colleague at that trial, Richard Peters, took the position that the question of party affiliation was irrelevant to the sentencing of Cooper, indicating perhaps how Chase was more inclined to let his personal ideology affect his sentencing than was Peters. Chase took the position that if a "party" was likely to indemnify Cooper for any fines levied the amount of the fines ought to be at a maximum. Id. at 209–10.

14. Somerville and Santori, supra note 6, at 277, 279.

15. Id. at 279.

16. See, e.g., Boorstin, supra note 5, and for a book-length account of how Jefferson could ignore even the law of civil liberties when he found it inconvenient, see L. Levy, *Jefferson and Civil Liberties: The Darker Side* (Quadrangle Paperback edition, 1973).

17. For Jefferson's support of Cooper and Callender, see, e.g., M. Peterson, *Adams and Jefferson: A Revolutionary Dialogue*, 78, 98, 100 (1976). Peterson notes that Callender reported, following Jefferson's freeing him from prison and remitting his fine as one of his first executive acts, that he (Cooper) "had been a paid hireling of the vice-president [Jefferson]. Id. at 98. Jefferson's thus supporting the writers of the vituperous attacks on his former friend John Adams led the latter to suspend their friendship, as he concluded that Jefferson's "patronage of Callender and a host of Republican libelers was not only a blot on his moral character but proof he was a captive of party." Id. at 100.

18. For John Adams's alarm at Jefferson's attacks on Christianity, see, e.g., id. at 100 (Adams was distressed because Jefferson "despised the wholesome sentiments of the Christian religion").

19. See, e.g., Jefferson's essay on Christianity and the common law, appendix I, in 1 *Virginia Reports* 137–42, and Roeber's discussion of that essay, Roeber, supra note 4, at 161–66. For Jefferson's suggestion on the extent of religous freedom that ought to be accorded particular groups, see his "Autobiography," quoted in Somerville and Santori, supra note 6, at 250.

20. For Pendleton and Mason's beliefs, see the evidence in Roeber, supra note 4, at 164–66.

21. See generally Presser and Hurley, "Saving God's Republic: The Jurisprudence of Samuel Chase," 1984 *Ill. L. Rev.* 771, 787–90, and sources there cited.

22. For Chase's views see id. at 788–90. For the Virginians, see, e.g., Roeber's comments on St. George Tucker and George Mason, Roeber, supra note 4, at 252.

23. See, e.g., *National Intelligencer*, May 20, 1803, at 3, col. 1 (accusing Chase of being a monarchist); *National Intelligencer*, Aug. 10, 1803, at 3, cols. 1 & 2 (suggesting that Chase had become an advocate of aristocracy and monarchy because of "party spirit, the love of power, the thirst for lucre").

24. On the notion that only sufficient virtue in the people can support a republic, see generally J. G. A. Pocock, *The Machiavellian Moment: Florentine Political Thought and the Atlantic Republican Tradition*, 462–551 (1975).

25. See the part of the *Notes on Virginia*, which set forth an essentially aristocratic system of education, with some students from all classes attending at state expense, but places made available to the wealthy in all instances, reproduced in S. Presser and

J. Zainaldin, supra note 13, at 127–28. Roeber, supra note 4, at 167, also notes the nonegalitarian character of Jefferson's thought.

Roeber presents Jefferson's philosophy as constant over time, but I think that Jefferson, unlike Chase, grew less aristocratic with age. Compare the tone in the *Notes on Virginia*, supra, where Jefferson explains that one of the most important features of his educational system is to make clear that happiness consists not in ambition, or the condition in which one finds one's self in society, but in "good conscience, good health, occupation, and freedom," with his comments on his educational system in a letter to John Adams, in 1813, toward the end of their lives, when they had resumed their correspondence, Thomas Jefferson to John Adams, October 28, 1813, J. Cappon, ed., *The Adams-Jefferson Letters*, 387–92 (1959). In that letter, also excerpted in Somerville and Santori, supra note 6, at 266–70, Jefferson claims that his educational system was designed to separate and train the "natural aristocrats," those possessing talent and virtue, from the "pseudo-aristos," those whose high position in society was simply due to wealth. For commentary on that letter see M. Peterson, *Adams and Jefferson: A Revolutionary Dialogue*, 112–15 (1976). To me at least, the educational proposals in the *Notes on Virginia*, with their talk of a very few students of superior parts "raked from the rubbish annually," Presser and Zainaldin, supra note 13, at 127, smack of what Jefferson called, sneeringly, in 1813 "pseudo-aristocracy." Any social mobility allowed in the *Notes* seems not to threaten the hierarchy of wealth and property which Jefferson there allows to perpetuate itself. For a recent reading of the *Notes*, stressing their "republican" character, and also stressing the mood of anxiety in which Jefferson wrote them, see R. Ferguson, *Law and Letters in American Culture*, 35–58 (1984).

26. Jefferson's attitude is set forth in his letter to Joseph H. Nicholson, May 13, 1803, in the Jefferson Papers, Library of Congress, reprinted in *The Writings of Thomas Jefferson*, vol. 10, at 390 (A. Bergh, ed., 1907), quoted in J. Haw, F. Beirne, R. Beirne, and R. Jett, *Stormy Patriot: The Life of Samuel Chase*, 216 (1980). A good account of Jefferson's orchestration of and involvement in the attempt to impeach Chase is in R. Ellis, *The Jeffersonian Crisis: Courts and Politics in the Young Republic*, 76–82 (1971).

27. See supra chapters 7 and 8.

28. The text of the impeachment articles against Chase appears at *Trial of Samuel Chase, An Associate Justice of the Supreme Court of the United States*, vol. 1, at 5–8 (S. Smith and T. Lloyd, eds., 1805).

29. For Chase's answer to the articles of impeachment, see id. at 25–103.

30. Id. at 80.

31. On the Yazoo land controversy, an attempt by land speculators to recover compensation for title to property taken away from them by the Georgia legislature, see generally C. Magrath, *Yazoo: Law and Politics in the New Republic: The Case of Fletcher v. Peck* (1966). There is a concise explanation of the career of John Randolph and his break with Jefferson. Id. at 39–49.

32. Ellis, supra note 26, at 103–7.

33. See, e.g., R. K. Newmyer, *Supreme Court Justice Joseph Story: Statesman of the Old Republic* (1985), passim.

34. For Chase's equanimity when his daughter married a Jeffersonian democrat, see J. Sanderson, *Biography of the Signers to the Declaration of Independence*, vol. 9, at 234 (1827).

35. For excerpts from his *Notes on Virginia* (1781) where these points are made, see Presser and Zainaldin, supra note 13, at 127–28.

36. Ibid.

37. Adams's most famous expression of such a belief in hierarchical society, and of his veneration for the British monarchical structure is to be found in his *Defense of the Constitutions of the United States Against the Attacks of M. Turgot* (1787), the first volume of a three-volume work, reprinted in *The Works of John Adams*, vol. 4, at 271 (C. F. Adams, ed., 1850–56). On this work, and on how it showed that Adams's thought was "irrelevant" to the future development of American political theory, a theory ostensibly based on "popular sovereignty," see G. Wood, *The Creation of the American Republic 1776–1787*, 567–92 (1969).

38. For the suggestion from Adams that his and Jefferson's views on aristocracy were essentially the same, whether Jefferson was prepared to admit it or not, and that these views included the need to defer to an aristocracy that inevitably would be at least partly hereditary, see John Adams to Thomas Jefferson, November 15, 1813, Cappon, supra note 25, at 400, discussed in Peterson, supra note 25, at 114–15.

39. For the essentially conservative views of Randolph, particularly in his later years, after the fiascos of the Chase impeachment and the Yazoo land controversy were behind him, see the writings collected in R. Kirk, *John Randolph of Roanoke* (3d ed., 1978), and the analysis of Randolph's conservatism in R. Kirk, *The Conservative Mind*, 130–46 (6th rev. ed., 1978).

40. See supra chapters 7 and 8.

41. One of the most prominent elements of English "country" political theory, imbibed by many American whigs, particularly the Jeffersonians, was that financial speculation and central banking (prominent tenets of American Hamiltonian federalism), led inevitably to corruption and a betrayal of the libertarian principles of the English constitution. This theme is explored in D. McCoy, *The Elusive Republic: Political Economy in Jeffersonian America* (1980).

42. Indeed, it has been observed that when Chase made his famous defense of judicial review (tracking the arguments of Hamilton in *Federalist* No. 78) in the *Callender* case, in Richmond, Virginia, John Marshall was in the audience, soaking up the arguments he would later reproduce in the *Marbury* case. For Marshall's attendance at the *Callender* trial, see A. Beveridge, *The Life of John Marshall*, vol. 3, at 39 (1919), and for the admission by Marshall's famous biographer that "Chase advanced most of the arguments used by Marshall in *Marbury v. Madison*," see id. at 40, n. 1.

43. For the latest expression of this traditional view, see G. Haskins and H. Johnson, *A History of the Supreme Court: Foundations of Power: John Marshall 1801–1815*, vol. 2, passim (1985). For skepticism regarding this traditional assertion that Marshall depoliticized the court, see Nedelsky, "Confining Democratic Politics: Anti-Federalists, Federalists, and the Constitution," 96 *Harv. L. Rev.* 340, 347–60 (1982) (reviewing Haskins and Johnson's *Foundations of Power*).

44. On the view of the Ancient Constitution as shared in common by Coke, Hale, and Burke, see J. G. A. Pocock, *The Ancient Constitution and the Feudal Law*, 242–43 (Norton, ed., 1967).

45. This may or may not be what is meant by H. Jefferson Powell, when he speaks of the "original intent" as having been to interpret the Constitution in the manner the

"common law" was interpreted in England. Powell, "The Original Understanding of Original Intent," 98 *Harv. L. Rev.* 885 894–902 (1985), but I think Powell's insight about original intention and the common law method is correct, and I think that in the hands of Chase and his pre-Marshall Federalist fellows, a common-law method of interpretation could only have been in accordance with the English "conservative" common lawyers, such as Mansfield, Blackstone, and Burke.

46. See generally chapter 3, supra.

47. See generally chapter 4, supra.

48. See, e.g., J. Reid, *The Authority of Rights* (1986), *The Authority to Tax* (1987), and *The Concept of Liberty in the Age of the American Revolution* (1988).

49. For this astonishing Marshallian behavior, viewed as something of an embarrassment by his greatest modern apologist, see A. Beveridge, supra note 42, at 176–78.

50. To be somewhat fairer to Marshall, he did squarely take on the Jeffersonians in his handling of the *Burr* trial, in which he refused to depart from strict construction of the treason laws in a manner to satisfy Jefferson, who had pronounced Burr guilty even before any proceedings against him. On the *Burr* trial see generally chapter 8 in Haskins and Johnson, *Foundations of Power*, supra note 43, at 246–91. It bears stressing, however, that this activity of Marshall's occurred *after* Chase's vindication before the Senate. Until Chase's victory for the independence of the judiciary, a victory which probably made Marshall's boldness in the *Burr* trial possible, Marshall seems to have kept a relatively low profile.

51. Given the belief in most of the Supreme Court judges in the federal common law of crimes, see supra chapter 6, it is difficult not to believe that Marshall and his fellows could not have concocted a simple common law basis for the granting of the relatively simple relief sought in *Marbury*. It would have been easy to turn, for example, to the kind of supraconstitutional principles which Chase outlined in *Calder v. Bull*, or which Richard Peters referred to in his *Worrall* opinion to justify some fashioning of relief.

52. Most notably in *Dartmouth College v. Woodward* 17 U.S. (4 Wheat.) 518 (1819), or *Gibbons v. Ogden*, 22 U.S. (9 Wheat.) 1 (1824). For Marshall's complex vision of democracy or "popular sovereignty," see Shevory, "John Marshall as Republican: Order and Conflict in American Political History," in *John Marshall's Achievement*, supra note 3, at 75.

53. For Chase's long letter to Marshall and its argument regarding the unconstitutionality of the 1802 act, see G. Haskins and H. Johnson, supra note 43, at 171–77, original letter from Samuel Chase to John Marshall (April 24, 1802), available at the New York Historical Society.

54. For interpretations of John Marshall's jurisprudence which stress the modern individualist Lockean liberal aspects of his work, in a manner that seems to accord with the treatment given Marshall in this and the following section, see R. Faulkner, *The Jurisprudence of John Marshall* (1968), and two of Faulkner's shorter treatments, "The Marshall Court and Era," in *Encyclopedia of the American Judicial System*, vol. 1, at 39 (R. Janosik, ed., 1987), and "The Marshall Court and the Making of Constitutional Democracy," in *John Marshall's Achievement*, supra note 3, at 13.

55. See generally the essays collected in *John Marshall's Achievement*, supra note 3, and particularly the introduction by Thomas C. Shevory.

56. See generally the materials on the religious aspect of Chase's jurisprudence supra chapter 8.

57. See generally Horwitz, *The Transformation of American Law 1780–1860* (1977). In fairness to Professor Horwitz, my original mentor in this business, his most recent writing on the 1790s appears to have abandoned this instrumentalist/preinstrumentalist model of analysis, and to have shifted to focus more on the dichotomy between early American republicanism and liberalism in the law, in order to arrive at conclusions which bear a strong resemblance to many of those articulated here. See, e.g., Horwitz, "Republicanism and Liberalism in American Constitutional Thought," 29 *Wm. & Mary L. Rev.* 57 (1987).

58. Horwitz, *Transformation*, supra note 57, at 16–30.

59. Again, for Horwitz's recent elaboration of these differences taking account of recent work by historians who have studied the "Civic-Republican" tradition, such as Pocock, Bailyn, and Wood, see, e.g., Horwitz, "Republicanism and Liberalism," supra note 57.

60. Supra chapter 7.

61. Supra chapter 8.

62. For an excerpt from Chase's answer to the House's articles of impeachment, see Presser and Zainaldin, supra note 13, at 240.

63. 3 U.S. (3 Dall.) 171 (1796) (tax on carriages is not a direct tax calling for apportionment). In his opinion in *Hylton*, Chase observed that "[t]he deliberate decision of the national legislature, [who did not consider a tax on carriages a direct tax, but thought it was within the description of a duty] would determine me, if the case was doubtful, to receive the construction of the legislature." Id. at 173.

64. 3 U.S. (3 Dall.) 199 (1796).

65. 17 U.S. (4 Wheat.) 316, 407, 421 (1819). In *McCulloch*, of course, Marshall adopted Alexander Hamilton's view of the Constitution, and from that day to this Marshall has been associated with Hamiltonian federalism, and Marshall has been thought to have expressed something close to the original intention of the Founders. See, e.g., Howe, "Anti-Federalist/Federalist Dialogue and Its Implications for Constitutional Understanding," 84 *Nw. U.L. Rev.* 1, 9 (1989) for the assertion that Marshall's Hamiltonian Federalist beliefs were in "close[r] approximation of the vision of the Framers of the Constitution," than was Chase's brand of "religious, organicist, and civic republican" thought. Howe's is a powerful and elegant piece, but if our focus is to be not on the unexpressed *intention* of the framers, but rather on the meaning of the document that one construing it according to common law principles would give it, see Powell, supra note 45, then I think that the views of Chase and his Federalist brethren before Marshall—Paterson, Wilson, Ellsworth, for example—are entitled to the most weight.

66. Or so, at least, Story believed. See R. K. Newmyer, *Supreme Court Justice Joseph Story: Statesman of the Old Republic*, 233 (1985).

67. For a review of the literature stressing that the operative "republicanism" of the Jacksonian era had become an individualistic acquisitive cultural norm, which differed from the rather more altruistic "republicanism" of Chase's era, see Wilentz, "On Class and Politics in Jacksonian America," 10 *Reviews in American History* 45 (1982), and,

for an excellent study in the thought of the great mid-nineteenth century Whig politi-
cians, stressing how their secular system differed from the thought of late eighteenth-
century and early nineteenth-century American thinkers, see D. Howe, *The Political
Culture of the American Whigs* (1979). Howe has recently indicated that "Samuel
Chase deserves to be noticed at least in passing as an ideological forerunner of the
American Whig party." Howe, supra note 65, at 9.

68. The most thoughtful scholarship on Hamilton, e.g., G. Stourzh, *Alexander Hamilton and the Idea of Republican Government* (1970); J. Miller, *Alexander Hamilton
and the Growth of the New Nation* (1959); F. McDonald, *Alexander Hamilton: A Biography* (1982), suggests that whatever else he was, he was too concerned with honor
blatantly to write hypocritically.

69. For the latest expression of this view, see R. Bork, *The Tempting of America: The
Political Seduction of the Law* (1990).

70. See, e.g., M. Tushnet, *Red, White, and Blue* (1988).

71. The goal of turning back the clock is condemned by Justice Earl Warren in *Brown
v. Board of Education*, 347 U.S. 483, 492 (1954). The idea of turning back the clock
in our constitutional jurisprudence is criticized as a misconceived quest for the original
understanding in Brest, "The Misconceived Quest for the Original Understanding," 60
B.U.L. Rev. 204 (1980).

72. J. Sanderson, *Biography of the Signers to the Declaration of Independence*, vol. 9,
at 232 (1827).

73. Id.

CHAPTER 10

1. For a good statement of the orthodox position that the American judicial tradition
started with John Marshall, see G. White, *The American Judicial Tradition* (1976):

> The advent of the Revolution and the introduction of the Constitution changed
> the structure of the appellate court system in America but did not dramatically
> change the status of judges. The history of the Supreme Court from 1789 to
> 1801, the year of John Marshall's appointment as Chief Justice, was marked by
> three phenomena: the minimal extent of Court business; the disorganization
> and disunity of the Court itself—most notably with regard to the question of its
> authority to pass on the constitutionality of Congressional legislation—and the
> increasing involvement of the Court in partisan politics.

Id. at 8. See also Stites, Book Review, 40 *Wm. & Mary Q.* (3d ser.) 336 (1983) ("It is
axiomatic that history of the United States Supreme Court as a coequal branch of government begins in 1801 with the appointment of John Marshall as chief justice"). For
the position that Marshall established "the rule of law as the basis of the Supreme
Court's jurisprudence," see G. Haskins and H. Johnson, *History of the Supreme Court
of the United States: Foundations of Power*, vol. 2 (1981). The quote is from Nelson,
Book Review (of Haskins and Johnson), 131 *U. Pa. L. Rev.* 489, 489 (1982).

2. J. Goebel, Jr., *A History of the Supreme Court of the United States: Antecedents
and Beginnings to 1801*, vol. 1, at xiv (1971).

3. Lerner, "The Supreme Court as Republican Schoolmaster," 1967 *Sup. Ct. Rev.*
127.

4. *United States v. Callender*, 25 F. Cas. 239 (C.C.D. Va. 1800) (No. 14,709), discussed supra chapter 8.

5. 5 U.S. (1 Cranch) 137 (1803).

6. See supra chapter 8.

7. 28 F. Cas. 1012 (C.C.D. Pa. 1795) (No. 16,857). Discussed supra chapter 5.

8. 10 U.S. (6 Cranch) 7 (1810).

9. For some introductory material and citations to secondary sources on liberal in-
tellectuals' opposition to the Supreme Court in the early twentieth century, see S.
Presser and J. Zainaldin, *Law and American History: Cases and Materials*, 674–734
(1980).

10. 17 U.S. (4 Wheat.) 316 (1819).

11. 22 U.S. (9 Wheat.) 1 (1824).

12. See, e.g., F. Frankfurter, *The Commerce Clause Under Marshall, Taney and Waite*
(1937); B. Palmer, *Marshall and Taney* (1939); C. Warren, *The Supreme Court in
United States History* (1926) (2 vols.); Lerner, "John Marshall and the Campaign of
History," 39 *Colum. L. Rev*, 396 (1939).

13. See, e.g., A. Cox, *The Role of the Supreme Court in American Government* (1976);
A. Cox, *The Warren Court* (1968); G. White, *Earl Warren* (1982); White, "The Evo-
lution of Reasoned Elaboration: Jurisprudential Criticism and Social Change," 59 *Va.
L. Rev* 279 (1973). For the best skeptical view of the accomplishments of the Warren
Court, see A. Bickel, *The Supreme Court and the Idea of Progress* (1970).

14. For works ritually praising Marshall, see G. White, *The American Judicial Tradition: Profiles of Leading American Judges* (1976); L. Baker, *John Marshall* (1974); F.
Stites, *John Marshall, Defender of the Constitution* (1981). A remarkable recent article
by Bruce A. Campbell makes the link with current issues even clearer by arguing that
the famous *Dartmouth College* case, *Trustees of Dartmouth College v. Woodward*, 17
U.S. (4 Wheat.) 517 (1819), usually thought to have been about economic and property
rights, was actually an important precursor of civil rights jurisprudence. Campbell,
"Dartmouth College as a Civil Liberties Case: The Formation of Constitutional Policy," 70 *Ky. L.J.* 643 (1982).

15. J. G. A. Pocock, *The Ancient Constitution and the Feudal Law* (Norton Library,
ed., 1967).

16. Id. at 119–23.

17. See generally in addition to Bailyn and Robbins, G. Wood, *The Creation of the
American Republic 1776–1787* (1969).

18. The starting points for understanding the importance of republicanism in early
American history and modern American historiography are two articles by Shalhope,
"Towards a Republican Synthesis: The Emergence of an Understanding of Republicanism in American Historiography," 29 *Wm. & Mary Q.* (3d Ser.) 49 (1972) [hereafter
cited as "Republican Synthesis"], and Shalhope, "Republicanism and Early American
Historiography," 39 *Wm. & Mary Q.* (3d Ser.) 334 (1982) [hereafter cited as "Republican Historiography"].

19. See, e.g., James T. Kloppenberg, "The Virtues of Liberalism: Christianity, Republicanism, and Ethics in Early American Political Discourse," 74 *Journal of American*

History 9, 28–29 (1987), and see also H. May, *The Enlightenment in America* (1976); H. May, *Ideas, Faith and Feelings: Essays in American Intellectual and Religious History* (1983).

20. This appears to be the basic argument made in Nedelsky, "Confining Democratic Politics: Anti-Federalists, Federalists, and the Constitution" (Book Review), 96 *Harv. L. Rev.* 340 (1982). For similar suggestions see Horwitz, "Republicanism and Liberalism in American Constitutional Thought," 29 *Wm. & Mary L. Rev.* 57 (1987), and Horwitz, "History and Theory," 96 *Yale L. J.* 1825 (1987).

21. See, e.g., Horwitz, "Republicanism and Liberalism in American Constitutional Thought," 29 *Wm. & Mary L. Rev.* 57 (1987), and the articles in the symposium, "Roads Not Taken: Undercurrents of Republican Thinking in Modern Constitutional Theory," 84 *Nw. U.L. Rev.* 1–232 (1989).

22. On the perils of "presentism," see Gordon, "Historicism in Legal Scholarship," 90 *Yale L. J.* 1017 (1981).

23. Cf. T. Kuhn, *The Structure of Scientific Revolutions* (2d ed., 1971). For an earlier essay in intellectual history investigating "climates of opinion," which seem to be the same thing as the trendier Kuhnian "paradigms," see C. Becker, *The Heavenly City of the Eighteenth-Century Philosophers* (1932).

24. This is not to suggest that Chase and his fellows were unaware that their opponents charged them with "partisan" activity, but rather that they believed it was their opponents who were the only "partisans." On this phenomenon see generally R. Hofstadter, *The Idea of a Party System: The Rise of Legitimate Opposition in the United States 1780–1840* (1969).

25. Id. Hofstadter explored the transition from an era when people believed that there could not be legitimate differences over politics that could lead to multiple political parties to the "liberal" social order we have today, when differences in politics in particular and differences in values in general are taken for granted. This book has sought to follow some of Hofstadter's insights, and in particular to illustrate how the early federal judiciary, believing in only one legitimate form for politics, could conceive of its task as both objective and essentially "political."

26. For one of the latest revelations of the complexity of the term "republican" in early American politics, and for a sensitive statement of the importance of several different incipient traditions, "republican," "Christian," and "liberal," in early American politics, see James T. Kloppenberg, "The Virtues of Liberalism: Christianity, Republicanism, and Ethics in Early American Political Discourse," 74 *Journal of American History* 9, 28–29 (1987). Kloppenberg has brilliantly demonstrated that discourse about "virtue" in early United States politics and society was done with several different "vocabularies," and that it leaves too much out of the picture to suggest, as have some scholars, that the debate was merely about republicanism. Two other themes stressed by Kloppenberg, the regional diversity of American political thought and the transformation of American society from one preoccupied with virtue to one preoccupied with consumption are also pursued here.

27. Supra chapter 9.

28. For the varying vicissitudes of Adams's and Jefferson's views on what they saw as they neared the ends of their lives, see their exchange of letters discussed in M. Peterson, *Jefferson and Adams: A Revolutionary Dialogue,* 116–28 (1976).

29. This is suggested not only by Chase's personal speculation in financial matters during his entire adult life, but also by his 1784 letter to his children, Nancy, Sammy, and Tommy, in which he praised both the "profession of the law" and "the Business of a Merchant" as offering those with the requisite abilities and inclination the opportunity to achieve private financial success and to discharge "the duties of a good citizen by . . . benevolence, charity, and good offices, and by . . . example of virtue, integrity, and Honour." Chase's Letter to His Children (Feb. 8, 1784), Ettings Jurists Collection vol 1, at 37 (unpublished collection of primary sources available at the Historical Society of Pennsylvania).

30. For the acceptance of Mansfieldian principles in American law, see generally M. Horwitz, *Transformation of American Law 1780–1860*, at 172–85 (1977). Mansfield's life and legal work are discussed in depth in C. H. S. Fifoot, *Lord Mansfield* (1936).

31. See generally W. Nelson, *The Americanization of the Common Law: The Impact of Legal Change on Massachusetts Society, 1760–1830* (1975) (in the late eighteenth and early nineteenth centuries, Massachusetts law changed from community-based to individualistic); see also J. Reid, *The Concept of Liberty in the Age of the American Revolution*, passim (1988) (detailing the English sources of the late eighteenth-century American conception of liberty).

32. The divorce of politics and popular moral principles from a new commercialized constitutional and private-law jurisprudence is discussed in M. Horwitz, supra note 30, and W. Nelson, supra note 31. See also Kairys, "Introduction," in *The Politics of Law*, 1–6 (D. Kairys, ed., 1982) (despite claims to the contrary, law is utterly infused with politics).

33. Supra chapters 3 and 9, supra.

34. This is the view now most commonly associated with the Critical Legal Studies Movement. For a subtle statement of that viewpoint, see M. Tushnet, *Red, White, and Blue* (1988).

35. See generally M. Perry, *The Constitution, the Court, and Human Rights: An Inquiry into the Legitimacy of Constitutional Policymaking by the Judiciary* (1982) (Supreme Court should perform a religious role in articulating the highest aspirations of the American people); M. Perry, *Morality, Politics, and Law: A Bicentennial Essay* (1988) (exploring the possibility of an objective morality on which constitutional law could be based); *The Politics of Law*, supra note 32 (collecting essays that explore the form of morality that ought to undergird constitutional law and politics).

36. Cf. M. Horwitz, "The Conservative Tradition in the Writing of American Legal History," 17 *Am. J. Leg. Hist.* 275 (1973) (understanding of the social forces confronted by Justice Joseph Story aids in understanding the transformation of American law in the nineteenth century).

37. F. Stites, *John Marshall: Defender of the Constitution* (1981).

38. Stites, *Book Review*, 40 *Wm. & Mary Q.* (3d Ser.) 336, 338 (1983).

39. See, e.g., Nedelsky, "Confining Democratic Politics: Anti-Federalists, Federalists, and the Constitution," 96 *Harv. L. Rev.* 340, 350–60 (1982). In the interests of fairness it should be pointed out that Stites, in the book review disparaged in the text, understands, as does Nedelsky, that there is a great need to integrate the examination

of ideology with the examination of early American jurisprudence, and also faults such scholars as George Haskins and Herbert Johnson, whose recently published *A History of the United States Supreme Court: Foundations of Power*, vol. 2 (1981), slights the importance of ideology and politics to legal development. Curiously, however, Stites at least still seems implicitly to accept the notion of a "nonpartisan" law.

40. See, e.g., J. O'Conner, *William Paterson: Lawyer and Statesman, 1745–1806* (1979) (suggesting throughout that Paterson's views on the need for order and hierarchy in the law, as well as for undergirding the law with morality and religion, were similar to those of Chase); Jay, "Origins of Federal Common Law: Part One," 133 *U. Pa. L. Rev.* 1003 (1984) (suggesting uniformity on the part of the Federalist judges in their jury charges).

41. For Chase's statement of these principles, see his Manuscript Grand Jury Charge Book, Vertical File, Maryland Historical Society, at 33–37, 38–44 (latter pages are the Baltimore grand jury charge of 1803 which led to his impeachment).

42. See, e.g., G. Haskins, and H. Johnson, supra note 39, at 201–4, 246, 400, 421 (suggesting that Marshall tried to take the Supreme Court out of politics, the better to implement some key Federalist principles).

43. This may be part of the implications from Kent Newmyer's contrast drawn between Story, who still adhered to much of the deferential ideology of Chase, and Marshall, who was not fond of "butting his head against a wall in sport." See K. Newmyer, *Supreme Court Justice Joseph Story: Statesman of the Old Republic*, 102, 205 (1985).

44. Stites, *Book Review*, quoted supra text accompanying note 38.

45. For the evolution of American republicanism from an ideology of deference to one of acquisitive individualism, see Shalhope, "Republicanism and Early American Historiography," 39 *Wm. & Mary Q.* (3d Ser.) 334 (1982), and sources there cited. For John Marshall's status as a "transitional figure" who moved jurisprudence from republicanism to individualistic liberalism, see Richard A. Brisbin, Jr., "John Marshall on History, Virtue and Legality" in *John Marshall's Achievement: Law, Politics, and Constitutional Interpretations*, 95, 108–9 (Thomas C. Shevory, ed. 1989) ("John Marshall stands as a transitional figure in American political thought. In his understanding of history and political time he remained wedded to many of the cyclical ideas of classical republicanism. Yet his understanding of history also recognized the need for commercial development and the security of the nation across a linear time frame"),

46. For recent reevaluations of the edifice of constitutional interpretation that Marshall erected, see generally *The Politics of Law*, supra note 32 (collecting essays that critique the notion that the law and the state are nonideological social forces); see also Nedelsky, supra note 39, at 347–60. For an analysis of the ideological split in the ranks of Jeffersonian Republicans, suggesting that this split was between Republicans who flirted with Marshall's new ideology of individual acquisitiveness and those, such as John Randolph and Colonel Taylor, who favored a more traditional and aristocratic morality, see Stites, supra note 38, at 336. For a comparison of the ideologies of Randolph, Taylor, and Chase, see chapter 9. For wide-ranging elaborations of the thought of John Marshall, see the essays in *The Achievement of John Marshall*, supra and sources there cited.

47. The late Carl Becker's characterization of the eighteenth-century philosophers applies equally well to Chase's jurisprudence, as well as to the thought of Thomas Jeffer-

son. See C. Becker, *The Heavenly City of the Eighteenth Century Philosophers*, passim (1932) (The "faith" of the eighteenth-century philosophers in a benevolent progress was marked by some of the same irrational aspects as the "medievalism" they disparaged).

48. For contemporary castigation of Chase for abandoning the democratic pretensions of his youth, see *National Intelligencer*, May 20, 1803, at 3, col. 3 (Chase's Baltimore grand jury charge enabled observers to "behold the cloven foot" and were an attempt to prepare the public mind for monarchy); id, August 10, 1803, at 3, col. 2 (Chase abandoned the republicanism and democracy that he once championed, because of "party spirit, the love of power, and the thirst [for] lucre").

49. Supra see chapter 9.

50. Chase's intention to try some popular miscreants when he was a Maryland judge apparently led to threats on his life. He was undeterred. "The life of one man," he reportedly said, "is of little consequence compared to the prostration of the laws of the land; with the blessing of God, I will do my duty, be the consequences what they may." J. Thomas Scharf, *History of Maryland*, vol. 2, at 590 (1879), quoted in Elsmere, *Justice Samuel Chase*, 47 (1980).

51. The great current growth industry in American legal scholarship might be the intersection of religion and the law, both the study of its past manifestations and calls for its present integration. See, e.g., S. Levinson, *Constitutional Faith* (1988) (exploring faith in the Constitution as a form of American civil religion); M. Perry, *The Courts, the Constitution, and Human Rights* (1982) (suggesting a religious basis for American constitutional law); R. Unger, *Knowledge and Politics*, 295 (1975) (asking for guidance in reconciling the contradictions of liberal legalism with the famous plea, "Speak, God"). See also Ball, "Cross and Sword, Victim and Law: A Tentative Response to Leonard Levy's *Treason Against God*," 35 *Stan. L. Rev.* 1007, 1027, n. 105 (1983) (listing recent works evincing "a growing interest among legal scholars in studying the relation of religion and theology to law").

52. See supra chapters 3 and 8.

53. For Morton Horwitz's view that this is what happened to Chase's great successor, Joseph Story, see Horwitz, "The Conservative Tradition in the Writing of American Legal History," 17 *Am. J. Leg. Hist.* 275, 292–93 (1973).

54. Holmes, "The Path of the Law," 10 *Harv. L. Rev.* 457, 466 (1897).

55. Joseph Story seems to have traveled much of the same ideological journey from left to right as Chase. Compare his early infatuation with radicalism, Newmyer, supra note 43, at 45–48, with his later reliance on the wisdom of Aristotle, Cicero, and Burke, G. Dunne, *Justice Joseph Story and the Rise of the Supreme Court*, 378 (1970).

56. See, e.g., M. Kammen, *The Past Before Us* (1980) (reporting on the state of American history, emphasizing the rise of "social history," and criticizing the enterprise of biography as making a limited contribution to historical knowledge); Botein, "Biography in Legal History," 69 *L. Libr. J.* 456 (1976) (finding individual legal biography of limited value).

57. Gerald Stourzh, *Alexander Hamilton and the Idea of Republican Government* (1970).

58. L. Kerber, *Federalists in Dissent: Imagery and Ideology in Jeffersonian America* (1970).

59. J. G. A. Pocock, *The Ancient Constitution and the Feudal Law*, 144–47 (Norton Library, ed., 1967).

60. For what may be Pocock's latest cut at the problem, see Pocock, "States, Republics, and Empires: The American Founding in Early Modern Perspective," in Terrence Ball and J. G. A. Pocock, eds., *Conceptual Change and the Constitution*, 55 (1988).

61. For a discussion of Theodore Sedgwick's contribution to the synthesis of these two jurisprudential strands, see R. Ellis, *The Jeffersonian Crisis: Courts and Politics in the New Republic*, 186–92 (1971).

62. *Penn's Lessees v. Pennington* (New Castle Circuit Court for Delaware, June 5, 1804), quoted in Rodney, "The End of the Penns' Claims to Delaware, 1789–1814," 61 *Pa. Mag. Hist. & Biog.*, 182, 195–96 (1937).

63. The classic studies of the manner in which the judge ceased to comment on the evidence are Wright, "The Invasion of the Jury: Temperature of the Water," 27 *Temp. L.Q.* 137 (1953–54); Wright, "Instructions to the Jury: Summary without Comment," 1954 *Wash. U.L.Q.* 177.

64. Lerner, "The Supreme Court as Republican Schoolmaster" 1967 *Sup. Ct. Rev.* 127.

65. Horwitz, *The Transformation of American Law 1780–1860*, at 7–30 (1977).

66. Cf. G. White, *The American Judicial Tradition* (1976) (suggesting that throughout American judicial history there have been self-acknowledged constraints placed upon American judges in the enterprise of lawmaking).

67. C. B. MacPherson, *The Political Theory of Possessive Individualism: Hobbes to Locke*, 3, 263–64 (1962) (defining "possessive individualism").

68. See, e.g., Kennedy, "The Structure of Blackstone's Commentaries," 28 *Buffalo L. Rev.* 209 (1979) (exploring the tension between the need for individuals in society to have autonomy and their need for solidarity with their fellows).

69. Bork, "Alexander M. Bickel, Political Philosopher," 1975 *Sup. Ct. Rev.* 419, 420–21 (reviewing Bickel's *Morality of Consent*).

70. Horwitz, "The Rule of Law: An Unqualified Human Good?" 86 *Yale L. J.* 561, 566 (1977).

71. Jennifer Nedelsky is quite correct that the effort undertaken here is not designed to reproduce in the modern era the precise conservative philosophy that Chase followed. Nedelsky, "Democracy, Justice, and the Multiplicity of Voices: Alternatives to the Federalist Vision," 84 *Nw. U.L. Rev.* 232, 248 (1989). Nevertheless, I think that his attempt, and that of his fellows, to combine law, morality, and religion, was a noble one which recognized some basic human needs, and offers at least some aspects worth emulating.

72. For some more present-minded attempts at what one might call "Burkean" solutions to modern jurisprudential problems, see G. Calabrisi, *A Common Law for the Age of Statutes* (1982), and I. Macneil, *The New Social Contract: An Inquiry into Modern Contractual Relations* (1980).

Bibliography

What follows is a simple lising of sources cited in the notes. Evaluative comments on many of the secondary sources are made in the notes where the individual works are cited. Citations follow the form used by lawyers, essentially in accordance with A Uniform System of Citation (14th ed., Cambridge: Harvard Law Review Association, 1986), except that places of publication and publishers have been added for books.

PRIMARY SOURCES

Manuscript

Coxe (Tench) Papers, Historical Society of Pennsylvania, Philadelphia
Chase Papers, Maryland Historical Society, Baltimore
Chase, Samuel, Manuscript Prayer of the Hon. Samuel Chase, Associate Justice of the United States Supreme Court, Haverford College Quaker Collection, No. 715 (n.p., n.d.)
Chase, Samuel, Jury Charge Book, 1798-1800, 1802-03, 1805-06, Vertical File, Manuscript Division, Maryland Historical Society, Baltimore
Dallas Papers, Historical Society of Pennsylvania
Dreer Collection of the Signers of the Declaration of Independence, Historical Society of Pennsylvania
Dudley Ryder notebook manuscripts, Lincoln's Inn, London
Ettings Jurists Collection, Historical Society of Pennsylvania
Gratz Collection, Historical Society of Pennsylvania
Peters Papers, Manuscript Collection, Historical Society of Pennsylvania

Printed

A Complete Collection of State Trials, vol. 4 (London: Printed for the Undertakers, J. Walthoe, Thomas Wotton, 2d ed., 1730)
J. Alexander, A Brief Narrative of the Case and Trial of John Peter Zenger (Cambridge: Belknap Press of Harvard University, S. Katz, ed. 1963)
Annals of Congress, vol. 8 (Washington, 1804)
Austin, Benjamin, Observations on the Pernicious Practice of the Law, as Published Occasionally in the Independent Chronicle, in the Year 1786 (1819), reprinted in 13 Am.J.Leg. Hist. 244 (1969)
Blackstone, William, Commentaries on the Law of England, vol. 4 (originally published 1769, Chicago: University of Chicago Press, Reprint, 1979)
Chase, Samuel, Objections to the Federal government (1788?) reprinted, introduced and annotated by Haw, 76 Md. Hist. Mag. 272 (1981)

G.Gibbs, ed., Memoirs of the Administrations of George Washington and John Adams, Vol. 1 (1846)

Hamilton, Alexander, The Papers of Alexander Hamilton, (New York and London: Columbia University Press) vol. 1 (H. Syrett, ed. 1961), vol. 25 (H. Syrett, ed. 1977)

Hamilton, Alexander, The Works of Alexander Hamilton, Vol. 1 (H.C. Lodge, ed., New York: Haskell House, 1971 reprint, originally published 1904)

A. Hamilton, J. Madison, and J. Jay, The Federalist (Middletown, Conn: Wesleyan University Press, J. Cooke, ed 1961)

J. Higgins, Sampson Against the Philistines or the Reformation of Lawsuits (Philadelphia: B. Granes, for W. Duane, 2d ed., 1805)

Hobbes, Thomas, The Elements of Law (originally published 1640, modern 2nd ed., London: Cass, Tonnies, ed., 1969)

Thomas Hutchinson, A Dialogue Between an American and a European Englishman, 4 Perspectives in American History 343 (B. Bailyn, ed. 1975, original manuscript dates from 1768)

Independent Chronicle (Boston), 1790, 1799

R. Kirk, ed., The Portable Conservative Reader (New York: Viking Press, 1982)

M. Marcus, J. Perry, *et. al.* eds. The Documentary History of the Supreme Court of the United States: Appointments and Proceedings, vol. 1 (New York: Columbia University Press, 1985), The Justices on Circuit 1789-1800, vol. 2 (New York: Columbia University Press, 1988)

Massachusetts Mercury, 1793

J. McRee, ed., Life and Correspondence of James Iredell, vol. 2 (New York: P. Smith, 1949)

National Gazette of Philadelphia, 1793

National Intelligencer, 1803

Philadelphia General Advertiser 1790, 1793

Philadelphia Aurora, 1800

Proceedings in the Circuit Court of the United States Held in Philadelphia, April 11, 1800 (T. Cooper, ed., Philadelphia, 1800), pamphlet in the collection of the Historical Society of Pennsylvania

Pufendorf, De Jure Naturae et Gentium Libri Octo, vol. 2 (trans. by C.H. and W.A. Oldfather, 1688 ed., 1934)

J. Somerville and R. Santori, eds., Social and Political Philosophy (Garden City, N.Y.: Anchor Books, 1963)

Vattel, Emmerich de, The Law of Nations, or Principles of the Law of Nature Applied to the conduct and Affairs of Nations and Sovereigns (English Translation, 1797)

F. Wharton, ed., State Trials of the United States During the Administrations of Washington and Adams (Philadelphia: Carey and Hart, 1849)

Trial of Samuel Chase, An Associate Justice of the Supreme Court of the United States, vol. 1 (Washington: Printed for Samuel H. Smith, and T. Lloyd, eds., 1805)

The Whole Proceeding on the King's Commission of the Peace, Oyer and Terminer and Gaol Delivery for the City of London and also the Gaol Delivery for the County of Middlesex held at Justice Hall in the Old Baily taken in short hand by E. Hodg-

son, on Wednesday the 19th of December, 1783, and on the following Days...
no.1, pt. 1 (1783) (Bound Pamphlets available in the Guild Hall, London)

Wolfe, Christian, Jus Gentium Methodo Scientifica Petractum, vol. 2 (trans. by Joseph H. Drake, 1764 ed., 1934)

SECONDARY SOURCES

Books

S. Ahlstrom, A Religious History of the American People (New Haven: Yale University Press, 1972).

J. Alden, The American Revolution (New York: Harper & Row, 1954).

L. Baker, John Marshall: A Life in the Law (New York: Macmillan, 1974).

B. Bailyn, The Ideological Origins of the American Revolution (Cambridge: Belknap Press of Harvard University, 1967).

B. Bailyn, The Origins of American Politics (New York: Knopf, 1968).

L. Baldwin, Whiskey Rebels: The Story of a Frontier Uprising (Pittsburgh: University of Pittsburgh Press, originally published 1939, Rev. ed., 1968).

C. Becker, The Heavenly City of the Eighteenth-Century Philosophers (New Haven: Yale University Press, 1932).

M. Belknap, ed., American Political Trials (Westport, Conn.: Greenwood Press, 1981).

H. Belz, A. Kelly, and W. Harbison, The American Constitution: Its Origins and Development (New York: Norton, 6th ed. 1983).

R. Berger, Impeachment: The Constitutional Problems (Cambridge, Harvard University Press, 1973).

A. Beveridge, The Life of John Marshall (Boston: Houghton-Mifflin, 1916).

A. Bickel, The Supreme Court and the Idea of Progress (New York: Harper & Row, 1970).

N. Black, ed., Richard Peters, His Ancestors and Decendents 1810-1889 (Philadelphia: privately printed, 1904).

D. Boorstin, The Lost World of Thomas Jefferson (New York: H. Holt, 1948).

R. Bork, The Tempting of America: The Political Seduction of the Law (New York: Free Press, 1989).

C. Bowen, The Lion and the Throne (Boston: Little, Brown, 1957).

S. Boyd, ed., The Whiskey Rebellion: Past and Present Perspectives (Westport, Conn.: Greenwood Press, 1985).

T. Breen, The Character of the Good Ruler (New Haven: Yale University Press, 1970).

J. Brewer, Party Ideology and Popular Politics at the Accession of George III (Cambridge; New York: Cambridge University Press, 1976).

C. Brinton, A Decade of Revolution (New York: Harper & Row Torchbook ed., 1963).

W. Brown, The Life of Oliver Ellsworth (New York: Macmillan, 1905).

R. Buel, Jr., Securing the Revolution: Ideology in American Politics 1789-1815 (Ithaca, New York: Cornell University Press, 1972).

J. Burgh, Political Disquisitions (New York: DaCapo Press, 1971, 3 vols. 1774-75).

E. Burke, Reflections on the Revolution in France (Harmondsworth, Middlesex: Penguin, C.C. O'Brien, ed., 1969).

H. Butterfield, The American Past: A History of the United States from Concord to Hiroshima (New York: Simon & Schuster, 1947).

G. Calabrisi, A Common Law for the Age of Statutes (Cambridge, Mass.: Harvard University Press, 1982).

I. Christie, Wilkes, Wyville and Reform (London: Macmillan, 1962).

A. Cox, The Role of the Supreme Court in American Government (New York: Oxford University Press, 1976).

A. Cox, The Warren Court (Cambridge, Mass.: Harvard University Press, 1968).

W.W. Crosskey, Politics and the Constitution (Chicago: University of Chicago Press, 1953).

M. Dauer, The Adams Federalists (Baltimore: Johns Hopkins Press, 1953).

H. Dickenson, Liberty and Property: Political Ideology in Eighteenth Century Britain (London: Weidenfeld and Nicolson, 1977).

J. Diggins, The Lost Soul of American Politics (New York: Basic Books, 1984).

G. Dunne, Justice Joseph Story and the Rise of the Supreme Court (New York: Simon & Schuster, 1971).

F. Eastman, The Fries Rebellion (New York: American Historical Society, 1922).

R. Ellis, The Jeffersonian Crisis: Courts and Politics in the New Republic (New York: Oxford University Press, 1971).

J. Elsmere, Justice Samuel Chase (Muncie, Ind.: Janevar Pub. Co., 1980).

R. Faukner, The Jurisprudence of John Marshall (Princeton, N.J.: Princeton University Press, 1968).

R. Ferguson, Law and Letters in American Culture (Cambridge, Mass.: Harvard University Press, 1984).

J. Flexner, George Washington: Anguish and Farewell 1793-1799 (Boston: Little, Brown, 1972).

E. Foner, Tom Paine and Revolutionary America (New York: Oxford University Press, 1976).

W. Forsyth, History of Trial by Jury (London: J.W. Parker and Son, 1852).

F. Frankfurter, The Commerce Clause Under Marshall, Taney and Waite (Chapel Hill: University of North Carolina Press, 1937).

F. Frankfurter & J. Landes, The Business of the Supreme Court (New York: Macmillan, 1928).

L. Friedman, A History of American Law (New York: Simon & Schuster, 1973).

G. Gawalt, The Promise of Power: The Emergence of the Legal Profession in Massachusetts, 1760-1840 (Westport, Conn.: Greenwood Press, 1979).

G. Gilmore & C. Black, The Law of Admiralty (Mineola, N.Y.: Foundation Press, 1975).

J. Goebel, Jr., A History of the Supreme Court Vol. I: Antecedents and Beginnings to 1801 (New York: Macmillan, 1971).

A. Goodwin, The Friends of Liberty: The English Democratic Movement in the Age of the French Revolution (Cambridge, Mass.: Harvard University Press, 1979).

T. Green, Verdict According to Conscience: Perspectives on the English Criminal Trial Jury 1200-1800 (Chicago: University of Chicago Press, 1985).

G. Gunther, Cases and Materials on Constitutional Law (Mineola, New York: Foundation Press, 9th ed., 1975).

T. Hanley, The American Revolution and Religion: Maryland (Washington: Catholic University of America Press, 1971).

H. Hartog, Public Property and Private Power: The Corporation of the City of New York in American Law 1730-1870 (Chapel Hill: University of North Carolina Press, 1983).

G. Haskins and H. Johnson, A History of the Supreme Court, Vol. 2: Foundations of Power: John Marshall 1801-1815 (New York: Macmillan, 1985).

J. Haw, F. Beirne, R. Beirne, and R. Jett, Stormy Patriot: The Life of Samuel Chase (Baltimore: Maryland Historical Society, 1980).

D. Henderson, Courts for a New Nation (Washington, D.C.: Public Affairs Press, 1971).

P. Hofer and N. Hull, Impeachment in America 1635-1805 (New Haven: Yale University Press, 1984).

R. Hofstadter, The American Political Tradition & The Men Who Made It (Vintage Books ed., 1973, originally published New York: A.A. Knopf, 1948).

R. Hofstadter, The Idea of A Party System: The Rise of Legitimate Opposition in the United States (Berkeley: University of California Press, 1969).

W. Holdsworth, A History of English law, Vol. 7 (7th ed., London: Methuen, 1956).

Homer, The Illiad of Homer (Chicago: University of Chicago Press, R. Lattimore, trans, 1951).

M. Horwitz, The Transformation of American Law, 1780-1860 (Cambridge, Mass.: Harvard University Press, 1977).

D. Howe, The Political Culture of the American Whigs (Chicago: University of Chicago Press, 1979).

T. Jefferson, The Life and Selected Writings of Thomas Jefferson
(A. Koch, and W. Peden, eds., Englewood Cliffs, New Jersey: Prentice Hall, 1944).

D. Kairys, ed., The Politics of Law (New York: Pantheon Books, 1982)

M. Kammen, The Past Before Us (Ithaca: Cornell University Press, 1980).

L. Kerber, Federalists in Dissent: Imagery and Ideology in Jeffersonian America, (Ithaca, New York: Cornell University Press, 1970).

R. Kirk, The Conservative Mind from Burke to Eliot (Chicago, IL.: Regnery Gateway, 6th rev. ed. 1978).

R. Kirk, John Randolph of Roanoke (3rd ed., 1978).

T. Kuhn, The Structure of Scientific Revolutions (Chicago: University of Chicago Press, 2d ed., 1970).

L. Levy, Emergence of a Free Press (New York: Oxford University Press, 1985).

L. Levy, Jefferson and Civil Liberties: The Darker Side (New York: Quadrangle, The New York Times Book Co., 1973).

E. Link, Democratic-Republican Societies, 1790-1800 (New York: Octagon Books, 1965).

T. Macaulay, History of England (London: Dent, Everyman's Library ed., 1972).

F. MacDonald, Alexander Hamilton (New York: Norton, 1979).

F. MacDonald, E. Pluribus Unum (Boston: Houghton Mifflin, 1965).

I. Macneil, The New Social Contract: An Inquiry into Modern Contractual Relations (New Haven: Yale University Press, 1980).

C.B. MacPherson, The Political Theory of Possessive Individualism: Hobbes to Locke (Oxford: Oxford University Press, 1962).

C. Magrath, Yazoo: Law and Politics in the New Republic (Providence, Rhode Island: Brown University Press, 1966).

D. Malone, The Public Life of Thomas Cooper (Rev. ed. 1961).

J. Marshall, Life of George Washington (New York: Walton Book Co., 1903).

R. Matthews, The Radical Politics of Thomas Jefferson (Lawrence, Kan.: University Press of Kansas, 1984).

H. May, Ideas, Faith and Feelings: Essays in American Intellectual and Religious History (New York: Oxford University Press, 1983).

H. May, The Enlightenment in America (New York: Oxford University Press, 1976).

J. McClellan, Joseph Story and the American Constitution: A Study in Political and Legal Thought with Selected Writings (Norman, University of Oklahoma Press, 1971).

D. McCoy, The Elusive Republic: Political Economy in Jeffersonian America (Chapel Hill: University of North Carolina Press, 1980).

J. Miller, Alexander Hamilton and the Growth of the New Nation (New York: Harper & Row, Torchbook ed., 1959).

J. Miller, Crisis in Freedom: The Alien And Sedition Acts (Boston: Little, Brown, 1951).

J. Miller, The Federalist Era (New York: Harper & Row, 1960).

E. Morgan, The Genius of George Washington (New York: Norton, 1981).

G. Nash, The Urban Crucible (Cambridge, Mass.: Harvard University Press, 1979).

J. Nedelsky, Private Property and The Limits of American Constitutionalism (Chicago: University of Chicago Press, 1990).

W. Nelson, The Americanization of the Common Law: The Impact of Legal Change on Massachusetts Society, 1760-1830 (Cambridge, Mass.: Harvard University Press, 1975).

R.K. Newmyer, Supreme Court Justice Joseph Story: Statesman of the Old Republic (Chapel Hill: University of North Carolina Press, 1985).

J. O'Conner, William Paterson: Lawyer and Statesman, 1745-1806 (New Brunswick, N.J.: Rutgers University Press, 1979).

T. Paine, Common Sense (New York: Penguin Books, I. Kramnick, ed., 1976).

B. Palmer, Marshall and Taney (Minneapolis: University of Minnesota Press, 1939).

R.R. Palmer, The Age of the Democratic Revolution (Princeton, N.J.: Princeton University Press, 2 vols. 1959, 1964).

M. Perry, Morality, Politics, and Law: A Bicentennial Essay (New York: Oxford University Press, 1988).

M. Perry, The Constitution, The Court, and Human Rights: An Inquiry into the Legitimacy of Constitutional Policymaking by the Judiciary (New Haven: Yale University Press, 1982).

M. Peterson, Adams and Jefferson: A Revolutionary Dialogue (Athens: University of Georgia Press, 1976).

J. Plumb, England in the Eighteenth Century (London: Penguin Books, 1953).

J.G.A. Pocock, The Ancient Constitution and the Feudal Law (Cambridge: Cambridge University Press, 1957).

J.G.A. Pocock, The Machiavellian Moment: Florentine Political Thought and the Atlantic Republican Tradition (Princeton, N.J.: Princeton University Press, 1975).

J.G.A. Pocock, Politics, Language, and Time (London: Methuen 1972).

R. Porter, English Society in the Eighteenth Century (London: Allen Lane, 1982).

S. Presser & J. Zainaldin, Law and Jurisprudence in American History (St. Paul, Minn.: West Publishing Co., 2nd ed., 1989).

J. Reid, The Authority of Rights (Madison, Wis.: University of Wisconsin Press, 1986).

J. Reid, The Authority to Tax (Madison, Wis.: University of Wisconsin Press, 1987).

J. Reid, The Concept of Liberty in the Age of the American Revolution (Chicago: University of Chicago Press, 1988).

C. Robbins, The Eighteenth Century Commonwealthman (Cambridge, Mass.: Harvard University Press, 1959).

A.G. Roeber, Faithful Magistrates and Republican Lawyers: Creators of a Virginia Legal Culture, 1680-1810 (Chapel Hill: University of North Carolina Press, 1981).

N. Rosenberg, Protecting the Best Men: An Interpretive History of the Law of Libel (Chapel Hill: University of North Carolina Press, 1986).

R. Scruton, A Dictionary of Political Thought (New York: Harper & Row, 1982).

G. Seed, James Wilson (Millwood, New York: KTO Press, 1978).

R. Shalhope, John Taylor of Caroline: Pastoral Republican (Columbia: University of South Carolina Press, 1980).

T. Shevory, ed., John Marshall's Achievement: Law, Politics, and Constitutional Interpretation (New York: Greenwood Press, 1989).

T. Slaughter, The Whiskey Rebellion: Frontier Epilogue to the American Revolution (Westport, Conn.: Greenwood Press, 1986).

J. Smith, Appeals to the Privy Council from the American Plantations (New York: Columbia University Press, 1950).

J. Smith, Freedom's Fetters: The Alien and Sedition Laws and American Civil Liberties (Ithaca, New York: Cornell University Press, 1956).

L.B. Smith, This Realm of England 1399-1688 (New York: D.C. Heath, 3d. ed., 1976).

D. Stewart, The Opposition Press of the Federalist Period (Albany, New York: State University of New York Press, 1969).

F. Stites, John Marshall, Defender of the Constitution (Boston: Little, Brown, 1981).

H. Storing, What the Antifederalists Were For (Chicago: University of Chicago Press, 1981).

W.W. Story, Life and Letters of Joseph Story (Boston: Little, Brown, 1851).

G. Stourzh, Alexander Hamilton and the Idea of Republican Government (Stanford: Stanford University Press, 1970).

M. Tachau, Federal Courts in the Early Republic (Princeton, New Jersey: Princeton University Press, 1978).

J. Taylor, An Inquiry Into the Principles and Policy of the Government of the United States (New Haven: Yale University Press, R.P. Nichols, ed., 1950).

M. Tushnet, Red, White and Blue (Cambridge, Mass.: Harvard University Press, 1988).

R. Unger, Knowledge and Politics 295 (New York: Free Press, 1975).

C. Warren, The Supreme Court in United States History (Boston: Little, Brown, rev. ed., 1947).

G.E. White, The American Judicial Tradition: Profiles of Leading American Judges (New York: Oxford University Press, 1976).

G. Wills, Explaining America: The Federalist (Garden City, New York: Doubleday, 1981).

G. Wills, Inventing America: Jefferson's Declaration of Independence (Garden City, New York: Doubleday, 1978).

W. Wilcox, The Age of Aristocracy (Lexington, Mass.: D.C. Heath, 3rd. ed., 1976).

G. Wood, The Creation of the American Republic 1776-1787 (Chapel Hill: University of North Carolina Press, 1969).

Articles and Book Chapters

A Collection of Puns and Witticism of Judge Richard Peters, 25 Pa. Mag. Hist & Biog. 366 (1901).

Appleby, *Republicanism in Old and New Contexts*, 63 Wm. & Mary Quarterly 3rd ser. 30 (1986).

Baker, *Criminal Courts and Procedure at Common Law 1550-1800*, in Crime in England 1550-1880 15 (Princeton, Princeton University Press, J. Cockburn ed., 1977).

Ball, *Cross and Sword, Victim and Law: A Tentative Response to Leonard Levy's* Treason Against God, 35 Stan. L. Rev. 1007 (1983).

Banning, *Jeffersonian Ideology Revisited: Liberal and Classical Ideas in the New American Republic*, 63 William and Mary Quarterly 3rd ser. 3 (1986).

Banning, *Quid Transit? Paradigms and Process in the Transformation of Republican Ideas*, Reviews in American History 199 (1989).

Binney, *The Leaders of the Old Bar of Philadelphia*, 14 Pa. Mag. Hist. & Biog. 1 (1859).

Bork, *Alexander M. Bickel, Political Philosopher*, 1975 Sup. Ct. Rev. 419.

Bork, *Neutral Principles and Some First Amendment Problems*, 47 Ind. L.J. 1 (1971).

Botein, *Biography in Legal History*, 69 L. Libr. J. 456 (1976).

Brest, *The Misconceived Quest for Original Understanding*, 60 B.U. L. Rev. 204 (1980)).

Brewer, *The Wilkites and the Law 1763-74*, in An Ungovernable People: The English and Their Law in the Seventeenth and Eighteenth Centuries (New Brunswick, N.J.: Rutgers University Press, 1980).

Brisbin, *John Marshall on History, Virtue, and Legality*, in T. Shevory, ed., John Marshall's Achievement: Law, Politics, and Constitutional Interpretation 95 (New York: Greenwood Press, 1989).

Campbell, *Dartmouth College As a Civil Liberties Case: The Formation of Constitutional Policy*, 70 Ky. L.J. 643 (1982).

Ellis, *The Impeachment of Samuel Chase* in M. Belknap, ed., American Political Trials 55 (Westport, Conn.: Greenwood Press, 1981).

Elsmere, *The Trials of John Fries*, 103 Pa. Mag. Hist. & Biog. 432 (1979).

Geertz, *Ideology as a Cultural System*, in Ideology and Discontent 47 (New York: Free Press, D. Apter, ed., 1964).

Gordon, *Historicism In Legal Scholarship*, 90 Yale L.J. 1017 (1981).

Gordon, *The Politics of Legal History and the Search for a Usable Past*, 4 Benchmark 269 (1990).

Greenawalt, *The Enduring Significance of Neutral Principles*, 78 Col. L. Rev. 982 (1978).

Grey, *Do We Have an Unwritten Constitution?* 27 Stan. L. Rev. 703 (1975).

Henderson, *The Background of the Seventh Amendment*, 80 Harv. L. Rev. 289 (1966).

Henderson, *Some Aspects of Sectionalism in Pennsylvania, 1790-1812*, 61 Pa. Mag. Hist. & Biog. 113 (1937).

Holmes, *The Path of the Law*, 10 Harv. L. Rev. 457 (1897).

Horwitz, *The Conservative Tradition in the Writing of American Legal History* 17 Am. J. Leg. Hist. 275 (1973).

Horwitz, *Republicanism and Liberalism in American Constitutional Thought*, 29 Wm. & Mary L. Rev. 57 (1987).

Horwitz, *The Rule of Law: An Unqualified Human Good?* 86 Yale L.J. 561 (1977).

Howe, *Juries as Judges of Criminal Law*, 52 Harv. L. Rev. 582 (1939).

Jay, *Origins of the Federal Common Law* Part One, 133 U. Pa. L. Rev. 1003 (1985).

Katz, "Introductory Note" to Hart and Wechsler, The Federal Courts and the Federal System 1 (Mineola, N.Y.: Foundation Press, 2nd. ed., 1973).

Kennedy, *The Structure of Blackstone's Commentaries*, 28 Buffalo L. Rev. 209 (1979).

Kenyon, *Men of Little Faith: The Anti-Federalists on the Nature of Representative Government*, 12 Wm. & Mary Q. (3d ser.) (1955).

Klare, *Judicial Deradicalization of the Wagner Act and the Origins of Modern Legal Consciousness*, 62 Minn. L. Rev. 265 (1978).

Kloppenberg, *The Virtues of Liberalism: Christianity, Republicanism, and Ethics in Early American Political Discourse*, 74 Journal of American History 9 (1987).

Kramnick, *The "Great National Discussion": The Discourse of Politics in 1787*, 65 Wm. & Mary Q. 3d ser. (1988).

Kurland, *Judicial Review Revisited: "Original Intent" and "The Common Law,"* 55 Cinc. L. Rev. 773.

Landsman, *A Brief Survey of the Development of the Adversary System*, 44 Ohio St. L. J. 713 (1984).

Landsman, *The Decline of the Adversary System: How the Rhetoric of Swift and Certain Justice Has Affected Adjudication in American Courts*, 29 Buff. L. Rev. 487 (1981).

Langbein, *The Criminal Trial Before the Lawyers*, 45 U. Chi. L. Rev. 263 (1978)

Langbein, *Shaping the Eighteenth Century Criminal Trial: A View from the Ryder Sources*, 50 U. Chi. L. Rev. 1 (1983)

LaTrobe, *Biographical Sketch of Daniel Dulaney*, 3 Pa. Mag. Hist. & Biog. (1879).

Lerner, *John Marshall and the Campaign of History*, 39 Colum. L. Rev. 396 (1939).

Lerner, *The Supreme Court as Republican Schoolmaster*, 1967 Sup. Ct. Rev. 127.

Levinson, *Escaping Liberalism: Easier Said Than Done* 96 Harv. L. Rev. 1466 (1983).

Marcus & Teir, *Hayburn's Case: A Misinterpretation of Precedent*, 1988 Wisconsin Law Review 527.

Matthews, *Beyond "Sanctimonious Reverence" for a "Sacred" Law*, in T. Shevory, ed., John Marshall's Achievement: Law Politics and Constitutional Interpretation (New York: Greenwood Press, 1989).

Nedelsky, *Confining Democratic Politics: Anti-Federalists, Federalists, and the Constitution*, 96 Harv. L. Rev. 340 (1982).

Nedelsky, *Democracy, Justice, and the Multiplicity of Voices: Alternatives to the Federalist Vision*, 84 NW. L. Rev. 232 (1989).

Nelson, *Changing Conceptions of Judicial Review in the States 1790-1860*, 120 U. Pa. L. Rev. 1166 (1972).

Nelson, *The Eighteenth Century Background of the Jurisprudence of John Marshall*, 76 Mich. L. Rev. 893 (1978).

Oldham, *The Origins of the Special Jury*, 50 U. Chi. L. Rev. 137 (1983).

Palmer, *The Federal Common Law of Crime*, 4 Law and History Review 267 (1986).

Phillips, *William Paine, Philadelphia's Democratic Republicans, and The Origins of Modern Politics*, 101 Pa. Mag. Hist. & Biog. 365 (1977).

Pocock, *Introduction*, in Three British Revolutions, 1640, 1688, 1776, 3 (Princeton, N.J., Princeton University Press, J. Pocock, ed., 1980).

Powell, *The Original Understanding of Original Intent*, 98 Harv. L. Rev. 885 (1985).

Presser, *The Supra-Constitution, the Courts, and the Federal Common Law of Crimes* 4 Law and History Review 325 (1986).

Presser, *A Tale of Two Judges: Richard Peters, Samuel Chase, and the Broken Promise of Federalist Jurisprudence*, 73 NW. L. Rev. 26 (1978).

Presser and Hurley, *Saving God's Republic: The Jurisprudence of Samuel Chase*, 1984 U. Ill. L. Rev. 771.

Preyer, *Jurisdiction to Punish: Federal Authority, Federalism and the Common Law of Crimes in the Early Republic*, 4 Law and History Review 223 (1986).

Rabban, *The Ahistorical Historian: Leonard Levy on Freedom of Expression in Early American History*, 37 Stan. L. Rev. 795 (1985).

Reid, *"In a Defensive Rage": The Uses of the Mob, The Justification in Law, and The Coming of the American Revolution*, 49 N.Y.U. L. Rev. 1043 (1974).

Riddell, *Benjamin Franklin's Mission to Canada and the Causes of Its Failure*, 48 Pa. Mag. Hist. & Biog. 111 (1924).

Rodney, *The End of the Penns' Claims to Delaware 1789-1814* , 61 Pa. Mag. Hist. & Biog. 182 (1937).

Shalhope, *Republicanism and Early American Historiography*, 39 Wm. & Mary Q. (3d Ser.) 334 (1982).

Shalhope, *Toward A Republican Synthesis: The Emergence of an Understanding of Republicanism in American Historiography*, 29 Wm. & Mary Q. (3d Ser.) (1972).

Stein, *The Attraction of the Civil Law in Post Revolutionary America*, 52 Va. L. Rev. 403 (1966).

Turner, *The Midnight Judges*, 109 U. Pa. L. Rev. 494 (1961).

Warren, *New Light on the History of the Federal Judiciary Act of 1789*, 37 Harv. L. Rev. 49 (1923).

White, *The Evolution of Reasoned Elaboration: Jurisprudential Criticism and Social Change*, 59 Va. L. Rev. 279 (1973).

Wright, *Instructions to the Jury: Summary Without Comment*, 1954 Wash. U. L. Q. 177.

Wright, *Professor Bickel, The Scholarly Tradition, and the Supreme Court*, 84 Harv. L.Rev. 769 (1971).

Wright, *The Invasion of the Jury: Temperature of the Water*, 27 Temp. L. Q. (1953-54).

Index

Daughter marries Jeffersonian, 158
Defense to impeachment charges,
156–157
Democratic fires of youth cooled in
middle age, 27, 200, n.42
Early career as popular champion, 22,
23, 27, 33
Early judicial career, 24–25, 40–43,
94–95
English sojourn, 47–48
Excoriated by Jeffersonian press, 4–5
Experience in England as formative
influence, 24
Failure to understand public opinion,
11–12
Flour futures scandal, 24–25
Grand jury charges, 39–40, 43, 141–
146
Influences Marshall, 242, n.42
John Marshall's synthesis as outcome
of Chase's impeachment, 19–20
Jurisprudence of Restraint, 14, 39–44
Mirrored pessimistic views of
Alexander Hamilton, 18
Natural law and instrumentalism in
jurisprudence of, 165–166, 177
Not an American Jeffries, 13–14
On jury prerogatives, 43–44, 109–
110, 111–112, 116–117, 137–138
On meaning of "Law," 111–112, 137–
138
On repeal of Midnight Judges Act,
163, 176–177
Opinion in Calder v. Bull, 41–42
Opponent of Constitution of 1787,
21–22, 23
Opposition to his judicial
appointment, 25–26
Peculiar personality, 11, 12–13, 179–
180
Presides over Callender trial, 4, 133–
141, 171–172
Presides over Fries's trial, 3–4, 14
Reasons for his judicial appointment
by Washington, 26–27, 200, n.39
Religious aspects of jurisprudence

generally, 146–150, 181, 236, n.74,
237, n.78
Burke's influence on, 148–149, 238,
n.86, 169
In Cooper's trial, 121–124, 128–
129
In Fries's trial, 114–117
On the nature of humankind, 148
Rejects judicial neutrality, 142–143
Views liberty in conservative
republican terms, 144–146,
149–150
Risks life for law, 250, n.50
Similarity in views to those of
Jefferson on social ordering,
158–159, 174–175, 183
Coke, Sir Edward
On artificial reason, 138
Commercial law
In Pennsylvania federal courts, 58–60,
64–66
Common Law interpretation
of constitution, 242–243, n.45
Conservatism
Modern judicial philosophy and, 189
Cooper, Thomas
Seditious libel trial before Chase, 118,
121–124
Tried for crimes in England and
America, 53
Critical legal studies, 188, 189
Crosskey, William
Opinion that Chase was not a
"Federalist," 21–22

Dallas, Alexander James
And radicalism in Pennsylvania, 126–
127, 129
As counsel for John Fries, with
William Lewis
First trial, 104–108
Second trial, 109–112, 116, 124,
125, 128, 227, n.47
Corresponds with St. John Tucker,
231, n.124
In Worral's case, 77–78, 85, 93